The Bloomsbury Reader in Cultural Approaches to the Study of Religion

ALSO AVAILABLE FROM BLOOMSBURY

A Beginner's Guide to the Study of Religion, Bradley L. Herling

The Bloomsbury Reader in Religion, Sexuality, and Gender,
edited by Donald L. Boisvert and Carly Daniel-Hughes

Cultural Approaches to the Study of Religion: An Introduction to Theories and Methods, edited by Sarah J. Bloesch and Meredith Minister

The Study of Religion, George D. Chryssides and Ron Geaves

The Bloomsbury Reader in Cultural Approaches to the Study of Religion

**EDITED BY
SARAH J. BLOESCH
AND MEREDITH MINISTER**

BLOOMSBURY ACADEMIC
LONDON • NEW YORK • OXFORD • NEW DELHI • SYDNEY

BLOOMSBURY ACADEMIC
Bloomsbury Publishing Plc
50 Bedford Square, London, WC1B 3DP, UK
1385 Broadway, New York, NY 10018, USA

BLOOMSBURY, BLOOMSBURY ACADEMIC and the Diana logo are trademarks of
Bloomsbury Publishing Plc

First published in Great Britain 2018

Cover design: Terry Woodley
Cover image: Street Art, Arts District, Los Angeles, California, USA
© LHB Photo / Alamy Stock Photo

A catalogue record for this book is available from the British Library.

Library of Congress Cataloging-in-Publication Data
Names: Bloesch, Sarah J., editor.
Title: The Bloomsbury reader in cultural approaches
to the study of religion / [edited by] Sarah J. Bloesch and Meredith Minister.
Description: 1 [edition]. | New York : Bloomsbury Academic, 2018. |
Includes bibliographical references and index.
Identifiers: LCCN 2018001834 (print) | LCCN 2018026482 (ebook) |
ISBN 9781350039810 (ePUB) | ISBN 9781350039827 (ePDF) |
ISBN 9781350039797 (hpod : alk. paper) | ISBN 9781350039803 (pbk. : alk. paper)
Subjects: LCSH: Religion–Methodology. | Religion and culture. Classification: LCC BL41 (ebook) |
LCC BL41 .B56 2018 (print) | DDC 200.7–dc23
LC record available at https://lccn.loc.gov/2018001834

ISBN: HB: 978-1-3500-3979-7
PB: 978-1-3500-3980-3
ePDF: 978-1-3500-3982-7
eBook: 978-1-3500-3981-0

Typeset by Newgen KnowledgeWorks Pvt. Ltd., Chennai, India
Printed and bound in India

To find out more about our authors and books visit www.bloomsbury.com
and sign up for our newsletters.

This book is dedicated to our tireless support networks,
first and foremost, Jes and Kevin.

Contents

Acknowledgments

Crafting this volume has been an enormous undertaking that would not have been possible without the support of our families, friends, colleagues, and institutions. Our partners, also both scholars of religion, were the first to support our dream and offer helpful insights as we began to outline our vision. They have continued to support us throughout this project, making it possible for us to be in the same place when critical steps in the project required us to have more extended meetings and edit endless drafts of our work. Our deepest thanks for the editorial assistance of Lalle Pursglove, with whom it has been an absolute pleasure to work. We also thank Lucy Carroll for her amazing persistence in obtaining the permissions for this volume. We received tireless support from a dedicated group of readers and conversation partners who read drafts of the manuscript and thoughtfully engaged the state of theory in religious studies: Kevin Minister, Jes Boon, and Rhiannon Graybill. We thank them and the initial reviewers for their insights and work on this volume. Any remaining faults are our responsibility.

On March 16, 2017, Meredith was diagnosed with stage IV colon cancer and immediately began treatment, which involved a surgery her medical oncologist later deemed "aggressive and risky" followed by six months of chemotherapy. When she received the diagnosis, one of her first questions (which she reactively asked a very patient gastroenterologist) was, am I going to be able to finish the books I have under contract? As she sat with a grim prognosis in the short week before surgery, she decided that her final acts might be to finish her current book projects.

This project would not have been possible without the support Meredith received through treatment from Sarah, from Meredith's and her partner's extended families, from her friends, from an extended network of colleagues, and from colleagues, students, and administrators at Shenandoah University. A few special mentions for unquantifiable support go to her partner Kevin Minister, friends who drove her to chemo when Kevin was out of town, Andrea Smith and Dana Baxter, Sarah, of course, who arranged her own working schedule around Meredith's treatment, Meredith's parents, grandmother, and aunt H. D. and Kay Williams, Glenda Cooper, and Ladonna Cooper, her in-laws Andy and Becky Minister, her brother-in-law Stephen Minister and his family, Justin Allen for being an information node, relieving Meredith of the responsibility, and, finally, to everyone who laughed at her jokes about death instead of staring at her with horror (an especially high mention to folks who crafted new jokes). A few local businesses also supported Meredith during her treatment including Shenandoah University, the

Hideaway Café, and Shine Yoga. This list leaves out so many who sent care packages and helpful readings (usually feminist authors writing about illness and speculative fiction), brought food, vacuumed, did laundry and dishes, walked the dog, mowed the lawn, took over classes and committee work for Meredith and her partner (including finishing program planning for a conference committee they were on), organized fundraisers and marches, wrote cards and jokes for Meredith to read during chemo, and generally managed things that Meredith ignored to work on this volume.

While finishing the manuscript, Meredith had the opportunity to go on two retreats for cancer patients. The first was sponsored by Mary's Place By The Sea, a house in Ocean Grove, New Jersey, where women with cancer gather near the ocean for spa-like healing services including massage, gentle yoga, and prepared meals. The other retreat was sponsored by First Descents, an organization that arranges adventure programming for young adults with cancer. At both retreats, Meredith met amazing people that helped her manage many of the side effects from treatment. These organizations are doing incredible work and Meredith wishes to thank them for the retreats and promote the work that they do to other women and/or young adults with cancer. She also wishes to thank the people who accompanied her on these retreats and their willingness to share laughter and grief, often at the same time. As we prepare to submit the volume, Meredith faces her final round of chemo before entering an intensive monitoring period. She is hopeful this volume and the other books that went under contract shortly following the diagnosis will not be her final accomplishment.

Sarah would like to thank her friends, colleagues, and students at Elon University who have provided a rich opportunity to discuss, debate, and refine the role of theory and methods in the discipline and the classroom. Further, Sarah cherishes her time with the Duke/UNC Theory Reading Group and the intellectual rigor and friendship it provides—these are the settings to which an academic aspires. Finally, Sarah would also like to thank her family for their love and support through the many stages that come before a book ever reaches publication.

Permissions

Introduction

A series of photos by Renée Cox titled *Yo Mama's Last Supper* features a reconstruction of the final meal Jesus shared with his disciples prior to his death. Cox's photos follow the style of Leonardo da Vinci's famous painting, *The Last Supper* (late fifteenth century), in which thirteen white men clothed in colorful robes appear on one side of a long table, spread with a tablecloth and the remains of a feast. With the exception of the seated Jesus figure in the middle, most of the men appear to be having a heated discussion in pairs or trios. These discussions are supposed to be about Jesus's announcement that one of the disciples would betray him, as reported in the Christian gospel, John 13:21. Cox's late twentieth-century version, which takes the form of a series of five photographs, also features thirteen figures positioned on one side of a table appearing to have a heated discussion over a meal. Unlike da Vinci's painting, however, the central Jesus figure of Cox's work is Cox herself: a standing Black woman, gazing up with arms outstretched, and clothed only with a cloth draped around both forearms. Styling an unclothed Black woman as Jesus is not Cox's only variation on da Vinci's theme; twelve of the figures in Cox's work are Black, one is white, and at least two appear to be women. The white man is portrayed as Judas.

When Cox's piece was featured at the Brooklyn Museum of Art as part of an exhibition titled *Committed to the Image: Contemporary Black Photographers*, then-mayor of New York City Rudy Giuliani called the piece "disgusting," "outrageous," and "anti-Catholic" and announced that he would appoint a committee to set "decency standards" for NYC's public museums (Bumiller 2001). In response to Giuliani and other critics, Cox stated: "I have a right to interpret the Last Supper just as Leonardo da Vinci created the Last Supper with people who look like him" (Williams 2001). Cox's statement alludes to the European artistic construction of Jesus as white, despite historical evidence that suggests that Jesus was more likely brown. Criticism of her work, therefore, disguises racism and sexism in the language of decency and the desire to protect (white) Christian sentiments.

The disagreements between Cox and Giuliani reflect different approaches to Cox's work and, importantly, these different approaches make a difference in the world we share. Having read these second-hand accounts, and presumably not having seen Cox's photos, are you prepared to intervene in the debate about Cox's work? If so, on what grounds will you make your argument? Perhaps the second-hand account has given you some resources, but will you look at the primary sources, in this case Cox's photos and da Vinci's painting, before reaching a conclusion? Will you need to evaluate the artwork directly or will copies be sufficient? Are there other sources, such as interviews, that you will consult in order to make an informed decision about the debate? How will you interpret these sources in light of dominant assumptions about race, gender, and religion? What will your interpretations reveal about you?

The contextual difference between Cox and Giuliani makes a difference for their interpretations. What frameworks fomented Cox's production of *Yo Mama's Last Supper*? Cox's piece did not emerge out of nothing but is itself the product of a particular time and place, that is, da Vinci was not Cox's only inspiration. As a Black female artist who grew up in the Catholic church, Cox sees things differently than Giuliani, a white male politician who also grew up Catholic. These different social locations are not mere neutral differences; rather, they reflect cultural logics of supremacy that marginalize people who are Black, women, and/or approach Christianity in a manner that challenges white Christian leaders. While anyone may, theoretically, offer an interpretation of da Vinci's famous painting, Cox's rendition of da Vinci challenges culturally appropriate interpretations of *The Last Supper*. As a result of this challenge, Cox encounters complex forces of money, race, and gender. Concretely, these cultural logics of supremacy result in a manifestation of Giuliani's power to remove the types of funding that support Cox's profession. This is not a mere difference of interpretation: Giuliani threatens Cox's livelihood while also inadvertently giving her a broader advertisement than she would have received without his critique.

Their disagreement suggests that what we bring to an encounter, whether that be an encounter of a work of art or a written text, makes a difference in the resulting explanation. This is a book that presents primary sources and encourages questions based on those primary sources. As the debate around *Yo Mama's Last Supper* suggests, interpretations matter. This volume, therefore, compiles texts that have made a difference in the study of religion. Many scholars disagree in their approaches to the texts collected here. Thus, going back to the sources instead of parroting what has been said helps us understand others, even others that we are inclined to agree with. Moreover, students' own engagement with the work in light of their life experiences and contexts contribute to the understanding of the value and limits of these sources. While we may be inclined to agree with Cox's interpretation of her photographs, perhaps a closer examination reveals something that might trouble us. Perhaps it is something that would not have troubled us in 1997 but troubles us in 2018.

As we respond to the Cox's photographs or da Vinci's painting, we employ modes of interpretation when we attempt to convey what we see, think, or feel. This struggle toward explanation is a hallmark characteristic of theory. Simply stating that "you love the photos," "you are offended by it," or "you don't understand the fuss" might be your position. However, when you begin to explain *why* you hold that specific position—what factors lead you to that conclusion—you enter the realm of theory. These theories make a difference in how we engage religious cooperation and conflict. Drawing on personal resources, experiences, or previous conversations to make your case is something we do often without being aware of it; it feels like second nature. However, we do not create our arguments out of thin air. The ways we approach our explanation tend to draw on factors we find important to the conversation—such as the role of economics, gender, race, or language. Beyond being merely an individual endeavor, how we craft our analyses of situations have broader histories. The scholars in this volume have explicitly thought about how and why people respond, what motivates them to act, and how the process of living takes specific forms in different social worlds.

a. Structure of the Volume

This book features selected texts from ten major theorists whose work has changed the course of religious studies during the past fifty years, reconfiguring how we study religion today: Mary Douglas (anthropology), Phyllis Trible (textual studies), Wendy Doniger (myth), Catherine Bell (ritual), Alice Walker (literature), Charles Long (colonialism), Caroline Walker Bynum (history), Gloria Anzaldúa (borders), Judith Butler (gender), and Saba Mahmood (secularization). The theories presented by these scholars in the following pages offer students of religion an opportunity to engage directly with influential theories used in studying religion. Reading these selections creates an opportunity to wrestle with complicated texts and competing interpretations. This volume allows students to interpret these texts for themselves, adding their own voices and experiences to the conversation and developing the study of religion today. Moreover, reading the selections presented in this volume alongside of each other reveals significant patterns and themes in the field of religious studies including textual interpretation, ritual study, and the importance of material bodies and social locations. In this introduction, we invite readers into these texts by making a case for studying theories of religion.

The authors represented in this volume have written extensively and often beyond the format of the standard book length monograph, including lectures, articles, coedited volumes, and blog posts. Faced with such diversity of sources, choosing selections for this volume felt quite limiting. Thus, one of the major criteria we used in selecting the readings that appear here was the impact of a reading's specific contribution to methodological approaches. A reader who is already familiar with a specific author, for example, Butler or Bell, might be able to identify their particular approaches that often remain implicit throughout their writings. However, we have chosen works that explicitly demonstrate the author's thinking on theory in that moment. In some instances, we looked for texts where the authors spent time self-consciously reflecting on their methods, such as the selections from Doniger, Trible, Bell, and Long. In some, their methodological writings emerge from autobiographical reflections, such as Walker and Anzaldúa, and others are concentrated studies in what an updated, revised, or new method should produce, such as Douglas, Bynum, Butler, and Mahmood.

Further, many authors' writings have spanned such a length of time that their interests and thinking have assumed many directions. For example, Wendy Doniger has a rich corpus on the role of women, gender, deities, and animals in Indian text and imagery; yet we chose to focus on her comparative mythology. Alice Walker has dozens of novels, essays, and poems ranging from topics on race, Buddhism, autobiography, and debates on activism versus scholarship; yet we decided to include a letter from a novel, a definition, and an interview. In each case, we tried to hold together the balance of what has, at the moment, contributed the most unique methodological advancements in studying the "religious" and what approaches scholars have used most widely in their own work. For example, the selection from Butler comes from her earlier explorations in gender, sexuality, identity, and performativity because these topics, at present, remain far more broadly influential to those studying religion than her more recent work on democracy, Zionism, and the Jewish-Palestinian debates. This may very well change in the following decades; however, at present scholars repeatedly turn to Butler's earlier material in their own scholarship.

Scholars of religion have drawn on and will continue to draw on the texts contained in this volume to advance the field of religious studies. At times, we can see that movement within the selections contained in this volume as Mahmood draws on the arguments of Butler who draws on the arguments of Douglas. An intellectual genealogy appears. These texts help us trace the genealogies that are giving life to religious studies today.

The texts are grouped into three main parts: "Comparative Approaches," "Examining Particularities," and "Expanding Boundaries." Each part maps a general trajectory used in studying religion. Broadly speaking, the scholars in the comparative section pursue a notion that religions should be studied in relationship to other religious traditions, or that theoretical approaches for a single tradition can be applied to the study of other religious traditions. The texts that comprise the second part, to the contrary, assert that maintaining a closer focus on the details of a select tradition, context, or identity position provides valuable insights. Finally, the scholars in the third part argue that specific religions should be studied as entities and experiences that are located within histories of power. In the following section, we detail each of these sections and why we categorized each of the theorists within a particular section.

Because many of these texts are difficult reading, we have included brief introductions to each author's selections prior to the selected readings themselves. These introductions give readers background to the theorist, highlight some of the themes in the readings, and describe the texts' impact for the field of religious studies. The introductions are followed by selected writings from each theorist. Then, questions for comprehension, analysis, and synthesis conclude each chapter. These questions give readers an opportunity to comprehend the primary ideas in the reading, analyze the selected readings in light of the reader's own previous knowledge and experiences, and synthesize the key ideas in the readings with other theories used in the study of religion.

Comparative Approaches

The first part, "Comparative Approaches," contains texts that deal with the promises and difficulties of understanding how distinct religious expressions in different times and across cultures relate to one another. Three of the theorists—Mary Douglas, Wendy Doniger, and Catherine Bell—work toward articulating theories for approaching religion as an analytical category by identifying methods that seem to (re)appear across times and places. Phyllis Trible's work is directed toward one set of Christian texts but then widely applied by subsequent scholars to other sacred literature.

Douglas's texts look at the specifics of purity, pollution, and hygiene practices of certain groups of people to identify broader themes that translate to other cultures. She says: "I am going to argue that our ideas of dirt also express symbolic systems and that the difference between pollution behavior in one part of the world and another is only a matter of detail" (Douglas [1966] 2018: 21). Douglas believes that the details of each specific location, time, and tradition remain important; yet regardless of the shape, she argues that those specificities seem to fit into a generalizable framework of purity and pollution with which we can compare religions.

Similarly, as Wendy Doniger formulates her visions of how scholars might approach Hindu myth in a specific place or time, she makes her argument by drawing from wide-ranging sources such as Chinese philosophers, Shakespearean texts, Jewish and Christian figures, and the writings of Karl Marx, Sigmund Freud, and Robert Frost, to name a few. She uses these disparate sources as parallels and analogies to explain the function of myth, both inside and outside of contexts that the reader might find familiar. This process assumes that people, practices, ideas, and writings can easily be put alongside one another to help explain the other.

Catherine Bell writes: "My starting point is an exploration of what makes us identify some acts as ritual, what such a category does for the production and organization of knowledge about other cultures, and how we might assess the assumptions that create and constrain the notion of ritual" (Bell [1992] 2009: 4). Even though Bell understands ritual and "ritual-like" practices to be historically located, she questions the historical constructions of the category of ritual itself. In reconceptualizing the contours of the definition of "ritual," she considers the phenomenon across time, geography, language, tradition, and social formation.

While Phyllis Trible does not articulate a theory of religion in the same way as Douglas, Doniger, and Bell do, Trible's method of depatriarchalizing biblical interpretation has become an important touchstone for feminist encounters with sacred texts. That is, Trible offers a method for a comparative study of religious texts even though she does not articulate that method in her own work. Trible's feminist approach to sacred texts compares the contexts in which biblical texts were authored to the contexts in which these texts are interpreted. Through this process, Trible creates a theoretical ground for the reinterpretation of sacred texts in light of the new contexts in which sacred texts continue to have meaning.

Examining Particularities

The second part, "Examining Particularities," includes methodological texts that do not work toward formulating a grand unifying theory of studying religion. The theorists in this section, Alice Walker, Charles Long, and Caroline Walker Bynum, argue that searching for and analyzing the details of a certain time, place, people, or tradition reveals insights that can then be used to challenge prevailing stereotypes in both academic and popular culture. The authors here want to complicate historic and social pictures that have been painted with broad brushstrokes. Walker's texts ask her readers to consider the lives of Black women in the individual-and-communal "woman" of her definition of womanism, her own narrative and influences, and in the lives of her characters Shug, Celie, Nettie, and even God. Through her development of specific characters, Walker uses these specific points of view to comment on broader themes of how religion functions in society.

Whereas both Long and Bynum incorporate longer stretches of time and place into their studies—Long asks about "signs, symbols, and images" that could be applied across traditions and Bynum includes examples that span hundreds of years and much of western Europe—the authors in this section deal with specific issues that arises when discussing religion. The selections from Long challenge readers to acknowledge that the construction of a universalizing perspective, one that religious studies has often assumed, comes at the expense of ignoring perspectives of those who have received and felt the colonizing effects of these so-called universal ideas. Long, therefore, calls for specificity in seeking out and realizing the construction of "primitive" voices. Thus, "Black religion" is not merely an extension of Christianity from across the Atlantic Ocean, but is its own historically located entity.

As a medievalist, Bynum emphasizes that scholars must be attuned to cultural, historic contexts of a tradition, instead of importing present-day assumptions into the material. Again, we cannot simply talk about universalizing categories that easily traverse time, geography, language, and social structures. Rather, to investigate the role of women, food, and (in)animate objects in their relationships to devotion and power, we must be attentive to the details of premodern life. This attentiveness, in turn, provides history and context to think through modern formulations of gender, bodies, materiality, and devotion. Bynum's work challenges simplistic binaries of medieval versus modern and, instead, points toward historical continuities from the medieval period to our own without overlooking the discontinuities.

Expanding Boundaries

The third part, "Expanding Boundaries" contains readings from Gloria Anzaldúa, Judith Butler, and Saba Mahmood that explicitly locate their subjects of study within broader, specific systems of power, examining how the broad concepts of the West, race, sexuality, gender, and secularity were produced. By locating their theories within networks of power, these authors build upon, contest, or transform layers of previous assumptions, scholarship, and methods—many of which are found in the earlier parts of this volume. The selections in this portion of the reader follow the trajectory of many of the earlier theorists and ask that scholars investigate what has been ignored in the creation and maintenance of previous theories of religious difference.

Anzaldúa theorizes expansive categories such as the US-Mexico border, the legacies of Spanish conquest of indigenous populations, masculinity, lesbianism, and the possibility of spirituality through the very specific location of her own body. She writes of the difficulties of her own self/body to reflect on the status and experience of a whole people: "As a person, I, as a people, we, Chicanos, blame ourselves, hate ourselves, terrorize ourselves" (Anzaldúa [1987] 1999: 67). Yet this shame and oppression do not remain at the individual/communal level; she draws out how the structural relationships of capitalism, imperialism, sexism, racism, and nationalism are implicated in producing these outcomes.

If Anzaldúa uses the body to think outward to expand categories, then Butler uses the body to question the bounded stability that flesh seems to ensure when conceptualizing an "individual." Butler's work contests the long-held way of describing the sex/gender divide, which states that gender is a cultural category whereas sex is a biological pre-given category. Butler argues that topics such as subjecthood, sexuality, and gender require that we conceive of humans as always enmeshed in relationships and in the process of publically living out lives that we (mistakenly, and, in part, because of Christian legacies) believe to be deeply personal and private. Scholars have applied Butler's work to studying religion in terms of how "repetition" and "performance" function to produce the gendered, sexual, nationalistic, and ritual categories through which scholars approach religion.

Finally, Mahmood also focuses on a binary that has been taken as a historical given, the divide between "religion" and "secularity." She explores the intertwining of these two categories by asking what we can learn about nonliberal (often termed, fundamentalist) articulations of gendered agency in Egypt's women's mosque movement. In tracing the interdependent histories and implications of assumptions about faith, family, and politics, Mahmood challenges readers to approach each specific context attentive to the often invisible forces, which nevertheless shape it.

b. Why Study Theories about Religion

Theory provides different questions with which to analyze our and others' responses. Theorist Gayle Rubin talks about the usefulness and pliability of theory. She writes: "I approach systems of thought as tools people make to get leverage and control over certain problems . . . A tool may do one job brilliantly, and be less helpful for another" (Rubin and Butler 1994: 90). Theory, according to Rubin, is meant to be useful for a certain task, and we have to select the tool we think is best for the job we have engaged. The selections in this volume provide different tools for analyzing and examining contexts; further, they provide multiple possible approaches for asking how we interpret or respond to works such as Cox's photographs or da Vinci's painting. You can think about using different theories as you would use different tools, depending on what you want to emphasize. For example, Douglas's work on purity and pollution frame a discussion for those who view either Cox's *Yo Mama's Last Supper* or da Vinci's *The Last Supper* with disgust or reverence. Mahmood's work contextualizes how certain understandings of gender, religion, and the historical prominence of Europe influence responses to female nudity in sacred art.

These controversies around art and interpretation are not merely individual concerns. The Catholic Church, the mayoral office of NYC, and the Brooklyn Museum of Art are influential organizations and institutions that have their own structural histories, power struggles, and leadership debates. Such controversies do not exist in a cultural vacuum. Legacies of slavery and immigration, relationships among Protestant, Catholic, and Jewish communities, the distribution of money, and selected representation (in both museums and government offices) influence debates about who has the right to depict Jesus and his disciples and where such depictions can be made. Regardless of whether someone is Catholic or has ever been to the Brooklyn Museum, each of us is enmeshed in systems that shift and change depending on geography, race, gender, sexuality, education, and language of origin. The force of these systems and institutions contribute to shaping not only how we face such controversies but also how our specificities are marked by these discussions. An Ashkenazi Jewish mother in New York will likely respond to the controversy differently than a third-generation Korean American Protestant Christian in Missouri than an agnostic Black indigenous college student in Idaho—just as those in systems of power will hear their responses differently based on geography, race, gender, disability, religion, and class. Each person exists within relationships to governmental, cultural, and institutional powers. Theories used in studying religion aid in parsing complicated histories and relationships.

The theories in this volume will not provide a "correct" answer as to who is a better artist or how *The Last Supper* should be represented. However, the readings in the volume present distinct methods (or "tools") that help participants or observers analyze the overlapping historical and institutional dynamics present in an interpretation. For example, Bynum studies medieval Christianity and might approach this debate by discussing the relevance of late fifteenth-century food and gender expectations that informed da Vinci's *Last Supper* or how contemporary understandings of food and gender have changed interpretations of da Vinci's painting. Long's scholarship helps us to inquire about the role of "high" art and "folk" art, asking why some art has been lauded as mainstream over the centuries while art produced by minoritized communities tends to be considered expressions of group "identity."

Understanding theory equips students to analyze how religion works in the world around them and figure out how to navigate an ever more complicated and diverse religious world. However, reading what the theories actually propose—learning how to use the tools—is also an art that requires intentional work. The selections from the ten scholars provide ten different ways to analyze art, media, texts, contexts, and relationships. Therefore, it is critical to not only identify the broad strokes of what a scholar proposes but also to read attending to the nuances and differences in their particular approaches.

c. How to Read Dense, Theoretical Texts

Many students of history will be familiar with the use of primary sources, that is, sources that are original first-hand accounts, in the classroom. While the selected readings compiled here are secondary sources in the sense that they often reflect on primary source documents in order to develop new theories about religious traditions and experiences, they might be considered primary sources in the sense that they have become primary theories in the field of religious studies. We, therefore, invite readers to explore the ideas in these texts as they would explore ideas in primary sources, including questioning the context and assumptions of the author, why the argument of the author is important to the author, and why the author's argument continues to be influential for religious studies scholars. Because there are no neutral theories of religion, these selections should be read as a product of a specific time and place.

Many of these texts will ask readers to grapple with context. Writing in the 1960s and drawing on research gleaned as a result of British colonialism, for example, Mary Douglas's anthropological insights ask readers to consider the human expense at which these insights were obtained. Phyllis Trible's selections locate readers in the 1970s male-dominated field of biblical studies and Alice Walker's selections locate readers in the racial and gender equality movements of the 1970s and 1980s. Both Trible and Walker are shaped by these movements for equality and their selections invite us to consider what has changed and what has not. More recent selections, including a selection from Saba Mahmood's 2005 *Politics of Piety*, insist that readers consider the implications of contemporary assumptions about religion and gender and how those assumptions continue, in part, colonial legacies. All of these selections ask readers to grapple with the context in which the work was authored and explore the continuing relevance of the author's key ideas in light of shifting contexts. Reading these theories with attention to the author's contexts develops an understanding of how theories respond to the realization that religion is constantly in flux.

Reading may seem like an activity that one can either do or cannot do; a person is either literate or illiterate. The texts contained in this volume reveal the limitations of this simple binary. Reading is not a matter of simply understanding the meaning of words and sentences but, rather, should be understood on a scale in relation to the material being encountered. As trained religion scholars, we access and read texts like the ones contained in this volume every day and, because we do this so often, we have developed an advanced skill for reading these texts. While this advanced skill sometimes aids us in other pursuits, it takes us considerably more effort to, for example, read an article we find on UpToDate (a resource for doctors to aid in clinical decision-making) because this is probably not something we do daily. The texts contained in this volume offer students of religion an opportunity to develop the skill of reading in the field of religious studies.

Theoretical texts present readers with a challenge of working through new language and uses of language in order to enter a rich and complex field of scholarship. The scholars whose work is excerpted in this reader use vocabulary that will probably be unfamiliar to readers new to the study of religion; their work excerpted here also draws on the ideas of previous theorists whose work will probably be unfamiliar to readers new to the study of religion. The vocabulary and reference to other theorists and schools of thought reveal how each excerpt selected here is part of an already existing conversation. These selections should be read with an eye toward that already-existing conversation. How does the author frame what has come before? How do they hope to change previous theories or ideas? What is at stake for each author in the claims that they are making? The answers to these questions create an existing dialogue, a field of scholarship, to which these texts contribute.

Most of the texts in this reader are dense. As students have sometimes said in our classes, "I have to read with a dictionary." Other selections in this reader are more accessible but their relevance for the study of religion may not be immediately apparent. If the texts contained in this reader are so influential in the field of religious studies, why not just read scholars of religion who accessibly discuss the influence of these difficult texts for the field of religious studies? We have compiled these texts because we think it is essential for students of religion to wrestle with the complicated ideas contained in the selections gathered here, to ask their own questions of these influential texts, and to grapple with the context.

Making these texts available empowers students with the difficult task of interpretation and allows students to ask their own questions of the reading and to draw new conclusions. While some of the selections in this reader will require more than one reading, struggling with these readings is an exercise in patience akin to more recent "slow movements," including slow food, slow cities, and slow fashion. In contrast to much advice for learning how to get key ideas from the reading through skimming or the practice of "gutting a book," many of these dense, theoretical selections ask readers to slow the pace of reading. For this reason, most of these selections are brief and can be reread.

As the debates over *Yo Mama's Last Supper* demonstrate, interpretations and the structures and histories that inform them make a difference. As we practice reading and interpretation, we become better readers and develop more nuanced interpretations. This volume invites readers into the process of reading and interpreting texts with attention to context and detail. This process is essential for navigating religious difference.

We have designed this compilation of texts in such a way that they may be encountered on their own or in light of the secondary essays in the companion volume *Cultural Approaches to Studying Religion: An Introduction to Theories and Methods.*

That volume features essays by renowned scholars of religion that describe many of the texts selected here in an accessible fashion and locate these texts within specific social and historical contexts. These two books may be used separately or in tandem.

Readers of the selections contained in this volume encounter these texts through a new context, with different debates in mind, and different assumptions than other readers have had about the texts. Returning to these writings that are shaping the field of religious studies, therefore, creates space to reevaluate the contributions of these authors in light of recent developments in understandings of religion, including new forms of religious conflict and cooperation around the globe.

References

Committed to the Image: Contemporary Black Photographers, Brooklyn Museum of Art, February 16–April 29, 2001. Selections available online: https://www.brooklynmuseum. org/opencollection/exhibitions/783 (accessed October 2, 2017).

Anzaldúa, Gloria. ([1987] 2007), "La conciencia de la mestiza/Towards a New Consciousness," in *Borderlands/La Frontera: The New Mestiza*, 99–120, San Francisco: Aunt Lute Books.

Anzaldúa, Gloria. (2015), *Light in the Dark: Luz en lo Obscuro: Rewriting Identity, Spirituality, Reality*, AnaLouise Keating (ed.), Durham: Duke University Press.

Bell, Catherine. ([1992] 2009), *Ritual Theory, Ritual Practice*, 2nd edn., New York and Oxford: Oxford University Press.

Bell, Catherine. ([1997] 2009), *Ritual: Perspectives and Dimensions*, Oxford: Oxford University Press.

Bloesch, Sarah J., and Meredith Minister. (2018), *Cultural Approaches to Studying Religion: An Introduction to Theories and Methods*, London and New York: Bloomsbury Academic Press.

Bumiller, Elisabeth. (2001), "Affronted by Nude 'Last Supper,' Giuliani Calls for Decency Panel," *New York Times*, February 16. Available online: http://www.nytimes.com/ 2001/02/16/nyregion/affronted-by-nude-last-supper-giuliani-calls-for-decency-panel. html?pagewanted=all&src=pm (accessed October 2, 2017).

Butler, Judith. ([1990] 2006), "Bodily Inscriptions, Performative Subversions" in *Gender Trouble: Feminism and the Subversion of Identity*, 175–193, New York: Routledge.

Butler, Judith. (1993), "Imitation and Gender Insubordination," in Henry Abelove, Michèle Aina Barale, David M. Halperin (eds.), *The Lesbian and Gay Studies Reader*, 307–320, New York: Routledge.

Bynum, Caroline Walker. (1987), *Holy Feast and Holy Fast: The Religious Significance of Food to Medieval Women*, Berkeley: University of California Press.

Bynum, Caroline Walker. (1991), *Fragmentation and Redemption: Essays on Gender and the Human Body in Medieval Religion*, New York: Zone Books.

Bynum, Caroline Walker. (2007), *Wonderful Blood: Theology and Practice in Late Medeival Northern Germany and Beyond*, Philadelphia: University of Pennsylvania Press.

Bynum, Caroline Walker. (2011), *Christian Materiality: An Essay on Religion in Late Medieval Europe*, New York: Zone Books.

Cox, Renee. (1996), *Yo Mama's Last Supper*, series of photographs, Brooklyn Museum of Art, New York.

Doniger, Wendy. (1998), *The Implied Spider: Politics and Theology in Myth*, New York: Columbia University Press.

Douglas, Mary. ([1966] 2002), *Purity and Danger: An Analysis of Concepts of Pollution and Taboo*, London and New York: Routledge.

Douglas, Mary. ([1970] 1996), *Natural Symbols: Explorations in Cosmology*, 2nd edn., New York: Routledge.

Fairfield, Hannah. (1998), "Caroline Walker Bynum is Named University Professor" *Columbia University in the City of New York Record*, October 30, 24 (8). Available online: http://www.columbia.edu/cu/newrec/2408/tmpl/story.2.html (accessed October 2, 2017).

Long, Charles. ([1986] 1999), *Significations: Signs, Symbols, and Images in the Interpretation of Religion*, 89–106, Aurora, CO: Fortress Press.

Mahmood, Saba. ([2005] 2012), *Politics of Piety: The Islamic Revival and the Feminist Subject*, Princeton: Princeton University Press.

Rubin, Gayle with Judith Butler. (1994), "Interview: Sexual Traffic", *differences: A Journal of Feminist Cultural Studies* 6 (2+3): 62–99.

Trible, Phyllis. (1973), "Depatriarchalizing in Biblical Interpretation," *Journal of the American Academy of Religion* 41 (1): 30–48.

Trible, Phyllis. (1978), *God and the Rhetoric of Sexuality*, Philadelphia: Fortress Press.

Trible, Phyllis. (1984), *Texts of Terror: Literary-Feminist Readings of Biblical Narratives*. Philadelphia: Fortress Press.

Walker, Alice. (1982), *The Color Purple*, Orlando, Austin, New York, San Diego, Toronto, and London: Harcourt Brace Jovanovich.

Walker, Alice. (1983), *In Search of Our Mothers' Garden: Womanist Prose*, San Diego, New York, and London: Harcourt Brace Jovanovich.

Williams, Monte. (2001), "Yo Mama' Artist Takes On Catholic Critic," *New York Times*, 21 February. Available online: http://www.nytimes.com/2001/02/21/nyregion/yo-mama-artist-takes-on-catholic-critic.html (accessed October 2, 2017). *UpToDate*. Available online: https://www.uptodate.com/home (accessed October 2, 2017).

PART ONE

Comparative Approaches

1

The Bounds of Hierarchy:
Mary Douglas

a. Introduction

Mary Douglas (1921–2007) was a British anthropologist who challenged common distinctions between advanced and so-called primitive religions made by religious studies scholars. Her argument that dirt and pollution are defined in specific cultural contexts continues to challenge religious studies scholars to look for systems that structure social life. Douglas became interested in social anthropology during World War II, while volunteering with the British Colonial Office. After the war, Douglas took anthropology courses at the University of Oxford and eventually began work on a doctorate in anthropology under the guidance of E. E. Evans-Pritchard, during which she worked in the Belgian Congo (contemporary Zaire) where she studied the Lele of Kasai. She completed her doctorate in 1951. During her career, Douglas authored many books, including *Purity and Danger: An Analysis of Concepts of Pollution and Taboo* (1966) and *Natural Symbols: Explorations in Cosmology* (1970). The second chapter from *Purity and Danger* follows. In this selection, Douglas reveals how ideas about dirt and order depend on social agreements instead of on natural or biological absolutes.

In *Purity and Danger*, Douglas's first chapter argues that religious studies scholars have (falsely) bought into the idea that there is a difference between magic and religion and that primitive religious traditions are focused on the arrangement of physical items and, therefore, lacking in internal ethics. Moreover, she argues that these (still widespread) ideas assume the social evolutionary theory that there is a fundamental difference between so-called primitive and civilized people. Douglas makes this argument by drawing on the work of anthropologist J. G. Frazer to describe how Frazer's differentiation of primitive and advanced forms of religion depended on Christian assumptions of faith and belief. These disembodied Christian assumptions cause scholars to "disregard the material circumstances and judge [groups] according to the motives and disposition of the agent" (Douglas [1966] 2002: 13). This distinction between material circumstances and internal motives allowed Frazer to, on the one hand, correlate primitive religion with a magical concern and, on the other hand, correlate advanced religion (read: Christianity) with the ethics of internal motives. Douglas argues that, although anthropologists have rejected the evolutionary hypotheses out of which Frazer's work developed, these same anthropologists continue to accept Frazer's distinction between magic and religion. For Douglas, Frazer's distinction between magical and religious perpetuates a hierarchy of people based on their traditions, whether magic or religion. Douglas concludes this chapter with an apt caution: "We shall not expect to understand other people's ideas of contagion, sacred or secular, until we have confronted our own" (Douglas [1966] 2002: 35).

In the second chapter that follows this introduction, Douglas considers how ritual reflects modern medical assumptions about cleanliness. Douglas argues that cleanliness cannot be a satisfactory explanation for so-called primitive rituals such as washing or the avoidance of pork. Yet, she also argues that there is a relationship between modern medical rituals that promote hygiene and so-called primitive practices. Douglas states: "I am going to argue that our ideas of dirt also express symbolic systems and that the difference between pollution behavior in one part of the world and another is only a matter of detail" (Douglas [1966] 2018: 21). Thus, both modern practices of hygiene and ritual attempt to establish a symbolic system that determine when matter is in place, and thus clean, and when matter is out of place, and thus dirty. Douglas's exploration of how dirt is categorized leads to her development of a theory of culture as that which maintains communal understandings of order, which are necessary to keep dirt at bay. Douglas writes:

> To conclude, if uncleanness is matter out of place, we must approach it through order. Uncleanness or dirt is that which must not be included if a pattern is to be maintained. To recognise this is the first step towards insight into pollution. It involves us in no clear-cut distinction between sacred and secular. The same principle applies throughout. Furthermore, it involves no special distinction between primitives and moderns: we are all subject to the same rules (Douglas [1966] 2018: 25).

With this statement, Douglas maintains that contagion cannot be used to distinguish primitive and advanced religions because all social systems have ideas of contagion. In order to effectively study a community outside of our own, we must first understand our own ideas of contagion and purity. Douglas's argument makes the case for the role of reflexivity, or being aware of our own assumptions, when we study how others distinguish between what is pure and what is polluted in religious traditions.

Douglas's work establishes at least two major themes that continue to be influential for understanding the relationship between the physical world, the individual, and culture. First, Douglas establishes the purity rule, or the rule that social systems seek to map forms of social control onto bodily activities. Second, her work challenges us to consider the distinctions between magic, religion, and science and the roots of these distinctions in the legacy of colonialism. Because these distinctions are rooted in colonial histories, the distinctions between magic, religion, and science (and the implied hierarchy of science over religion over magic) are not insignificant but, rather, reflect colonial attempts to value people groups in accordance with their acceptance of higher orders of thinking. Scholars must, according to Douglas, be careful not to import their own understandings of the world into the categories they develop to understand the practices of others.

Through this anthropological work, Douglas creates a theory of religion. Religion, for her, becomes a social agreement that controls and regulates individual bodies. Part of this social agreement is the division of things that are considered to be polluting from things that are considered to be pure. This division protects the sacred or pure from the profane. Although she was trained outside of the discipline of religious studies, Douglas's work continues to be influential within religious studies, particularly around questions of social meaning and the relationship between social and individual meaning.

b. Secular Defilement (*Purity and Danger: An Analysis of Concepts of Pollution and Taboo*) *Mary Douglas*

Comparative religion has always been bedevilled by medical materialism. Some argue that even the most exotic of ancient rites have a sound hygienic basis. Others, though agreeing that primitive ritual has hygiene for its object, take the opposite view of its soundness. For them a great gulf divides our sound ideas of hygiene from the primitive's erroneous fancies. But both these medical approaches to ritual are fruitless because of a failure to confront our own ideas of hygiene and dirt.

On the first approach, it is implied that if we only knew all the circumstances we would find the rational basis of primitive ritual amply justified. As an interpretation this line of thought is deliberately prosaic. The importance of incense is not that it symbolises the ascending smoke of sacrifice, but it is a means of making tolerable the smells of unwashed humanity. Jewish and Islamic avoidance of pork is explained as due to the dangers of eating pig in hot climates.

It is true that there can be a marvellous correspondence between the avoidance of contagious disease and ritual avoidance. The washings and separations which serve the one practical purpose may be apt to express religious themes at the same time. So it has been argued that their rule of washing before eating may have given the Jews immunity in plagues. But it is one thing to point out the side benefits of ritual actions, and another thing to be content with using the by-products as a sufficient explanation. Even if some of Moses's dietary rules were hygienically beneficial, it is a pity to treat him as an enlightened public health administrator, rather than as a spiritual leader.

I quote from a commentary on Mosaic dietary rules, dated 1841:

It is probable that the chief principle determining the laws of this chapter will be found in the region of hygiene and sanitation... The idea of parasitic and infectious maladies, which has conquered so great a position in modern pathology, appears to have greatly occupied the mind of Moses, and to have dominated all his hygienic rules. He excludes from the Hebrew dietary animals particularly liable to parasites; and as it is in the blood that the germ or spores of infectious diseases circulate, he orders that they must be drained of their blood before serving for food....

(Kellog)

He goes on to quote evidence that European Jews have a longer expectation of life and immunity in plagues, advantages which he attributes to their dietary restrictions. When he writes of parasites, it is unlikely that Kellog is thinking of the trichiniasis [sic] worm, since it was not observed until 1828 and was considered harmless to man until 1860 (Hegner, Root & Augustine, 1929, p. 439).

For a recent expression of the same kind of view, read Dr. Ajose's account of the medical value of ancient Nigerian practices (1957). The Yoruba cult of a smallpox deity, for example, requires the patients to be isolated and treated only by a priest, himself recovered from the disease and therefore immune. Furthermore, the Yoruba use the left hand for handling anything dirty:

... because the right hand is used for eating, and people realise the risk of contamination of food that might result if this distinction were not observed.

Father Lagrange also subscribed to the same idea:

Alors l'impurité, nous ne le nions pas, a un caractère religieux, ou du moins touche au surnaturel prétendu; mais, dans sa racine, estce autre chose qu'une mesure de préservation sanitaire? L'eau ne remplace-t-elle pas ici les antiseptiques? Et l'esprit redouté n'a-t-il pas fait des siennes en sa nature propre de microbe?

(p. 155)

It may well be that the ancient tradition of the Israelites included the knowledge that pigs are dangerous food for humans. Anything is possible. But note that this is not the reason given in Leviticus for the prohibition of pork and evidently the tradition, if it ever existed, was lost. For Maimonides himself, the great twelfth-century prototype of medical materialism, although he could find hygienic reasons for all the other dietary restrictions of Mosaic law, confessed himself baffled by the prohibition on pork, and was driven back to aesthetic explanations, based on the revolting diet of the domestic pig:

I maintain that the food which is forbidden by the Law is unwholesome. There is nothing among the forbidden kinds of food whose injurious character is doubted, except pork, and fat. But also in these cases the doubt is not justified. For pork contains more moisture than necessary (for human food), and too much of superfluous matter. The principal reason why the Law forbids swine's flesh is to be found in the circumstance that its habits and its food are very dirty and loathsome....

(p. 370 seq.)

This at least shows that the original basis of the rule concerning pig flesh was not transmitted with the rest of the cultural heritage, even if it had once been recognised.

Pharmacologists are still hard at work on Leviticus XI. To give one example, I cite a report by David I. Macht to which Miss Jocelyne Richard has referred me. Macht made muscle extract from swine, dog, hare, coney (equated with guinea-pigs for experimental purposes) and camel, and also from birds of prey and from fishes without fins and scales. He tested the extracts for toxic juices and found them to be toxic. He tested extracts from animals which counted as clean in Leviticus and found them less toxic, but still he reckoned his research proved nothing either way about the medical value of the Mosaic laws.

For another example of medical materialism read Professor Kramer, who lauds a Sumerian tablet from Nippur as the only medical text received from the third millennium BC.

> The text reveals, though indirectly, a broad acquaintance with quite a number of rather elaborate medical operations and procedures. For example, in several of the prescriptions the instructions were to 'purify' the simples before pulverisation, a step which must have required several chemical operations.

Quite convinced that purifying here does not mean sprinkling with holy water or reciting a spell, he goes on enthusiastically:

> The Sumerian physician who wrote our tablet did not resort to magic spells and incantations ... the startling fact remains that our clay document, the oldest 'page' of medical text as yet uncovered, is completely free from mystical and irrational elements.
>
> (1956, pp. 58–9)

So much for medical materialism, a term coined by William James for the tendency to account for religious experience in these terms: for instance, a vision or dream is explained as due to drugs or indigestion. There is no objection to this approach unless it excludes other interpretations. Most primitive peoples are medical materialists in an extended sense, in so far as they tend to justify their ritual actions in terms of aches and pains which would afflict them should the rites be neglected. I shall later show why ritual rules are so often supported with beliefs that specific dangers attend on their breach. By the time I have finished with ritual danger I think no one should be tempted to take such beliefs at face value.

As to the opposite view – that primitive ritual has nothing whatever in common with our ideas of cleanness – this I deplore as equally harmful to the understanding of ritual. On this view, our washing, scrubbing, isolating and disinfecting has only a superficial resemblance with ritual purifications. Our practices are solidly based on hygiene, theirs are symbolic: we kill germs, they ward off spirits. This sounds straightforward enough as a contrast. Yet the resemblance between some of their symbolic rites and our hygiene is sometimes uncannily close. For example, Professor Harper summarises the frankly religious context of Havik Brahmin pollution rules. They recognise three degrees of religious purity. The highest is necessary for performing an act of worship; a middle degree is the expected normal condition; and finally there is a state of impurity. Contact with a person in the middle state will cause a person in the highest state to become impure, and contact with anyone in an impure state will make either higher categories impure. The highest state is only gained by a rite of bathing.

> A daily bath is absolutely essential to a Brahmin, for without it he cannot perform daily worship to his gods. Ideally, Haviks say, they should take three baths a day, one before each meal. But few do this. In practice all Haviks whom I have known rigidly observe the custom of a daily bath, which is taken before the main meal of the day and before the household gods are worshipped... Havik males, who belong to a relatively wealthy caste and who have a fair amount of leisure time during certain seasons, nevertheless do a great deal of the work required to run their areca nut estates. Every attempt is made to finish work that is considered dirty or ritually defiling – for example, carrying manure to the garden or working with an untouchable servant – before the daily bath that precedes the main meal. If for any reason this work has to be done in the afternoon, another bath should be taken when the man returns home....
>
> (p. 153)

A distinction is made between cooked and uncooked food as carriers of pollution. Cooked food is liable to pass on pollution, while uncooked food is not. So uncooked foods may be received from or handled by members of any caste – a necessary rule from the practical point of view in a society where the division of labour is correlated with degrees of inherited purity. Fruit and nuts, as long as they are whole, are not subject to ritual defilement, but once a coconut is broken or a plantain cut, a Havik cannot accept it from a member of a lower caste.

> The process of eating is potentially polluting, but the manner determines the amount of pollution. Saliva – even one's own – is extremely defiling. If a Brahmin inadvertently touches his fingers to his lips, he should bathe or at least change his clothes. Also, saliva pollution can be transmitted through some material substances. These two beliefs have led to the practice of drinking water by pouring it into the mouth instead of putting the lips on the edge of the cup, and of smoking cigarettes ... through the hand so that they never directly touch the lips. (Hookas are virtually unknown in this part of India) ... Eating of any food – even drinking coffee – should be preceded by washing the hands and feet.
>
> (p. 156)

Food which can be tossed into the mouth is less liable to convey saliva pollution to the eater than food which is bitten into. A cook may not taste the food she is preparing, as by touching her finger to her lips she would lose the condition of purity required for protecting food from pollution. While eating, a person is in the middle state of purity and if by accident he should touch the server's hand or spoon, the server becomes impure and should at least change clothes before serving more food. Since pollution is transmitted by sitting in the same row at a meal, when someone of another caste is entertained he is normally seated separately. A Havik in a condition of grave impurity should be fed outside the house, and he is expected himself to remove the leaf-plate he fed from. No one else can touch it without being defiled. The only person who is not defiled by touch and by eating from the leaf of another is the wife who thus, as we have said, expresses her personal relation to her husband. And so the rules multiply. They discriminate in ever finer and finer divisions, prescribing ritual behaviour concerning menstruation, childbirth and death. All bodily emissions, even blood or pus from a wound, are sources of impurity. Water, not paper must be used for washing after defecating, and this is done only with the left hand, while food may be eaten only with the right hand. To step on animal faeces causes impurity. Contact with leather causes impurity. If leather sandals are worn they should not be touched with the hands, and should be removed and the feet be washed before a temple or house is entered.

Precise regulations give the kinds of indirect contact which may carry pollution. A Havik, working with his Untouchable servant in his garden, may become severely defiled by touching a rope or bamboo at the same time as the servant. It is the simultaneous contact with the bamboo or rope which defiles. A Havik cannot receive fruit or money directly from an Untouchable. But some objects stay impure and can be conductors of impurity even after contact. Pollution lingers in cotton cloth, metal cooking vessels, cooked food. Luckily for collaboration between the castes, ground does not act as a conductor. But straw which covers it does.

> A Brahmin should not be in the same part of his cattle shed as his Untouchable servant, for fear that they may both step on places connected through overlapping straws on the floor. Even though a Havik and an Untouchable simultaneously bathe in the village pond, the Havik is able to attain a state of *Madi* (purity) because the water goes to the ground, and the ground does not transmit impurity.
>
> (p. 173)

The more deeply we go into this and similar rules, the more obvious it becomes that we are studying symbolic systems. Is this then really the difference between ritual pollution and our ideas of dirt: are our ideas hygienic where theirs are symbolic? Not a bit of it: I am going to argue that our ideas of dirt also express symbolic systems and that the difference between pollution behaviour in one part of the world and another is only a matter of detail.

Before we start to think about ritual pollution we must go down in sack-cloth and ashes and scrupulously re-examine our own ideas of dirt. Dividing them into their parts, we should distinguish any elements which we know to be the result of our recent history.

There are two notable differences between our contemporary European ideas of defilement and those, say, of primitive cultures. One is that dirt avoidance for us is a matter of hygiene or aesthetics and is not related to our religion . . . The second difference is that our idea of dirt is dominated by the knowledge of pathogenic organisms. The bacterial transmission of disease was a great nineteenth-century discovery. It produced the most radical revolution in the history of medicine. So much has it transformed our lives that it is difficult to think of dirt except in the context of pathogenicity. Yet obviously our ideas of dirt are not so recent. We must be able to make the effort to think back beyond the last 150 years and to analyse the bases of dirt avoidance, before it was transformed by bacteriology; for example, before spitting deftly into a spittoon was counted unhygienic.

If we can abstract pathogenicity and hygiene from our notion of dirt, we are left with the old definition of dirt as matter out of place. This is a very suggestive approach. It implies two conditions: a set of ordered relations and a contravention of that order. Dirt then, is never a unique, isolated event. Where there is dirt there is system. Dirt is the by-product of a systematic ordering and classification of matter, in so far as ordering involves rejecting inappropriate elements. This idea of dirt takes us straight into the field of symbolism and promises a link-up with more obviously symbolic systems of purity.

We can recognise in our own notions of dirt that we are using a kind of omnibus compendium which includes all the rejected elements of ordered systems. It is a relative idea. Shoes are not dirty in themselves, but it is dirty to place them on the dining table; food is not dirty in itself, but it is dirty to leave cooking utensils in the bedroom, or food be spattered on clothing; similarly, bathroom equipment in the drawing room; clothing lying on chairs; outdoor things indoors; upstairs things downstairs; under-clothing appearing where over-clothing should be, and so on. In short, our pollution behaviour is the reaction which condemns any object or idea likely to confuse or contradict cherished classifications.

We should now force ourselves to focus on dirt. Defined in this way it appears as a residual category, rejected from our normal scheme of classifications. In trying to focus on it we run against our strongest mental habit. For it seems that whatever we perceive is organised into patterns for which we, the perceivers, are largely responsible. Perceiving is not a matter of passively allowing an organ – say of sight or hearing – to receive a ready made impression from without, like a palette receiving a spot of paint. Recognising and remembering are not matters of stirring up old images of past impressions. It is generally agreed that all our impressions are schematically determined from the start. As perceivers, we select from all the stimuli falling on our senses only those which interest us, and our interests are governed by a pattern-making tendency, sometimes called *schema* (see Bartlett, 1932). In a chaos of shifting impressions, each of us constructs a stable world in which objects have recognisable shapes, are located in depth, and have permanence. In perceiving we are building, taking some cues and rejecting others. The most acceptable cues are those which fit most easily into the pattern that is being built up. Ambiguous ones tend to be treated as if they harmonised with the rest of the pattern. Discordant ones tend to be rejected. If they are accepted, the structure of assumptions has to be modified. As learning proceeds objects are named. Their names then affect the way they are perceived next time: once labelled they are more speedily slotted into the pigeon-holes in future.

As time goes on and experiences pile up, we make a greater and greater investment in our system of labels. So a conservative bias is built in. It gives us confidence. At any time we may have to modify our structure of assumptions to accommodate new experience, but the more consistent experience is with the past, the more confidence we can have in our assumptions. Uncomfortable facts which refuse to be fitted in, we find ourselves ignoring or distorting so that they do not disturb these established assumptions. By and large, anything we take note of is preselected and organised in the very act of perceiving. We share with other animals a kind of filtering mechanism which at first only lets in sensations we know how to use.

But what about the other ones? What about the possible experiences which do not pass the filter? Is it possible to force attention into less habitual tracks? Can we even examine the filtering mechanism itself?

We can certainly force ourselves to observe things which our schematising tendencies have caused us to miss. It always gives a jar to find our first facile observation at fault. Even to gaze steadily at distorting apparatus makes some people feel physically sick, as if their own balance was attacked. Mrs. Abercrombie put a group of medical students through a course of experiments designed to show them the high degree of selection we use in the simplest observations. 'But you can't have all the world a jelly,' one protested. 'It is as though my world has been cracked open,' said another. Others reacted in a more strongly hostile way (p. 131).

But it is not always an unpleasant experience to confront ambiguity. Obviously it is more tolerable in some areas than in others. There is a whole gradient on which laughter, revulsion and shock belong at different points and intensities. The experience can be stimulating. The richness of poetry depends on the use of ambiguity, as Empson has shown. The possibility of seeing a sculpture equally well as a landscape or as a reclining nude enriches the work's interest. Ehrenzweig has even argued that we enjoy works of art because they enable us to go behind the explicit structures of our normal experience. Aesthetic pleasure arises from the perceiving of inarticulate forms.

I apologise for using anomaly and ambiguity as if they were synonymous. Strictly they are not: an anomaly is an element which does not fit a given set or series; ambiguity is a characteristic of statements capable of two interpretations. But reflection on examples shows that there is very little advantage in distinguishing between these two terms in their practical application. Treacle is neither liquid nor solid; it could be said to give an ambiguous sense-impression. We can also say that treacle is anomalous in the classification of liquids and solids, being in neither one nor the other set.

Granted, then, that we are capable of confronting anomaly. When something is firmly classed as anomalous, the outline of the set in which it is not a member is clarified. To illustrate this I quote from Sartre's essay on stickiness. Viscosity, he says, repels in its own right, as a primary experience. An infant, plunging its hands into a jar of honey, is instantly involved in contemplating the formal properties of solids and liquids and the essential relation between the subjective experiencing self and the experienced world (1943, p. 696 seq.). The viscous is a state half-way between solid and liquid. It is like a cross-section in a process of change. It is unstable, but it does not flow. It is soft, yielding and compressible. There is no gliding on its surface. Its stickiness is a trap, it clings like a leech; it attacks the boundary between myself and it. Long columns falling off my fingers suggest my own substance flowing into the pool of stickiness. Plunging into water gives a different impression. I remain a solid, but to touch stickiness is to risk diluting myself into viscosity. Stickiness is clinging, like a too-possessive dog or mistress. In this way the first contact with stickiness enriches a child's experience. He has learnt something about himself and the properties of matter and the interrelation between self and other things.

I cannot do justice, in shortening the passage, to the marvellous reflections to which Sartre is provoked by the idea of stickiness as an aberrant fluid or a melting solid. But it makes the point that we can and do reflect with profit on our main classifications and on experiences which do not exactly fit them. In general, these reflections confirm our confidence in the main classifications. Sartre argues that melting, clinging viscosity is judged an ignoble form of existence in its very first manifestations. So from these earliest tactile adventures we have always known that life does not conform to our most simple categories.

There are several ways of treating anomalies. Negatively, we can ignore, just not perceive them, or perceiving we can condemn. Positively, we can deliberately confront the anomaly and try to create a new pattern of reality in which it has a place. It is not impossible for an individual to revise his own personal scheme of classifications. But no individual lives in isolation and his scheme will have been partly received from others.

Culture, in the sense of the public, standardised values of a community, mediates the experience of individuals. It provides in advance some basic categories, a positive pattern in which ideas and values are tidily ordered. And above all, it has authority, since each is induced to assent because of the assent of others. But its public character makes its categories more rigid. A private person may revise his pattern of assumptions or not. It is a private matter. But cultural categories are public matters. They cannot so easily be subject to revision. Yet they cannot neglect the challenge of aberrant forms. Any given system of classification must give rise to anomalies, and any given culture must confront events which seem to defy its assumptions. It cannot ignore the anomalies which its scheme produces, except at risk of forfeiting confidence. This is why, I suggest, we find in any culture worthy of the name various provisions for dealing with ambiguous or anomalous events.

First, by settling for one or other interpretation, ambiguity is often reduced. For example, when a monstrous birth occurs, the defining lines between humans and animals may be threatened. If a monstrous birth can be labelled an event of a peculiar kind, the categories can be restored. So the Nuer treat monstrous births as baby hippopotamuses, accidentally born to humans and, with this labelling, the appropriate action is clear. They gently lay them in the river where they belong (Evans-Pritchard, 1956, p. 84).

Second, the existence of anomaly can be physically controlled. Thus, in some West African tribes the rule that twins should be killed at birth eliminates a social anomaly, if it is held that two humans could not be born from the same womb at the same time. Or take the night-crowing cocks. If their necks are promptly wrung, they do not live to contradict the definition of a cock as a bird that crows at dawn.

Third, a rule of avoiding anomalous things affirms and strengthens the definitions to which they do not conform. So where Leviticus abhors crawling things, we should see the abomination as the negative side of the pattern of things approved.

Fourth, anomalous events may be labelled dangerous. Admittedly, individuals sometimes feel anxiety confronted with anomaly. But it would be a mistake to treat institutions as if they evolved in the same way as a person's spontaneous reactions. Such public beliefs are more likely to be produced in the course of reducing dissonance between individual and general interpretations. Following the work of Festinger it is obvious that a person, when he finds his own convictions at variance with those of friends, either wavers or tries to convince the friends of their error. Attributing danger is one way of putting a subject above dispute. It also helps to enforce conformity, as we shall show below in a chapter on morals.

Fifth, ambiguous symbols can be used in ritual for the same ends as they are used in poetry and mythology, to enrich meaning or to call attention to other levels of existence. We shall see in the final chapter of Purity and Danger how ritual, by using symbols of anomaly, can incorporate evil and death along with life and goodness, into a single, grand, unifying pattern.

To conclude, if uncleanness is matter out of place, we must approach it through order. Uncleanness or dirt is that which must not be included if a pattern is to be maintained. To recognise this is the first step towards insight into pollution. It involves us in no clear-cut distinction between sacred and secular. The same principle applies throughout. Furthermore, it involves no special distinction between primitives and moderns: we are all subject to the same rules. But in the primitive culture the rule of patterning works with greater force and more total comprehensiveness. With the moderns it applies to disjointed, separate areas of existence.

c. Questions

Comprehension

1. In the first statement of this selection, Douglas argues that comparative religion has been "bedeviled by medical materialism." What does she mean?

2. Why does Douglas argue that medical materialism is an insufficient reason for ritual practices?

3. Identify at least three examples of a symbolic system that distinguishes between cleanliness and pollution that Douglas identifies in this selection.

4. What is the role of anomaly and ambiguity in these symbolic systems?

Analysis

5. Douglas argues: "If uncleanness is matter out of place, we must approach it through order. Uncleanness or dirt is that which must not be included if a pattern is to be maintained. To recognize this is the first step towards insight into pollution. It involves us in no clear-cut distinction between sacred and secular. The same principle applies throughout. Furthermore, it involves no special distinction between primitives and moderns: we are all subject to the same rules." ([1966] 2018: 25). What are some of your ideas about dirt (what is gross, contagious, or polluting)? How does reading Douglas help you understand these ideas about dirt?

6. In the final paragraph of the chapter, Douglas argues that ideas about pollution are insufficient in order to distinguish between religious and secular and to distinguish between primitive and modern. On what basis, then, can or should we distinguish between what is religious and what is secular or what is primitive and what is modern?

Synthesis

7. How does Douglas's position as an anthropologist enable or constrain her contribution to the field of religious studies? What do you think are some of the different perspectives scholars trained in anthropology bring to their work? Based on your reading of Douglas, what can religious studies scholars learn from reading anthropologists?

References

Bartlett, F. C. (1932), *Remembering*. Cambridge: Cambridge University Press.
Evans-Pritchard, E. E. (1956), *Nuer Religion*. Oxford: Oxford University Press.
Hegner, R., F. Root and D. Augustine. (1929), *Animal Parasitology*. New York and London: The Century Company.
Kramer, Noah. (1956), *From the Tablets of Sumer*. Denver: The Falcon's Wing Press.
Sartre, J.- P. (1943), *L'Etre et le néant*. 3rd ed. Gallimard, Paris: Gallimard.

2

Feminist Textual
Critique: Phyllis Trible

a. Introduction

Phyllis Trible (1932–) is a US-born feminist biblical scholar whose method for biblical interpretation continues to open new avenues for the study of religious texts. Trible attended Meredith College and Union Theological Seminary before enrolling at Columbia University, where she finished her PhD in 1973. During her career, Trible authored several notable books, including *God and the Rhetoric of Sexuality* (1978) and *Texts of Terror: Literary-Feminist Readings of Biblical Narratives* (1984). With this body of work, Trible authorized feminist textual criticism in the field of biblical studies. The selection that follows highlights key features of Trible's method of feminist textual interpretation. Her central claim is that feminist textual interpretation and, in particular, the method of depatriarchalizing does not impose an outside worldview on the biblical text but, rather, is already present within the text itself.

In this selection, an article in the premier journal in the field of religious studies, the *Journal of the American Academy of Religion* (*JAAR*), Trible explores biblical interpretation in the context of the 1970s movement for women's liberation. "Depatriarchalizing in Biblical interpretation" challenges the impossible choice that biblical studies scholars assume they must make between "biblical faith and Women's Liberation" (Trible [1973] 2018: 29). Rather than accept this choice, Trible makes a case for translating biblical faith without sexism. According to Trible, "Depatriarchalizing is not an operation which the exegete performs on the text. It is a hermeneutic operating within Scripture itself. We expose it; we do not impose it" (Trible [1973] 2018: 42). Trible insists that scholars are not bringing an external mode of interpretation to understanding scripture but, rather, that the seeds of depatriarchalizing are built into the text itself. In this process of depatriarchalizing, Trible looks to three biblical themes that disavow descriptions of God that defy sex (such as God as a caring mother), the Ex of liberation and its relevance for gender dynamics, and the idea of corpora that connects everyone and, thus, makes gender oppression limiting for

Trible also reinterprets the exegesis of two passages that are often used to support male dominance: the story of the fall in Genesis 2–3 and the Song of Songs. According to Trible, the three biblical themes that disavow sexism along with the exegesis of Genesis 2–3 and the Song of Songs reveal biblical breaks with patriarchy. Interpreters of biblical texts who assume the patriarchal nature of the text fail to recognize these biblical breaks with patriarchy. As an alternative, Trible urges interpreters as follows: "For our day we need to perceive the depatriarchalizing principle, to recover it in those texts and themes where it is present, and to accent it in our translations" (Trible [1973] 2018: 42). For Trible, this is a crucial exercise not only for the liberation of women but also for the understanding of the biblical text.

While Trible's work is focused on biblical studies, her methods of depatriarchalizing have been foundational to the feminist pursuit of interpreting texts in multiple religious traditions. As a textual scholar, she is trained in a field traditionally housed under the umbrella of "religious studies." Trible's work does not offer a theory of religion in the way that Douglas's theory of pollution does; instead, Trible offers a theory for religion, meaning that her method of feminist textual interpretation is a theory often applied to the study of religious texts. With her literary criticism, Trible invites readers of sacred texts to set their own assumptions aside and to see what is happening in the text.

b. Depatriarchalizing in Biblical Interpretation (*Journal of the American Academy of Religion*) *Phyllis Trible*

BIBLICAL FAITH CHALLENGES the faithful to explore treasures old and new. In this context I propose to examine interactions between the Hebrew Scriptures and the Women's Liberation Movement. I am aware of the risks. Some claim that the task is impossible and ill-advised. The two phenomena have nothing to say to each other. As far as the East is from the West, so far are they separated. To attempt to relate them is to prostitute them. Others aver that the Bible and the Women's Movement are enemies. "Patriarchy has God on its side," declares Kate Millett, introducing her sexually-oriented discussion of the Fall. She maintains that this myth is "designed as it is expressly in order to blame all this world's discomfort on the female."[1] Making a similar point from within the Christian faith, Mary Daly writes of "the malignant view of the man-woman relationship which the androcentric myth itself inadvertently 'reveals' and perpetuates."[2] For her this story belongs to a patriarchal religion oppressive to women.

It is superfluous to document patriarchy in Scripture.[3] Yahweh is the God of Abraham, Isaac, and Jacob as well as of Jesus and Paul. The legal codes of Israel treat women primarily as chattel. Qoheleth condemns her "whose heart is snares and nets and whose hands are fetters," concluding that although a few men may seek the meaning of existence, "a woman among all these I have not found" (7:23–29). In spite of his eschatology, Paul considers women subordinate to their husbands,[4] and, even worse, I Timothy makes woman responsible for sin in the world (2:11–15).[5] Considerable evidence indicts the Bible as a document of male supremacy. Attempts to acquit it by tokens such as Deborah, Huldah, Ruth, or Mary and Martha only reinforce the case.

If these views are all which can be said or primarily what must be said, then I am of all women most miserable. I face a terrible dilemma: Choose ye this day whom you will serve: the God of the fathers or the God of sisterhood. If the God of the fathers, then the Bible supplies models for your slavery. If the God of sisterhood, then you must reject patriarchal religion and go forth without models to claim your freedom.[6] Yet I myself perceive neither war nor neutrality between biblical faith and Women's Liberation. The more I participate in the Movement, the more I discover my freedom through the appropriation of biblical symbols. Old and new interact. Let me not be misunderstood: I know that Hebrew literature comes from a male dominated society. I know that biblical religion is patriarchal, and I understand the adverse effects of that religion for women. I know also the dangers of eisegesis. Nevertheless, I affirm that the intentionality of biblical faith, as distinguished from a general description of biblical religion, is neither to create nor to perpetuate patriarchy but rather to function as salvation for both women and men. The Women's Movement errs when it dismisses the Bible as inconsequential or condemns it as enslaving. In rejecting Scripture women ironically accept male chauvinistic interpretations and thereby capitulate to the very view they are protesting. But there is another way: to reread (not rewrite) the Bible without the blinders of Israelite men or of Paul, Barth, Bonhoeffer, and a host of others.[7] The hermeneutical challenge is to translate biblical faith without sexism.

Themes Disavowing Sexism

One approach to translation *is* through themes which implicitly disavow sexism. Israel's theological understanding of Yahweh is such a theme. Here is a deity set apart from the fertility gods of the ancient Near East; a deity whose worship cannot tolerate a cult of sexuality; a deity described as one, complete, whole, and thus above sexuality (cf. Deut 6:4). To be sure, the masculine pronoun regularly denotes this God, but just as faithfully the Hebrew Scriptures proclaim that Yahweh is not a male who requires a female. There is no *hieros gamos* in Yahweh religion.[8] Moreover, the danger of a masculine label for Deity is recognized. While depicting Yahweh as a man, Israel repudiates both anthropomorphisms and andromorphisms. God repents, we read in some passages.[9] According to others, God is not a man that he should repent.[10] In his poem on Israel the faithless son and Yahweh the loving deity, Hosea beautifully presents this paradox of affirming while denying anthropomorphic language (11:1–11). Yahweh is the parent who teaches the child to walk, who heals tender wounds, and who feeds the hungry infant. Strikingly, these activities belonged to the mother, not to the father, in ancient Israel.[11] Like a human being, Yahweh agonizes, struggles, and suffers over the wayward child. Then as love overcomes anger, this Deity accounts for a verdict of mercy by denying identification with the male. Thus comes the wonderful climax, "for I am God (*'el*) and not man (*'ish*), the Holy One in your midst" (11:9).

Feminine imagery for God is more prevalent in the Old Testament than we usually acknowledge.[12] It occurs repeatedly in traditions of the Exodus and Wanderings. The murmuring themes focus often on hunger and thirst.[13] Providing food and drink is woman's work, and Yahweh assumes this role. Even as women fetch water for their families,[14] so the Lord supplies water in the desert for the people.[15] As mothers feed their household,[16] so Yahweh prepares manna and quail for the children of Israel.[17] But the children continue to complain, and an angry Moses reproaches God in a series of rhetorical questions:

> Did I conceive all this people? Did I bring them forth, that thou shouldst say to me, "Carry them in your bosom, as a nurse carries the sucking child, to the land which thou didst swear to give their fathers"?
>
> (Num. 11:12)

This extraordinary language indicates that Yahweh was indeed mother and nurse of the wandering children.[18] Further, the recital of *Heilsgeschichte* in Nehemiah 9 introduces Yahweh as seamstress:

> Forty years didst thou sustain them in the wilderness, and they lacked nothing; *their clothes did not wear out* and their feet did not swell.
>
> (Neh. 9:21)

The role of dressmaker is not unique to the God of the Wilderness. This same Deity made garments of skin to clothe the naked and disobedient couple in the Garden (Genesis 3:21). As a woman clothes her family,[19] so Yahweh clothes the human family.

Second Isaiah boldly employs gynomorphic speech for God. Yahweh speaks of her birth pangs:[20]

> Now I will cry out like a woman in travail,
>   I will gasp and pant. (42:14b)

The Deity compares her loving remembrance of Zion to a mother nursing her child:

> Can a woman forget her sucking child,
>   that she should have no compassion
>   on the son of her womb?
> Even these may forget,
>   yet I will not forget you. (49:15)

Third Isaiah continues the maternal picture. Yahweh is like Zion in labor, bringing forth children:[21]

Shall I bring to the birth and not cause
> to bring forth?
> says the Lord;
> shall I, who cause to bring forth, shut the womb?
> says your God. (66:9)

Yahweh is a comforting mother:

As one whom his mother comforts,
> so I will comfort you. (66:13)

The maternal Deity may also be a midwife:[22]

Yet thou are he who took me from the womb;
Thou didst keep me safe upon my mother's breast.
Upon thee was I cast from my birth....
> (Psalm 22:9-10a; cf. Psalm 71:6; Job 3:12)

Midwife, seamstress, housekeeper, nurse, and mother: all these feminine images characterize Yahweh, the God of Israel.

To summarize: Although the Old Testament often pictures Yahweh as a man, it also uses gynomorphic language for the Deity.[23] At the same time, Israel repudiated the idea of sexuality in God. Unlike fertility gods, Yahweh is neither male nor female; neither he nor she. Consequently, modern assertions that God is masculine, even when they are qualified,[24] are misleading and detrimental, if not altogether inaccurate. Cultural and grammatical limitations (the use of masculine pronouns for God) need not limit theological understanding. As Creator and Lord, Yahweh embraces and transcends both sexes. To translate for our immediate concern: the nature of the God of Israel defies sexism.

The Exodus speaks forcefully to Women's Liberation. So compelling is this theme of freedom from oppression that our enthusiasm for it may become unfaithfulness to it.[25] Yet the story does teach that the God of Israel abhors slavery; that Yahweh acts through human agents to liberate (agents who may not even acknowledge him; agents who may be *personae non gratae* not only to rulers but also to slaves); that liberation is a refusal of the oppressed to participate in an unjust society and thus it involves a withdrawal; and that liberation begins in the home of the oppressor. More especially, women nurture the revolution. The Hebrew midwives disobey Pharaoh. His own daughter thwarts him, and her maidens assist. This Egyptian princess schemes with female slaves, mother and daughter, to adopt a Hebrew child whom she names Moses. As the first to defy the oppressor, women *alone* take the initiative which leads to deliverance (Exod. 1:15–2:10).[26] If Pharaoh had realized the power of these women, he might have reversed his decree (Exod. 1:16, 22) and had females killed rather than males! At any rate, a patriarchal religion which creates and preserves such feminist traditions contains resources for overcoming patriarchy.

A third theme disavowing sexism is corporate personality.[27] All are embraced in the fluidity of transition from the one to the many and the many to the one. Though Israel did not apply this principle specifically to the issue of women, in it she has given us a profound insight to appropriate. "For the wound of the daughter of my people is my heart wounded," says Jeremiah (8:21). To the extent that women are enslaved, so too men are enslaved. The oppression of one individual or one group is the oppression of all individuals and all groups. Solidarity marks the sexes. In sexism we all die, both victim and victor. In liberation we all live equally as human beings.

Exegesis: Genesis 2–3

Another approach to translation is the exegesis of passages specifically concerned with female and male. With its focus on the concrete and the specific, this method complements and checks the generalizing tendencies of themes. Hence, I propose to investigate briefly the Yahwist story of creation and fall in Genesis 2–3. Many feminists reject this account because they accept the traditional exegesis of male supremacy. But interpretation is often circular. Believing that the text affirms male dominance and female subordination, commentators find evidence for that view. Let us read with an opposing concern: Does the narrative break with patriarchy? By asking this question, we may discover a different understanding.

Ambiguity characterizes the meaning of 'adham in Genesis 2–3. On the one hand, man is the first creature formed (2:7). The Lord God puts him in the garden "to till it and keep it," a job identified with the male (cf. 3:17–19). On the other hand, 'adham is a generic term for humankind. In commanding 'adham not to eat of the tree of the knowledge of good and evil, the Deity is speaking to both the man and the woman (2:16–17). Until the differentiation of female and male (2:21–23), 'adham is basically androgynous: one creature incorporating two sexes.

Concern for sexuality, specifically for the creation of woman, comes last in the story, after the making of the garden, the trees, and the animals. Some commentators allege female subordination based on this order of events.[28] They contrast it with Genesis 1:27 where God creates 'adham as male and female in one act.[29] Thereby they infer that whereas the Priests recognized the equality of the sexes, the Yahwist made woman a second, subordinate, inferior sex.[30] But the last may be first, as both the biblical theologian and the literary critic know. Thus the Yahwist account moves to its climax, not its decline, in the creation of woman.[31] She is not an afterthought; she is the culmination. Genesis 1 itself supports this interpretation, for there male and female are indeed the last and truly the crown of all creatures. The last is also first where beginnings and endings are parallel. In Hebrew literature the central concerns of a unit often appear at the beginning and the end as an *inclusio* device.[32] Genesis 2 evinces this structure. The creation of man first and of woman last constitutes a ring composition whereby the two creatures are parallel. In no way does the order disparage woman. Content and context augment this reading.

The context for the advent of woman is a divine judgment, "It is not good that *'adham* should be alone; I will make him a helper fit for him" (2:18). The phrase needing explication is "helper fit for him." In the Old Testament the word helper (*'ezer*) has many usages. It can be a proper name for a male.[33] In our story it describes the animals and the woman. In some passages it characterizes Deity. God is the helper of Israel. As helper Yahweh creates and saves.[34] Thus *'ezer* is a relational term; it designates a beneficial relationship; and it pertains to God, people, and animals. By itself the word does not specify positions within relationships; more particularly, it does not imply inferiority. Position results from additional content or from context. Accordingly, what kind of relationship does *'ezer* entail in Genesis 2:18, 20? Our answer comes in two ways: 1) the word *neged*, which joins *'ezer*, connotes equality: a helper who is a counterpart.[35] 2) The animals are helpers, but they fail to fit *'adham*. There is physical, perhaps psychic, rapport between *'adham* and the animals, for Yahweh forms (*yaṣar*) them both out of the ground (*'adbamah*). Yet their similarity is not equality. *'Adham* names them and thereby exercises power over them. No fit helper is among them. And thus the narrative moves to woman. My translation is this: God is the helper superior to man; the animals are helpers inferior to man; woman is the helper equal to man.

Let us pursue the issue by examining the account of the creation of woman (21–22). This episode concludes the story even as the creation of man commences it. As I have said already, the ring composition suggests an interpretation of woman and man as equals. To establish this meaning, structure and content must mesh. They do. In both episodes Yahweh alone creates. For the last creation the Lord God "caused a deep sleep (*tardemab*) to fall upon the man." Man has no part in making woman; he is out of it. He exercises no control over her existence. He is neither participant nor spectator nor consultant at her birth. Like man, woman owes her life solely to God. For both of them the orgin of life is a divine mystery. Another parallel of equality is creation out of raw materials: dust for man and a rib for woman. Yahweh chooses these fragile materials and in both cases processes them before human beings happen. As Yahweh shapes dust and then breathes into it to form man, so Yahweh takes out the rib and then builds it into woman.[36] To call woman "Adam's rib" is to misread the text which states carefully and clearly that the extracted bone required divine labor to become female, a datum scarcely designed to bolster the male ego. Moreover, to claim that the rib means inferiority or subordination is to assign the man qualities over the woman which are not in the narrative itself. Superiority, strength, aggressiveness, dominance, and power do not characterize man in Genesis 2. By contrast he is formed from dirt; his life hangs by a breath which he does not control; and he himself remains silent and passive while the Deity plans and interprets his existence.

The rib means solidarity and equality. *'Adham* recognizes this meaning in a poem:[37]

This at last is bone of my bones
    and flesh of my flesh.
She shall be called *'ishshah* (woman)
    because she was taken out of *'ish* (man). (2:23)

The pun proclaims both the similarity and the differentiation of female and male. Before this episode the Yahwist has used only the generic term *'adham*. No exclusively male reference has appeared. Only with the specific creation of wom-words, sexuality is simultaneous for woman and man. The sexes are interrelated and interdependent. Man as male does not precede woman as female but happens concurrently with her. Hence, the first act in Genesis 2 is the creation of an (*'ishshah*) occurs the first specific term for man as male (*'ish*). In other androgyny (2:7) and the last is the creation of sexuality (2:23).[38] Male embodies female and female embodies male. The two are neither dichotomies nor duplicates. The birth of woman corresponds to the birth of man but does not copy it. In responding to the woman, man speaks for the first time and for the first time discovers himself as male. No longer a passive creature, *'ish* comes alive in meeting *'ishshah*.

Some read in (to) the poem a naming motif. The man names the woman and thereby has power and authority over her.[39] But again I suggest that we reread. Neither the verb nor the noun *name* is in the poem. We find instead the verb *qara'*, to call: "she shall be called woman." Now in the Yahwist primeval history this verb does not function as a synonym or parallel or substitute for *name*. The typical formula for naming is the verb *to call* plus the explicit object *name*. This formula applies to Deity, people, places, and animals. For example, in Genesis 4 we read:

> Cain built a city and *called* the *name* of the city after the *name* of his son Enoch (v. 17).
> And Adam knew his wife again, and she bore a son and *called* his *name* Seth (v. 25).
> To Seth also a son was born and he *called* his *name* Enoch (v. 26*a*).
> At that time men began to *call* upon the *name* of the Lord (v. 26*b*).

Genesis 2:23 has the verb *call* but does not have the object *name*. Its absence signifies the absence of a naming motif in the poem. The presence of both the verb *call* and the noun *name* in the episode of the animals strengthens the point:

> So out of the ground the Lord God formed every beast of the field and every bird of the air and brought them to the man to see what he would *call* them; and whatever the man *called* every living creature, that was its *name*. The man gave *names* to all cattle, and to the birds of the air and to every beast of the field. (2:19–20)

In calling the animals by name, *'adham* establishes supremacy over them and fails to find a fit helper. In calling woman, *'adham* does not name her and does find in her a counterpart. Female and male are equal sexes. Neither has authority over the other.[40]

A further observation secures the argument: *Woman* itself is not a name. It is a common noun; it is not a proper noun. It designates gender; it does not specify person. *'Adham* recognizes sexuality by the words *'ishshah* and *'ish*. This recognition is not an act of naming to assert the power of male over female. Quite the contrary. But the true skeptic is already asking: What about Genesis 3:20 where "the man called his wife's name Eve"? We must wait to consider that question. Meanwhile, the words of the ancient poem as well as their context proclaim sexuality originating in the unity of 'adham. From this one (androgynous) creature come two (female and male). The two return to their original unity as 'ish and 'ishshah become one flesh (2:24):[41] another instance of the ring composition.

Next the differences which spell harmony and equality yield to the differences of disobedience and disaster. The serpent speaks to the woman. Why to the woman and not to the man? The simplest answer is that we do not know. The Yahwist does not tell us anymore than he explains why the tree of the knowledge of good and evil was in the garden. But the silence of the text stimulates speculations, many of which only confirm the patriarchal mentality which conceived them. Cassuto identifies serpent and woman, maintaining that the cunning of the serpent is "in reality" the cunning of the woman.[42] He impugns her further by declaring that "for the very reason that a woman's imagination surpasses a man's, it was the woman who was enticed first." Though more gentle in his assessment, von Rad avers that "in the history of Yahweh-religion it has always been the women who have shown an inclination for obscure astrological cults" (a claim which he does not document).[43] Consequently, he holds that the woman "confronts the obscure allurements and mysteries that beset our limited life more directly than the man does," and then he calls her a "temptress." Paul Ricoeur says that woman "represents the point of weakness," as the entire story "gives evidence of a very masculine resentment."[44] McKenzie links the "moral weakness" of the woman with her "sexual attraction" and holds that the latter ruined both the woman and the man.[45] But the narrative does not say any of these things. It does not sustain the judgment that woman is weaker or more cunning or more sexual than man. Both have the same Creator, who explicitly uses the word "good" to introduce the creation of woman (2:18). Both are equal in birth. There is complete rapport, physical, psychological, sociological, and theological, between them: bone of bone and flesh of flesh. If there be moral frailty in one, it is moral frailty in two. Further, they are equal in responsibility and in judgment, in shame and in guilt, in redemption and in grace. What the narrative says about the nature of woman it also says about the nature of man.

Why does the serpent speak to the woman and not to the man? Let a female speculate. If the serpent is "more subtle" than its fellow creatures, the woman is more appealing than her husband. Throughout the myth she is the more intelligent one, the more aggressive one, and the one with greater sensibilities.[46] Perhaps the woman elevates the animal world by conversing theologically with the serpent. At any rate, she understands the hermeneutical task. In quoting God she interprets the prohibition ("neither shall you touch it"). The woman is both theologian and translator. She contemplates the tree, taking into account all the possibilities. The tree is good for food; it satisfies the physical drives. It pleases the eyes; it is aesthetically and emotionally desirable. Above all, it is coveted as the source of wisdom (haskîl). Thus the woman is fully aware when she acts, her vision encompassing the gamut of life. She takes the fruit and she eats. The initiative and the decision are hers alone. There is no consultation with her husband. She seeks neither his advice nor his permission. She acts independently. By contrast the man is a silent, passive, and bland recipient: "She also gave some to her husband and he ate." The narrator makes no attempt to depict the husband as reluctant or hesitating. The man does not theologize; he does not contemplate; he does not envision the full possibilities of the occasion. His one act is belly-oriented, and it is an act of quiescence, not of initiative. The man is not dominant; he is not aggressive; he is not a decision-maker. Even though the prohibition not to eat of the tree appears before the female was specifically created, she knows that it applies to her. She has interpreted it, and now she struggles with the temptation to disobey. But not the man, to whom the prohibition came directly (2:6). He follows his wife without question or comment, thereby denying his own individuality. If the woman be intelligent, sensitive, and ingenious, the man is passive, brutish, and inept. These character portrayals are truly extraordinary in a culture dominated by men. I stress their contrast not to promote female chauvinism but to undercut patriarchal interpretations alien to the text.

The contrast between woman and man fades after their acts of disobedience. They are one in the new knowledge of their nakedness (3:7). They are one in hearing and in hiding. They flee from the sound of the Lord God in the Garden (3:8). First to the man come questions of responsibility (3:9, 11), but the man fails to be responsible: "The woman whom Thou gavest to be with me, she gave me fruit of the tree, and I ate" (3:12). Here the man does not blame the woman; he does not say that the woman seduced him;[47] he blames the Deity. The verb which he uses for both the Deity and the woman is *ntn* (cf. 3:6). So far as I can determine, this verb neither means nor implies seduction in this context or in the lexicon. Again, if the Yahwist intended to make woman the temptress, he missed a choice opportunity. The woman's response supports the point. "The serpent beguiled me and I ate" (3:13). Only here occurs the strong verb *nsb'*, meaning to deceive, to seduce. God accepts this subject-verb combination when, immediately following the woman's accusations, Yahweh says to the serpent, "Because you have done this, cursed are you above all animals" (3:14).

Though the tempter (the serpent) is cursed,[48] the woman and the man are not. But they are judged, and the judgments are commentaries on the disastrous effects of their shared disobedience. They show how terrible human life has become as it stands between creation and grace. We misread if we assume that these judgments are mandates. They describe; they do not prescribe. They protest; they do not condone. Of special concern are the words telling the woman that her husband shall rule over her (3:16). This statement is not license for male supremacy, but rather it is condemnation of that very pattern.[49] Subjugation and supremacy are perversions of creation. Through disobedience the woman has become slave. Her initiative and her freedom vanish. The man is corrupted also, for he has become master, ruling over the one who is his God given equal. The subordination of female to male signifies their shared sin.[50] This sin vitiates all relationships: between animals and human beings (3:15); mothers and children (3:16); husbands and wives (3:16); man and the soil (3:17, 18); man and his work (3:19). Whereas in creation man and woman know harmony and equality, in sin they know alienation and discord. Grace makes possible a new beginning.

A further observation about these judgments: They are culturally conditioned. Husband and work (childbearing) define the woman; wife and work (farming) define the man. A literal reading of the story limits both creatures and limits the story. To be faithful translators, we must recognize that women as well as men move beyond these culturally defined roles, even as the intentionality and function of the myth moves beyond its original setting. Whatever forms stereotyping takes in our own culture, they are judgments upon our common sin and disobedience. The suffering and oppression we women and men know now are marks of our fall, not of our creation.

It is at this place of sin and judgment that "the man calls his wife's name Eve" (3:20), thereby asserting his rule over her. The naming itself faults the man for corrupting a relationship of mutuality and equality. And so Yahweh evicts the primeval couple from the Garden, yet with signals of grace. Interestingly, the conclusion of the story does not specify the sexes in flight. Instead the narrator resumes use of the generic and androgynous term 'adham, with which the story began, and thereby completes an overall ring composition (3:22–24).

We approached this myth by asking if it presages a break with patriarchy. Our rereading has borne fruit. Remarkable is the extent to which patriarchal patterns fade; the extent to which the Yahwist stands over against his male dominated culture; the extent to which the vision of a trans-sexual Deity shaped an understanding of human sexuality.

Exegesis: Song of Songs

On this issue the Yahwist is not alone in Israel. Among his companions are the female and the male who celebrate the joys of erotic love in the Song of Songs. This poetry contains many parallels to the Yahwist narrative. Perhaps the Paradise described in Genesis 2 and destroyed in Genesis 3 has been regained, expanded, and improved upon in the Song of Songs. At any rate, its words and images embody simultaneously several layers of meaning. The literal, the metaphoric, and the euphemistic intertwine in content and nuance.[51]

Canticles begins with the woman speaking.[52] She initiates love-making:

Let him kiss me with the kisses of his mouth,
        for your love is sweeter than wine (1:2).

In this first poem (1:2–2:6) she calls herself keeper of vineyards (1:6). In the last poem (8:4–14) she returns to this motif (8:12), even as she concludes the unit by summoning her beloved (8:14). Thus the overall structure of the Song is a ring composition showing the prominence of the female. Within this design another *inclusio* emphasizes women. The daughters of Jerusalem commence and close the second poem (2:7 and 3:5).

As in Genesis 2–3, the ring composition of the Song of Songs encircles a garden.[53] Person and place blend in this imagery.

> Let my beloved come to his garden
>   and eat its choicest fruit (4:16c).

The woman is the garden (4:10–15), and to the garden her lover comes (5:1, 6:2, 11). Together they enjoy this place of sensuous delight. Many trees adorn their garden, trees pleasant to the sight and good for food:[54] the apple tree (2:3; 7:8; 8:5), the fig tree (2:13), the pomegranate (4:3, 13; 6:7), the cedar (5:15), the palm (7:8) and "all trees of frankincense" (4:14). Spices give pleasure as does the abundance of fruits, plants, and flowers: the meadow saffron (2:1), the lotus (2:1f, 16; 4:5; 5:13; 7:2), the mandrake (7:13), and others (2:12, 13; 4:13, 16; 6:11). Fountains of living water enhance further this site (4:12, 15), inviting comparisons with the subterranean stream watering the earth (Gen. 2:6) and with the rivers flowing out of Eden to water the garden (Gen. 2:10–14).

Animals inhabit two gardens. In the first they were formed, both beasts and birds, and received their names. As foils they participated in the creation of woman and provided a context for the total joy of 'ish and 'ishshah. In Canticles their names become explicit as does their contextual and metaphorical participation in the encounters of lovers. The woman describes her mate:

> My beloved is like a gazelle
>   or a young stag (2:9)
> ......
>   his locks are wavy,
>   black as a raven (5:11).
> His eyes are like doves
>   beside springs of water (5:12).

The man also uses animal imagery to describe the woman:

> Behold, you are beautiful, my love
>   behold, you are beautiful!
> Your eyes are doves
>   behind your veil.
> Your hair is like a flock of goats,
>   moving down the slopes of Gilead.
> Your teeth are like a flock of shorn ewes
>   that have come up from the washing,
> Each having its twin,
>   and not one of them is bereaved (4:1–2)
>   ......

Your two breasts are like two fawns,
> twins of a gazelle,
> that feed among the lilies (4:5).

The mare (1:9), the foxes (2:15), the turtledove (2:12), the lions and the leopards (4:8) also dwell in this garden where all nature extols the love of female and male.

The sensuality of Eden broadens and deepens in the Song. Love is sweet to the taste, like the fruit of the apple tree (2:3; cf. 4:16; 5:1, 13). Fragrant are the smells of the vineyards (2:13), of the perfumes of myrrh and frankincense (3:6), of the scent of Lebanon (4:11), and of beds of spices (5:13; 6:2). The embraces of lovers confirm the delights of touch (1:2; 2:3–6; 4:10, 11; cf. 5:1; 7:6–9; 8:1, 3). A glance of the eyes ravishes the heart (4:9; 6:13), as the sound of the beloved thrills it (5:4).

Work belongs both to the garden of creation and to the garden of eroticism. Clearly man works in Eden and implicitly woman too. The Song alters this emphasis. The woman definitely works. She keeps vineyards (1:6; cf. 8:12), and she pastures flocks (1:8). Her lover may be a shepherd also (1:7), though the text does not secure this meaning.[55] By analogy he is a king (1:4, 12; 8:11, 12), but he neither rules nor dispenses wisdom. He provides luxury for the sake of love (3:9–11).[56] Together Genesis 2 and the Song of Songs affirm work in gardens of joy, and together they suggest fluidity in the occupational roles of woman and man. In Canticles nature and work are pleasures leading to love, as indeed they were before the primeval couple disobeyed and caused the ground to bring forth thorns and thistles and work to become pain and sweat (Gen. 2:15; 3:16, 18, 19).

Neither the primeval couple nor the historical couple bear names, but both are concerned with naming. When 'adham names the animals, it is an act of authority consonant with creation. When he names the woman, it is an act of perversion preceding expulsion. In the erotic garden roles reverse, authority vanishes, and perversion is unknown. The woman names the man:

For your love is better than wine,
> your anointing oils are fragrant,
Your *name* is oil poured out;
> therefore the maidens love you (1:2b-3).

Her act is wholly fitting and good. Naming is ecstasy, not exercise; it is love, not control. And that love marks a new creation.

Song of Songs extends beyond the confines of Eden to include other places, people, and professions. We move from the countryside (2:14; 4:11; 6:11; 7:12) to the city with its squares, streets, and walls (2:9; 3:2, 3; 5:7). We hear of kings (1:9; 3:7; 4:4) and warriors (3:7; 6:4); queens, concubines, and maidens (6:8, 9); watchmen (3:3; 5:7) and merchants (3:6); brothers (1:6), sisters (8:8), mothers (6:9; 8:1, 2, 5), and companions male (1:7) and female (2:2, 7). Paradise expands to civilization. History, like nature, contributes to the encounter of the sexes.

Parental references merit special attention. Seven times the lovers speak of mother, but not once do they mention father.[57] The man calls his beloved the special child of the mother who bore her (6:9), even as the woman cites the travail of the mother who bore him (8:5). This concern with birth is also reminiscent of the theme of creation in Genesis 2. In yearning for closeness with her lover, the woman wishes he were a brother nursing at the breast of her mother (8:1). But these traditional images do not exhaust the meaning of mother. It is his mother who crowns Solomon on the day of his wedding (3:11). The female lover identifies her brothers as sons of her mother, not of her father (1:6). And most telling of all, the woman leads her lover to the "house of her mother" (3:4; 8:2). Neither the action nor the phrase bespeaks patriarchy.[58] This strong matriarchal coloring in the Song of Songs recalls the primeval man leaving his father and his mother to cleave to his wife (Gen. 2:24; cf. Gen. 24:28; Ruth 1:8).

Like Genesis 2, Canticles affirms mutuality of the sexes. There is no male dominance, no female subordination, and no stereotyping of either sex. The woman is independent, fully the equal of the man. Her interests, work, and words defy the connotations of "second sex." Unlike the first woman, this one is not a wife. Her love does not include procreation.[59] At times the man approaches her, and at other times she initiates their meetings. In one poem the man moves vigorously and quickly over the hills and mountains to stand at her window. He calls her to join him outside:

Arise, my love, my fair one
    and come away;
for lo, the winter is past,
    the rain is over and gone (2:10,11).

Next the woman actively seeks the man (3:1–4). Upon her bed she desires him. She rises to search in the streets and squares. Her movements are bold and open. She does not work in secret or in shame. She asks help of the night watchman: "Have you seen him whom my *nephesh* loves?" Finding him, she clasps him securely:

I held him and would not let go
    until I had brought him into
        my mother's house,
    and into the chamber of her that
        conceived me (3:4).

This theme of alternating initiative for woman and man runs throughout the poetry.[60] Further, each lover exalts the physical beauty and charm of the other in language candid and covert. Their metaphorical speech reveals even as it conceals. They treat each other with tenderness and respect, for they are sexual lovers, not sexual objects. They neither exploit nor escape sex; they embrace and enjoy it.[61] Both are naked and they are not ashamed (cf. Gen. 2:25).

On occasion the woman expresses their relationship by the formula, "My beloved is mine and I am his" (2:16; 6:3). Once she says, "I am my beloved's and his desire is for me" (7:10). This word *desire* occurs only three times in the Old Testament: once in Canticles and twice in the Yahwist Epic (Gen. 3:16; 4:7). "Your desire shall be for your husband, and he shall rule over you" is the divine judgment upon the woman. As we have seen, its context is sin and perversion. *Desire* in the Song of Songs reverses this meaning of the male–female relationship. Here desire is joy, not judgment. Moreover, the possessive reference has switched from the wife's desire for her husband to the desire of the male lover for the female. Has one mark of sin in Eden been overcome here in another garden with the recovery of mutuality in love? Male dominance is totally alien to Canticles. Can it be that grace is present?

Let us stress that these lovers are not the primeval couple living before the advent of disobedience. Nor are they an eschatological couple, as Karl Barth would have us believe.[62] They live in the "terror of history" (Eliade) but their love knows not that terror. To be sure, the poetry hints of threats to their Paradise. If the first garden had its tree and its serpent, the second has its potential dangers too. There is the sterile winter now past (2:11); the little foxes which spoil the vineyards (2:15); the anger of the brothers (1:6);[63] a knowledge of jealously (8:6); and the anxiety of the woman seeking her beloved, finding him not (3:1–4; 5:6–8; 6:1), and suffering at the hands of the watchmen (5:7). In addition, death threatens eroticism even as it haunted creation (Gen 2:17); 3:3, 4, 19). But all these discordant notes blend into the total harmony of love. If death did not swallow the primeval couple, neither does it overpower the historical couple. "Love is strong as death" (8:6). The poetry speaks triumphantly to all terror when it affirms that not even the primeval waters of chaos can destroy love:

Many waters cannot quench love, (*'ahabah*)
    neither can floods drown it (8:7).

In many ways, then, Song of Songs is a midrash on Genesis 2–3.[64] By variations and reversals it creatively actualizes major motifs and themes of the primeval myth. Female and male are born to mutuality and love. They are naked without shame; they are equal without duplication. They live in gardens where nature joins in celebrating their oneness. Animals remind these couples of their shared superiority in creation as well as of their affinity and responsibility for lesser creatures. Fruits pleasing to the eye and to the tongue are theirs to enjoy. Living waters replenish their gardens. Both couples are involved in naming; both couples work. If the first pair pursue the traditional occupations for women and men, the second eschews stereotyping. Neither couple fits the rhetoric of a male dominated culture. As equals they confront life and death. But the first couple lose their oneness through disobedience. Consequently, the woman's desire becomes the man's dominion. The second couple affirm their oneness through eroticism. Consequently, the man's desire becomes the woman's delight. Whatever else it may be, Canticles is a commentary on Genesis 2–3. Paradise Lost is Paradise Regained.

Yet the midrash is incomplete. Even though Song of Songs is the poetry of history, it speaks not at all of sin and disobedience. Life knows no prohibitions. And most strikingly, no Deity acts in that history. God is not explicitly acknowledged as either present or absent (though eroticism itself may be an act of worship in the context of grace). Some may conclude that these omissions make the setting of Canticles a more desirable paradise than Eden. But the silences portend the limits. If we cannot return to the primeval garden (Gen. 3:23–24), we cannot live solely in the garden of eroticism. Juxtaposing the two passages, we can appropriate them both for our present concern.

Conclusion: A Depatriarchalizing Principle

Suffice it to conclude that the Hebrew Scriptures and Women's Liberation do meet and that their encounter need not be hostile. Contrary to Kate Millett, the biblical God is not on the side of patriarchy, and the myth of the Fall does not "blame all this world's discomfort on the female." Indeed, this myth negates patriarchy in crucial ways; it does not legitimate the oppression of women. It explores the meaning of human existence for female and male. It reveals the goodness yet frailty of both creatures; their intended equality under God and with each other; their solidarity in sin and in suffering; and their shared need of redemption. Thereby its symbols illuminate a present issue, even as they exercise a sobering check on it. In Yahwist theology neither male nor female chauvinism is warranted. Both are perversions of creation which signify life under judgment.

Song of Songs counterbalances this "undertone of melancholy" (von Rad) by showing woman and man in mutual harmony after the Fall. Love is the meaning of their life, and this love excludes oppression and exploitation. It knows the goodness of sex and hence it knows not sexism. Sexual love expands existence beyond the stereotypes of society. It draws unto itself the public and the private, the historical and the natural. It transforms all life even as life enhances it. Grace returns to female and male.[65]

Alongside Genesis 2–3 and the Song of Songs we place the themes of the nature of Yahweh, of the Exodus, and of corporate personality. In various ways they demonstrate a depatriarchalizing principle at work in the Hebrew Bible. Depatriarchalizing is not an operation which the exegete performs on the text. It is a hermeneutic operating within Scripture itself. We expose it; we do not impose it. Tradition history teaches that the meaning and function of biblical materials is fluid. As Scripture moves through history, it is appropriated for new settings. Varied and diverse traditions appear, disappear, and reappear from occasion to occasion. We shall be unfaithful readers if we neglect biblical passages which break with patriarchy or if we permit our interpretations to freeze in a patriarchal box of our own construction. For our day we need to perceive the depatriarchalizing principle, to recover it in those texts and themes where it is present,[66] and to accent it in our translations. Therein we shall be explorers who embrace both old and new in the pilgrimage of faith.

c. Questions

Comprehension

1. What is depatriarchalization? Why does it matter for Trible? What difference does it makes in biblical studies?

2. Describe the three biblical themes that, according to Trible, disavow sexism.

3. In what ways does Trible argue Genesis 2–3 and the Song of Songs are texts that describe the equality of men and women?

Analysis

4. Trible argues that the biblical text can be "depatriarchalized." Explain why you agree or disagree with her argument.

5. Trible's method is articulated specifically in relation to the Bible. Are there limitations to Trible's method when applied to the sacred texts of other traditions?

Synthesis

6. How is Trible's engagement of texts similar to or different than the method of Douglas, who studies both texts and living communities in her fieldwork?

Notes

1 Kate Millett, *Sexual Politics* (Garden City, NY: Doubleday & Company, 1970), pp. 51–54.

2 Mary Daly, "The Courage to See," *The Christian Century,* September 22, 1971, p. 1110. See also *The Church and the Second Sex* (New York: Harper & Row, 1968), pp. 32–42.

3 On the status of women in the male dominated society of Israel, see Roland de Vaux, *Ancient Israel* (New York: McGraw-Hill Book Company, 1961), p. 39f; J. Pederson, *Israel* I (Oxford, 1959), pp. 60–81; 231–33; W. Eichrodt, *Theology of the Old Testament,* I (Philadelphia: The Westminister Press, 1961), pp. 80–82.

4 I Cor. 14:34–35; Col. 3:18; cf. Eph. 5:22–24.

5 On Paul see Krister Stendahl, *The Bible and the Role of Women* (Philadelphia: Fortress Press, 1966); Madeleine Boucher, "Some Unexplored Parallels to 1 Cor 11, 11–12 and Gal 3, 28: The NT on the Role of Women," *Catholic Biblical Quarterly,* January, 1969: 50–58. For efforts to exonerate Paul, see Robert C. Campbell, "Women's Liberation and the Apostle Paul," *Baptist Leader,* January, 1972; Robin Scroggs, "Paul: Chauvinist or Liberationist?," *The Christian Century,* March 15, 1972: 307–9; *ibid.,* "Paul and the Eschatological Woman," *Journal of the American Academy of Religion* XL, no. 3

(September, 1972): 283–303; G. B. Caird, "Paul and Women's Liberty," *Bulletin of the John Rylands Library* 54, no. 2 (Spring, 1972): 268–81.

6 Happily, the paradigm in Josh. 24:14–15 resolves the predicament. It poses a choice between competing gods only if the people are unwilling to serve Yahweh.

7 Cf. Peggy Ann Way, "An Authority of Possibility for Women in the Church," in *Women's Liberation and the Church*, ed. Sarah Bentley Doely (New York: Association Press, 1970), pp. 78–82.

8 Eichrodt, *Theology,* I, pp. 121, 151f; cf. Helmer Ringgren, *Israelite Religion* (Philadelphia: Fortress Press, 1966), p. 197f.

9 E.g., Gen. 6:6; Ex. 32:14; I Sam. 15:11, 35; Jonah 3:10.

10 E.g., Num. 23:19; I Sam. 15:29.

11 Cf. Ludwig Köhler, *Hebrew Man* (New York: Abingdon Press, 1956), p. 58ff.

12 For much of this material I am indebted to an unpublished paper, "Yahweh's Relationship as Mother to Israel" (June, 1972), by Ms. Toni Craven of Andover Newton Theological School. We have only begun to explore the topic.

13 Martin Noth, *Exodus* (Philadelphia: The Westminster Press, 1962), pp. 128–140. For a technical discussion of the murmuring theme, see George W. Coats, *Rebellion in the Wilderness* (New York: Abingdon Press, 1968), pp. 47–127, 249–54.

14 Gen. 21:19; 24:11; 13–20; 43–46; Exod. 2:16ff; I Sam. 9:11; I Kings 17:10.

15 Exod. 17:1–7; Num. 20:2–13; Neh. 9:15.

16 Prov. 31:14–15; Gen. 18:6; 27:9, 14; cf. II Sam. 13:7–10.

17 Exod. 16:4–36; Num. 11; Neh. 9:15; cf. Deut. 32:13–14; Hos. 11:4; Psalm 36:8; 81:10, 16.

18 Martin Noth comments tellingly on this passage in *Numbers,* Philadelphia: The Westminster Press, 1968, p. 86f.

19 Prov. 31:21f.

20 See James Muilenburg, "Isaiah 40–66," *The Interpreter's Bible,* V (New York: Abingdon Press, 1956), p. 473.

21 Muilenburg, *op. cit.,* p. 765f.

22 See the discussion on birth in de Vaux, *op. cit.,* p. 42f. Whether or not fathers were present at birth is debatable (cf. Jer. 20:15 and Gen. 50:23); certainly midwives were present (Gen. 35:17; 38:28; Exod. 1:15). While Samuel Terrien sees paternal imagery underlying Ps. 22:9–10, it is more likely that the metaphor is maternal (S. Terrien, *The Psalms and their Meaning for Today* (New York: Bobbs-Merrill, 1952), p. 154f).

23 See James Muilenburg, "The History of the Religion of Israel," *The Interpreter's Bible,* I (New York: Abingdon Press, 1952), p. 301f.

24 E.g., John L. McKenzie, *The Two-Edged Sword* (Garden City, NY: Image, 1966), p. 116; Bishop C. Kilmer Myers, *United Church Herald,* January, 1972, p. 14; Albert J. du-Bois, "Why I Am Against the Ordination of Women," *The Episcopalian* (July, 1972): 22.

25 For instance, the exodus theme is not a paradigm for "leaving home" and developing a community without models (so Mary Daly, "The Spiritual Revolution: Women's Liberation as Theological Re-education," *Andover Newton Quarterly,* March, 1972: 172f.) The Exodus itself is a return home, with its models drawn from the traditions of the Fathers (e.g., Exod. 3:15–17; 6:2–8).

26 Cf. Hans Walter Wolff, "The Elohistic Fragments in the Pentateuch," *Interpretation* XXVI (April, 1972): 165: "… it is women whose actions are decisive for the formation of God's people."

27 H. Wheeler Robinson, "The Hebrew Conception of Corporate Personality," in *Werden und Wesen des Alten Testaments,* ed. Paul Volz, Friedrich Stummer and Johannes Hempel (Berlin: Verlag von Alfred Topelmann, 1936), pp. 49–62.

28 Cf. E. Jacob, *Theology of the Old Testament* (New York: Harper & Row, 1958), p. 172f; S. H. Hooke, "Genesis," *Peake's Commentary on the Bible* (London: Thomas Nelson, 1962), p. 179.

29 E.g., Elizabeth Cady Stanton observed that Gen. 1:26–28 "dignifies woman as an important factor in the creation, equal in power and glory with man," while Gen. 2 "makes her a mere afterthought" (*The Woman's Bible,* Part I, New York: European Publishing Company, 1895, p. 20). See also Elsie Adams and Mary Louise Briscoe, *Up Against the Wall, Mother …* Beverly Hills: Glencoe Press, 1971, p. 4, and Sheila D. Collins, "Toward a Feminist Theology," *The Christian Century* (August 2, 1972): 798.

30 Cf. Eugene H. Maly, "Genesis," *The Jerome Biblical Commentary* (Englewood Hills: Prentice Hall, 1968), p. 12: "But woman's existence, psychologically and in the social order, is dependent on man."

31 See John L. McKenzie, "The Literary Characteristics of Gen. 2–3," *Theological Studies* 15 (1954): 559; John A. Bailey, "Initiation and the Primal Woman in Gilgamesh and Genesis 2–3," *Journal of Biblical Literature* (June, 1970): 143. Bailey writes emphatically of the remarkable importance and position of the woman in Gen. 2–3, "all the more extraordinary when one realizes that this is the only account of the creation of woman as such in ancient Near Eastern literature." He hedges, however, in seeing the themes of helper and naming (Gen. 2:18–23) as indicative of a "certain subordination" of woman to man. These reservations are unnecessary; see below. Cf. also Claus Westermann, *Genesis, Bibliscber Kommentar* 1/4 (Neukirchen-Vluyn: Neukirchener Verlag, 1970), p. 312.

32 James Muilenburg, "Form Criticism and Beyond," *Journal of Biblical Literature,* March, 1969, p. 9f; Mitchell Dahood, *Psalms* I, The Anchor Bible (New York: Doubleday & Company, 1966), *passim* and esp. p. 5.

33 I Chron. 4:4; 12:9; Neh. 3:19.

34 Psalms 121:2; 124:8; 146:5; 33:20; 115:9–11; Exod. 18:4; Deut 33:7, 26, 29.

35 L. Koehler and W. Baumgartner, *Lexicon in Veteris Testamenti Libros,* Leiden: E. J Brill, 1958, p. 591f.

36 The verb *bnb* (to build) suggests considerable labor. It is used of towns, towers, altars, and fortifications, as well as of the primeval woman (Koehler-Baumgartner, p. 134). In Gen. 2:22 it may mean the fashioning of clay around the rib (Ruth Amiran, "Myths of the Creation of Man and the Jericho Statues," *BASOR* no. 167 (October, 1962): 24f).

37 See Walter Brueggemann, "Of the Same Flesh and Bone (Gn 2, 23a)," *Catholic Biblical Quarterly* (October, 1970): 532–42.

38 In proposing as primary an androgynous interpretation of *'adham,* I find virtually no support from (male) biblical scholars. But my view stands as documented from the text, and I take refuge among a remnant of ancient (male) rabbis (see George Foot Moore, *Judaism,* I, Cambridge: Harvard University Press, 1927, p. 453; also Joseph Campbell, *The Hero with a Thousand Faces,* Meridian Books, World Publishing Company, 1970, pp. 152ff, 279f).

39 See, e.g., G. von Rad, *Genesis* (Philadelphia: The Westminster Press, 1961), pp. 80–82; John H. Marks, "Genesis," *The Interpreter's One-Volume Commentary on the Bible* (New York: Abingdon Press, 1971), p. 5; John A. Bailey, *op. cit.,* p. 143.

40 Cf. Westermann, *op. cit.,* pp. 316ff.

41 Verse 24 probably mirrors a matriarchal society (so von Rad, *Genesis,* p. 83). If the myth were designed to support patriarchy, it is difficult to explain how this verse survived without proper alteration. Westermann contends, however, that an emphasis on matriarchy misunderstands the point of the verse, which is the total communion of woman and man (*op. cit.,* p. 317).

42 U. Cassuto, *A Commentery on the Book of Genesis,* Part I (Jerusalem: The Magnes Press, n.d.), p. 142f.

43 von Rad, *op. cit.,* pp. 87–88.

44 Ricoeur departs from the traditional interpretation of the woman when he writes: "Eve n'est donc pas la femme en tant que "deuxième sexe"; toute femme et tout homme sont Adam; tout homme et toute femme sont Ève." But the fourth clause of his sentence obscures this complete identity of Adam and Eve: "toute femme peche "en" Adam, tout homme est seduit "en" Ève." By switching from an active to a passive verb, Ricoeur makes only the woman directly responsible for both sinning and seducing. (Paul Ricoeur, *Finitude ét Culpahilite,* II. *La Symbolique du Mal,* Aubier, Éditions Montaigne, Paris, 1960. Cf. Ricoeur, *The Symbolism of Evil,* Boston: Beacon Press, 1969, p. 255.)

45 McKenzie, "The Literary Characteristics of Gen 2–3," p. 570.

46 See Bailey, *op. cit.,* p. 148.

47 So Westermann (*op. cit.,* p. 340), *contra* Gunkel.

48 For a discussion of the serpent, see Ricoeur, *The Symbolism of Evil,* pp. 255–60.

49 Cf. Edwin M. Good, *Irony in the Old Testament* (Philadelphia: The Westminster Press), 1965, p. 84, note 4: "Is it not surprising that, in a culture where the subordination of woman to man was a virtually unquestioned social principle, the etiology of the subordination should be in the context of man's primal sin? Perhaps woman's subordination was not unquestioned in Israel." Cf. also Henricus Renckens, *Israel's Concept of the Beginning* (New York: Herder and Herder, 1964), p. 217f.

50 *Contra* Westermann, *op. cit.,* p. 357.

51 I hold a natural (rather than an allegorical, typological, mythological, or cultic) interpretation of the Song of Songs as erotic love poetry. For various views, see Otto Eissfeldt, *The Old Testament* (New York: Harper & Row, 1965), pp. 483–91, and Ernst Sellin and Georg Fohrer, *Introduction to the Old Testament* (Nashville: Abingdon Press, 1968), pp. 299–303. A recent exposition of the cultic view, which revives the general theory of T. J. Meek, is Samuel Noah Kramer, "The Sacred Marriage and Solomon's Song of Songs," *The Sacred Marriage Rite* (Bloomington: Indiana University Press, 1969), pp. 85–106.

52 For structure I am dependent on the forthcoming article by J. Cheryl Exum, "A Literary and Structural Analysis of the Song of Songs," *Zeitschrift für die Alten Testamentum.* See also L. Krinetski, *Das Hobelied,* Düsseldorf, 1964.

53 In addition to the ring composition, Gen. 2–3 and the Song of Songs share other literary and rhetorical features: (1) Chiasmus: e.g., the order of serpent/woman/ man, man/woman/serpent, serpent/woman/man (Genesis 3); face/voice, voice/face (Song 2:14) as well as the structure of Song 2:8–17. (2) Paranomasia: e.g., *'adham* and *'adhamah* (Gen. 2:7); *'ish* and *'ishshah* (Gen. 2:23); *shemen and sh*meka* (Song 1:3b); *ṣ*'i* and *haṣṣo'n* and *r*'i* and *haro'im* (Song 1:8). For rhetorical devices in Canticles, see Exum, *op. cit.*

54 Cf. Gen. 2:9 and Song of Songs 2:3.

55 In Song of Songs 1:7 the verb *r'h* (to feed or to pasture) has no direct object, thereby producing ambiguous meanings. Some translators supply the object *flock* (or *sheep*) to make the man a shepherd (so RSV, NEB, JB, NJV). More likely, the verb is a *double entendre* for erotic play. In 2:16 and 6:3 the same verb occurs, again without objects in MT: the man pastures among the lilies. In 2:1,2 the woman is the lily.

56 See Albert Cook, *The Root of the Thing* (Bloomington: Indiana University Press, 1968), pp. 106, 125.

57 Cook, *op. cit.*, p. 103.

58 Cf. de Vaux, *op. cit.*, p. 20f.

59 It is a moot question whether or not procreation is implied in the relationship of the primeval couple before their fall. Certainly it is not specified. Von Rad holds that "one flesh" (Gen. 2:24) signifies progeny (*op. cit.*, p. 824). Gunkel maintains that the phrase means sexual intercourse (*Genesis*, HAT, Göttingen, Vandenhoeck und Ruprecht, 1902, p. 10). Westermann claims neither view is adequate; "one flesh" means the total communion of woman and man (*op. cit.*, p. 317).

60 Cf. Cook, *op. cit.*, pp. 131–46.

61 See Brevard S. Childs, *Biblical Theology in Crisis* (Philadelphia: The Westminster Press, 1970), pp. 191–93.

62 Karl Barth, *Church Dogmatics,* III/2 (Edinburgh: T. and T. Clark, 1960), pp. 291–300.

63 The meaning of the word anger (*nbr*) is uncertain; see Köhler-Baumgartner, *op. cit.*, p. 609.

64 I use midrash here to designate a type of exegesis, not a literary genre. See Addison G. Wright, *Midrash* (New York: Alba House, 1967), pp. 43–45, 143, and Roger Le Deaut, "Apropos a Definition of Midrash," *Interpretation* XXV (July, 1971): 259–82.

65 Cook, *op. cit.*, p. 103f.

66 The task of recovering the depatriarchalizing principle in Scripture has only begun. For another recent effort, see William L. Holladay, "Jeremiah and Women's Liberation," *Andover Newton Quarterly* (March, 1972): 213–23.

3

Myth and the Religious Imaginary: Wendy Doniger

a. Introduction

Wendy Doniger (1940–, also published as Wendy Doniger O'Flaherty) studies the religious traditions of India and, through this study, has made significant contributions to the understanding of myth. She completed her doctoral studies at Harvard University in 1968 and at Oxford University in 1973 and began teaching at the University of Chicago in 1978 where, as of 2017, she continues to teach. In the selection that follows, "Microscopes and Telescopes," Doniger develops a robust understanding of the multiple perspectives through which myth should be approached.

The selection is a chapter from *The Implied Spider: Politics and Theology in Myth* (1998), which is based on a series of lectures given as part of the American Lectures in the History of Religions series.[1] In "Microscopes and Telescopes" Doniger identifies three levels for the study of myths: the big view (the telescope), the middle view (the naked eye), and the small view (the microscope). In the big view, we can see unifying themes across myths, in the middle view, we can see how a myth operates for a community in a particular time and place, and in the small view, we can see how a myth produces individual insight. By keeping these three levels of analysis in focus, we can interpret myth in a way that prevents us from "drawing our own eye," or studying ourselves when we think we are studying another (Dongier [1998] 2018: 49).

Throughout her work, Doniger develops a robust theory of myth that includes several components. First, she describes myth as a mixture of the cosmic and the banal, the telescope through which we see the cosmos and the microscope through which we see the minute. Second, she describes how myths emerge from a particular time and place but are comparable and often commensurable across time and place. This allows her to compare material that may seem at first glance to be quite disparate. Third, she describes myths as political. For Doniger, this means that myths employ and demand radical shifts in perspective. Myths allow us to see ourselves in the eyes of others. Finally, she maintains that there is no neutral or objective study of myths. This does not mean that the study of myths is not rigorous or challenging. Rather, the lack of neutrality forces us to constantly negotiate our own biases and reactions to myths, a negotiation that becomes part of the challenge of studying myths.

In this selection and her other writings on mythology, Doniger develops a theory of religion. Unlike Mary Douglas, who was trained as an anthropologist, Doniger is trained as a scholar of religion, but they both offer theories of religion. While Douglas draws out the ways religious traditions use purity as an implicit rule, Dongier describes myth as an explicit aspect of religious traditions. In this work, Dongier creates a robust theory of religion that works comparatively across religious traditions. Doniger focuses on the comparative study of mythology, a study that considers how the myths of multiple traditions are so different but often speak to human concerns that transcend context. The process of comparison, however, is not easy and continues to be fraught with tensions that must be constantly negotiated, including the position of the scholar in the interpretation of myths. Navigating this tension, according to Doniger, is the challenge and the promise of the comparative study of myths.

b. Microscopes and Telescopes (*The Implied Spider: Politics and Theology in Myth*) *Wendy Doniger*

Myths as Textual Lenses

In this first chapter I will consider the metaphor of the microscope and the telescope in the functions and the analysis of myths, and will demonstrate my method by comparing texts from two traditions, the Hebrew Bible and Hindu mythology. Let me begin by arguing that the microscopic and telescopic levels are intrinsically combined within the myths themselves.

One way to begin to define myth is to contextualize it on a continuum of all the narratives constructed of words (poems, realistic fiction, histories, and so forth)—all the various forms of narrations of an experience. If we regard this textual continuum as a visual spectrum, we may use the metaphor of the microscope and/or telescope to epitomize the extreme ends of this narrative vision. The end of the continuum that deals with the entirely personal (a realistic novel, or even a diary), the solipsistic ("This never happened to anyone but me"), is the microscope; this is where I would situate a dream or the entirely subjective retelling of an experience. Some novels on this end of the continuum may he contrasted with myths in several respects. These novels depend on the individual; character is all-important; these novels say, this could only happen to this one person or at least only did happen to this one person. In most myths, by contrast, character, except in the broadest terms (young or old, wise or foolish), doesn't count at all; myths say, this could happen to anyone. Yet some novels are more like myths than others; many novels assume that the drama of a few representative men and women speaks to our condition. And while "romantic realism," a phrase denoting a detailed description of a particular event or person that simultaneously conveys another meaning, is often used to categorize some novels, it also applies to certain myths in which a detailed description of an actor vividly suggests the myths' applicability not only to many individuals but also, sometimes, to certain abstract concepts.

T. S. Eliot hoped that James Joyce would beget a lineage of mythological novelists; "In using the myth, in manipulating a continuous parallel between contemporaneity and antiquity, Mr. Joyce is pursuing a method which others must pursue after him... Instead of narrative method, we may now use the mythical method."[2] To me, the mythical method *is* the narrative method, but a very special sort of narrative method, which Joyce employed not only in the obvious way of fashioning his novel after Homer's *Odyssey* (as John Updike built the double focus, contemporary and realistic on the one hand and ancient mythic on the other, into his novel *The Centaur*), but also in constantly invoking mythic tropes, constantly fiddling with the lenses. Writing about the novels of John Dos Passos, Joseph Epstein said, "Use a wide-angle lens and you cannot expect to go very deep; use the closeup and you lose breadth of detail. It has been given to very few novelists—Balzac. Dickens, Tolstoy, and, at moments, Stendhal—to do both things well."[3] But in my view, it has been given to a number of mythmakers. It is in part a matter of degree: the mixture of the cosmic and the banal is different in different novels, and also in different myths.

At the other end of the continuum from the personal, the abstract end—the telescope—is the entirely general and the formal: a theoretical treatise, or even a mathematical formula. "Euclid alone has looked on beauty bare," as Edna St. Vincent Millay entitles a poem, and we might locate the barest beauty of a myth in the sort of geometrical abstractions that the anthropologist Claude Lévi-Strauss ends up with, the ultimate algebraic formula into which he distills a myth.[4] On one occasion when scientists wished to send a message to possible life-forms on other planets, who could not be expected to know any of our languages, they sent radio waves with such data as the figure of *pi* (the ratio between the radius and circumference of a circle), which is presumably the same everywhere, outside the range of language. Here at the telescope end is where we might locate experiences unimaginably great ("This has happened to two million Armenians, six million Jews," or even, "This is happening every day in some one of the billions of other planets in the galaxy"). It is also where we might imagine an ideal experience devoid of any human telling, devoid of subjectivity—though this is a purely theoretical construct.

On this continuum between the personal and the abstract, myth vibrates in the middle; of all the things made of words, myths span the widest range of human concerns, human paradoxes. Epics, too, so closely related to myths, have as their central theme the interaction of the two planes, the human and the divine, as the gods constantly intervene in human conflicts. Myths range from the most highly detailed (closest to the personal end of the continuum) to the most stripped down (closest to the artificial construct at the abstract end of the continuum); and each myth may be rendered by the scholar in its micro- or macro- form. If prose is general and translatable, poetry particular and untranslatable, myth is prose at its most general, which is one of the reasons Lévi-Strauss was able to claim that the essence of myth, unlike the essence of poetry, is translatable.[5] And, I would add, myth is cross-culturally translatable, which is to say comparable, commensurable. The simultaneous engagement of the two ends of the continuum, the same and the different, the general and the particular, requires a peculiar kind of double vision, and myth, among all genres, is uniquely able to maintain that vision. Myth is the most interdisciplinary narrative.

The reflecting telescope uses a concave mirror as its eye,[6] and some scholars of myth have used the related images of reflection and transparency to express the ability of myth to capture simultaneously the near and far view, as in the title of A. K. Ramanujan's article about myths: "Where Mirrors Are Windows."[7] Also writing about myths (though he was using the word *myth* to describe something very different from what I am talking about in this book), Roland Barthes said, "If I am in a car and I look at the scenery through the window. I can at will focus on the scenery or on the window-pane. At one moment I grasp the presence of the glass and the distance of the landscape; at another, on the contrary, the transparence of the glass and the depth of the landscape; but the result of this alternation is constant; the glass is at once present and empty to me, and the landscape unreal and full. The same thing occurs in the mythical signifier: its form is empty but present, its meaning absent but full."[8]

Scholarly Lenses on Myths

Turning from the myths themselves to scholarly approaches to them, we can choose to focus a microscope on any of an infinite number of levels of magnification within any text and see something very different, from submolecular structures to large patterns that are also visible to the naked eye. As Cyril Stanley Smith pointed out, speaking of metallurgy but also of much more, you must constantly change the scale on which you view any particular phenomenon, for there are always at least two significant levels above and two levels below what you are looking at at any given moment.[9] Through the microscope end of a myth, we can see the thousands of details that each culture, indeed each version, uses to bring the story to life—what the people in the story are eating and wearing, what language they are speaking, and all the rest. "God is in the details," as Mies van der Rohe said (though he also said that the devil is in the details). But through the telescope end, we can see the unifying themes.

We might distinguish three levels of lenses in methods for the analysis of myths: the big view (the telescope) is the universalist view sought by Freud, Jung, Eliade; the middle view (the naked eye) is the view of contextualized cultural studies; and the small view (the microscope) is the focus on individual insight. Elsewhere, I suggest two different, specific ways the big view and the small view can be combined in a scholar's work; here let me approach the more general question of scholarly focus.[10]

Where do we set the f-stop? When do we use a wide-angle lens, a zoom lens? Victor Hugo posed this question: "Where the telescope ends, the microscope begins Which of the two has the grander view? Choose."[11] The subjective nature of this choice, and of vision through any lens, is best demonstrated, I think, by a story that James Thurber told of his youth, when his eyesight was already very poor. It seems that in botany class Thurber could never see anything through the microscope, despite the persistent fiddling of his teacher; but one day, as he stared into it and focused up and down, he saw "a variegated constellation of flecks, specks, and dots," which he promptly drew. The instructor came over hopefully, looked at the drawing, squinted into the microscope, and shouted in fury, "You've fixed the lens so that it reflects! You've drawn your own eye!"[12] Annie Dillard too, in her essay "Lenses," describes vividly the difficulties in looking through microscopes and telescopes:

> You get used to looking through lenses; it is an acquired skill. When you first look through binoculars, for instance, you can't see a thing. You look at the inside of the barrel; you blink and watch your eyes; you play with the focus knob till one eye is purblind. The microscope is even worse. You are supposed to keep both eyes open as you look through its single eyepiece.[13]

You "watch your eyes," like half-blind Thurber, in the binoculars; but you must also willingly half blind yourself to see the world of a microscope.

We are always in danger of drawing our own eye, for we depict our own vision of the world when we think we are depicting the world; often when we think we are studying an other we are really studying ourselves through the narrative of the other. Our choice of lens level is arbitrary, but not entirely so, for it is circumscribed by certain boundaries that we ignore to our peril. The choice is heuristic; we choose a specific level in order to make possible a specific task. Where we focus depends on the sorts of continuities we are looking for; in all instances, something is lost and something is gained. One particular focus lets us ask just one set of questions, but does not stop other people from focusing in other ways. Taking the two extreme ends, the microscope and the telescope, as I propose to do, at the cost of the middle focus (or the focus provided by normal human vision), is another way of expressing my choice to focus on the individual and the human race in general, at the cost of the focus on any ethnic group or historic moment or cultural milieu—a choice I will defend in my chapter "Implied Spiders an the Politics of Individualism" and apply in the micromyth and the macromyth in "Micromyths, Macromyths, and the Multivocality", though I will now qualify it.[14] My choice of these two extreme points of focus is sustained, though hardly validated, by the tendency of the myths themselves to maintain these polarized foci—though always, of course, with the mediation of culturally specific materials. Let us therefore turn to the myths, to see how they do it.

Myths as Theological Lenses in Job and the Bhagavata Purana

How do texts provide us with microscopes and telescopes? Why do we need them? I will approach these questions first by taking a look at two texts from two different cultures, the Book of Job in the Hebrew Bible and the Sanskrit text of the *Bhagavata Purana,* and then by considering the role of the double focus in human life.

When, in the Book of Job, Job confronts God, the level of focus of the text changes, and that changes the level of focus of the text's readers or hearers. What precedes this transitional point in the text is Job's sufferings, not the sufferings of a Greek hero or a Shakespearean king, but everyday sufferings (admittedly raised to the nth degree), "the heartaches and the thousand natural shocks that flesh is heir to":[15] the loss of our possessions (the destruction of Job's livestock), the deaths of those we love (friends and parents, Job's children), physical illness (cancer and heart disease, boils), injustice. Job tries, in vain, to deal with these problems in the normal human way, with words— words of acceptance, words of denial, arguments with his friends, arguments with his wife, arguments with God. That is, he naturally enough confronts the problem on the plane on which he experiences it, the plane of human experience, human injustice, human grief.

Instead of giving a direct answer to any of Job's arguments—for they cannot be answered—God sends him the voice from the whirlwind. Refusing to deal on the level of argument, of *logos,* on which the problem remains insoluble, the text catapults Job out of the plane of his existence onto another plane altogether, that of *muthos.* It whips the microscope of self-pity out of his hand and gives him, in its place, a theological telescope. The voice of God begins at the beginning, with cosmogony, the making of the world: "Where were you when I planned the Earth? Tell me, if you are so wise. Do you know who took its dimensions, measuring its length with a cord?" This image of the measuring cord holds out a transitory hope of returning us once again to the comfortable and comforting scale of human actions, human trades, something that can be counted, counted on, comprehended, encompassed, measured, "as if God were really a gigantic carpenter."[16] And responding on the same domestic level, Job's reply begins, "If ever my grief were measured/or my sorrow put on a scale,/it would outweigh the sands of the ocean:/that is why I am desperate." But that personal image is immediately swamped by the spectacular, impersonal image of cosmic power: "the morning stars burst out singing and the angels shouted for joy." We are robbed even of the comfort of an everyday metaphor.

The juxtaposition of the comforting image of the measuring cord and the overpowering riddle of creation also occurs in another of the great cosmogonies of the world, the one in the *Rig Veda,* composed in the mountains of northern India over a thousand years before the Common Era: "The measuring cord was extended across. Was there below? Was there above? Who really knows? Who will here proclaim it?"[17] But the comfort of this metaphor is undercut by two verses that frame it, for the hymn begins, most confusingly, with the statement, "There was neither existence nor nonexistence then," and it ends, most unsatisfyingly, with the suggestion, "Whence this creation has arisen—perhaps it formed itself, or perhaps it did not—the one who looks down on it in the highest heaven, only he knows—or perhaps he does not know."[18] And when the image of measuring recurs in the *Rig Veda,* again it is submerged in cosmic splendor, and again it is undercut by the unanswered cosmic question: "He by whom the awesome sky and the Earth were made firm, by whom the dome of the sky was propped up, and the sun, who measured out the middle realm of space—who is the god whom we should worship with the oblation?"[19]

Later Hindu tradition was troubled by this open-ended refrain and invented a god whose name was the interrogative pronoun *ka* (cognate with the Latin *quis*, French *qui*). Who. One text explained it. The creator asked the sky god, Indra, "Who am I?," to which Indra replied, "Just who you just said" (i.e., "I am Who"), and that is how the creator got the name of Who.[20] Read back into the Vedic hymn, as it was in some of the Vedic commentaries,[21] this resulted in an affirmative statement ("Indeed Who *is* the god whom we should honor with the oblation") somewhat reminiscent of the famous Abbott and Costello routine ("Who's on first?").

In the Book of Job, too, God poses riddles: "Does the rain have a father?" Stephen Mitchell, the author of the beautiful translation that I am using, comments on this in his introduction. *"Does the rain have a father? The whole meaning is the lack of an answer. If you say yes, you're wrong. If you say no, you're wrong. God's humor here is rich and subtle beyond words."*[22] Beyond words, indeed. The power of the passage lies not in its arguments, its words, but in its images, more precisely in the dizzying way it ricochets back and forth between images of cosmic machismo and of familiar, treasured things. First, the cosmic (though even here connected to the personal, for the great constellations are called by their nicknames): "Can you tie the Twins together or loosen the Hunter's cords? Can you light the Evening Star or lead out the Bear and her cubs? ... If you shout commands to the thunder-clouds, will they rush off to do your bidding? If you clap for the bolts of lightning, will they come and say, 'Here we are'?" Then, in contrast, familiar things evoke family and human reproduction, viewed in the mirror of animal metaphor: "Do you tell the antelope to calve or ease her when she is in labor? Do you count the months of her fullness and know when her time has come? She kneels; she tightens her womb, she pants, she presses, gives birth. Her little ones grow up; they leave and never return." This passage—which repeats the motif of counting and time, measuring again—sets up a tension in the outer frame of the story too, for Job has lost the one thing that is most precious to him of all: his children, his posterity. And is God mocking this value in Job when he tells him of an ostrich who has lost her offspring and does not care?

When in the end, God has the last word, it is the word beyond words. He mocks Job—"Has my critic swallowed his tongue?" And Job replies, lamely, "I had heard of you with my ears; but now my eyes have seen you. Therefore I will be quiet, comforted than [sic] I am dust." This is a comfort that renders words irrelevant; Job says, "I am *speechless*: what can I *answer*? I put my hand on my *mouth*. I have said too much already; now I will speak no more." But this vision, and its brand of comfort, is of course expressed in words, the words of the text, the words of the myth—*muthos*, not *logos*.

Does Job forget the image of the beast who "chews clubs to splinters and laughs at the quivering spear"? We are not told, but it is clear at the end of the story that Job is caught up once again in the snug and smug world of material wealth and family pleasures, in which we first encountered him: "So the Lord blessed the end of Job's life more than the beginning. Job now had fourteen thousand sheep, six thousand camels, a thousand yoke of oxen, and a thousand donkeys. He also had seven sons and three daughters"—and a partridge in a pear tree. We are back in the world of account books and dowries, business as usual. We have moved back from the cosmic measuring cord to the cash register. But we have also moved back to a world in which God has restored to Job what is most precious to him in real life: another set of children, his posterity.

There are many who find this ending a rather lame afterthought, like the second endings that Orson Welles and F. Scott Fitzgerald were asked to write for their Hollywood screenplays, or the Hayes office endings in films where the audience knew that the protagonists really did get away with adultery or murder, or the happy endings that Melina Mercouri tacked on to the Greek tragedies in the 1959 film *Never On Sunday* (Medea and the children all went to the seashore).[23] In fact, we have been prepared for this ending by the prologue, in which God and Satan look down through their telescopes and decide to use Job as a pawn in a test of their own powers, much as the Greek gods manipulate men in their own quarrels (as Gloucester says in *King Lear*: "As flies to wanton boys, are we to the gods; they kill us for their sport"[24]). It has not been a game to Job, of course, but at least he does not die at the end, like Lear or a Greek tragic hero; the final restoration attempts to make the story, retroactively, a kind of game to him too, as if he were being invited to see through the divine telescope, to see the god's-eye view of his own sufferings, to torment himself for his own sport. Many readers refuse to accept this invitation. For them, if they identify with Job, it is certainly not a game—it has real consequences in their lives. For the author, perhaps, who kills Job's children (fictional creations, after all) for his sport, and more than sport, and who moves the reader for his sport, and more than sport, it is a very serious game indeed.

The trick of undoing it all at the end ("It was all a dream") is not typical of the Hebrew Bible, and so its appearance at the end of the Book of Job adds yet one more puzzle to this puzzling book. (The trick is also used at the end of the story of Abraham and Isaac, when God at the last minute allows Abraham to sacrifice a ram instead of his son. Woody Allen's version of this myth has God answer Abraham's complaints by saying. "I jokingly suggest thou sacrifice Isaac and thou immediately runs out to do it." And when Abraham protests, "I never know when you're kidding," God replies, "No sense of humor."[25] Or, as Stephen Mitchell argued of the Book of Job, "God's humor here is rich and subtle.")

But the "it was just a dream" ending is a staple of myths enacting Hindu theories of illusion, and it makes sense in Hindu mythology, where the idea that evil itself is an illusion is widely accepted.[26] Let us consider some Hindu parallels that use this trick of illusion-shattering epiphany and thus shed light on the dynamics of the Book of Job. One of these is the *Bhagavad Gita*, a test [sic] composed in Sanskrit in the centuries before the Common Era, in which, on the eve of the great battle in the great epic the *Mahabharata*, the hero Arjuna asks the incarnate god Krishna a lot of difficult, indeed unanswerable, moral questions about the justice of war.[27] Krishna gives a series of rather abstract answers, and then Arjuna asks Krishna to display his true cosmic form. Krishna shows him his doomsday form, the form that J. Robert Oppenheimer recalled when he saw the first explosion of an atomic bomb.[28] And Arjuna cries out, "I see your mouths with jagged tusks, and I see all of these warriors rushing blindly into your gaping mouths, like moths rushing to their death in a blazing fire. Some stick in the gaps between your teeth, and their heads are ground to powder."[29] And right in the middle of the terrifying epiphany, Arjuna apologizes to Krishna for all the times that he has rashly and casually called out to him, saying, "Hey, Krisha! Hey, pal!" And he begs him to turn back into his pal Krishna, which the god consents to do. Again the worshipper is comforted by the banality, the familiarity of human life. Outside the text, however, the reader has been persuaded that since war is unreal, it is not evil; the warrior with ethical misgivings has been persuaded to kill, just as God kills. And this political message is made palatable by God's resumption of his role as close human companion.

The casual intimacy of that brief passage is enhanced by the reader's (or listener's) memory of a kind of fun-house mirror image of the *Gita* that occurs in the epic just two books earlier: Arjuna is living in disguise as an impotent transvestite dancing master, who offers his services as charioteer to a certain young prince, Uttara, giving as his reference none other than Arjuna himself, for whom, he says, he used to serve as charioteer. As the battle approaches, Uttara gets cold feet and doesn't want to fight; Arjuna tries to talk him into it, with a kind of parody of the speech that Krishna will give to Arjuna in the *Gita*: "People will laugh at you if you don't fight." Reflexively, in the *Gita* Krishna begins his exhortation by saying to Arjuna, "Don't act like an impotent transvestite; stand up!"[30] (a line whose sexual double entendre was almost certainly unintended but may have operated on a subconscious level). In this proleptic parody, Prince Uttara jumps off the chariot and runs away, and Arjuna, in drag, his skirts flapping, runs after him (people who see him run say, "Gosh, he looks more like Arjuna than an impotent transvestite; that *must* be Arjuna"). Arjuna catches Uttara by the hair and says, "If you won't fight, why don't you at least drive the chariot?" And the prince (whom the text describes as "witless and terrified") agrees to this.[31] So the initial apparent inversion of power and status is turned right side up after all; Arjuna is the warrior, and his inferior is his charioteer. Finally Arjuna reveals himself to the prince, who doesn't believe him at first and asks him to recite, and then to explain, Arjuna's ten names (which Arjuna does); then Uttara is convinced, and Arjuna wins the battle. When Arjuna finally reveals his true identity to the king, Uttara's father, the king says, as Arjuna says to Krishna in the *Gita*, "Whatever we may have said to you [when we didn't know who you were]—please forgive us."[32] As Arjuna was to Prince Uttara, so Krishna in the *Gita* is to Arjuna: a creature of great destructive power who velvets his claws for the sake of human affection. (Another brief satire occurs elsewhere in the *Mahabharata*, when Arjuna's blustery brother Bhima meets the great monkey Hanuman [hero of the other epic, the *Ramayana*] and tries in vain to lift the monkey's massive tail; when he asks Hanuman to expand to his full form, Hanuman stops halfway, saying, "This is about as much as you can stand." Bhima agrees that he can't stand to look at Hanuman in this form, any more than he could stare at the sun.)[33]

The passage in the *Gita* is about war and destruction, the passage in Job about creation and destruction. And there are other differences; the illusion in Job has just happened (God "unsays" the sufferings, the deaths), while in the *Gita* the illusory battle is about to happen. But the parallels between them are rightly noted by Stephen Mitchell:

> The only scriptural analogy to God's answer (the other Biblical examples, except for the burning bush, are of a lesser god) is the vision granted to Arjuna in chapter 11 of the [*Bhagavad*] *Gita*... But Job's vision is the more vivid, I think, because its imagination is so deeply rooted in the things of this world.[34]

Mitchell is certainly right about the *Bhagavad Gita*. But there are other Hindu texts that, like Job—perhaps even more than Job—take refuge "in the things of this world," and do so through the image of looking inside the mouth of god. One such text occurs elsewhere in the *Mahabharata* (3.186), when the sage Markandeya, wandering about in the cosmic ocean, stumbles on a sleeping child who is in fact Vishnu/Krishna; Markandeya enters the god's mouth and sees, inside his belly, the entire universe. This motif is repeated in several *Puranas*, often with variations. Here is one:

> When the world was in darkness, Vishnu slept in the middle of the cosmic ocean. A lotus grew out of his navel. Brahma came to him and said, "Tell me, who are you?" Vishnu replied, "I am Vishnu, creator of the universe. All the worlds, and you yourself, are inside me. And who are you?" Brahma replied, "I am the creator, self-created, and everything is inside me." Vishnu then entered Brahma's body and saw all three worlds in his belly. Astonished, he came out of Brahma's mouth and said, "Now, you must enter my belly in the same way and see the worlds." And so Brahma entered Vishnu's belly and saw all the worlds. Then, since Vishnu had shut all the openings. Brahma came out of Vishnu's navel and rested on the lotus.[35]

The *Bhagavata Purana*, composed in Sanskrit in South India, probably during the tenth century of the Common Era, adds another layer to the image when it tells a story about the same incarnate god Krishna when he was a little boy, here with his mortal mother, Yashoda:

> One day when the children were playing, they reported to Yashoda, "Krishna has eaten dirt." Yashoda took Krishna by the hand and scolded him and said, "You naughty boy, why have you eaten dirt? These boys, your friends, and your elder brother say so" "Mother, I have not eaten," said Krishna. "They are all lying. If you believe them instead of me, look at my mouth yourself." "Then, open up," she said to the god, who had in play taken the form of a human child; and he opened his mouth.

Then she saw in his mouth the whole universe, with the far corners of the sky, and the wind, and lightning, and the orb of the Earth with its mountains and oceans, and the moon and stars, and space itself; and she saw her own village and herself. She became frightened and confused, thinking, "Is this a dream or an illusion fabricated by God? Or is it a delusion in my own mind? For God's power of delusion inspires in me such false beliefs as, 'I exist,' 'This is my husband,' 'This is my son.'" When she had come to understand true reality in this way, God spread his magic illusion in the form of maternal love. Instantly Yashoda lost her memory of what had occurred. She took her son on her lap and was as she had been before, but her heart was flooded with even greater love for God, whom she regarded as her son.[36]

What could be more personal, more "deeply rooted in the things of this world," more literally *down to earth* or *earthy* than a small, dirty boy lying about *dirt*? But taking off from this modest moment, the myth plummets down and turns the universe inside out, shifting gears entirely into the warp speed of *muthos*. It is surely relevant that this cosmic vision takes place inside the child's *mouth*, the place of useless words, the place of *logos*, now silenced by the wordless images of the myth—images conveyed, as always, by words. For death, as well as words, comes out of the mouth of God. Yashoda, like Arjuna, like Job, cannot sustain the vertiginous vision of the world beyond the world that she has always regarded as real. T. S. Eliot pointed out (in *Burnt Norton*), "Humankind cannot bear very much reality"; apparently; humankind can't bear very much *un*reality, either, or very much of what the text presents as an alternative reality.

The myth returns the mother to what the text regards as the level of comfortable illusion. She forgets that her child's mouth is the mouth of God, just as Job, perhaps, forgets the image of the beast whose mouth "chews clubs to splinters" and Arjuna forgets the beast whose teeth grind the heads of warriors to powder in his mouth. Indeed, later in the *Mahabharata,*[37] Arjuna reminds Krishna of the time right before the battle when Krishna revealed his divine form, and he adds: "But I have lost all that you said to me in friendship, O tiger among men, for I have a forgetful mind. And yet I am curious about those things again, my lord." Krishna, rather crossly, remarks that he is displeased that Arjuna failed to understand or grasp the eternal secret, and he adds, "I cannot tell it again just like that." Like Arjuna, Yashoda has a forgetful mind, but in this instance Krishna himself gives her that forgetfulness as a gift.

More than that: it is unlikely that anyone, even a Vedantic Hindu, could believe for long that her life was totally unreal.[38] Most people's gut reactions to such stories, as to the end of Job, is that the banal is the real, and the astronomical vision is just so much cosmic bullshit. But the myth as a whole offers a way of balancing the two views so that the reader is not in fact forced to accept either one, or to choose between them.

The telescope and microscope are famously conflated in the opening stanza of William Blake's poem, "Auguries of Innocence":

To see a World in a Grain of Sand,
And a Heaven in a Wild Flower,

Hold Infinity in the palm of your hand,
And Eternity in an hour.

In fact, Hindu philosophers saw a world in a grain of sand in a most literal and detailed way, in a twelfth-century Kashmiri philosophical text, the *Yogavasistha,* in which a man goes inside a stone to find a whole new universe, and a beautiful girl.[39]

Seamus Heaney drew upon Blake in his insightful comments on Elizabeth Bishop's poem, "The Sandpiper":

> Part of the purpose of this writing is to blur the distinction between what is vast and what is tiny. The student of Blake, after all, will see a world in a grain of sand... We might in fact go so far as to say that the poem is about the way in which obsessive attention to detail can come through into visionary understanding; the way in which an intense focus can amplify rather than narrow our sense of scope. The last two lines of the poem do transform what is tiny and singular and project it on a cosmic screen. They make radiant and marvelous that which is in danger of being overlooked and disregarded. Again, the small and the great are brought into contact, and the small brings the great into question.[40]

Sand itself brings the small and the great into contact, for while each grain is infinitely small, their cumulative number is infinite. It is in this latter sense that Job, searching for an image of unimaginable greatness, says that his sorrows "would outweigh the sands of the ocean."

A different threat posed by the combination of the telescopic and microscopic views is well expressed by the eponymous hero of Saul Bellow's novel, *Henderson the Rain King.*

> Being in point of size precisely halfway between the sun and the atoms, living among astronomical conceptions, with every thumb and fingerprint a mystery, we should get used to living with huge numbers. In the history of the world many souls have been, are, and will be, and with a little reflection this is marvelous and not depressing. Many jerks are made gloomy by it, for they think quantity buries them alive. That's just crazy.[41]

Just as the Earth mediates between the sun (seen through a telescope) and the atoms (seen through a microscope), so the myth allows us to ground the "huge numbers" in such a way that we do not go crazy or get "gloomy."

There is an old story about a lady who went to a lecture and heard the lecturer say that the universe was going to self-destruct in five billion years, at which she fainted. When they asked her why she was so upset about an event that was five billion years away, she heaved a sigh of relief and said, "Oh thank God. I thought he said five *million* years." (Annie Dillard once remarked about such figures, "These astronomers are nickel-diming us to death."[42] And a boy in her novel, *The Living,* feels as if "The spaces between the stars were pores, out of which human meaning evaporated."[43]) The enormous scale of the theological visions in Job and the *Gita* and the *Bhagavata Purana* would, if accepted on their own terms, threaten to dwarf human enterprise. The much underrated theologian Woody Allen made the point well in the episode in *Annie Hall* when Alvy stops doing his homework because, he explains to his mother when she presses him for an explanation, "The universe is expanding, ... and ... someday it will break apart and that would be the end of everything!" His mother replies, "What has the universe got to do with it? You're here in Brooklyn! Brooklyn is not expanding!" and the family doctor says, "It won't be expanding for billions of years yet, Alvy. And we've gotta try to enjoy ourselves while we're here!" The myth does not demand that we accept the theological vision; even within the text the actors end up in the everyday world. But the myth is not necessarily saying that the ending is more real than the vision that precedes it. On the contrary, its purpose is to challenge us simultaneously to see that our lives are real, and to see that they are unreal. To the question, "Which is the reality?" the myth replies, "Yes."

Myths as Political Lenses

We have seen how myths use different scales of words, different verbal lenses, to link theology with daily reality. The abstract end of the textual continuum may be antipolitical (though certainly not a-political) if it withdraws the gaze from human affairs entirely, to a life of philosophical contemplation or renunciation—religious or other—or eschatological expectation. But the process of generalization, of abstraction from local detail, has a political aspect as well: it is where we begin to look beyond our selfish personal concerns and think globally, environmentally; think of the future; think of what is happening elsewhere on the planet Earth; think of the consequences of what we say and do and write for people in political circumstances very different from our own. The wide-angle lens can be political and theological simultaneously, as when we realize the political implications of our own theological assumptions or begin to respect the humanity of political others by appreciating their theologies. And myth is particularly qualified to forge these links. Using microscopes and telescopes to link daily reality with global—indeed, galaxial—politics, myth enables us to do what the bumper sticker urges: think globally, act locally.[44]

The human instinct, the common sense, that resists the theological argument that we are unreal is a political instinct; but there are also ways political narratives offer us a telescope not to turn us away from our own lives but to turn us toward the lives of others, including political others. Just as our theological vision is opened up by myths like those discussed above, so too our political vision may be opened up by our own myths: by the juxtaposition of certain texts with the events of our lives; by the comparison of myths from other cultures; and, most of all, by the interaction of political and theological texts acting as lenses for one another, so that we see each differently, better, through the insights of the other. Here again, if one should ask of politics and theology, "Which is the reality?" the answer is "Yes."

In Thomas Keneally's book *Schindler's List* (and in the film),[45] the hero stands on a high hill, mounted on a high horse, and views, as if through a telescope, the panorama of the liquidation of the Krakow ghetto. Amid all the carnage he sees one little girl, in a red coat, and follows her as she wanders through the scenes of horror, a red thread through the genocidal murder mystery, like the inevitable red dot in a landscape by Corot. (The red dot is the only piece of color in this part of the black-and-white film, producing a genre shock akin to the sudden burst of Technicolor in *The Wizard of Oz*).[46] By seeing her, Schindler sees what he must do. Here, switching from a telescope to a microscope is the move from indifference to compassion; for Job, the move in the other direction is the move from self-pity to something more than indifference— resignation, perhaps, or acceptance. Myth is a narrative that employs, and demands, radical shifts in perspective.

A fine example of this mythic scope, and an image beyond words (though I must use words to tell about it), occurs in a film about World War I, *Oh What a Lovely War* (1969).[47] This film ends with a kind of quotation of the end of *All Quiet on the Western Front* (1930),[48] the classic film about that war, in which we hear a shot, our hero falls, and we see, against the background of a field of white crosses, a line of soldiers marching away, each turning and staring into the camera for a moment, accusingly, before turning back and fading into the field of graves. At the end of *Oh What a Lovely War*, the hero whom we have come to know and care about in the course of the film— through the cinematic microscope—is fighting in the trenches. He is shot, the movie shifts into slow motion and silence, and we see him sitting on the grass at a picnic on a hill in England with his family, full of the mellow drowsiness of sunshine and wine. He leans back against a tree to take a nap, but the tree becomes a white cross that marks his grave, and he vanishes. As the camera zooms back farther and farther from the cross, enlarging our field of vision, we see that the cross on the grave of the soldier we know is just one among the millions of crosses marking the graves on the battlefields of France, one small white tree in a great forest of death. For a second, or perhaps ten seconds, we are able to experience, simultaneously, the intensity of personal grief that we feel for that one soldier and our more general, cosmic sorrow for the astronomical numbers of young men who, as we have long known and long ceased to notice, died in World War I. A similar double vision of another war, the American Civil War, is achieved in the scene in *Gone With the Wind* (1939)[49] when Scarlett O'Hara's horror at the suffering of one soldier is suddenly magnified as the camera zooms back to reveal the horrifying dimensions of the full slaughter, the enormous Atlantan square full of wounded and dying soldiers.

In a *Star Trek* episode,[50] the half-Vulcan Mr. Spock, who has the ability to "bond" with other minds, suddenly experiences agonizing pain when he senses the death screams of four hundred Vulcans on a star ship some distance from him. When Dr. McCoy expresses his amazement, Spock says, "I have noticed this insensitivity among wholly human beings. It is easier for you to feel the death of one fellow-creature than to feel the deaths of millions." And when McCoy asks if Spock would wish that empathy upon humans, Spock replies, "It might have rendered your history a bit less bloody." Our myths allow us "wholly humans" a glance through the telescope of Vulcan vision.

"One man's death is a tragedy; the death of a million is a statistic," said Joseph Stalin (who knew whereof he spoke). The myth turns the statistic back into a tragedy, turns the telescope back into a microscope. But sometimes, like Job, we need to change the lens in the other direction. In fury and despair, Job gazes through the microscope at the millions of tiny gnats that are gnawing away at his peace of mind. And the poet magnifies them for us, magnifies the banality of human suffering, the banality of evil, as Hannah Arendt put it. "A mote it is to trouble the mind's eye," as Horatio says to Hamlet,[51] speaking of the way our own eyes magnify the small things that trouble us. This same mote, as Matthew tells us (7.3), is the sign of our selfishness, our inability to see ourselves in proper proportion to other people: "Why beholdest thou the mote that is in thy brother's eye but considerest not the beam that is in thine own eye?"

Whenever the microscope of our ego rivets our gaze to the minutiae of our daily lives, myths may catch our eye and make us see with our telescopes, make us think about the stars and the galaxy and how small the planet Earth is. And it is difficult for us to think like this for long. It is difficult for us to go on living with care and concern and at the same time to stay fully aware that "Our lives don't really amount to a hill of beans," as Rick (Humphrey Bogart) says at the end of *Casablanca*[52] when his own love affair, which had seemed all that mattered in the world, is dwarfed by the giant reality of the Nazi threat, seen through the political telescope. But just as Job and Yashoda could not believe for long that their lives were unreal, so we can't live our lives if we think only about the galaxies, or the Nazis, or the children who are dying of starvation or disease or gunshot wounds on the streets of our own cities as well as in wars and famines throughout the world. We can't think about those things for long because we are human and we care about *our* lives, about what film we're going to watch tonight. Yet at the same time we know that there are all those galaxies out there, and all those children. We never entirely forget. This tension in us, in either direction, haunts us and threatens either to dim the intensity of the pleasure that we rightly take in our lives or to weaken our commitment to causes beyond our lives, causes that we undertake for the sake of those who will inhabit this planet hundreds of years after we have died.

The difficult choice between the two foci is captured in Reinhold Neibuhr's prayer (now best known as Alcoholics Anonymous's "Serenity Prayer"), which asks for the serenity to bear the things we cannot change, the courage to change the things we can, and the wisdom to tell the difference. But wisdom often nudges us in the direction of "serenity" or acceptance of other peoples' lives, which we can simply ignore. The sorts of stories I have been discussing—myths like the Book of Job and the story of Krishna—and other sorts as well may inspire a number of different reactions in the reader—regret, guilt, rage. Too often they fail to produce comfort. But sometimes they shake us out of whatever focus we happen to be stuck in. The tension gives rise to the myth. And this tension may affect us in many different ways, of which one, perhaps the most idealized but very real nevertheless, is to inspire us to strive to keep both of these levels of political vision, the microscopic and the telescopic, alive in us at the same time. But how?

The myth offers a fictive solution to the problem that it raises, but we may carry it back into our lives to make it real. The myth balances simultaneously the conviction that each of us is such a tiny part of the universe that nothing we do is real (in the sense that the Buddha taught, that nothing is permanent); and the conviction that a picnic with our friends and family is a great thing, not a small thing. Myths form a bridge between the terrifying abyss of cosmological ignorance and our comfortable familiarity with our recurrent, if tormenting, human problems. Myths make us reverse the focus, viewing through the telescope of detachment the personal lives that we normally view through the microscope and viewing the cosmic questions through the microscope of intimate involvement.

In the theological myths of Job and Krishna, it was the telescope that provided the shock of another reality. But in political myths, as in *Schindler's List,* it may be the microscope rather than the telescope that gives the shock, when a myth balances simultaneously the comfort of an ancient, general, commonplace truth and the surprise of totally new, totally specific details. In fact, the myth can work in either direction, both in theology and in politics. Lévi-Strauss used the idea of an optical image (a kind of crude microscope) to describe the process of inversions in myths:

> Similar inversions occur in optics. An image can be seen in full detail when observed through any adequately large aperture. But as the aperture is narrowed the image becomes blurred and difficult to see. When, however, the aperture is further reduced to a pinpoint, that is to say, when *communication* is about to vanish, the image is inverted and becomes clear again. This experiment is used in schools to demonstrate the propagation of light in straight lines, or in other words to prove that rays of light are not transmitted at random, but within the limits of a structural field… The field of mythical thought, too, is structured.[53]

One such inversion is precisely the ability of "the field of mythical thought" to move us from the infinitely small to the infinitely large. The myths suggest that if your microscope is powerful enough it turns into a telescope, that things really deep inside and really far away become one another.

Lévi-Strauss's image of inversion is an inversion of the use of the same image by Marcel Proust:

> Soon I was able to shew a few sketches. No one understood a word. Even those who were favourable to my conception of the truths which I intended later to carve within the temple congratulated me on having discovered them with a microscope

when I had, on the contrary; used a telescope to perceive things which, it is true, were very small but situated afar off and each of them a world in itself. Whereas I had sought great laws, they called me one who grubs for petty details.[54]

The "world in itself" inside each "very small" thing, each "petty detail," is the grand vision, the panorama of "great laws," of a great novelist, a mythological novelist.

As we have seen, the microscope too can be an instrument of empathy, but as Andrew Delbanco points out: "If a man surrenders to his designated function, his victims will be no clearer to him than microbes smeared on a slide as seen with the unaided eye. He will not see beyond the blur to the lives consumed—each singular, each a world unto itself."[55] The world within each life is precisely what is embodied in the Hindu image of the world that the mother sees inside the mouth of her child, and that Proust saw in each "very small" thing.

Annie Dillard, in her essay on lenses, describes the experience of looking at whistling swans through binoculars, and the experience of coming back out of the world of the binoculars afterward:

As I rotated on my heels to keep the black frame of the lenses around them, I lost all sense of space. If I lowered the binoculars I was always amazed to learn in which direction I faced—dazed, the way you emerge awed from a movie and try to reconstruct, bit by bit, a real world, in order to discover where in it you might have parked the car.[56]

To find our place in the world after we emerge from the magnified mythological vision, the world of the truly wide screen; to avoid getting the metaphysical equivalent of culture shock or a deep-sea diver's "bends" from coming up (or down) too fast, or from awakening too fast from that other world that we also enter sometimes when we dream but usually forget; and to find our car in a different place from the place where we parked it—that's the trick, and myth is the key.

Myths as Human Lenses

Sometimes the myth is formed not within a text, but rather in the intersection of our own lives with a text,[57] a telescope that provides a political as well as a theological shock, Delbanco writes of the time when Franklin Roosevelt discovered Kierkegaard and understood, for the first time, the Nazi evil; it was "a moment at which this feeling of theatrical distance was obliterated by a shock of recognition."[58] The double vision of a dead philosopher writing about the human condition in general and the immediate problem posed by totally new, totally specific human details produced this particular shock of recognition. Kierkegaard's general insights into human nature allowed Roosevelt to understand not *that* the Nazi evil had occurred (which, by then, he knew) but *how* it could have occurred.

Delbanco also wrote about the effect of the publication of John Hersey's *Hiroshima* in a 1946 *New Yorker* magazine:

> Hersey gave the anonymous victims of the nuclear firestorm faces and names. He showed the citizens of Hiroshima in the kitchen, on the porch, putting their children in pajamas in the moments before the bomb fell. He showed them blown about like tossed debris amid window shards and the splinters of what had been roofs and walls. He made it difficult to represent them with a number (70,000 or 100,000, depending on whether one took account of post-blast radiation effects) and a dismissive name (Japs).[59]

Sometimes only fiction can make reality real. A radio advertisement for the play *Miss Saigon* declared, "Saigon: it used to be just a name in the news, but now it's real."[60] The mythic drama claims to make the war real, implying that the "name in the news" was *not* real because it was just a name, not a story. Here I am reminded of the epilogue of George Bernard Shaw's play *Saint Joan*, when Cauchon asks, "Must then a Christ perish in torment in every age to save those that have no imagination?"[61]

But sometimes life itself is the text in which we read the myth of double vision. On the wall of the central room in the house in Amsterdam where Anne Frank and her family hid from the Nazis, two charts are preserved, side by side. One is a column of short, parallel, horizontal lines by which Otto Frank marked the growth of his children over the years, as my father used to mark mine, and I marked my son's. The other is a map of Europe with pins marking the advance of the Allied forces—too late, as we now know, to allow that first chart to grow more than a few poignant inches. They are roughly the same size, those two charts, and they represent the tragic intersection of the tiniest, most banal personal concern and a cataclysmic world event. For me, they are the microscopic and telescopic view of the Holocaust, side by side.

We can use these lenses either to see or to blur a world that we cannot fathom. In great myths, the microscope and the telescope together provide a parallax that allows us to see ourselves in motion against the stream of time, like stars viewed from two different ends of the Earth's orbit, one of the few ways to see the stars move. And when we take into account myths not, perhaps, from different ends of the Earth's orbit, but at least from different ends of the Earth, we have made our mythical micro-telescope a bit longer than the one provided by our own cultures, and we can use it to see farther inside and also farther away—a double helix of the human paradox. To jump ahead to the argument that I will make in subsequent chapters, not just for myths but for comparative mythology, the individual text is the microscope that lets us see the trees; the comparison is the telescope that lets us see the forest. The myth allows us to look through both ends of the human kaleidoscope at once, simultaneously to view the personal, the details that make our lives precious to us, through the microscope of our own eye and, through the telescope provided by the eye of other cultures, to view the vast panorama that dwarfs even the grand enterprises of great powers, that dwarfs the sufferings of Job and of ourselves. Every time we listen to a story with mythic dimensions, about human beings in crisis, and really listen and think about the ways it is telling us the story of our own lives—and *not* the story of our own lives—we see for a moment with the double vision of the human microscope and cosmic telescope.

c. Questions

what's going on ab Shankae. The myth of how the dirt was found

Comprehension

1. How does Doniger describe myth?

2. Describe the three levels at which Doniger argues myths can be analyzed, and provide an example of each.

3. How do myths themselves offer microscopes and telescopes on the world?

4. How does myth offer a way to balance the banal, or everyday, and the cosmic?

Analysis

5. On the reading of myths, Doniger claims: "We are always in danger of drawing our own eye, for we depict our own vision of the world when we think we are depicting the world; often when we think we are studying an other we are really studying ourselves through the narrative of the other" (Dongier [1998] 2018: 49). Explain this statement. Do you agree or disagree?

6. On the purpose of myths, Doniger argues: "The myth does not demand that we accept the theological vision … its purpose is to challenge us simultaneously to see that our lives are real, and to see that they are unreal" (Dongier [1998] 2018: 57). Do you agree with Doniger that the purpose of myths is to challenge us to see our lives differently or do myths demand that we accept their view of reality? What is the purpose of myths? Is it possible to separate theological vision from myths?

Synthesis

7. Consider the two different theories of religion proffered by Mary Douglas and Wendy Doniger. What are the similarities and differences of these two theories of religion? Do you find one more appealing than the other? Explain why or why not.

8. Consider the two different approaches to religious texts offered by Phyllis Trible and Wendy Doniger. What are the similarities and differences of these two approaches to religious texts? Do you find one more appealing than the Explain why or why not.

Notes

1   From the American Academy of Religion website: "Founded in 1891 to encourage path-breaking scholarship through a lecture and book series, the American Lectures in the History of Religions flourished under the auspices of the American Council of Learned Societies and Columbia University from 1936. At the request of the ACLS, the American Academy of Religion assumed administrative responsibility for the series in 1994." (https://www.aarweb.org/programs-services/history-of-religions-lectures)

2   T. S. Eliot, "*Ulysses,* Order, and Myth," pp. 177–78.

3   Joseph Epstein, " 'U.S.A.' Today," p. 72.

4   Doniger, *The Implied Spider*, chapter 6.

5   Claude Lévi-Strauss, *Structural Anthropology*, p. 210.

6   Benjamin Goldberg, *The Mirror and Man.*

7   A. K. Ramanujan, "Where Mirrors Are Windows."

8   Ronald Barthes, *Mythologies*, p. 123. Again, he uses *form* and *meaning* in different senses from mine; my point is simply that he uses the same metaphor to talk about them.

9   Cyril Stanley Smith, "Metallurgical Footnotes to the History of Art," pp. 280–92.

10 Doniger, *The Implied Spider*, chapters 3 and 4.

11 Victor Hugo, *Les Misérables,* St. Denis, Book III, "The House in the Rue Plumet," chapter 3, "Foliis ac Frondibus." I am grateful to Ronald Lane Reese, professor of physics and astronomy at Washington and Lee University, for this quote.

12 James Thurber, "University Days," pp. 222–23.

13 Annie Dillard, "Lenses," in *Teaching a Stone to Talk,* p. 104.

14 Doniger, *The Implied Spider*, chapters 3 and 4.

15 Shakespeare, *Hamlet,* 3.4.

16 Stephen Mitchell, *The Book of Job,* p. xxii.

17 *Rig Veda* 10.129.5–6; Wendy Doniger O'Flaherty, *The Rig Veda*, pp. 25–26.

18 *Rig Veda* 10.129, 7.

19 *Rig Veda* 10.121.5; Doniger O'Flaherty, *The Rig Veda,* pp. 26–28.

20 *Aitareya Brahmana* 3.21.

21 Sayana's commentary on *Rig Veda* 1.121.

22 Mitchell, *The Book of Job,* p. xxv.

23 *Never on Sunday* (1959), written and directed by Jules Dassin, starring Melina ... Dassin. Rossini tacked a happy ending onto his opera based ... on one occasion when it was to be performed at the ... sisted on certain changes: when Desdemona says (as ... sini version), "I am innocent," this time Othello replies, ... he believes Desdemona and kicks Iago out. Philip Gossett, ... lition of this opera, pointed out to me that he reproduced ... ive ending and gave the reader a reference to the place ... ld be found, but deliberately did *not* reproduce that score in

the critical apparatus, in order to discourage anyone from performing the mutilated variant. Philip Gossett, personal communication, December 7, 1996.

24 Shakespeare, *King Lear,* 4.1.

25 Woody Allen, "The Scrolls," p. 27.

26 Wendy Doniger O'Flaherty, *The Origins of Evil* and *Dreams, Illusion, and Other Realities.*

27 *Mahabharata* 6.23–40.

28 Doniger O'Flaherty, *Other Peoples' Myths,* p. 157.

29 *Bhagavad Gita,* 11.25–29 (*Mahabharata* 6.33.25–29).

30 *Bhagavad Gita* 2.3: klaibyam ma sma gamah, Partha … tyakva' ottishta, Paramtapa.

31 *Mahabharata* 4.32–42.

32 *Mahabharata* 4.66.20.

33 *Mahabharata* 3.148–49. See also the more serious imitation of the *Gita* in the text that Hindus explicitly regard as the "anu-*Gita,*" the "after-*Gita,*" at *Mahabharata* 14.16–50.

34 Mitchell, *The Book of Job,* pp. xxvi–xxvii.

35 *Kurma Purana* 1.9.

36 *Bhagavata Purana* 10.8.21–45; Doniger O'Flaherty, *Dreams, Illusion,* pp. 109–10; *Hindu Myths,* pp. 218–20.

37 *Mahabharata* 14.16.6–12.

38 Doniger O'Flaherty, *Dreams, Illusion.*

39 *Yogavasistha* 6.2.56–94; Doniger O'Flaherty, *Dreams, Illusion,* p. 234.

40 Heaney, *The Redress of Poetry;* "Counting to a Hundred: On Elizabeth Bishop" (164–185), p. 177.

41 Saul Bellow, *Henderson the Rain King,* p. 137.

42 Annie Dillard, *For the Time Being.*

43 Annie Dillard, *The Living,* p. 70.

44 I believe it was Eli Lilly who first coined this phrase.

45 Thomas Keneally, *Schindler's List; Schindler's List* (1993), written by Steven Zaillian, from the novel by Thomas Keneally; directed by Steven Spielberg; starring Liam Neeson.

46 *The Wizard of Oz* (1939), written by L. Frank Baum; directed by Victor Fleming; starring Judy Garland, Bert Lahr, and Ray Bolger. For the color shift, see Doniger O'Flaherty, *Other Peoples' Myths,* pp. 158–59.

47 *Oh What a Lovely War* (1969), written by Len Deighton from the stage show by Joan Littlewood; directed by Richard Attenborough.

48 *All Quiet on the Western Front* (1930), written by Lewis Milestone, Maxwell Anderson et al. from the novel by Erich Maria Remarque, directed by Lewis Milestone.

49 *Gone With the Wind* (1939), written by Sidney Howard from the novel by Margaret Mitchell; directed by Victor Fleming et al.; starring Clark Gable, Vivien Leigh, Olivia de Havilland, Leslie Howard.

50 *Star Trek,* "The Immunity Syndrome," written by Robert Sabaroff, directed by Joseph Pevney, and first aired on January 19, 1968. I am grateful to Peter Gottschalk for finding this episode for me.

51 Shakespeare, *Hamlet,* 1.1.

52 *Casablanca* (1942), written by Julius J. Epstein, Philip G. Epstein, and Howard Koch, from the play *Everybody Comes to Rick's,* by Murray Burnett and Joan Allison; directed by Michael Curtiz, starring Humphrey Bogart, Ingrid Bergman, Claude Raines, Paul Henreid.

53 Claude Lévi-Strauss, "The Story of Asdiwal," p. 42.

54 Marcel Proust, *Remembrance of Things Past,* English translation cited here, vol. 2, p. 1118. He is referring to his first book, *Les Plaisirs et les Jours,* according to the editor of the French edition, vol. 4, p. 618.

55 Andrew Delbanco, *The Death of Satan,* p. 231.

56 Dillard, "Lenses," p. 104.

57 Doniger O'Flaherty, *Other Peoples' Myths.*

58 Delbanco, *The Death of Satan,* p. 191.

59 Delbanco, *The Death of Satan,* p. 200.

60 Advertisement broadcast on January 18, 1992, on WFMT in Chicago.

61 George Bernard Shaw, *Saint Joan,* p. 223; cited in Doniger O'Flaherty, *Other Peoples' Myths,* p. 130.

4

Ritual and Belief: Catherine Bell

a. Introduction

Catherine Bell (1953–2008) was a scholar trained in the study of religion at the University of Chicago and who focused on ritual studies, particularly in Chinese traditions. Bell's work called on religious studies scholars to reconsider an established dichotomy between belief and ritual and, in particular, to think about ritual as generative instead of repetitive. After completing her studies, she taught in Japan and at the University of California, Berkley, before taking a position at Santa Clara University, where she spent most of her career effectively balancing research, teaching, and administrative duties until her retirement in 2005.

The selection, "Constructing Ritual," is from Bell's first book, *Ritual Theory, Ritual Practice* published by Oxford University Press first in 1992 and again in 2009. In this selection, Bell describes the field of ritual studies by categorizing the contributions of the field's leading theorists into what she calls three structural patterns. According to Bell, these patterns assume a difference between thought and action that she hopes to challenge. In the first structural pattern, Bell observes that ritual theorists associate ritual with action and then differentiate "ritual-as-action" from "thought," which tends to be associated with belief. In the second structural pattern, Bell observes that theorists of ritual portray ritual as a means of integrating thought and action. The third pattern, theorized by Clifford Geertz, describes how ritual becomes the place where thought and action are not only fused for ritual participants but also for ritual observers. That is to say that ritual reveals the integration of thought and action for people who are not participating in the ritual and, thus, becomes the place where ritual theorists can recognize the meaningfulness of the ritual for participants. According to Bell, Geertz sets up "a third permutation of the thought-action dichotomy. That is, ritual participants act, whereas those observing them think" (Bell [1992] 2018: 73). Geertz's attempt to theorize the position of the ritual observer forces scholars to reckon with how perspective affects observation.

By describing these structural patterns of ritual theory, Bell offers a means of understanding multiple approaches to ritual. More importantly, she challenges anyone who hopes to observe ritual (a group that includes both the authors and readers of this text) to account for our own positions in that observation of ritual. According to Bell, the perspective of the ritual observer (an outsider perspective) can impose theoretical frameworks that fail to describe ritual or account for a ritual participant (or insider) perspective. She states, "The implicit structure of ritual theory, while effective in identifying a distinctive phenomenon for cultural analysis, has imposed a powerful limit on our theoretical flexibility, our divisions of human experience, and our ability to perceive the logical relations inscribed within these divisions" (Bell [1992] 2009: 17). In other words, she thinks that the structures that guide scholars also limit scholars. In response, Bell calls for theorists of ritual to consider the assumptions that limit how scholars think about ritual, including the distinction between thought and action. Scholars in ritual and religious studies continue to take up this call by adopting theoretical flexibility that allows ritual to be studied from multiple angles.

In this selection, we first see how studying ritual becomes a means of making the familiar strange and the strange familiar. With Bell, we can look with renewed curiosity at the singing of the national anthem prior to the super bowl while components of the Muslim practice of prayer simultaneously become more recognizable to Christians. Bell also describes differences between insider and outsider perspectives of ritual, offering an explanation for why ritual participants give different reasons for their actions than ritual observers. Finally, Bell's description of ritual reveals how they sustain a sense of group unity by naturalizing activities that are socially constructed. These three themes have continued to impact the study of ritual long after the publication of Bell's arguments.

Bell's ritual theory offers an explanation of how religion works and how we understand the meaning of religion and other social practices. That is, she draws on specific religious rituals in order to develop a theory of ritual that works across religious contexts. These themes appear in Bell's later work, *Ritual: Perspectives and Dimensions* (1997), where she develops a theory of ritual that helps explain the "ritual-like" activities that many religious studies scholars would argue have some relation to religious practices even though they are not often popularly identified as religious. Bell's work remains influential for redefining boundaries for theorizing ritual. The following selection was chosen to offer an introduction into Bell's rich theoretical world.

b. Constructing Ritual (*Ritual Theory, Ritual Practice*) *Catherine Bell*

Theoretical descriptions of ritual generally regard it as action and thus automatically distinguish it from the conceptual aspects of religion, such as beliefs, symbols, and myths. In some cases added qualifications may soften the distinction, but rarely do such descriptions question this immediate differentiation or the usefulness of distinguishing what is thought from what is done. Likewise, beliefs, creeds, symbols, and myths emerge as forms of mental content or conceptual blueprints: they direct, inspire, or promote activity, but they themselves are not activities.[1] Ritual, like action, will act out, express, or perform these conceptual orientations. Sometimes the push for typological clarity will drive such differentiations to the extreme. Ritual is then described as particularly *thoughtless* action—routinized, habitual, obsessive, or mimetic—and therefore the purely formal, secondary, and mere physical expression of logically prior ideas. Just as the differentiation of ritual and belief in terms of thought and action is usually taken for granted, so too is the priority this differentiation accords to thought. For example, Edward Shils argues that ritual and belief are intertwined and yet separable, since it is conceivable that one might accept beliefs but not the ritual activities associated with them. He concludes that logically, therefore, "beliefs could exist without rituals; rituals, however, could not exist without beliefs."[2] Claude Lévi-Strauss takes this logic much further when an initial distinction between ritual and myth eventuates in a distinction between living and thinking.[3]

Aside from this basic structural pattern in which ritual is differentiated from mental categories as readily as action is differentiated from thought, there is a second structural pattern in theoretical discussions of ritual. This second pattern describes ritual as a type of functional or structural mechanism to reintegrate the thought–action dichotomy, which may appear in the guise of a distinction between belief and behavior or any number of other homologous pairs. Both of these structural patterns—the differentiation of ritual as action from thought and the portrayal of ritual as a mechanism for integrating thought and action—can be demonstrated in several representative approaches to ritual.

Durkheim argued that religion is composed of beliefs and rites: beliefs consist of representations of the sacred; rites are determined modes of action that can be characterized only in terms of the representations of the sacred that are their object. "Between these two classes of facts," he wrote, "there is all the difference which separates thought from action."[4] Yet despite the secondary nature of ritual given in these initial definitions, Durkheim's important discussion of cult at the end of *The Elementary Forms* reintroduces ritual as the means by which collective beliefs and ideals are simultaneously generated, experienced, and affirmed as real by the community. Hence, ritual is the means by which individual perception and behavior are socially appropriated or conditioned.[5] In Durkheim's model the ritual activity of cult constitutes the necessary interaction between the collective representations of social life (as a type of mental or metamental category) and individual experience and behavior (as a category of activity).[6]

These two patterns turn up also in another, loosely structural, model employed with great sophistication by Stanley Tambiah but more simplistically by many others. There ritual is provisionally distinguished as the synchronic, continuous, traditional, or ontological in opposition to the diachronic, changing, historical, or social. However, ritual is also subsequently portrayed as the arena in which such pairs of forces interact. It is the mediating process by which the synchronic comes to be reexpressed in terms of the diachronic and vice versa.[7]

A third model, presented most fully in the early work of V. Turner, also portrays these two patterns. Turner initially described ritual as the affirmation of communal

rast to the frictions, constraints, and competitiveness of social life and
8 Rite affords a creative 'antistructure' that is distinguished from the
nance of social orders, hierarchies, and traditional forms. However, when
.ly portrayed as embodying aspects of both structure and antistructure, he
describes rituals as those special, paradigmatic activities that mediate or orchestrate the necessary and opposing demands of both *communitas* and the formalized social order.

Each of these examples employs the two structural patterns described previously: ritual is first differentiated as a discrete object of analysis by means of various dichotomies that are loosely analogous to thought and action; then ritual is subsequently elaborated as the very means by which these dichotomous categories, neither of which could exist without the other, are reintegrated. These two structural patterns are rarely explicit and the first, in particular, in which ritual is differentiated from conceptual categories, is routinely taken for granted. However, the relationship that develops *between* these two patterns when they are simultaneously operative in a theoretical description of ritual is even less acknowledged and much more powerful. In effect, the dichotomy that isolates ritual on the one hand and the dichotomy that is mediated by ritual on the other become loosely homologized with each other. Essentially, as I will demonstrate, the underlying dichotomy between thought and action continues to push for a loose systemization of several levels of homologized dichotomies, including the relations between the ritual observer and the ritual actor. It is this invisible process of 'homologization', driven by the implicit presence of an opposition between conceptual and behavioral categories, that begins to construct a persuasive and apparently logical body of discourse.

Dichotomies and Dialectics

Jameson analyzes a type of logical structure within linguistical theory that is similar to the two patterns sketched out earlier for ritual theory.[9] The structured argument that he isolates provides a useful contrast to the one I am recovering here. Jameson points to a logical structure in which an initial differentiation, originally proposed to enable the theorist to concentrate on just one of the differentiated terms, surfaces again and again within subsequent analysis of that term. Specifically addressing Ferdinand Saussure's system of linguistics, Jameson shows that an initial distinction between structure and history (synchrony and diachrony) enables Saussure to focus upon and systematically elucidate one aspect of language, the synchronic or structural aspect. However, Saussure never resolved or transcended the dichotomy between synchrony and diachrony but reproduced it even in the final terms of his system.[10] How did such a replication occur?

In reaction against historicism in linguistics, Jameson explains, Saussure attempted to talk about the nonhistorical aspects of language. On a primary level, he distinguished between diachrony and synchrony, thereby providing himself a clear focus on the synchronic side of linguistics as opposed to the other side, where, he argued, everyone else was working. On a second level, and therefore within the synchronic system itself, Saussure also distinguished between *langue* and *parole* in order to further differentiate synchronic language from speech. He therein had his first internal replication of the original opposition. On yet a third level, Saussure took *langue* as a system and within it distinguished two ways in which signs are related, the syntagmatic and the associative (or paradigmatic), replicating his original dichotomy for a second time within the system as a whole.[11] The original differentiation between diachrony and synchrony was applied, through various pairs of categories, to three levels of analysis. In other words, the continual application of the dichotomy between synchrony and diachrony systematically generated successive and homologous levels of analysis.

At this point, Jameson suggests that it becomes quite "problematical to what degree the object of study is the thought pattern of the linguist himself, rather than that of the language." Moreover, this is also the point at which the originality of Saussure's initial distinction becomes a constraint on the whole system he has generated from it. Saussure's "initial repudiation of history," remarks Jameson, "which at the very outset resulted in an inability to absorb change into the system as anything but a meaningless and contingent datum, is now reproduced, at the very heart of the system itself, as an inability to deal with syntax as such."[12]

Theoretical discourse on ritual displays a similar logical structure: a distinction between belief and rite, made as readily as the heuristic distinction between thought and action, clears the way to focus on ritual alone. This is the first structural pattern noted previously. Ritual, however, becomes in turn a new starting point at which to differentiate once again between conceptual and behavioral components. This is the second structural pattern described earlier. However, ritual theory goes on to do something that Saussure, in the rigor of his focus and logic, according to Jameson, failed to do, namely, provide a stage of synthetic integration. Differentiated from belief in the first structural pattern, ritual becomes a second point at which to distinguish thought and action. Yet at this second stage ritual is seen as synthetic, as the very mechanism or medium through which thought and action are integrated. The elaboration of ritual as a mechanism for the fusion of opposing categories simultaneously serves both to differentiate and unite a set of terms. That is, the second structural pattern in ritual theory, in which ritual mediates thought and action, posits a dialectical relation between the differentiated entities instead of replicating an unmediated dichotomy. Ritual emerges as the means for a provisional synthesis of some form of the original opposition.

Saussure generated his linguistic system by positing an initial distinction, the successive and systematic replication of which rendered the distinction an ahistorical, nondialectical, or pure opposition.[13] Most ritual theory avoids this by incorporating the notion of dialectic or synthesis: ritual is a dialectical means for the provisional convergence of those opposed forces whose interaction is seen to constitute culture in some form.

The three representative theories of ritual briefly described clearly present ritual as just such a medium of integration or synthesis for opposing sociocultural forces. These are not isolated examples. There is a strong impetus within theoretical studies of religion and culture for this type of dialectic. This impetus can be seen, for example, in contemporary evaluations of Durkheim's theory of ritual. Some argue that his notion of ritual contains a dialectical mediation of the social and the individual; others argue that its fundamental weakness is precisely that his notion of ritual lacks such a dialectic. E. E. Evans-Pritchard has pinpointed Durkheim's theory of ritual as the central but "most obscure" and "unconvincing" part of his notion of society and religion.[14] Nancy Munn, on the other hand, has found it to be of "signal importance" for ritual studies today.[15] She argues that Durkheim developed a model of "social (ritual) symbolism as the switch point between the external moral constraints and groupings of the socio-political order, and the internal feelings and imaginative concepts of the individual actor."[16] Although it is precisely the nature of this switch point that Evans-Pritchard finds obscure, Munn is clearly attempting to find rooted in Durkheim a dialectical relationship between two irreducible entities, the individual's subjective state and the communal order, a dialectic mediated therefore by the collective representations generated and appropriated in the cult.

Sahlins has also looked for a synthetic reintegration of thought and action, self and society within Durkheim's theory and not found it. He argues that Durkheim's collective representations fail to mediate at all. Rather, as idealized representations of social values and structures, they merely act upon subjective states to mold them. For Sahlins, Durkheim's collective representations are unable to mediate or rearticulate individual experience within social categories; all they can do is simply appropriate and organize it into a "metalanguage."[17] In a somewhat similar argument, Lévi-Strauss suggested that Durkheim lacked an "adequate" notion of a symbol and symbolic action.[18] That is, in contrast to how symbols function, Durkheim's collective representations are mere signs, idealizations of the forms of social morphology that have become independent of these forms, and thus act solely to subordinate and structure individual perception and experience.[19]

Ultimately, Sahlins and Lévi-Strauss find Durkheim's theory of cult and ritual action less than complete for two reasons: first, it does not generate a level of cultural analysis as such; and second, it does not overcome the fundamental duality that resurfaced for Durkheim even in his portrayal of human nature itself. "This is the objective foundation of the idea of the soul: Those representations whose flow constitutes our interior life are of two different species which are irreducible one into another. Some concern themselves with the external and material world; others, with an ideal world to which we attribute a moral superiority over the first." For Durkheim, therefore, "we are really made up of two beings facing in different and almost contrary directions, one of whom exercises a real pre-eminence over the other. Such is the profound meaning of the antithesis which all men have more or less clearly conceived between the body and the soul, the material and the spiritual beings who coexist within us."[20]

Whether Durkheim provides a complete notion of ritual or not, we can see in his work and in the arguments of those reading him a tendency to isolate two types of sociocultural processes or entities and then to seek in ritual theory a model of their necessary reintegration. Indeed, given any initial avowal or assumption of such differentiated processes, a theoretician would have to come up with some phenomenon structured to mediate them if it did not already exist. Hence, I am suggesting that descriptions of how rituals work have been constructed according to a logic rooted in the dynamics of theoretical speculation and the unconscious manipulation of the thought–action dichotomy is intrinsic to this construction.

Saussure could not see how his initial distinctions radically limited the descriptive power of his system. Likewise, we do not see how such dichotomies as continuity and change, individual experience and social forms, and beliefs and behavior invoke an assumption about thought and action that runs particularly deep in the intellectual traditions of Western culture. We do not see that we are wielding a particularly powerful analytical tool, nor do we see how our unconscious manipulation of it is driven not only by the need to resolve the dichotomy it establishes, but also simultaneously to affirm *and* resolve the more fundamental opposition it poses—the opposition between the theoretician and the object of theoretical discourse. In other words, we do not see how such dichotomies contribute to the relational definition of a knower, a known, and a particular type of knowledge.

Geertz and the Window of Ritual

To clarify the relationship between dichotomies and dialectics within the structure of ritual theory, a fuller example is needed to demonstrate how a coherent discourse on ritual is generated. The work of Geertz provides an excellent extended illustration for this purpose. Geertz has been a major influence in the study of religion and ritual, as well as a navigator for many through the shoals and reefs of various methodological issues. This is due in part to the symmetry of his terminology, its appeal to common sense, and his richly anecdotal ethnographies in which texture and nuance appear to defy ethnographic reductionism.

Geertz maintains that the thrust of his theoretical approach is the explanation of "meaning" in cultural phenomena.[21] With this focus he wishes to go beyond the functional or mechanistic analyses of human activity that he correlates with the reductionism of subordinating either the social to the cultural or vice versa.[22] Basic to this project is a distinction between "ethos" and "worldview." Ethos designates the moral and aesthetic aspects of a culture—a people's "underlying attitude toward themselves and their world."[23] Elsewhere Geertz describes ethos in terms of "dispositions," defined not as activity but as the likelihood of activity taking place under certain circumstances. Such dispositions are, in turn, further differentiated into two kinds: moods and motivations.[24] Worldview, on the other hand, indicates for Geertz the "cognitive, existential aspects" of a culture, a people's sense of the really real, their most comprehensive idea of a general order of existence.[25] Understood in this way, these two terms clearly lend themselves to a polarization in which ethos is to worldview as action is to thought.

At times Geertz explicitly correlates religious ritual with ethos and religious belief with worldview, thus invoking the first structural pattern in which ritual is taken for activity in contrast to belief as thought.[26] At other times he presents ethos and worldview as synthesized, fused, or stored in symbols that are arranged in various systems, patterns, or control mechanisms such as ritual, art, religion, language, and myth.[27] However, these systems do not only store a synthesis of ethos and worldview; they are also seen to effect it. Geertz argues with regard to ritual that "any religious ritual no matter how apparently automatic or conventional … involves this symbolic fusion of ethos and world view."[28] Here the second structural pattern appears in which ritual involves the integration of thought and action categories.

The dialectical nature of this fusion of ethos and worldview is made clear in Geertz's related discussion of symbolic systems, such as religion, which involve both "models for" and "models of" reality. These systems are "culture patterns." That is, they "give meaning … [or] objective form, to social and psychological reality both by shaping themselves to it and by shaping it to themselves."[29] With regard to ritual per se, Geertz suggests that "it is in some sort of ceremonial form—even if that form be hardly more than the recitation of a myth, the consultation of an oracle, or the decoration of a grave—that the moods and motivations which sacred symbols induce in men and the general conceptions of the order of existence which they formulate for men meet and reinforce one another." He goes on: "In ritual, the world as lived and the world as imagined, fused under the agency of a single set of symbolic forms, turns out to be the same world."[30]

Here the simplest ritual activities are seen to "fuse" a people's conceptions of order and their dispositions (moods and motivations) for action. For Geertz, this opposition of conceptions and dispositions, or the world as imagined and the world as lived, constitutes cultural life per se. Moreover, our perception and analysis of their opposition and resolution constitute a theoretical explanation of 'meaning' in culture. Indeed, failure to grasp the interaction of these two fundamentally differentiated categories—conceptions and dispositions—is tantamount to the reductionism that Geertz specifically decries, the reductionism of the social to the cultural or the cultural to the social.[31] Thus, the dichotomous nature of conceptions of order (worldview) and dispositions for action (ethos) is fundamental to Geertz's approach, as is their resolution in such symbolic systems as ritual. The temporary resolution of a dichotomy is cast as the central dynamic of cultural life.

So far this analysis of Geertz has simply invoked the two structural patterns discussed earlier. However, Geertz also reveals a third pattern and the further implications of his model of ritual. He goes on to explain that cultural performances such as religious ritual are "not only the point at which the dispositional and conceptual aspects of religious life converge *for the believer,* but also the point at which the interaction between them can be most readily examined *by the detached observer.*"[32]

What does he mean by this? Since ritual enacts, performs, or objectifies religious beliefs (action gives expression to thought) and in so doing actually fuses the conceptual and the dispositional aspects of religious symbols (ritual integrates thought and action), Geertz must be concluding that ritual offers a special vantage point for the theorist to observe these processes. Why and how, we might ask, does ritual work to facilitate the theorist's project? The answer is left implicitly in Geertz's text. To answer explicitly, we need to retrace the homologizations that silently push his argument forward.

Outsiders, states Geertz, will see in ritual only the mere presentation of a particular religious perspective which they may appreciate aesthetically or analyze scientifically.[33] Neither response, he implies, penetrates to the real meaning and dynamics of such a cultural phenomenon. For participants, on the other hand, rites are "enactments, materializations, realizations" of a particular religious perspective, "not only models of what they believe, but also models for the believing of it."[34] Thus, the outsider has only conceptual categories with which he or she approaches the ritual activity. Participants, in contrast, actually experience in the rite the integration of their own conceptual framework and dispositional imperatives. In this argument, Geertz is setting up a third structural pattern and a third permutation of the thought–action dichotomy. That is, ritual participants act, whereas those observing them think. In ritual activity, conceptions and dispositions are fused for the participants, which yields meaning. Meaning for the outside theorist comes differently: insofar as he or she can perceive in ritual the true basis of its meaningfulness for the ritual actors—that is, its fusion of conceptual and dispositional categories—then the theorist can go beyond mere thoughts about activity to grasp the meaningfulness of the ritual. By recognizing the ritual mechanism of meaningfulness for participants, the theorist in turn can grasp its meaningfulness as a cultural phenomenon. Ritual activity can then become meaningful *to the theorist*. Thus, a cultural focus on ritual activity renders the rite a veritable window on the most important processes of cultural life.[35]

Slipping in by virtue of its homologization with the other two structural patterns, the third one organizes the argument in such a way that the theoretical explanation of 'meaning' is itself a fusion of thought and action—the theorist's thought (conceptual categories) and the activity of the ritual participants (which is also a fusion of conceptions and dispositions in its own right). Herein lies the implicit structural homology: the fusion of thought and action described within ritual is homologized to a fusion of the theoretical project and its object, ritual activity. Both generate meaning—the first for the ritual actor and the second for the theorist.

Another example of an argument for a particular relationship between the project of the outside observer and the project of the ritual is laid out by Theodore Jennings.[36] Jennings describes ritual as, first of all, a display to an observer (god, theorist, etc.) or observers (the community itself) and, second, as an epistemological project. Both of these dimensions of ritual act as a "point of contact" between the rite and the attempt by outside observers to grasp a "theoretical-critical understanding of it."[37] We need not castigate our pursuit of the meaning of ritual as "voyeurism or whoring," Jennings asserts, since our cognitive concerns are simply an "extension" of those of the ritual we are "invited" to watch.[38]

All the delicate assumptions of Jennings's approach find their inevitable contrast in Stephen Greenblatt's account of the epistemological project of the amateur ethnographer Captain John G. Bourke. Bourke "witnessed among the Zuñi Indians extreme and simultaneous violations of the codes governing food and waste, and hence experienced extreme disgust." His reaction, Greenblatt speculates, was "not simply an occupational hazard; after all, it is the ethnographer's nausea that gives him his particular discursive field." The parameters of Bourke's lengthy 1891 opus, *Scatologic Rites of All Nations,* were defined, asserts Greenblatt, "precisely by the rising of his gorge." "It would be absurd," he continues, "to conclude that a similar, if better disguised, revulsion lies at the constitutive moment of *all* ethnography, but one may easily find other and more respectable instances than the work of Captain Bourke, in which aversion serves to transform behavior and material substances into the objects of representation and interpretation."[39]

Greenblatt suggests that Bourke instinctively depended on his revulsion to define his epistemological project and the 'otherness' it both required and established. Geertz and Jennings, in contrast, would have us depend on the essential congruity or likeness of doing ritual and generating theoretical interpretations of ritual to establish both our difference from and access to the "other."

c. Questions

Comprehension

1. What aspects of ritual make it appear to be natural?

2. Explain what Bell refers to as "two structural patterns."

3. Describe the third structural pattern Bell attributes to Geertz ([1992] 2018: 72).

4. How, according to Bell's interpretation of Geertz, does ritual create meaning in different ways for the participants and the observers?

Analysis

5. What does it mean that ritual participants give a different reason for their actions than ritual observers? Identify and discuss at least two examples of ritualized activity that people understand differently as a result of participating in that ritual activity versus observing that ritual activity. What's at stake in these disagreements between participants and observers?

Synthesis

6. Is it fair to categorize myth as thought and ritual as action? What is helpful about distinguishing myth as thought and ritual as action? Why is it inappropriate to consider myth to be thought while ritual is considered action? Why is ritual often understood to be a fusion of thought and action? How would Doniger respond to these questions?

Notes

1 Gilbert Lewis discusses the general application of the notion of ritual to conduct or behavior rather than thought or feelings in *Day of Shining Red*, pp. 10–11.

2 Edward Shils, "Ritual and Crisis," in *The Religious Situation: 1968*, ed. Donald R. Cutler (Boston: Beacon Press, 1968), p. 736. (This version of "Ritual and Crisis" differs substantially from a paper with the same name included in Sir Julian Huxley, ed., "A Discussion of Ritualization of Behavior in Animals and Man," *Philosophical Transactions of the Royal Society*, series B, 251 [1966]: 447–50.)

3 Lévi-Strauss, *The Naked Man*, pp. 669–75, 679–84.

4 Durkheim, p. 51.

5 Durkheim, pp. 463ff.

6 James Peacock has noted how Weber's model, which he finds to be "the most systematic and comprehensive conceptualization of the relationship between belief and action," contrasts with the Durkheimian model. See Peacock, "Weberian, Southern Baptist, and Indonesian Muslim Conceptions of Belief and Action," in *Symbols and Society: Essays on Belief Systems in Action*, ed. Carole E. Hill (Athens: University of Georgia Press, 1975), p. 82. Action (*Handeln*) is the "fundamental unit" of Weber's sociology, a unit that represents the act *and* its subjective meaning to the actor, which cannot he separated from each other. Hence, for Weber action cannot be analyzed "independently of belief" (Peacock, p. 82). As such, Weberian analysis focuses on the relationship between the individual and his or her acts and involves the interpretation of the meanings of those acts to the actor. It does not focus on the relationship of beliefs to society as in the Durkheimian approach. This Weberian perspective was elaborated into a full theory of action by Talcott Parsons, of course, in *The Structure of Social Action* (New York: Free Press, 1937) and with Edward Shils in *Toward a General Theory of Action* (New York: Harper and Row, 1962). Yet the objection can be made that the results of both the Durkheimian and the Weberian approaches are rather similar. The Durkheimian is left with a vividly constructed social self (or spiritual being) oddly contrasted with that other vaguely noted being, the physical individual self. In his opposition of self and society, the self is left in somewhat mystical shadows. The Weberian on the other hand is left with a vivid construction of the subjective meanings attached to the objective acts of the individual in contrast to the social significance of these acts. Their social significance, or meaningfulness for others in the culture, cannot be depicted. Rather their transpersonal significance can be described only in terms of logical and idealized systems of socioeconomic behavior completely dissociated from real people and their activities. In both Durkheimian and Weberian conceptualizations, an underlying distinction between the individual and society, or belief and action, pushes the analysis to a dualism in which two entities or forces are simply juxtaposed and not really integrated. Numerous Durkheimians and Weberians have attempted to complete the "integration" that their masters left incomplete. See Robert Wuthnow's discussion of such dualisms and their resolution in *Meaning and Moral Order* (Berkeley: University of California Press, 1987), pp. 23, 26–27, 37–41. For a critique of Parsons and his separate systems of culture and personality, see Marcus and Fisher (pp. 9–11) and Sherry B. Ortner, "Theory in Anthropology Since the Sixties," *Comparative Studies in Society and History* 26 (1984): 150.

7 Stanley J. Tambiah, *Buddhism and the Spirit Cults in North-East Thailand* (Cambridge: Cambridge University Press, 1970).

8 Victor W. Turner, *The Ritual Process: Structure and Anti-Structure* (Chicago: Aldine, 1966).

9 Jameson, *The Prison-House of Language,* pp. 17–32.

10 Jameson, *The Prison-House of Language,* pp. 18–21.

11 Jameson, *The Prison-House of Language,* pp. 18–39 passim.

12 Jameson, *The Prison-House of Language,* p. 39.

13 Jameson, *The Prison-House of Language,* p. 22.

14 E. E. Evans-Pritchard, *Theories of Primitive Religion* (Oxford: Clarendon Press, 1965), pp. 61–62.

15 Nancy D. Munn, "Symbolism in a Ritual Context," in *Handbook of Social and Cultural Anthropology,* ed. John J. Honigmann (Chicago: Rand McNally, 1973), p. 583.

16 Munn, p. 583. This is the basis for Munn's own view according to which "ritual can be seen as a symbolic intercom between the level of cultural thought and other complex meanings, on the one hand, and that of social action and immediate event, on the other" (p. 579).

17 Marshall Sahlins, *Culture and Practical Reason* (Chicago: University of Chicago Press, 1976), pp. 110–13, especially p. 111.

18 Claude Lévi-Strauss, "French Sociology," in *Twentieth Century Sociology,* ed. George Gurvitch and Wilbert E. Moore (New York: The Philosophical Library, 1945), p. 518.

19 In this context, Sahlins (*Culture and Practical Reason,* p. 111) draws attention to W. Doroszewski's theory of the influence of Durkheim's notion of a "sign" on Saussure, in Doroszewski's "Quelques rémarques sur les rapports de la sociologie et de la linguistique: Durkheim et F. de Saussure," *Journal de Psychologie* 30 (1933): 82–91.

20 Durkheim, p. 298.

21 Geertz, *The Interpretation of Cultures,* p. 89. According to Sperber, Radcliffe-Brown regarded anthropology as a "natural science of society," while Evans-Pritchard put it among the humanities. Geertz, on the other hand, is a major representative of a third approach according to which "the only way to *describe* cultural phenomena is, precisely, to *interpret* them." Sperber goes on to criticize this approach and to "develop a fourth view of anthropological knowledge" (*On Anthropological Knowledge,* pp. 9–10).

22 Geertz, *The Interpretation of Cultures,* pp. 143–44.

23 Geertz, *The Interpretation of Cultures,* pp. 89, 126–27.

24 Geertz, *The Interpretation of Cultures,* pp. 95–97.

25 Geertz, *The Interpretation of Cultures,* pp. 89, 98, 126–27.

26 Geertz, *The Interpretation of Cultures,* pp. 127 and 131.

27 Geertz, *The Interpretation of Cultures,* pp. 44–45, 48, 89, 113, 127, 137, etc.

28 Geertz, *The Interpretation of Cultures,* pp. 113 and 127. Also see Geertz's discussion of how symbols "synthesize" ethos and worldview (p. 89).

29 Geertz, *The Interpretation of Cultures,* pp. 92–93.

30 Geertz, *The Interpretation of Cultures,* pp. 112–13.

31 Geertz, *The Interpretation of Cultures,* pp. 143 and 163.

32 Geertz, *The Interpretation of Cultures,* p. 113. Emphasis added.

33 Geertz, *The Interpretation of Cultures,* p. 113.

34 Geertz, *The Interpretation of Cultures,* p. 114.

35 Frits Staal gives an interesting demonstration of the problems that arise when ritual is seen as "pure activity." By this characterization, made in the context of a clear and complete opposition between thought and action, Staal wishes to maintain the total resistance of pure activity to any theoretical appropriation whatsoever. Thus, Staal concludes that ritual cannot be understood, that it is "meaningless" ("The Meaninglessness of Ritual," pp. 2–22).

36 Theodore Jennings, "On Ritual Knowledge," *Journal of Religion* 62, no, 2 (1982): 111–27.

37 Jennings, pp. 113, 124.

38 Jennings, pp. 124–27.

39 Stephen Greenblatt, "Filthy Rites," *Daedalus* 111, no. 3 (1982): 3–4.

PART TWO

Examining Particularities

5

Womanist Religious Interpretation: Alice Walker

a. Introduction

Alice Walker (1944–) is primarily known as an American novelist but her novels have unarguably contributed to movements in the field of religious studies. Walker's definition of womanism is often cited as the foundation of womanist theology, a subfield in religious studies that draws on the perspectives of Black women, and her use of Buddhism continues to be a source of study for religious studies scholars. In addition to her writing, Walker has also been an activist for civil rights and, more recently, the Boycott, Divestment, and Sanctions movement against Israel's occupation of Palestine. Walker attended Spelman College beginning in 1961 but transferred to Sarah Lawrence to complete her degree after disagreeing with Spelman's decision to fire Howard Zinn, who was accused of radicalizing Spelman students. Walker's work has been taken up by scholars in religious studies to consider the value of particular perspectives and approaches that emerge from racial and gender differences. While the authors in the first part of this reader looked for comparisons across cultural and bodily difference, Walker and the other authors featured in this part ask us to consider the unique perspectives that emerge from the experiences of specific bodies. The three selections chosen to represent the work of Walker, the first two from a book of essays titled *In Search of Our Mothers' Garden* (1983) and the third from Walker's award winning novel, *The Color Purple* (1982), describe Black women's experiences. The experiences Walker describes require scholars to move beyond universal categories of whiteness and maleness.

The first two selections, from Walker's book of essays, contains both Walker's famous definition of womanism as well as a selection titled, "From an Interview." Walker's four-part definition of womanism, a preface to *In Search of Our Mothers' Gardens* (1983), offers a concise articulation of Black women's experiences. This definition describes a space for the willfulness of Black women, the value of women's culture, self-love, and a poetic difference between womanist and feminist. The final part of the definition states that "Womanist is to feminist as purple to lavender" (Walker [1983] 2018: 79). For Walker, there is something more brilliant—with more color than a washed-out pastel—about the experience of Black women that cannot be ignored as it has been in the predominantly white feminist movement. This definition marks an important early voice for the specificity of Black women's experience and the difference that experience makes.

In the interview, Walker describes her experience with suicidal thoughts and how that experience informed her writing. She states: "I wish it had never happened. But if it had not, I firmly believe I would never have survived to be a writer. I know I would not have survived at all . . . Writing poems is my way of celebrating with the world that I have not committed suicide the evening before" (Walker [1983] 2018: 82–83). The celebration with the world Walker describes in this essay is similar to the theology of Walker's character Shug in *The Color Purple*. Both, according to Walker, are inspired by African American and Native American beliefs. In the interview, Walker states: "Everything is inhabited by spirit. This belief encourages knowledge perceived intuitively. It does not surprise me, personally, that scientists now are discovering that trees, plants, flowers, have feelings" (Walker [1983] 2018: 84). Whether or not this spirit can be called God remains an open question for Walker. Walker states: "Like many, I waver in my convictions about God, from time to time. In my poetry I seem to be for; in my fiction, against" (Walker [1983] 2018: 91). Thus, the medium of communication, poetry versus fiction, makes a difference for religious understanding.

Additionally in the interview, Walker calls particular attention to the experiences of young Black woman writers because she argues that Black male writers are taken more seriously than Black female writers (Walker [1983] 2018: 89). Drawing on portrayals of Zora Neale Hurston, Walker describes how critics discuss the lives and the likeability of Black female authors instead of their writing. While Walker pays particular attention to Hurston, this essay also describes the wide-ranging influence of other writers on Walker's work.

The third selection, a brief vignette from Walker's third novel, *The Color Purple* (1982), comes from a climactic moment in the novel where Walker's main character, Celie, stops writing to God and starts writing to her sister, Nettie. Because the entire novel is in the form of first-person perspective letters, this shift in address marks an important change. The letters are, at first, addressed from Celie to God, then from Nettie to Celie, and finally from Celie to Nettie. In the selection, Celie describes God as, "a man. And act just like all the other mens I know. Trifling, forgitful, and lowdown" (Walker [1982] 2018: 95). In this letter, Walker describes Celie's conversation with Shug on the nature of the white God, the white Bible, and the white church. Celie gives up on God because, according to Shug, Celie can only see the white man's God. Shug instructs her: "Whenever you trying to pray, and man plop himself on the other end of it, tell him to git lost, say Shug. Conjure up flowers, wind, water, a big rock" (Walker [1982] 2018: 98). Although Celie seems receptive to Shug's theology, the novel continues without Celie addressing God until the final letter. In this letter, Celie begins: "Dear God. Dear stars, dear trees, dear sky, dear peoples. Dear Everything. Dear God" (Walker 1982: 285). In this final letter, Walker offers a reconciliation of the problems that plague Celie in the novel, symbolized by the return of Nettie. This final shift in address signals Celie's own coming to terms with a new perspective on God. *The Color Purple* draws attention to narrative ways of knowing and the legacy of slavery and its continued impact on Black religious life. Overall, this vignette offers a primer to understanding the racial and gender specificity of religious experience.

While Walker is not trained in religious studies, her work asks religious studies scholars to take the specificity of experience seriously and to hesitate before making comparative, cross-cultural claims. In these selections, Walker offers a theory for religion that is different from the theories of religion that attempt broad, universalistic explanations of religious experiences including Douglas's theory of pollution, Dongier's theory of myth, and Bell's theory of ritual. In place of these theories of religion, Walker draws on the lives, thoughts, actions, and conflicts of specific characters, including herself at times, in order to narrate Black women's experience. By articulating the particularity of these experiences in her novels, poems, and essays, Walker offers an approach to religious studies that asks scholars to take difference seriously.

b. Womanist (*In Search of our Mothers' Gardens*) *Alice Walker*

Womanist

1. From *womanish*. (Opp. of "girlish," i.e., frivolous, irresponsible, not serious.) A black feminist or feminist of color. From the black folk expression of mothers to female children, "You acting womanish," i.e., like a woman. Usually referring to outrageous, audacious, courageous or *willful* behavior. Wanting to know more and in greater depth than is considered "good" for one. Interested in grown-up doings. Acting grown up. Being grown up. Interchangeable with another black folk expression: "You trying to be grown." Responsible. In charge. *Serious*.

***

2. *Also:* A woman who loves other women, sexually and/or nonsexually. Appreciates and prefers women's culture, women's emotional flexibility (values tears as natural counterbalance of laughter), and women's strength. Sometimes loves individual men, sexually and/or nonsexually. Committed to survival and wholeness of entire people, male *and* female. Not a separatist, except periodically, for health. Traditionally universalist, as in: "Mama, why are we brown, pink, and yellow, and our cousins are white, beige, and black?" Ans.: "Well, you know the colored race is just like a flower garden, with every color flower represented." Traditionally capable, as in: "Mama, I'm walking to Canada and I'm taking you and a bunch of other slaves with me." Reply: "It wouldn't be the first time."

***

3. Loves music. Loves dance. Loves the moon. *Loves* the Spirit. Loves love and food and roundness. Loves struggle. *Loves* the Folk. Loves herself. *Regardless*.

***

4. Womanist is to feminist as purple to lavender.

c. From an Interview (*In Search of Our Mothers' Gardens*) Alice Walker

I have always been a solitary person, and since I was eight years old (and victim of a traumatic accident that blinded and scarred one eye[1]), I have daydreamed—not of fairy tales—but of falling on swords, of putting guns to my heart or head, and of slashing my wrists with a razor. For a long time I thought I was very ugly and disfigured. This made me shy and timid, and I often reacted to insults and slights that were not intended. I discovered the cruelty (legendary) of children, and of relatives, and could not recognize it as the curiosity it was.

I believe, though, that it was from this period—from my solitary, lonely position, the position of an outcast—that I began really to see people and things, really to notice relationships and to learn to be patient enough to care about how they turned out. I no longer felt like the little girl I was. I felt old, and because I felt I was unpleasant to look at, filled with shame. I retreated into solitude, and read stories and began to write poems.

But it was not until my last year in college that I realized, nearly, the consequences of my daydreams. That year I made myself acquainted with every philosopher's position on suicide, because by that time it did not seem frightening or even odd—but only inevitable. Nietzsche and Camus made the most sense, and were neither maudlin nor pious. God's displeasure didn't seem to matter much to them, and I had reached the same conclusion. But in addition to finding such dispassionate commentary from them—although both hinted at the cowardice involved, and that bothered me—I had been to Africa during the summer, and returned to school healthy and brown, and loaded down with sculptures and orange fabric—and pregnant.

I felt at the mercy of everything, including my own body, which I had learned to accept as a kind of casing over what I considered my real self. As long as it functioned properly I dressed it, pampered it, led it into acceptable arms, and forgot about it. But now it refused to function properly. I was so sick I could not even bear the smell of fresh air. And I had no money, and I was, essentially—as I had been since grade school—alone. I felt there was no way out, and I was not romantic enough to believe in maternal instincts alone as a means of survival; in any case, I did not seem to possess those instincts. But I knew no one who knew about the secret, scary thing abortion was. And so, when all my efforts at finding an abortionist failed, I planned to kill myself, or—as I thought of it then—to "give myself a little rest." I stopped going down the hill to meals because I vomited incessantly, even when nothing came up but yellow, bitter bile. I lay on my bed in a cold sweat, my head spinning.

While I was lying there, I thought of my mother, to whom abortion is a sin; her face appeared framed in the window across from me, her head wreathed in sunflowers and giant elephant-ears (my mother's flowers love her; they grow as tall as she wants); I thought of my father, that suspecting, once-fat, slowly shrinking man, who had not helped me at all since I was twelve years old, when he bought me a pair of ugly saddle oxfords I refused to wear. I thought of my sisters, who had their own problems (when approached with the problem I had, one sister never replied, the other told me—in forty-five minutes of long-distance carefully enunciated language—that I was a slut). I thought of the people at my high-school graduation who had managed to collect seventy-five dollars, to send me to college. I thought of my sister's check for a hundred dollars that she gave me for finishing high school at the head of my class: a check I never cashed, because I knew it would bounce.

I think it was at this point that I allowed myself exactly two self-pitying tears; I had wasted so much, how dared I? But I hated myself for crying, so I stopped, comforted by knowing I would not have to cry—or see anyone else cry—again.

I did not eat or sleep for three days. My mind refused, at times, to think about my problem at all—it jumped ahead to the solution. I prayed to—but I don't know Who or What I prayed to, or even if I did. Perhaps I prayed to God a while, and then to the Great Void a while. When I thought of my family, and when—on the third day—I began to see their faces around the walls, I realized they would be shocked and hurt to learn of my death, but I felt they would not care deeply at all, when they discovered I was pregnant. Essentially, they would believe I was evil. They would be ashamed of me.

For three days I lay on the bed with a razor blade under my pillow. My secret was known to three friends only—all inexperienced (except verbally), and helpless. They came often to cheer me up, to bring me up to date on things as frivolous as classes. I was touched by their kindness, and loved them. But each time they left, I took out my razor blade and pressed it deep into my arm. I practiced a slicing motion. So that when there was no longer any hope, I would be able to cut my wrists quickly, and (I hoped) painlessly.

In those three days, I said good-bye to the world (this seemed like a high-flown sentiment, even then, but everything was beginning to be unreal); I realized how much I loved it, and how hard it would be not to see the sunrise every morning, the snow, the sky, the trees, the rocks, the faces of people, all so different (and it was during this period that all things began to flow together; the face of one of my friends revealed itself to be the friendly, gentle face of a lion, and I asked her one day if I could touch her face and stroke her mane. I felt her face and hair, and she really was a lion; I began to feel the possibility of someone as worthless as myself attaining wisdom). But I found, as I had found on the porch of a building in Liberty County, Georgia—when rocks and bottles bounced off me as I sat looking up at the stars—that I was not afraid of death. In a way, I began looking forward to it. I felt tired. Most of the poems on suicide in *Once* come from my feelings during this period of waiting.

On the last day for miracles, one of my friends telephoned to say someone had given her a telephone number. I called from school, hoping for nothing, and made an appointment. I went to see the doctor and he put me to sleep. When I woke up, my friend was standing over me holding a red rose. She was a blonde, gray-eyed girl, who loved horses and tennis, and she said nothing as she handed me back my life. That moment is engraved on my mind—her smile, sad and pained and frightfully young—as she tried so hard to stand by me and be my friend. She drove me back to school and tucked me in. My other friend, brown, a wisp of blue and scarlet, with hair like thunder, brought me food.

That week I wrote without stopping (except to eat and go to the toilet) almost all of the poems in *Once*—with the exception of one or two, perhaps, and these I do not remember.

I wrote them all in a tiny blue notebook that I can no longer find—the African ones first, because the vitality and color and friendships in Africa rushed over me in dreams the first night I slept. I had not thought about Africa (except to talk about it) since I returned. All the sculptures and weavings I had given away, because they seemed to emit an odor that made me more nauseated than the smell of fresh air. Then I wrote the suicide poems, because I felt I understood the part played in suicide by circumstances and fatigue. I also began to understand how alone woman is, because of her body. Then I wrote the love poems (love real and love imagined), and tried to reconcile myself to all things human. "Johann" is the most extreme example of this need to love even the most unfamiliar, the most fearful. For, actually, when I traveled in Germany I was in a constant state of terror, and no amount of flattery from handsome young German men could shake it. Then I wrote the poems of struggle in the South. The picketing, the marching, all the things that had been buried, because when I thought about them the pain caused a paralysis of intellectual and moral confusion. The anger and humiliation I had suffered were always in conflict with the elation, the exaltation, the *joy* I felt when I could leave each vicious encounter or confrontation whole, and not—like the people before me—spewing obscenities or throwing bricks. For, during those encounters, I had begun to comprehend what it meant to be lost.

Each morning, the poems finished during the night were stuffed under Muriel Rukeyser's door—her classroom was an old gardener's cottage in the middle of the campus. Then I would hurry back to my room to write some more. I didn't care what she did with the poems. I only knew I wanted someone to read them as if they were new leaves sprouting from an old tree. The same energy that impelled me to write them carried them to her door.

This was the winter of 1965, and my last three months in college. I was twenty-one years old, although *Once* was not published till three years later, when I was twenty-four. (Muriel Rukeyser gave the poems to her agent, who gave them to Hiram Haydn at Harcourt Brace Jovanovich—who said right away that he wanted them; so I cannot claim to have had a hard time publishing, yet). By the time *Once* was published, it no longer seemed important—I was surprised when it went, almost immediately, into a second printing—that is, the book itself did not seem to me important; only the writing of the poems, which clarified for me how very much I loved being alive. It was this feeling of gladness that carried over into my first published short story, "To Hell with Dying," about an old man saved from death countless times by the love of his neighbor's children. I was the children, and the old man.

I have gone into this memory because I think it might be important for other women to share. I don't enjoy contemplating it; I wish it had never happened. But if it had not,

I firmly believe I would never have survived to be a writer. I know I would not have survived at all.

Since that time, it seems to me that all of my poems—and I write groups of poems rather than singles—are written when I have successfully pulled myself out of a completely numbing despair, and stand again in the sunlight. Writing poems is my way of celebrating with the world that I have not committed suicide the evening before.

Langston Hughes wrote in his autobiography that when he was sad, he wrote his best poems. When he was happy, he didn't write anything. This is true of me, where poems are concerned. When I am happy (or neither happy nor sad), I write essays, short stories, and novels. Poems—even happy ones—emerge from an accumulation of sadness…

The writing of my poetry is never consciously planned; although I become aware that there are certain emotions I would like to explore. Perhaps my unconscious begins working on poems from these emotions long before I am aware of it. I have learned to wait patiently (sometimes refusing good lines, images, when they come to me, for fear they are not lasting), until a poem is ready to present itself—*all* of itself, if possible. I sometimes feel the urge to write poems way in advance of ever sitting down to write. There is a definite restlessness, a kind of feverish excitement that is tinged with dread. The dread is because after writing each batch of poems I am always convinced that I will never write poems again. I become aware that I am controlled by them, not the other way around. I put off writing as long as I can. Then I lock myself in my study, write lines and lines and lines, then put them away, underneath other papers, without looking at them for a long time. I am afraid that if I read them too soon they will turn into trash; or, worse, something so topical and transient as to have no meaning—not even to me—after a few weeks. (This is how my later poetry-writing differs from the way I wrote *Once*.) I also attempt, in this way, to guard against the human tendency to try to make poetry carry the weight of half-truths, of cleverness. I realize that while I am writing poetry, I am so high as to feel invisible, and in that condition it is possible to write anything.

I am preoccupied with the spiritual survival, the survival *whole* of my people. But beyond that, I am committed to exploring the oppressions, the insanities, the loyalties, and the triumphs of black women. In *The Third Life of Grange Copeland,* ostensibly about a man and his son, it is the women and how they are treated that colors everything. In my new book, *In Love & Trouble: Stories of Black Women,* thirteen women—mad, raging, loving, resentful, hateful, strong, ugly, weak, pitiful, and magnificent—try to live with the loyalty to black men that characterizes all of their lives. For me, black women are the most fascinating creations in the world.

Next to them, I place the old people—male and female—who persist in their beauty in spite of everything. How do they do this, knowing what they do? Having lived what they have lived? It is a mystery, and so it lures me into their lives. My grandfather, at eighty-five, never been out of Georgia, looks at me with the glad eyes of a three-year-old. The pressures on his life have been unspeakable. How can he look at me in this way? "Your eyes are widely open flowers. / Only their centers are darkly clenched / To conceal Mysteries / That lure me to a keener blooming / Than I know. / And promise a secret / I must have." All of my "love poems" apply to old, young, man, woman, child, and growing things. . . .

It is possible that white male writers are more conscious of their own evil (which, after all, has been documented for several centuries—in words and in the ruin of the land, the earth) than black male writers, who, along with black and white women, have seen themselves as the recipients of that evil and therefore on the side of Christ, of the oppressed, of the innocent.

The white women writers that I admire—Kate Chopin, the Brontes, Simone de Beauvoir, and Doris Lessing—are well aware of their own oppression and search incessantly for a kind of salvation. Their characters can always envision a solution, an evolution to higher consciousness on the part of society, even when society itself cannot. Even when society is in the process of killing them for their vision. Generally, too, they are more tolerant of mystery than is Ahab, who wishes to dominate, rather than be on equal terms with, the whale.

If there is one thing African-Americans and Native Americans have retained of their African and ancient American heritage, it is probably the belief that everything is inhabited by spirit. This belief encourages knowledge perceived intuitively. It does not surprise me, personally, that scientists now are discovering that trees, plants, flowers, have feelings ... emotions, that they shrink when yelled at; that they faint when an evil person is about who might hurt them.

One thing I try to have in my life and my fiction is an awareness of and openness to mystery, which, to me, is deeper than any politics, race, or geographical location. In the poems I read, a sense of mystery, a deepening of it, is what I look for—because that is what I respond to. I have been influenced—especially in the poems in *Once*—by Zen epigrams and Japanese haiku. I think my respect for short forms comes from this. I was delighted to learn that in three or four lines a poet can express mystery, evoke beauty and pleasure, paint a picture—and not dissect or analyze in any way. The insects, the fish, the birds, and the apple blossoms in haiku are still whole. They have not been turned into something else. They are allowed their own majesty, instead of being used to emphasize the majesty of people; usually the majesty of the poets writing.

I believe in change: change personal, and change in society. I have experienced a revolution (unfinished, without question, but one whose new order is everywhere on view) in the South. And I grew up—until I refused to go—in the Methodist church, which taught me that Paul *will* sometimes change on the way to Damascus, and that Moses—that beloved old man—went through so many changes he made God mad. So Grange Copeland was *expected* to change. He was fortunate enough to be touched by love of something beyond himself. Brownfield did not change, because he was not prepared to give his life for anything, or *to* anything. He was the kind of man who could never understand Jesus (or Che or King or Malcolm or Medgar) except as the white man's tool. He could find nothing of value within himself and he did not have the courage to imagine a life without the existence of white people to act as a foil. To become what he hated was his inevitable destiny.

A bit more about the "Southern Revolution." When I left Eatonton, Georgia, to go off to Spelman College in Atlanta (where I stayed, uneasily, for two and a half years), I deliberately sat in the front section of the Greyhound bus. A white woman, complained to the driver. He—big and red and ugly—ordered me to move. I moved. But in those seconds of moving, everything changed. I was eager to bring an end to the South that permitted my humiliation. During my sophomore year I stood on the grass in front of Trevor-Arnett Library at Atlanta University and I listened to the young leaders of SNCC. John Lewis was there, and so was Julian Bond, thin, well starched and ironed in light-colored jeans; he looked (with his cropped hair that still tried to curl) like a poet (which he was). Everyone was beautiful, because everyone (and I now think of Ruby Doris Robinson, who has since died) was conquering fear by holding the hands of the persons next to them. In those days, in Atlanta, springtime turned the air green. I've never known this to happen in any other place I've been—not even in Uganda, where green, on hills, plants, trees, begins to dominate the imagination. It was as if the air turned into a kind of water—and the short walk from Spelman to Morehouse was like walking through a green sea. Then, of course, the cherry trees—cut down, now, I think—that were always blooming away while we—young and bursting with fear and determination to change our world—thought, beyond our fervid singing, of death. It was not surprising, considering the intertwined thoughts of beauty and death, that the majority of the people in and around SNCC at that time were lovers of Camus.

Random memories of that period: Myself, moving like someone headed for the guillotine, with (as my marching mate) a beautiful girl who spoke French and came to Spelman from Tuskegee, Alabama ("Chic Freedom's Reflection" in *Once*), whose sense of style was unfaltering, in the worst of circumstances. She was the only really black-skinned girl at Spelman who would turn up dressed in stark white from head to toe—because she knew, instinctively, that white made an already beautiful black girl look like the answer to everybody's prayer. Myself, marching about in front of a restaurant, seeing—inside—the tables set up with clean napkins and glasses of water, the owner standing in front of us barring the door, a Jewish man who went mad on the spot, and fell to the floor. Myself, dressed in a pink faille dress, with my African roommate, my first real girl friend, walking up the broad white steps of a broad white church. And men (white) in blue suits and bow ties materializing on the steps above with ax handles in their hands ("The Welcome Table" in *In Love & Trouble*). We turned and left. It was a bright, sunny day. Myself, sitting on a porch in Liberty County, Georgia, at night, after picketing the jailhouse (where a local black schoolteacher was held) and holding in my arms the bleeding head of a little girl—where is she now?—maybe eight or ten years old, but small, who had been cut by a broken bottle wielded by one of the mob in front of us. In this memory there is a white girl I grew to respect because she never flinched and never closed her eyes, no matter what the mob—where are they now?—threw. Later, in New York, she tried to get me to experiment with LSD with her, and the only reason I never did was because on the night we planned to try it I had a bad cold. I believe the reason she never closed her eyes was because she couldn't believe what she was seeing. We tried to keep in touch—but, because I had never had very much (not even a house that didn't leak), I was always conscious of the need to be secure; because she came from an eleven-room house in the suburbs of Philadelphia and, I assume, never had worried about material security, our deepest feelings began to miss each other. I identified her as someone who could afford to play poor for a while (her poverty interrupted occasionally by trips abroad), and she probably identified me as one of those inflexible black women black men constantly complain about: the kind who interrupt light-hearted romance by saying, "Yes, well … but what are the children going to eat?"

The point is that less than ten years after all these things I walk about Georgia (and Mississippi) eating, sleeping, loving, singing, burying the dead—the way men and women are supposed to do in a place that is the only "home" they've ever known. There is only one "For Coloreds" sign left in Eatonton, and it is on a black man's barbershop. He is merely outdated. Booster, if you read this, *change* your sign!

I see the work that I have done already as a foundation. That being so, I suppose I knew when I started *The Third Life of Grange Copeland* that it would have to cover several generations, and over half a century of growth and upheaval. It begins around 1900 and ends in the sixties. But my first draft (which was never used, not even one line, in the final version) began with Ruth as a Civil Rights lawyer in Georgia going to rescue her father, Brownfield Copeland, from a drunken accident, and to have a confrontation with him. In that version she is married—also to a lawyer—and they are both committed to insuring freedom for black people in the South. In Georgia, specifically. There was lots of love-making and courage in that version. But it was too recent, too superficial—everything seemed a product of the immediate present. And I believe nothing ever is.

So, I brought in the grandfather. Because all along I wanted to explore the relationship between parents and children, specifically between daughters and their fathers (this is most interesting, I've always felt; for example, in "The Child Who Favored Daughter" in *In Love & Trouble,* the father cuts off the breasts of his daughter because she falls in love with a white boy; why this, unless there is sexual jealousy?), and I wanted to learn, myself, how it happens that the hatred a child can have for a parent becomes inflexible. And I wanted to explore the relationship between men and women, and why women are always condemned for doing what men do as an expression of their masculinity. Why are women so easily "tramps" and "traitors" when men are heroes for engaging in the same activity? Why do women stand for this?

My new novel will be about several women who came of age during the sixties and were active (or not active) in the Movement in the South. I am exploring their backgrounds, familial and sibling connections, their marriages, affairs, and political persuasions, as they grow toward a fuller realization (and recognition) of themselves.

Since I put together my course on black women writers, which was taught first at Wellesley College and later at the University of Massachusetts, I have felt the need for real critical and biographical work on these writers. As a beginning; I am writing a long personal essay on my own discovery of these writers (designed, primarily, for lectures), and hope soon to visit the birthplace and home of Zora Neale Hurston, Eatonville,

Florida. I am so involved with my own writing that I don't think there will be time for me to attempt the long, scholarly involvement that all these writers require. I am hopeful, however, that as their books are reissued and used in classrooms across the country, someone will do this. If no one does (or if no one does it to my satisfaction), I feel it is my duty (such is the fervor of love) to do it myself.

I read all of the Russian writers I could find in my sophomore year in college. I read them as if they were a delicious cake. I couldn't get enough: Tolstoy, especially his short stories, and the novels *The Kreutzer Sonata* and *Resurrection,* which taught me the importance of diving through politics and social forecasts to dig into the essential spirit of individual persons, because otherwise characters, no matter what political or current social issue they stand for, will not live), and Dostoevsky, who found his truths where everyone else seemed afraid to look, and Turgenev, Gorky, and Gogol, who made me think that Russia must have something floating about in the air that writers breathe from the time they are born. The only thing that began to bother me, many years later, was that I could find almost nothing written by a Russian woman writer.

Unless poetry has mystery, many meanings, and some ambiguities (necessary for mystery) I am not interested in it. Outside of Basho and Shiki and other Japanese haiku poets, I read and was impressed by the poetry of Li Po, the Chinese poet, Emily Dickinson, E. E. Cummings (deeply), and Robert Graves, especially his poems in *Man Does, Woman Is*—which is surely a male-chauvinist title, but I did not think about that then. I liked Graves because he took it as given that passionate love between man and woman does not necessarily last forever. He enjoyed the moment, and didn't bother about the future. My poem "The Man in the Yellow Terry" is very much influenced by Graves.

I also loved Ovid and Catullus. During the whole period of discovering haiku and the sensual poems of Ovid, the poems of E. E. Cummings and William Carlos Williams, my feet did not touch the ground. I ate, I slept, I studied other things (like European history) without ever doing more than giving it serious thought. It could not change me from one moment to the next, as poetry could.

I wish I had been familiar with the poems of Gwendolyn Brooks when I was in college. I stumbled upon them later. If there was ever a *born* poet, I think it is Brooks. Her natural way of looking at anything, of commenting on anything, comes out as a vision, in language that is peculiar to her. It is clear that she is a poet from the way your whole spiritual past begins to float around in your throat when you are reading, just as it is clear from the first line of *Cane* that Jean Toomer is a poet, blessed with a soul that is surprised by nothing. It is not unusual to weep when reading Brooks, just as when reading Toomer's "Song of the Sun" it is not unusual to comprehend— in a flash—what a dozen books on black people's history fail to illuminate. I have embarrassed my classes occasionally by standing in front of them in tears as Toomer's poem about "some genius from the South" flew through my body like a swarm of golden butterflies on their way toward a destructive sun. Like Du Bois, Toomer was capable of comprehending the black soul. It is not "soul" that *can* become a cliché, but something to be illuminated rather than explained.

The poetry of Arna Bontemps has strange effects on me too. He is a great poet, even if he is not recognized as such until after his death. Or is never acknowledged. The passion and compassion in his poem "A Black Man Talks of Reaping" shook the room I was sitting in the first time I read it. The ceiling began to revolve and a breeze— all the way from Alabama—blew through the room. A tide of spiritual good health tingled the bottoms of my toes. I changed. Became someone the same, but different. I understood, at last, what the transference of energy was.

It is impossible to list all of the influences on one's work. How can you even remember the indelible impression upon you of a certain look on your mother's face? But random influences are the following.

Music, which is the art I most envy.

Then there's travel—which really made me love the world, its vastness, and variety. How moved I was to know that there is no center of the universe. Entebbe, Uganda, or Bratislava, Czechoslovakia, exist no matter what we are doing here. Some writers— Camara Laye, and the man who wrote *One Hundred Years of Solitude* (Gabriel García Márquez)—have illumined this fact brilliantly in their fiction. Which brings me to African writers I *hope* to be influenced by: Okot p'Bitek has written my favorite modern poem, "Song of Lawino." I am crazy about *The Concubine* by Elechi Ahmadi (a perfect story, I think), *The Radiance of the King,* by Camara Laye, and *Maru,* by Bessie Head. These writers do not seem afraid of fantasy, of myth and mystery. Their work deepens one's comprehension of life by going beyond the bounds of realism. They are like musicians: at one with their cultures and their historical subconscious.

Flannery O'Connor has also influenced my work. To me, she is the best of the white Southern writers, including Faulkner. For one thing, she practiced economy. She also knew that the question of race was really only the first question on a long list. This is hard for just about everybody to accept, we've been trying to answer it for so long.

I did not read *Cane* until 1967, but it has been reverberating in me to an astonishing degree. *I love it passionately;* could not possibly exist without it. *Cane* and *Their Eyes Were Watching God* are probably my favorite books by black American writers. Jean Toomer has a very feminine sensibility (or, phrased another way, he is both feminine and masculine in his perceptions), unlike most black male writers. He loved women.

Like Toomer, Zora Neale Hurston was never afraid to let her characters be themselves, funny talk and all. She was incapable of being embarrassed by anything black people did, and so was able to write about everything with freedom and fluency. My feeling is that Zora Neale Hurston is probably one of the most misunderstood, least appreciated writers of this century. Which is a pity. She is great. A writer of courage, and incredible humor, with poetry in every line.

When I started teaching my course in black women writers at Wellesley (the first one, I think, ever), I was worried that Zora's use of black English of the twenties would throw some of the students off. It didn't. They loved it. They said it was like reading Thomas Hardy, only better. In that same course I taught Nella Larsen, Frances Watkins Harper (poetry and novel), Dorothy West, Ann Petry, Paule Marshall, among others. Also Kate Chopin and Virginia Woolf—not because they were black, obviously, but because they were women and wrote, as the black women did, on the condition of humankind from the perspective of women. It is interesting to read Woolf's *A Room of One's Own* while reading the poetry of Phillis Wheatley, to read Larsen's *Quicksand* along with *The Awakening*. The deep-throated voice of Sojourner Truth tends to drift across the room while you're reading. If you're not a feminist already, you become one.

There are two reasons why the black woman writer is not taken as seriously as the black male writer. One is that she's a woman. Critics seem unusually ill-equipped to discuss and analyze the works of black women intelligently. Generally, they do not even make the attempt; they prefer, rather, to talk about the lives of black women writers, not about what they write. And, since black women writers are not, it would seem, very likable—until recently they were the least willing worshipers of male supremacy—comments about them tend to be cruel.

In Nathan Huggins's very readable book *Harlem Renaissance,* he hardly refers to Zora Neale Hurston's work, except negatively. He quotes from Wallace Thurman's novel *Infants of the Spring* at length, giving us the words of a character, "Sweetie Mae Carr," who is allegedly based on Zora Neale Hurston. Sweetie Mae is a writer noted more "for her ribald wit and personal effervescence than for any actual literary work. She was a great favorite among those whites who went in for Negro prodigies." Huggins goes on for several pages, never quoting Zora Neale Hurston herself, but, rather, the opinions of others about her character. He does say that she was "a master of dialect," but adds that "her greatest weakness was carelessness or indifference to her art."

Having taught Zora Neale Hurston, and, of course, having read her work myself, I am stunned. Personally, I do not care if Zora Hurston was fond of her white women friends. When she was a child in Florida, working for nickels and dimes, two white women helped her escape. Perhaps this explains it. But even if it doesn't, so what? Her work, far from being done carelessly, is done (especially in *Their Eyes Were Watching God*) almost too perfectly. She took the trouble to capture the beauty of rural black expression. She saw poetry where other writers merely saw failure to cope with English. She was so at ease with her blackness it never occurred to her that she should act one way among blacks and another among whites (as her more "sophisticated" black critics apparently did).

It seems to me that black writing has suffered because even black critics have assumed that a book that deals with the relationships between members of a black family—or between a man and a woman—is less important than one that has white people as primary antagonists. The consequences of this is that many of our books by "major" writers (always male) tell us little about the culture, history, or future, imagination, fantasies, and so on, of black people, and a lot about isolated (often improbable) or limited encounters with a nonspecific white world. Where is the book by an American black person (aside from *Cane*) that equals Elechi Ahmadi's *The Concubine,* for example? A book that exposes the *subconscious* of a people, because the people's dreams, imaginings, rituals, legends are known to be important, are known to contain the accumulated collective reality of the people themselves. Or *The Radiance of the King,* where the white person is shown to be the outsider he is, because the culture he enters in Africa *itself* expells him. Without malice, but as nature expells what does not suit. The white man is mysterious, a force to be reckoned with, but he is not glorified to such an extent that the Africans turn their attention away from themselves and their own imagination and culture. Which is what often happens with "protest literature." The superficial becomes—for a time—the deepest reality, and replaces the still waters of the collective subconscious.

When my own novel was published, a leading black monthly admitted (the editor did) that the book itself was never read; but the magazine ran an item stating that a *white* reviewer had praised the book (which was, in itself, an indication that the book was no good—so went the logic) and then hinted that the reviewer had liked my book because of my life style. When I wrote to the editor to complain, he wrote me a small sermon on the importance of my "image," of what is "good" for others to see. Needless to say, what others "see" of me is the least of my worries, and I assume that "others" are intelligent enough to recover from whatever shocks my presence or life choices might cause.

Women writers are supposed to be intimidated by male disapprobation. What they write is not important enough to be read. How they live, however, their "image," they owe to the race. Read the reason Zora Neale Hurston gave for giving up her writing. See what "image" the Negro press gave her, innocent as she was. I no longer read articles or reviews unless they are totally about the work. I trust that someday a generation of men and women will arise who will forgive me for such wrong as I do not agree I do, and will read my work because it is a true account of my feelings, my perception, and my imagination, and because it will reveal something to them of their own selves. They will also be free to toss it—and me—out of a high window. They can do what they like....

When I take the time to try to figure out what I am doing in my writing, where it is headed, and so on, I almost never can come up with anything. This is because it seems to me that my poetry is quite different from my novels (*The Third Life of Grange Copeland* and the one I am working on now); for example, *Once* is what I think of as a "happy" book, full of the spirit of an optimist who loves the world and all the sensations of caring in it; it doesn't matter that it began in sadness; *The Third Life of Grange Copeland*, though sometimes humorous and celebrative of life, is a grave book in which the characters see the world as almost entirely menacing. The optimism that closes the book makes it different from most of my short stories, and the political and personal content of my essays makes them different—again—from everything else. So I would not, as some critics have done, categorize my work as "gothic." I would not categorize it at all. Eudora Welty, in explaining why she rebels against being labeled "gothic," says that to her "gothic" conjures up the supernatural, and that she feels what she writes has "something to do with real life." I agree with her.

I like those of my short stories that show the plastic, shaping, almost painting quality of words. In "Roselily" and "The Child Who Favors Daughter" the prose is poetry, or, prose and poetry run together to add a new dimension to the language. But the most that I would say about where I am trying to go is this: I am trying to arrive at that place where black music already is; to arrive at that unself-conscious sense of collective oneness; that naturalness, that (even when anguished) grace.

The writer—like the musician or painter—must be free to explore, otherwise she or he will never discover what is needed (by everyone) to be known. This means, very often, finding oneself considered "unacceptable" by masses of people who think that the writer's obligation is not to explore or to challenge, but to second the masses' motions, whatever they are. Yet the gift of loneliness is sometimes a radical vision of society or one's people that has not previously been taken into account. Toomer was, I think, a lonely, wandering man, accustomed to being tolerated and misunderstood— a man who made choices many abhorred—and yet, *Cane* is a great reward; though Toomer himself probably never realized it.

The same is true of Zora Neale Hurston. She is probably more honest in her fieldwork and her fiction than she is in her autobiography, because she was hesitant to reveal how different she really was. It is interesting to contemplate what would have been the result and impact on black women—since 1937—if they had read and taken to heart *Their Eyes Were Watching God*. Would they still be as dependent on material things—fine cars, furs, big houses, pots and jars of face creams—as they are today? Or would they, learning from Janie that materialism is the dragrope of the soul, have become a nation of women immune (to the extent that is possible in a blatantly consumerist society like ours) to the accumulation of things, and aware, to their core, that love, fulfillment as women, peace of mind, should logically come before, not after, selling one's soul for a golden stool on which to sit. Sit and be bored.

Hurston's book, though seemingly apolitical, is, in fact, one of the most radical novels (without being a tract) we have. Although I am constantly involved, internally, with religious questions—and I seem to have spent all of my life rebelling against the church and other people's interpretations of what religion is—the truth is probably that I don't believe there is a God, although I would like to believe it. Certainly I don't believe there is a God beyond nature. The world is God. Man is God. So is a leaf or a snake … So, when Grange Copeland refuses to pray at the end of the book, he is refusing to be a hypocrite. All his life he has hated the church and taken every opportunity to ridicule it. He has taught his granddaughter, Ruth, this same humorous contempt. He does, however, appreciate the humanity of man-womankind as a God worth embracing. To him, the greatest value a person can attain is full humanity, which is a state of oneness with all things, and a willingness to die (or to live) so that the best that has been produced can continue to live in someone else. He "rocked himself in his own arms to a final sleep" because he understood that man is alone—in his life as in his death— without any God but himself (and the world).

Like many, I waver in my convictions about God, from time to time. In my poetry I seem to be for; in my fiction, against.

I am intrigued by the religion of the Black Muslims. By what conversion means to black women, specifically, and what the religion itself means in terms of the black American past: our history, our "race memories," our absorption of Christianity, our *changing* of Christianity to fit our needs. What will the new rituals mean? How will this new religion imprint itself on the collective consciousness of the converts? Can women be free in such a religion? Is such a religion, in fact, an anachronism? So far I have dealt with this interest in two stories, "Roselily," about a young woman who marries a young Muslim because he offers her respect and security, and "Everyday Use," a story that shows respect for the "militance" and progressive agricultural programs of the Muslims, but at the same time shows skepticism about a young man who claims attachment to the Muslims because he admires the rhetoric. It allows him to acknowledge his contempt for whites, which is all he believes the group is about.

In other stories, I am interested in Christianity as an imperialist tool used against Africa ("Diary of an African Nun") and in voodoo used as a weapon against oppression ("The Revenge of Hannah Kemhuff"). I see all of these as religious questions.

The poem "Revolutionary Petunias" did not have a name when I sat down to write it. I wanted to create a person who engaged in a final struggle with her oppressor, and won, but who, in every other way, was "incorrect." Sammy Lou in the poem is everything she should not be: her name is Sammy Lou, for example; she is a farmer's wife; she works in the fields. She goes to church. The walls of her house contain no signs of her blackness—though that in itself reveals it; anyone walking into that empty house would know Sammy Lou is black. She is so incredibly "incorrect" that she is only amused when the various poets and folk singers rush to immortalize her heroism in verse and song. She did not think of her killing of her oppressor in that way. She thought—and I picture her as tall, lean, black, with short, badly straightened hair and crooked teeth—that killing is never heroic. Her reaction, after killing this cracker-person, would be to look up at the sky and not pray or ask forgiveness but to say—as if talking to an old friend—"Lord, you know my heart. I never wanted to have to kill nobody. But I couldn't hold out to the last, like Job. I had done took more than I could stand."

Sammy Lou is so "incorrect" she names her children after Presidents and their wives: she names one of them after the founder of the Methodist church. To her, this does not mean a limitation of her blackness; it means she feels she is so black she can absorb—and change—all things, since everybody knows that a black-skinned Jackie Kennedy still bears resemblance only to her own great-aunt, Sadie Mae Johnson.

But the most "incorrect" thing about Sammy Lou is that she loves flowers. Even on her way to the electric chair she reminds her children to water them. This is crucial, for I have heard it said by one of our cultural visionaries that whenever you hear a black person talking about the beauties of nature, that person is not a black person at all, but a Negro. This is meant as a put-down, and it is. It puts down all of the black folks in Georgia, Alabama, Mississippi, Texas, Louisiana—in fact, it covers just about everybody's mama. Sammy Lou, of course, is so "incorrect" she does not even know how ridiculous she is for loving to see flowers blooming around her unbearably ugly gray house. To be "correct" she should consider it her duty to let ugliness reign. Which is what "incorrect" people like Sammy Lou refuse to do.

Actually, the poem was to claim (as Toomer claimed the people he wrote about in *Cane,* who were all as "incorrect" as possible) the most "incorrect" black person I could, and to honor her as my own—on a level with, if not above, the most venerated saints of the black revolution. It seems our fate to be incorrect (look where we live, for example), and in our incorrectness stand.

Although Sammy Lou is more a rebel than a revolutionary (since you need more than one for a revolution) I named the poem "Revolutionary Petunias" because she is not—when you view her kind of person historically—isolated. She is part of an ongoing revolution. Any black revolution, instead of calling her "incorrect," will have to honor her single act of rebellion.

Another reason I named the poem "Revolutionary Petunias" is that I like petunias and like to raise them because you just put them in any kind of soil and they bloom their heads off—exactly, it seemed to me, like black people tend to do. (Look at the blues and jazz musicians, the blind singers from places like Turnip, Mississippi, the poets and writers and all-around blooming people you know, who—from all visible evidence— achieved their blooming by eating the air for bread and drinking muddy water for hope.) Then I thought, too, of the petunias my mother gave me when my daughter was born, and of the story (almost a parable) she told me about them. Thirty-seven years ago, my mother and father were coming home from somewhere in their wagon—my mother was pregnant with one of my older brothers at the time—and they passed a deserted house where one lavender petunia was left, just blooming away in the yard (probably to keep itself company)—and my mother said Stop! let me go and get that petunia bush. And my father, grumbling, stopped, and she got it, and they went home, and she set it out in a big stump in the yard. It never wilted, just bloomed and bloomed. Every time the family moved (say twelve times) she took her petunia—and thirty-seven years later she brought me a piece of that same petunia bush. It had never died. Each winter it lay dormant and dead-looking, but each spring it came back, livelier than before.

What underscored the importance of this story for me is this: modern petunias do not live forever. They die each winter and the next spring you have to buy new ones.

In a way, the whole book is a celebration of people who will not cram themselves into any ideological or racial mold. They are all shouting Stop! I want to go get that petunia!

Because of this they are made to suffer. They are told that they do not belong, that they are not wanted, that their art is not needed, that nobody who is "correct" could love what they love. Their answer is resistance, without much commentary; just a steady knowing that they stand at a point where—with one slip of the character—they might be lost, and the bloom they are after wither in the winter of self-contempt. They do not measure themselves against black people or white people; if anything, they learn to walk and talk in the presence of Du Bois, Hurston, Hughes, Toomer, Attaway, Wright, and others—and when they bite into their pillows at night these spirits comfort them. They are aware that the visions that created them were all about a future where all people—and flowers too—can bloom. They require that in the midst of the bloodiest battles or revolution this thought not be forgotten.

When I married my husband there was a law that said I could not. When we moved to Mississippi three years after the lynching of Cheney, Schwerner, and Goodman, it was a punishable crime for a black person and a white person of opposite sex to inhabit the same house. But I felt then—as I do now—that in order to be able to live at all in America I must be unafraid to live anywhere in it, and I must be able to live in the fashion and with whom I choose. Otherwise, I'd just as soon leave. If society (black or white) says, Then you must be isolated, an outcast, then I will be a hermit. Friends and relatives may desert me, but the dead—Douglass, Du Bois, Hansberry, Toomer, and the rest—are a captive audience… These feelings went into two poems, "Be Nobody's Darling" and "While Love Is Unfashionable."

"For My Sister Molly Who in the Fifties" is a pretty real poem. It really is about one of my sisters, a brilliant, studious girl who became one of those Negro wonders— who collected scholarships like trading stamps and wandered all over the world. (Our hometown didn't even have a high school when she came along.) When she came to visit us in Georgia it was—at first—like having Christmas all during her vacation. She loved to read and tell stories; she taught me African songs and dances; she cooked fanciful dishes that looked like anything but plain old sharecropper food. I loved her so much it came as a great shock—and a shock I don't expect to recover from—to learn she was ashamed of us. We were so poor, so dusty and sunburnt. We talked wrong. We didn't know how to dress, or use the right eating utensils. And so, she drifted away, and I did not understand it. Only later did I realize that sometimes (perhaps) it becomes too painful to bear: seeing your home and family—shabby and seemingly without hope—through the eyes of your new friends and strangers. She had felt—for her own mental health—that the gap that separated us from the rest of the world was too wide for her to keep trying to bridge. She understood how delicate she was.

I started out writing this poem in great anger; hurt, really. I thought I could write a magnificently vicious poem. Yet, even in the first draft, it did not turn out that way, which is one of the great things about poetry. What you really feel, underneath everything else, will present itself. Your job is not to twist that feeling. So that although being with her now is too painful with memories for either of us to be comfortable, I still retain (as I hope she does), in memories beyond the bad ones, my picture of a sister I loved, "Who walked among the flowers and brought them inside the house, who smelled as good as they, and looked as bright."

This poem (and my sister received the first draft, which is hers alone, and the way I wish her to relate to the poem) went through fifty drafts (at least) and I worked on it, off and on, for five years. This has never happened before or since. I do not know what to say about the way it is constructed other than to say that as I wrote it the lines and words went, on the paper, to a place comparable to where they lived in my head.

I suppose, actually, that my tremendous response to the poems of William Carlos Williams, Cummings, and Basho convinced me that poetry is more like music—in my case, improvisational jazz, where each person blows the note that she hears—than like a cathedral, with every stone in a specific, predetermined place. Whether lines are long or short depends on what the poem itself requires. Like people, some poems are fat and some are thin. Personally, I prefer the short, thin ones, which are always like painting the eye in a tiger (as Muriel Rukeyser once explained it). You wait until the energy and vision are just right, then you write the poem. If you try to write it before it is ready to be written you find yourself adding stripes instead of eyes. Too many stripes and the tiger herself disappears. You will paint a photograph (which is what is wrong with "Burial") instead of creating a new way of seeing.

The poems that fail will always haunt you. I am haunted by "Ballad of the Brown Girl" and "Johann" in *Once*, and I expect to be haunted by "Nothing Is Right" in *Revolutionary Petunias*. The first two are dishonest, and the third is trite.

The poem "The Girl Who Died # 2" was written after I learned of the suicide of a student at the college I attended. I learned, from the dead girl's rather guilty-sounding "brothers and sisters," that she had been hounded constantly because she was so "incorrect"; she thought she could be a black hippie. To top that, they tried to make her feel like a traitor because she refused to limit her interest to black men. Anyway, she was a beautiful girl. I was shown a photograph of her by one of her few black friends. She was a little brown-skinned girl from Texas, away from home for the first time, trying to live a life she could live with. She tried to kill herself two or three times before, but I guess the brothers and sisters didn't think it "correct" to respond with love or attention, since everybody knows it is "incorrect" to even think of suicide if you are a black person. And, of course, black people do not commit suicide. Only colored people and Negroes commit suicide. (See "The Old Warrior Terror": Warriors, you know, always die on the battlefield.) I said, when I saw the photograph, that I wished I had been there for her to talk to. When the school invited me to join the Board of Trustees, it was her face that convinced me. I know nothing about boards and never really trusted them; but I can listen to problems pretty well… I believe in listening—to a person, the sea, the wind, the trees, but especially to young black women whose rocky road I am still traveling.

d. Selection from *The Color Purple Alice Walker*

Dear Nettie,

I don't write to God no more, I write to you.

What happen to God? ast Shug.

Who that? I say.

She look at me serious.

Big a devil as you is, I say, you not worried bout no God, surely.

She say, Wait a minute. Hold on just a minute here. Just because I don't harass it like some peoples us know don't mean I ain't got religion.

What God do for me? I ast.

She say, Celie! Like she shock. He gave you life, good health, and a good woman that love you to death.

Yeah, I say, and he give me a lynched daddy, a crazy mama, a lowdown dog of a step pa and a sister I probably won't ever see again. Anyhow, I say, the God I been praying and writing to is a man. And act just like all the other mens I know. Trifling, forgitful and lowdown.

She say, Miss Celie. You better hush. God might hear you.

Let 'im hear me, I say. If he ever listened to poor colored women the world would be a different place, I can tell you.

She talk and she talk, trying to budge me way from blasphemy. But I blaspheme much as I want to.

All my life I never care what people thought bout nothing I did, I say. But deep in my heart I care about God. What he going to think. And come to find out, he don't think. Just sit up there glorying in being deef, I reckon. But it ain't easy, trying to do without God. Even if you know he ain't there, trying to do without him is a strain.

I is a sinner, say Shug. Cause I was born. I don't deny it. But once you find out what's out there waiting for us, what else can you be?

Sinners have more good times, I say.

You know why? she ast.

Cause you ain't all the time worrying bout God, I say.

Naw, that ain't it, she say. Us worry bout God a lot. But once us feel loved by God, us do the best us can to please him with what us like.

You telling me God love you, and you ain't never done nothing for him? I mean, not go to church, sing in the choir, feed the preacher and all like that?

But if God love me, Celie, I don't have to do all that. Unless I want to. There's a lot of other things I can do that I speck God likes.

Like what? I ast.

Oh, she say. I can lay back and just admire stuff. Be happy. Have a good time.

Well, this sound like blasphemy sure nuff.

She say, Celie, tell the truth, have you ever found God in church? I never did. I just found a bunch of folks hoping for him to show. Any God I ever felt in church I brought in with me. And I think all the other folks did too. They come to church to *share* God, not find God.

Some folks didn't have him to share, I said. They the ones didn't speak to me while I was there struggling with my big belly and Mr. _____ children.

Right, she say.

Then she say: Tell me what your God look like, Celie.

Aw naw, I say. I'm too shame. Nobody ever ast me this before, so I'm sort of took by surprise. Besides, when I think about it, it don't seem quite right. But it all I got. I decide to stick up for him, just to see what Shug say.

Okay, I say. He big and old and tall and graybearded and white. He wear white robes and go barefooted.

Blue eyes? she ast.

Sort of bluish-gray. Cool. Big though. White lashes, I say.

She laugh.

Why you laugh? I ast. I don't think it so funny. What you expect him to look like, Mr. _____?

That wouldn't be no improvement, she say. Then she tell me this old white man is the same God she used to see when she prayed. If you wait to find God in church, Celie, she say, that's who is bound to show up, cause that's where he live.

How come? I ast.

Cause that's the one that's in the white folks' white bible.

Shug! I say. God wrote the bible, white folks had nothing to do with it.

How come he look just like them, then? she say. Only bigger? And a heap more hair. How come the bible just like everything else they make, all about them doing one thing and another, and all the colored folks doing is gitting cursed?

I never thought bout that.

Nettie say somewhere in the bible it say Jesus' hair was like lamb's wool, I say.

Well, say Shug, if he came to any of these churches we talking bout he'd have to have it conked before anybody paid him any attention. The last thing niggers want to think about they God is that his hair kinky.

That's the truth, I say.

Ain't no way to read the bible and not think God white, she say. Then she sigh. When I found out I thought God was white, and a man, I lost interest. You mad cause he don't seem to listen to your prayers. Humph! Do the mayor listen to anything colored say? Ask Sofia, she say.

But I don't have to ast Sofia. I know white people never listen to colored, period. If they do, they only listen long enough to be able to tell you what to do.

Here's the thing, say Shug. The thing I believe. God is inside you and inside everybody else. You come into the world with God. But only them that search for it inside find it. And sometimes it just manifest itself even if you not looking, or don't know what you looking for. Trouble do it for most folks, I think. Sorrow, lord. Feeling like shit.

It? I ast.

Yeah, It. God ain't a he or a she, but a It.

But what do it look like? I ast.

Don't look like nothing, she say. It ain't a picture show. It ain't something you can look at apart from anything else, including yourself. I believe God is everything, say Shug. Everything that is or ever was or ever will be. And when you can feel that, and be happy to feel that, you've found It.

Shug a beautiful something, let me tell you. She frown a little, look out cross the yard, lean back in her chair, look like a big rose.

She say, My first step from the old white man was trees. Then air. Then birds. Then other people. But one day when I was sitting quiet and feeling like a motherless child, which I was, it come to me: that feeling of being part of everything, not separate at all. I knew that if I cut a tree, my arm would bleed. And I laughed and I cried and I run all round the house. I knew just what it was. In fact, when it happen, you can't miss it. It sort of like you know what, she say, grinning and rubbing high up on my thigh.

Shug! I say.

Oh, she say. God love all them feelings. That's some of the best stuff God did. And when you know God loves 'em you enjoys 'em a lot more. You can just relax, go with everything that's going, and praise God by liking what you like.

God don't think it dirty? I ast.

Naw, she say. God made it. Listen, God love everything you love—and a mess of stuff you don't. But more than anything else, God love admiration.

You saying God vain? I ast.

Naw, she say. Not vain, just wanting to share a good thing. I think it pisses God off if you walk by the color purple in a field somewhere and don't notice it.

What it do when it pissed off? I ast.

Oh, it make something else. People think pleasing God is all God care about. But any fool living in the world can see it always trying to please us back.

Yeah? I say.

Yeah, she say. It always making little surprises and springing them on us when us least expect.

You mean it want to be loved, just like the bible say.

Yes, Celie, she say. Everything want to be loved. Us sing and dance, make faces and give flower bouquets, trying to be loved. You ever notice that trees do everything to git attention we do, except walk?

Well, us talk and talk bout God, but I'm still adrift. Trying to chase that old white man out of my head. I been so busy thinking bout him I never truly notice nothing God make. Not a blade of corn (how it do that?) not the color purple (where it come from?). Not the little wildflowers. Nothing.

Now that my eyes opening, I feels like a fool. Next to any little scrub of a bush in my yard, Mr. _____'s evil sort of shrink. But not altogether. Still, it is like Shug say, You have to git man off your eyeball, before you can see anything a'tall.

Man corrupt everything, say Shug. He on your box of grits, in your head, and all over the radio. He try to make you think he everywhere. Soon as you think he everywhere, you think he God. But he ain't. Whenever you trying to pray, and man plop himself on the other end of it, tell him to git lost, say Shug. Conjure up flowers, wind, water, a big rock.

But this hard work, let me tell you. He been there so long, he don't want to budge. He threaten lightening, floods and earthquakes. Us fight. I hardly pray at all. Every time I conjure up a rock, I throw it.

Amen

e. Questions

Comprehension

1. Why does Walker argue that Black women writers aren't taken as seriously as Black male writers?

2. Who are Walker's literary influences and what does she find compelling about these influences?

3. Describe the understanding of God to which Celie objects when she stops writing to God.

4. Describe Shug's understanding of sin, God, sex, the Bible, and how humans relate to God.

5. Why does Celie have a hard time accepting Shug's theology, even though she agrees?

Analysis

6. Compare Walker's ideas about belief in "From an Interview" to the beliefs articulated in Shug and Celie's conversation in *The Color Purple*. How are Walker's beliefs articulated in the essay similar to or different from the beliefs described in the novel?

7. Walker argues that the writing of Black women is not taken seriously and that, instead, critics focus on their lives or their likeability. Is this still an issue for Black women authors today? Can you think of specific examples?

8. How might religious studies scholars heed Walker's words to listen "to a person, the sea, the wind, the trees, but especially to young Black women whose rocky road I am still traveling"? ([1982] 2018: 95) What difference might that make in theorizing religion?

Synthesis

9. How does the specificity of Black women's experience as articulated by Walker challenge existing categories for religious studies, including the categories described in the first section of this reader?

Note

1 See "Beauty: When the Other Dancer Is the Self."

6

Signifying Religion in the Modern World: Charles H. Long

a. Introduction

Charles H. Long (1926–) is a leader in the field of religious studies in recognizing and challenging how the European colonial perspective biased the study of religion through institutional structures that ignored indigenous peoples and labeled them as "the other." Long trained at the University of Chicago and is professor emeritus at the University of California, Santa Barbara, in religious studies where he also directed the Center for Black Studies. In the first of the two selections here, Long explores the larger structural problem of studying a relationship only from one side. In the second selection offered here, he moves to a closer perspective that examines the neglected side, nuancing what is often portrayed as monolithic.

The first essay, "Primitive/Civilized: The Locus of a Problem," ([1986] 1999) focuses on how the study of religion has historically created and relied on the foundational binary of primitive and civilized to conceptualize scholarly categories of investigation. His is a call to consider how scholarship has erased the voices of non-European/non-Western people. In this essay, Long makes three moves. These moves trace the assumption that privileged "civilization" is the epitome of Enlightenment thinking. The first move is the tendency of using "others" to make empirical claims. Long notes: "The self-conscious realization of the Western European rise to the level of civilization must be seen simultaneously in its relationship to the discovery of a new world which must necessarily be perceived as inhabited by savages and primitives who constitute the lowest rung on the ladder of cultural reality" ([1999] 2018: 107). He observes how identity is based on a zero-sum equation—for one group to be higher on the ladder it must be measured against other groups who reside in lower positions. Second, he evokes the power of the image of "utopia" as religious studies came to distinguish itself from Christian theological, confessional stances. Incorporating and intertwining with methods from previous and emerging fields in the social sciences and natural sciences, the category of "primitive" is the foil against which civilization can maintain visions of "utopia" through religious archetypes, cartography, and the imperial pursuit.

In the third and final move of the essay, Long calls for a demythologizing of this binary construction that separates people into positively valued, historical people (civilized) and negatively valued, atemporal people (primitive). Destructive on multiple levels, one problem of labeling peoples and geographies as primitive is that Western scholarship is written from only one perspective, and religious nuance is afforded to only the conquering side.

In Long's second essay included here, "Perspectives for a Study of Afro-American Religion in the United States," ([1971] 1999) he writes: "For some time I have felt the need to present a systematic study of black religion" that is "an attempt to see what kinds of images and meanings lie behind the religious experiences of the black communities in America" ([1999] 2018: 117). In the pursuit of studying "religious experiences," Long designates "black communities in America" as their own, unique religious tradition, which should be examined as a discrete unit. Long identifies two problems that have plagued, and thus hindered, scholarly approaches to analyzing black religious traditions in the United States—either black communities are studied through social scientific methods, which do not adequately address the religious elements, or religion in black communities tends to be conflated and equated simply with black Christianity. Long presents three approaches that demonstrate the specific realities and histories of black communities in the United States, using each of these to nuance and contour black religious experiences. The first, "Africa as historical reality and religious image," focuses on the importance of land—alienation from, longing for, mythical and historical relation to land—as a religious image. The second approach Long recommends for demonstrating the specific realities and histories of black communities in the United States is recognizing that black presence in the United States is not voluntary. The history of slavery presented an "opaqueness," resulting from the multiple contradictions associated with chattel slavery in a purportedly democratic nation. Long argues that navigating, living in, and resisting this opacity should be read as a religious element. Finally, "the experience and symbol of God" looks at the holy literature of black communities, including "slave narratives, sermons, the words and music of spirituals and the blues, the cycles of Brer Rabbit and High John, the Conqueror, stories" (Long [1999] 2018: 121). Accounting for both biblical and non-biblical traditions used in a variety of "nontraditional" contexts, the study of black religion in the United States requires a more nuanced view of important materials and reveals the complexity of what was too often skimmed over as monolithic.

Long's work takes on the very categories that have shaped how a scholar knows something should be classified as religion. The act of boundary-drawing, which produces the value-laden categories of insiders and outsiders, is upended when multiple perspectives actually enter the discourse. Long's call to consider religious studies from its multiple relationships of conquest and its privileging of some groups has far reaching implications. Not only does his work speak to historical contexts of often forced migration and movement but his methods also help us examine other ways in which traditions move and are defined, such as missionary endeavors and chosen immigration patterns. The emphasis cannot be to study only one side; rather, the scholar needs to investigate the whole system and relationship present in each situation.

b. Primitive/Civilized: The Locus of a Problem (*Significations: Signs, Symbols, and Images in the Interpretation of Religion*) Charles H. Long

In 1967, Professor Charles J. Adams published an article, "The History of Religions and the Study of Islam."[1] In his essay Adams expressed a singular problem regarding methodology in the discipline of the history of religions. While the discipline purports to study, investigate, and render a systematic and comprehensive understanding of all religious phenomena, the source of most of its important theories is derivative from an interpretation of primitive and prehistoric religious cultures. This trend may be seen in the works of Nathan Söderblom, Gerardus van der Leeuw, and Mircea Eliade. Even when nonprimitive historical-cultural forms of religion — for example, Hebrew, Christian, Islam — are dealt with, they are confronted on the levels of their "primitive" aspects to conform to the methodological orientation of the historian of religions. One does not have to agree with every detail of this criticism to acknowledge that the study of primitive religions has loomed large in the history of the history of religions. This may be explained historically by showing how the origins of the discipline took place in the milieu of E. B. Tylor's researches into primitive cultures, of Charles Darwin's evolutionary theories, and of the popularity of James Frazer's *Golden Bough*. The central cultural issues were expressed in terms of "origins," of the search for the first and simplest forms, and of explanatory systems that traced the evolutionary course of human development over historical time.

This milieu accounts for certain initiatory emphases in method, but it does not explain the continuing and inordinate concern for the data of primitive religions and methods growing from their interpretations. Let us explore this problem by relating the concern for primitive religion to the more general orientation of primitivism.

Arthur O. Lovejoy and George Boas in their classical work define two generic forms of primitivism.[2] One form, chronological primitivism, is concerned with the question of the temporal distribution of good or value in the history of humankind, whether this has occurred in the past, is in the present, or will be in the future. Cultural primitivism, the second form, expresses the discontent of the civilized with civilization or with some conspicuous or characteristic feature of it. It is the expression of a nostalgia for a simpler and less sophisticated form of life than that obtaining in the present situation.

In both forms, chronological or cultural primitivism, one notes a generic ingredient of civilization. Lovejoy and Boas are not careful to define what they mean by civilization; for them, it is a relative term which might extend from the cultures of prehistory to the present. What is important for them is the critical element in the orientation of primitivism, for it expresses the inquietude of human consciousness itself. We might also note that the documents of their text are from West Asian, Indian, and Greco-Roman cultures.

The concern for primitive religion in our time might well be the expression of either or both kinds of primitivism in late modern Western culture. I think, however, that something much more fundamental is at stake in this concern. The texts of Lovejoy and Boas cover literary, philosophical, and imaginary genres; the worlds embodied in primitivism exist as modes of thought and imaginative speculation.

The milieu that forms the context for Tylor, Darwin, and Frazer is of a different kind.[3] It is different in at least two senses. First of all, the term "civilization" has a definite and self-conscious meaning for the intellectuals of this period. Second, the meaning of this term cannot be understood apart from the geographies and cultures of the New World that are both "other" and empirical.

It is clear that the New World itself — the new worlds of the western hemisphere and later the South Pacific — made an extraordinary impact on the European consciousness. Nothing before or since has equaled this discovery. This should not imply, however, that the modality and structure of the "empirical other" is unknown in Western culture prior to this time. Initial perceptual forms for the New World were more often than not based upon a prior history.

Empirical Others

I use the phrase "empirical others" to define a cultural phenomenon in which the extraordinariness and uniqueness of a person or culture is first recognized negatively. However, because the recognition of the person or culture is necessary for interpreters of cultural identity, various stratagems of description and/or diagnosis are employed to represent the other in the relationship.

One example of this kind of meaning can be gained from Ilza Veith's history of the disease hysteria.[4] In her research she traces the history of the disease from ancient Egypt to the work of Freud.

Hysteria throughout this history is classified as a woman's disease; its name is derived from the Greek *hystera,* which means uterus. The symptom of this disease is a marked emotional tension expressing itself in fainting spells or violent pathological behavior. Throughout the history of this disease, various diagnoses are made, many defining the uterus as an animal that tends to wander through the body out of its place. A standard remedy prescribed for this disease throughout its history is heightened heterosexual activity. In other cases, vapors or watery solutions were to be inserted into the vagina. It is especially interesting to note that in the Kahun Papyrus of the Egyptian Middle Kingdom, aromatic agents were to be incorporated in the shape of the ibis. The aroma from this wax upon entering the womb is supposed to pacify the womb. The ibis, a bird, is the symbol of Thoth. Thoth is a male deity personified by the moon and related to the sun. He is also the inventor of writing and the scribe of all the other gods.

Veith notes that "this specific instance of the ibis used for vulvar insufflation inevitably gives rise to further speculations that bear on modern psychological theories.

The employment of the image of a powerful male deity to lure a wandering female organ is highly suggestive of the nature of the underlying ideas concerning hysteria even if it is nowhere spelled out in detail."[5]

Another instance of "empirical other" in the modality of an internal European "otherness" may be seen in the mythological structure of the wild man.[6] Elements of this mythological structure may be traced from Enkidu in the Gilgamesh epic to the Tarzan of the cinema, but the exemplary form of this figure is found in its medieval European manifestation. This figure is neither human nor beast; falling somewhere in between these species, it expresses in a grotesque way some of the proclivities of both. It is usually pictured as a hairy creature that walks on two legs, possesses a tail, and is often endowed with boar's tusks growing from the comers of his mouth.

The wild man is a child of nature, his natural habitat is the forest. His great strength is matched by his appetite for carnal connections with human female and the flesh of human beings. Nothing about the wild man prepares him for participation in civil society. When confronted with human beings, he may take to flight or, conversely, offer steadfast resistance to the death. This mythological figure is found on the folkloric, literary, theatrical, and artistic levels of medieval society.

Richard Bernheimer's history of the mythology of the wild man is matched by Michel Foucault's history of madness.[7] Foucault sees a connection between the disappearance of leprosy at the end of the Middle Ages and the confinement of persons considered to be mad.

Prior to the confinement of mad persons, they were able to lead a wandering existence. As a matter of fact, the *Narrenschiff* of mythological lore became literally a "ship of fools," a ship on which mad persons, driven from various cities, were forced to embark. While all mad persons were not placed on ships of this kind, the symbolic meaning of the navigation of mad persons expressed a peculiar valuation.

> But water adds to this dark mass its own values; it carries off, but it does more, it purifies. Navigation delivers now to the uncertainty of fate; on water, each man's voyage is at once a rigorous division and an absolute Passage. In one sense, it simply develops, across a half-real, half-imaginary geography, a mad-man's liminal position on the horizon of medieval concern.[8]

But the watery wanderings of the mad did not continue; in the course of time since, mad persons have been confined, first of all in the abandoned leprosariums, then in places built especially for them. The locus of this confinement is sometimes on the periphery of the city and sometimes in the center of the city.

This brief discussion of certain extraordinary behaviors and beliefs within Europe was undertaken to form a basis for the symbolic and mythological languages used to describe and interpret the new worlds discovered by the Europeans since the fifteenth century. First of all, attention is given to biology and anatomy, but what is the normal anatomical and biological structure of the "other" appears to the authoritative interpreter as the mode of the extraordinary, or the pathological and the irrational.

Second, there is the issue of loci. In the case of hysteria, we are confronted with a wandering animal within the body of the female, an animal that will not stay in its place and must be induced to do so by clinical procedures or actions that have the salutary side effect of providing pleasure for men.

Wild men are separated from human society. The natural place for these ambiguous creatures is the forest, removed from human habitation. Wild men are tempted to leave the wilds out of an inordinate and destructive desire for human flesh, expressed carnally or cannibalistically. Their biological structure is ambiguous, partaking of the human and the beast, uncontrolled by human reason; their great natural and bestial strength poses a threat to human society.

In the case of madness, if we follow Foucault, until the middle of the sixteenth century mad persons were wanderers, their lack of fixity of mind paralleled by their abandonment in space.[9] Their first confinement was in a kind of quasi prison — a ship of fools that confined them in a pilgrimage over the waters. Later confinements were within old leprosariums, where they inherited many of the valuations of the former lepers simply by being in those places. Subsequently, confinement in places built for the mad expresses the ambivalence of the society regarding the locus of unreason. Is the place of confinement to be, as in the case of Bedlam, located within the city? And again, what are the functions of unreason? Is it a mysterious malady that should be isolated or is it a spectacle to be observed for the sake of amusement or sober reflection?

It is not at all strange that notions such as these formed the archetypes for the descriptions and taxonomies that Europeans used to make sense of the new worlds. It is normal to describe the new by reference to the old that is already known. However, a new factor of necessity must be observed in regard to the New World. This factor has to do with those movements — political, economic, and religious — which took place within Western Europe from the late fifteenth century to the end of the eighteenth century. In a word, this is symbolized by the notion of civilization. While civilization is used most often as a term to describe the ideas, technology, religion, manners, morals, and so on, of citied traditions throughout the world since the Near Eastern urban development, the precise word "civilization" does not appear in Western languages until the late eighteenth century, first in France in the writings of Marquis de Mirabeau and fifteen years later in England in 1772 in Boswell's *Life of Johnson*.[10] The incident of the appearance of the word in the English language is instructive regarding the new range of meanings implied by the term.

On Monday March 23, [1772] found [Dr. Johnson] busy preparing a fourth edition of his folio Dictionary... He would not admit *civilization,* but only *civility.* With great deference to him I thought *civilization,* from to *civilize,* better in the sense opposed to barbarity than civility, as it is better to have a distinct word for each sense, than one word for two senses, which civility is, in his way of using it.[11]

Émile Benveniste surmises from this statement of Boswell's that the term "civilization" was already in use in England and not a neologism of his own invention.

It may, therefore, be the case that the term has an earlier appearance in England than the year 1772.

In any case, one is able to find a proliferation of usages within a short time after this date, and one is led to presuppose that it was part of the *lingua franca* of the intellectual class. Adam Smith, in his *An Inquiry Into the Nature and Causes of Wealth of Nations,* makes use of the term in almost a casual manner.[12] As a matter of fact, Benveniste was able to find the term used as common parlance among Scottish intellectuals in John Millar's *Observations Concerning the Distinction of Ranks in Society,* published in 1771.[13] It is safe to say that by the middle of the eighteenth century the word had become a necessary descriptive term for certain cultural processes at work in France and England. Norbert Elias has described these processes as "civilizing processes" that find expression in what he terms sociogenetic and psychogenetic processes. These processes refer to the gradual changes taking place in Western Europe over a two- or three-century period — changes on the psychic and social levels that produced the culture we refer to as modern Western civilization.

> This concept [civilization] expresses the self-consciousness of the West. One could even say: the national consciousness. It sums up everything in which Western society of the last two or three centuries believes itself superior to earlier societies or 'more primitive' contemporary ones. By this term Western society seeks to describe what constitutes its special character and what it is proud of: the level of *its* technology, the nature of *its* manners, the development of *its* scientific knowledge or view of the world and much more.[14]

Outside of internal developments in Western Europe, this formation of culture is caused by or correlative with the discovery of the New World by the West. The self-conscious realization of the Western European rise to the level of civilization must be seen simultaneously in its relationship to the discovery of a new world which must necessarily be perceived as inhabited by savages and primitives who constitute the lowest rung on the ladder of cultural reality.

The sociogenesis and psychogenesis of this formation are equally formed by the explorers, adventurers, merchants, and literary artists whose field of opportunity and expression was the brave New World of savages and primitives beyond the Atlantic sea.

Hermeneutical Excursus

It would be easy, too easy, at this point to interpret the formation of modern Western culture in political and ideological terms, pointing out the relationship between universal education and literacy as aspects of mercantile imperialism and a tool of the rising bourgeoisie, the primitives and primitivism in general serving only as a camouflage and justification for conquest.

Resistance to this temptation should not imply that these kinds of factors are not at work and even though inordinate attention to these features might render a too simplistic interpretation, this is not why such a temptation must be resisted. The resistance is, rather, based on the hermeneutical nature of this enterprise. What is at stake and what has appeared is the symbol, civilization—a symbol that includes the meaning and definition of primitive. This symbol, at least as far as our interpretation has gone, is an expression of the will to power, and at this juncture the problem of truth and error must be subordinated. One must employ at this juncture what Paul Ricoeur has called the hermeneutics of suspicion.[15]

The issue is whether the symbol civilization is simply the context for a necessary lie (the appearance of crude and debased cultures and the demonstration of the superior power of the Europeans) or a new sacred power in the world (the bringing of all cultures into communication with one another and the beginnings of the possibility for a new meaning of human freedom in the world). Both interpretations are equally as true as they are false. Both inhere within the epistemological valence of civilization. Both are products of false consciousness as much as each makes a claim for truth. The very notion of civilization is now suspended within the web of a hermeneutic of suspicion.

And this is as true for those who form its heritage as it is for those who see themselves as its victims. The champions of civilization still speak in continuity with the rhetoric of imperialists and mercantile classes, and its victims clamor for recognition and authenticity of their histories and heritages in the name of civilization, protesting against the unfairnesses of civilization for reducing them to the semantics of tribes and primitives within the very taxonomies of the civilization, which is in point of fact their *bête noir*.[16] Both come to know themselves and define their presence within the rhetoric of "civilization."

The hermeneutics of suspicion reveals the authenticity residing within the ambiguities of the existential. It may be seen as part and parcel of our history after the Second World War, the vogue of anticolonialism, the rise of the Third World, and so on. In this sense, it emphasizes a capacity for iconoclasm, destruction, and nihilism. But all of this in the name of true human authenticity and being. It is, however, impossible to make sense of the being of the human in strictly existential language. The being of the human requires a recognition of depth, whether that depth is defined as history, givenness, creation, or in terms of the vague shadows that accompany the clarity of identity. And so this critical iconoclastic element within a hermeneutics of suspicion already anticipates a hermeneutic of recollection and memory.

Utopias and Hermeneutics

The term "civilization" — a term that embodies the notion of the primitive — became a part of Western languages in the eighteenth century. Elias has shown that this term is the synthesis of a number of processes that can be understood empirically in Western culture since its medieval period. But if civilization represents a clarity and an identity regarding cultural formation, it throws shadows on histories, imaginations, and meanings that are obscured by the very clarity of the symbol of civilization.

The West as a symbol is historically and logically prior to civilization as a symbol. The West as symbol has had many and varied moments of authenticity, but from the point of view of civilization, the West evokes a dialectical and synthetic orientation to the meaning of "human world." The semantic range engenders a history that is both ideological (suspicious) and normative (a curiosity regarding the nature of being human).

> Two relations, separate but indivisible, are always apparent in the European consciousness. One is the realm of political life in its broadest sense, in the atmosphere of — if I may describe it so — concrete relations with concrete non-European countries, peoples and worlds... The other relationship has reigned in the minds of men. Its domain is that of the imagination, of all sorts of images of non-Western peoples and worlds which have flourished in our cultures — images derived not from observation, experience, and perceptible realities, but from a psychological urge. That urge creates its own realities that are totally different from the political realities of the first category. But they are in no way subordinate in either strength or clarity since they have always possessed that absolute reality value so characteristic of the rule of myth.[17]

Henri Baudet's statement regarding the formative elements in Western culture goes far in explaining its penchant for the dialectical and the binary and the exemplary form of the symbol as the coherence of paradoxical elements.

Many of these structures were alive in the history of the Renaissance and medieval period prior to the rise of that extension of Western cultural formation which we denote by the term "civilization." It is represented not by symbols and images of an empirical other, but by symbolic imaginative others. It opens us to the symbol of the noble savages of antiquity, of paradisial myths, of imaginary geographies and other worlds.

It is against such a background that the cartographers and explorers of the fifteenth century prepared for their explorations of new worlds.[18] Since the time of the Crusades, the myth of the kingdom of Prester John, who ruled a Christian kingdom in Ethiopia, reigned in the minds of Europeans. This kingdom had a vague basis in biblical and classical literature, and the existence of such a kingdom raised hopes for aid against the assault of the Muslims. In addition to this, according to biblical sources, the kingdom of Ethiopia should lie close to the geographical location of the paradisiacal Garden of Eden. The image of Ethiopia led to concrete expression in the search for its geographical and cartographic reality.

In concert with this image, the legend of the Magi underwent new interpretations.[19] To the symbol of time represented by them originally is added the geographical symbol of space. The Magi appear already in a sixth-century Armenian gospel as King Melchior of Persia, King Casper of India-Ethiopia, and King Balthazar of Ethiopia. Another version of this spatial morphology has them recapitulating sons of Noah: Ham with Africa, Shem with the East, and Japheth with Greece, the West.

These myths of recollection and reminiscence are the basis for the geographical and cartographic images regarding the nature of the world during the Renaissance. This geographical and cartographic interest indicates how the imaginary was used as a clue and tool for the understanding of the concrete world; it actually became the basis for voyages into the *terra incognita*. It is this historical and imaginary background which forms the latent structures of thought for the discovery of America and the extension of the power of modern civilization.

Through an ingenious form of logical and philosophical reasoning, Edmundo O'Gorman has sought to dispel the notion that Christopher Columbus *discovered America*.[20] The reasons for this critique are not ideological; the aim is not to put forward a previous discovery by the Norse or the Phoenicians, nor to make the obvious claim that the aborigines of this continent came from somewhere at sometime before the appearance of Europeans.

O'Gorman's critique presupposes the European understanding of America — and his point of departure is the adventures of the Admiral of the Ocean Sea — as an extension of the meaning of the West. His critique is logical and historical, but because it is so, both the history and the logic must be seen in terms of that structure wherein cartographies lead to historical consequences.

Succinctly put, Columbus did not discover *America*, for in terms of the imaginary cartographic and geographical knowledge of his time, the meaning and existence of a space that could be America did not exist. Is it possible to discover that which does not exist? Added to this logic are the facts of Columbus's biography; to his dying day and after four voyages across the Atlantic, he believed that he had discovered what did in fact exist, either the shores of Cathay or a watery route to the Indian seas.

O'Gorman does not rest his case on the history of this period, nor on the biography of Columbus. As a historian, his method must verify his historical judgment. Two rather long quotes from O'Gorman will reveal that philosophical logic undergirding his historiography.

This conclusion led me to understand that the basic concept for the historian is that of "invention," because the concept of creation which assumes that something is produced *ex nihilo* can have meaning only within the sphere of religious faith. Thus I came to suspect that the clue to the problem of the historical appearance of America lay in considering the event a result of an inspired invention of Western thought not as the result of a purely physical discovery, brought about, furthermore, by accident.[21]

We ask whether or not the idea that the American continent was "discovered" was acceptable as a satisfactory way of explaining its appearance on the historical scene of Western culture. We may now answer that it is not satisfactory, because this interpretation does not account adequately for the facts that it interprets; it reduces itself to an absurdity when it reaches the limits of its logical possibilities. The reason for this absurdity is the substantialistic concept of America as a thing in itself. We must conclude that it is necessary to discard both this obsolete notion and the interpretation that depends on it... If one ceases to conceive of America as a ready-made thing that had always been there and that one day miraculously revealed its hidden unknown, and unforeseeable being to an awe-struck world, then the event which is thus interpreted [the finding by Columbus of unknown oceanic lands] takes on an entirely different meaning, and so, of course does the long series of events that followed. All of these happenings which are now known as the exploration, the conquest, and the colonization of America, the establishment of colonial systems in all their diversity and complexity; the gradual formation of nationalities; the movement toward political independence and the economic autonomy; in a word, the sum total of all American history, both Latin and Anglo-American, will assume a new and surprising significance… Historical events will no longer appear as something external and accidental that in no way alters the supposed essence of an America ready-made since the time of Creation, but as something internal which constitutes its ever-changing mobile, and perishable being, as is the being of all that partakes of life; and its history will no longer be that which has happened to America, but that which it has been, is, and is in the act of being.[22]

It is O'Gorman's argument that Amerigo Vespucci really discovered America, for in his voyage of 1501–02 along the coast of what is called South America, Vespucci discerned that he had found a "New World." His interpretation was based on an *a posteriori* foundation. Vespucci's voyage became the empirical determinant that opened up the possibility of explaining the new-found lands in a way different from and contradictory to the accepted picture of the world.[23] Vespucci says in his description of this New World that he is going to write about things unknown by either ancient or modern authors.

It is through this process, according to O'Gorman, that the *being* of America, the New World, unfolds. The imaginary cartography of the Renaissance that led Europeans to undertake their initial voyages is broken by the sheer facticity of the existence of the new land mass and the impossibility of fitting it into the older symbolic structure without doing violence to the structure or the empiricity of the new lands. But if the geographical images were broken, the historical elements of this image remained intact. The inhabitants of the new world would bear the name "Indians," a carryover from the imaginary geography of Columbus. Their historical meaning would fluctuate between those of Western antiquity, biblical and classical, as archetypes, on the one hand, and would be deciphered in the terms of a norm of nature on the other. The norm of nature often combined in one image that of the older "empirical others" of Europe and a passive paradisiacal understanding of nature.

From this process several images of the primitive emerge. The aboriginal inhabitants of North America appear as noble savages, as metaphors of the wilderness and as wild men. These images come to fruition through a combined fertilization of theological-philosophical, economic-political, artistic-literary, and scientific concerns on the part of the Europeans.[24]

The semantic range, from a virgin land in North America inhabited alternatively by noble or ignoble savages to models based on the extension of the archetypes of the crusades in Mesoamerica and South America, indicates the speculative arena in which these images took shape. In the South Pacific, that other vital source of primitivism in the modern period, the varying meanings of the norm of nature as a deciphering tool were dependent on two European traditions of artistic depiction, both traditions represented simultaneously on Captain Cook's voyage of 1768. On this voyage were two kinds of painters. One type had been trained by the British navy and were revered by the Royal Society for their accuracy and scientific attention to detail. The second type represented the tradition of neoclassicism. For them, nature was to be depicted not with imperfections clinging to it but in ideal perfected forms. Both traditions of painting and the literary traditions of high and popular culture stemming from them in England contributed to the ambiguous image of the natives of the South Pacific.[25]

These images, in spite of their variations, constitute a coherency to the extent that they all refer to the "other world" of the primitives, for coherency was based on a singular contrast with the mode of civilization. The voyages from Vespucci to the end of the nineteenth century had almost dispelled the earlier imaginary cartography and providential history of the late fifteenth and sixteenth centuries; the actual and empirical outlines of all the lands of the world were known. The inhabitants of these lands became the loci of a new *terra incognita*. They were not imagined in the symbols of a totally imaginary archetype, reminiscent of, let us say, that of Prester John; more often than not, they immediately became confined within the structures of the prison of medieval Europe's "empirical others," and European contact with them created a new modality of primitivism in the West that was experienced as a fatal impact by the natives of these new worlds.[26] The utopian quest of the Renaissance had been altered. The aesthetic satisfaction and scientific knowledge to be gained from exploration had already been blunted in the motivations of the first voyages by the search for riches; thus political considerations were already present, but vestiges of the aesthetic and scientific meaning of perfection in knowledge of the world continued as one of the reasons for undertaking a voyage of exploration. However, given the inner dynamics of Western civilization during this period, the Utopias were more often than not defined in more concrete economic terms. It is the Hakluyts, the Purchases, the Hawkesworths of the rising mercantile class who promise the Utopias in the new world, and their manipulation of the primitives or the ideology of primitivism is related directly to their existential concerns.[27] The utopia of the new world from this point of view must necessarily create its fatal impact in the creation of the primitive.

Demythologizing and Reorientation

The concern for primitivism may well be as Lovejoy and Boas indicated, a concern of civilization throughout the history of this cultural form. However, that concern for primitivism which has expressed itself in the imaginary and empirical knowledge of extra-European peoples from the fifteenth century to the present represents a unique form for several reasons. In the first sense, the peoples and culture who were the data for this form of primitivism were not *simply* imaginary structures of reality either in terms of their cultural reality or their geographical loci.

Second, this present meaning of primitivism contained an imaginary dimension, but it possessed more than an imaginary meaning for the civilization that had defined it in those terms. The civilization of Western Europe during this period could not have defined itself apart from the empirical existence of the primitive cultures and their exploitation. The range of significations for the meaning of primitivism during this period is much wider and bears a greater depth of meaning. Third, the background and context for this understanding are within the framework of the democratization of western Europe and the universalizing of Western civilization.

There is obviously not a relationship of identity between the academic community and ordinary citizens, but they share common semantic orientations especially as cultural meanings affect the economic and popular levels of culture. To the extent that learned societies expressed a meaning of truth that was not simply class oriented — a truth arrived at through scientific investigations — such truths about the primitives were communicated quite easily to persons on the popular levels of culture.[28] For this reason, the ideology of primitivism constitutes a pervasive influence in modern Western cultures, on the learned as well as the popular level. The problem surrounding the usage of the term "primitive" as a proper designation for certain cultures, histories, and religions must therefore be seen as a crisis of the term "civilization."

Other terms have been forthcoming to replace the term "primitive" — noncivilized, nonliterate, cold cultures, and so on. These changes will not suffice, for the cultural language of civilization that brought forth the structure of the primitive has not changed.

The problem defines a hermeneutical situation. Since the beginning of the modern period in the West the primitives have been understood as religious and empirical "others," empirical from the point of view of those disciplines and sciences which take these peoples and their cultures as the data of their inquiry — for example, anthropology, ethnology, and history of religions. These "others" are religious in two senses. In the first sense, the primitives form one of the most important bases of data for a non-theological understanding of religion in the post-Enlightenment West. In the second sense, the "primitives" define a vague "other"; their significance lies not in their own worth and value but in the significance this other offers to civilization when contrasted with it. The primitives operate as a negative structure of concreteness that allows civilization to define itself as a structure superior to this ill-defined and inferior "other."

The disciplines of hermeneutics are responses to this crisis of civilization. The importance of hermeneutics for our time can be seen in the movement from hermeneutics as the interpretation of biblical texts to a general hermeneutics — a field in which the problem of understanding covers the range of the disciplines of the human sciences. These disciplines, whether economics, depth psychology, or the history of religions, are related to certain existential problems of our civilization.

A favorite pattern can be discerned in their methodological procedures. Once an issue has been raised as problematical or pathological within our culture — for example, the problem of production and class structure in economics; the problem of the sexual in depth psychology; the loss or absence of the religious sensibility in modern culture — primitivism or the primitives appear as a methodological tool or stratagem that enables one to analyze the problem or pathology in a culture and history where it appears nonpathological or problematical and fully expressive. This other situation for modern Western civilization has become the world of the ethnological primitives.

We began with the citation of a suspicion about the relationship of the history of religions to the study of primitive religions. A discourse concerning primitives, primitivism, and civilization then followed. Another suspicion is encountered, this time a suspicion surrounding the necessary relationship obtaining between primitives, primitivism and civilization. By implication, this second suspicion is at the same time a suspicion regarding civilization and religion.

Our discussion of the designation of those "others" referred to as "primitives" occurred in the attempt to demythologize the symbolic myth of civilization. We must now ask whether we are able to discern a structure of symbols and meanings that will establish a new integrity for the status of primitive religions, on the one hand, and demonstrate the proper place for this study within the history of religions on the other.

The religions of the "primitives" are too often seen as static, externally existing in the present, and as such they constitute the basis for a minimum definition of religion. Some elements of all religions appear under this guise, for to the extent that religions manifest the status of the human in relationship to the transcendent, myths and symbols express this atemporal dimension. Too often this dimension of primitive religions is taken to define the total meaning of the religion, so that the temporal dimension is entirely lost or neglected. In the case of the New World, we must take account of these religions as they are described in their pre-European integrity, as well as their existence during and after the European contact and subsequent conquest.

The movement of Europeans to the West was undertaken in many cases under the aegis of utopian and eschatological symbols. America is the result of a European diaspora. But there have been eschatological dimensions in the pre-European traditions of aborigines in several parts of the world. An understanding of this form of sacrality in non-European traditions would throw light on the nature of this religious symbol.

But more important than this is the possibility of studying the living traditions of the contact between Europeans and aborigines in the various situations in which this happened. It is the myths of conquest, or the myths of virgin lands, that have obscured the traditions and languages of this religious meaning. We have, to be sure, several studies of cargo cult movements in various parts of the world; these studies are important and we shall return to them in the last essay in this section, but we are speaking here more of the kinds of studies represented by Nathan Wachtel's study of the religious tradition for the conquest itself in the history of Mesoamerica and South America.[29] Jacques Lafaye's work on the Mexican tradition is a more elaborate description, but the possibility of this kind of study is not unique to the history of Mexico.[30] Eva Hunt's work is also situated in Mexico, but like Wachtel's, its fundamental data are those of the folkloric tradition, as in Gary Gossen's study of the Chamulas.[31]

For North America, Francis Jennings's study reveals a rich mine of data available for the study of the Puritans and the aborigines.[32] I am pointing to a simple fact: scientific studies and reports on the primitives are usually made after some two hundred years of cultural contact with Europeans. This fact must be understood as part of the religious meaning of these traditions. If primordial structures are revealed in these religions, such symbols might simultaneously refer to a mythical past and a history of cultural contact.

One aspect of this religion of contact is the phenomenon of cargo cults. They provide a unique and alternate meaning of human freedom in the modern world. Their traditions demythologized through contact with the modern world, the cargo cult prophets undertake a new quest for a world of sacred meaning. This quest is not a return to the precontact situation, nor a mere acquiescence to the conquerors. The ingredients of the past and the present are reconceived as sacred forms, and from this sacrality new human beings are to be created. A revalorization of matter, time, money, and human exchanges is adumbrated in these movements, for they represent one of the most powerful attempts of modern human beings to live an authentic sacred life.[33]

The problematical character of Western modernity created the language of the primitives and primitivism through their own explorations, exploitations, and disciplinary orientations. Recourse to the "primitives" cannot bring about new insight. The world and language that emerged from the imaginary geographies of the Renaissance through the conquest of the Americas and the later conquest of the South Pacific can no longer be returned to as a lively hermeneutical option.

The marks that provided the basis for internal distinction and contrast between the primitive and civilization are no longer valid. This is as true of nudity (the sexuality of savages) as it is for language (writing) and for rationality. From Lucien Lévy-Bruhl's recantation to Claude Lévi-Strauss's enunciation of the logic of the concrete, from E. B. Tylor's theory of animism to Mircea Eliade's notion of a primitive ontology, the distinctions are blurred. The ultimate contrast based upon writing has evoked the most brilliant critical analyses from the pen of Jacques Derrida.[34]

No one denies that there were and are peoples and cultures in the world who possess different technologies, customs, manners, and so forth; the general designation of these forms of human reality as primitive is less than a description and more than a definition. The withering away of the distinction represents a critique of civilization itself. A new and different "other" is present for our understanding.

We can only come to terms with this reality through the tools and data we have at hand. A first step would be to reexamine the modes by which this primitive other came to be in the beginnings of our civilization and its disciplinary orientations. This would include a careful analysis of the problem of internal others as well as the others of exoticism. But the most important task would be epistemological. This combines the issues of knowing and naming. If the symbol of civilization is demythologized, if this symbol no longer possesses an ontological prestige among the other symbols of human culture, in what manner do the others appear?

What is now the proper *topos* for the modalities of rationality, the sacred, civilization? There may well be a prerational that is the correlate of the rational consciousness; a primordial that undergirds the existential; a primitive that is a modality of the civilized, and, as Derrida has argued, there may be a writing before writing. But if any of these assertions are admitted for investigation, they should be so as expressions of universal human conditions and should not be imputed to or limited to one time or place.

If the West demythologized and demystified the religious traditions of aboriginal cultures throughout the modern period, a proper study of these traditions might enable us to demythologize in turn our own discipline, and thereby extend our understanding of religion.

c. Perspectives for a Study of Afro-American Religion in the United States (*Significations: Signs, Symbols, and Images in the Interpretation of Religion) Charles H. Long*

Americans of African descent have for some time been the subject of countless studies and research projects — projects extending from the physical through the social sciences. The religion of this culture has not been overlooked.[35]

Most of the studies of religion have employed the methodology of the social sciences; hardly any of the studies have come to terms with the specifically religious elements in the religion of black Americans. We have not yet seen anything on the order of Pierre Verger's[36] study of African religion in South America or of Alfred Métraux's[37] study of the same phenomenon in the Atlantic islands.

On the contemporary scene, a group of black scholars have been about the task of writing a distinctively "black theology." I refer here to the works of Joseph Washington (*Black Religion* [Boston, 1961]) and James Cone (*Black Theology and Black Power* [New York, 1969]), and to Albert Cleage's sermons (*The Black Messiah* [New York, 1968]). In this enterprise these men place themselves in the religious tradition of David Walker, Henry Garnett, Martin Delaney, and W. E. B. DuBois. They are essentially apologetic theologians working implicitly and explicitly from the Christian theological tradition.

What we have, in fact, are two kinds of studies: those arising from the social sciences, and an explicitly theological apologetic tradition. This limitation of methodological perspectives has led to a narrowness of understanding and the failure to perceive certain creative possibilities in the black community in America.

One of the most telling examples of this limitation of perspectives in the study of black religion is to be found in Joseph Washington's work cited above. Washington has correctly seen that black religion is not to be understood as a black imitation of the religion of the majority population. His religious norm is Christianity, and the internal norm for Christianity is faith expressing itself in theology. From his analysis he concludes that black religion is not Christian, thus does not embody faith, and therefore has produced no theology. Black religion has, in his view, been more concerned with civil rights and protest, and hardly, if ever, concerned with genuine Christian faith.

I do not wish to take issue with Washington regarding his understanding of Christian faith and theology, for this lies outside the scope of the concerns in this essay. However, a word or two must be said in passing. Washington seems to conceive of Christianity and theology in static terms unrelated to historical experience. He seems to be unaware of the historical situations that were correlative to European and American theology, and he seems equally unaware that Americans have produced few theologians of the variety that would meet his norm. In short, his critique of black religion from the stance of Christian theology is blunted by the lack of his historical understanding of theology.

But now, to the point that is most relevant for this discussion: the distinctive nature of black religion. Washington's insights here are very accurate, for he shows in his work how folkloric materials, social protest, and Negro fraternalism, along with biblical imagery, are all aspects of black religion. He experiences a difficulty here, for he is unable to deal with religion outside the normative framework of Christian theology But even if one is to have a theology, it must arise from religion, something that is prior to theology.

For some time I have felt the need to present a systematic study of black religion — a kind of initial ordering of the religious experiences and expressions of the black communities in America. Such a study should not be equated with Christianity, or any other religion for that matter. It is, rather, an attempt to see what kinds of images and meanings lie behind the religious experiences of the black communities in America. While recognizing the uniqueness of this community, I am also working as a historian of religions. These perspectives constitute symbolic images as well as methodological principles. They are:

1. Africa as historical reality and religious image

2. The involuntary presence of the black community in America

3. The experience and symbol of God in the religious experience of blacks.

Africa as Historical Reality and Religious Image

It is a historical fact that the existence of the black communities in America is due to the slave trade of numerous European countries from the seventeenth to the nineteenth century (slaves were still being illegally smuggled into the United States as late as the 1880s). The issue of the persistence of African elements in the black community is a hotly debated issue. On the one hand, we have the positions of E. Franklin Frazier and W. E. B. DuBois,[38] emphasizing the lack of any significant persisting elements of Africanism in America. Melville Herskovits held this same position but reversed his position in the *Myth of the Negro Past* (Boston, 1958), where he places a greater emphasis on the persistence of African elements among the descendants of the slaves in North America. One of the issues in this discussion had to do with the comparative level of the studies. Invariably, the norm for comparison was the black communities in the Atlantic islands and in South America. In the latter, the African elements are very distinctive, and, in the case of Brazil, Africans have gone back and forth between Africa and Brazil.[39] African languages are still spoken by blacks in Brazil. Indeed, Pierre Verger first became interested in Yoruba religion when he saw it being practiced in South America!

It is obvious that nothing of this sort has existed in the United States. The slave system of the United States systematically broke down the linguistic and cultural patterns of the slaves, but even a protagonist for the loss of all Africanisms, such as E. Franklin Frazier, acknowledges the persistence of "shout songs," African rhythm, and dance in American culture. Frazier, and in this matter DuBois, while acknowledging such elements, did not see these elements of ultimate significance, for they could not see these forms playing an important role in the social cohesion of the black community. Without resolving this discussion, we need to raise another issue. The persistence of elements of what some anthropologists have called "soft culture" means that, given even the systematic breakdowns of cultural forms in the history of North American slavery, the slaves did not confront America with a religious *tabula rasa*. If not the content of culture, a characteristic mode of orienting and perceiving reality has probably persisted. We know, for example, that a great majority of the slaves came from West Africa, and we also know from the studies of Daryll Forde that West Africa is a cultural as well as a geographical unit.[40] Underlying the empirical diversity of languages, religions and social forms, there is, according to Forde, a structural unity discernible in language and religious forms.[41] With the breakdown of the empirical forms of language and religion as determinants for the social group, this persisting structural mode and the common situation as slaves in America may be the basis for the persistence of an African style among the descendants of the Africans.

In addition to this, in the accounts of the slaves and their owners we read of "meetings" which took place secretly in the woods. It is obvious that these "meetings" were not devoted to the practice of the masters' religion. They were related to what the slaves themselves called "conjuring," and the connotation reminds one of voodoo rites in Haiti.

Added to this is the precise manner in which slaves, by being slaves, black persons, were isolated from any self-determined legitimacy in the society of which they were a part and were recognized by their physiological characteristics. This constituted a complexity of experience revolving around the relationship between their physical being and their origins. So even if they had no conscious memory of Africa, the image of Africa played an enormous part in the religion of the blacks. The image of Africa, an image related to historical beginnings, has been one of the primordial religious images of great significance. It constitutes the religious revalorization of the land, a place where the natural and ordinary gestures of the blacks were and could be authenticated. In this connection, one can trace almost every nationalistic movement among the blacks and find Africa to be the dominating and guiding image. Even among religious groups not strongly nationalistic, the image of Africa or Ethiopia still has relevance.[42] This is present in such diverse figures as Richard Allen, who organized the African Methodist Episcopal Church in the late eighteenth century, through Martin Delaney in the late nineteenth century, and then again in Marcus Garvey's,[43] "back to Africa movement" of the immediate post-World War I period, and finally in the taking up of this issue again among black leaders of the present time.

The image of Africa as it appears in black religion is unique, for the black community in America is a landless people. Unlike the American Indian, the land was not taken from them, and unlike the black Africans in South Africa or Zimbabwe (Rhodesia), the land is not occupied by groups whom they consider aliens. Their image of the land points to the religious meaning of land even in the absence of these forms of authentication. It thus emerges as an image that is always invested with historical and religious possibilities.

The Involuntary Presence of the Black Community in America

Implied in the discussion concerning the land and the physiological characteristics of the blacks is the significance attributed to this meaning in America. The stance has, on the one hand, been necessitated by historical conditions and, on the other hand, been grasped as creative possibility. From the very beginning, the presence of slaves in the country has been involuntary; they were brought to America in chains, and this country has attempted to keep them in this condition in one way or another. Their very presence as *human beings* in the United States has always constituted a threat to the majority population. From the point of view of the majority population, they have been simply and purely legal entities, first as slaves defined in terms of property, and then, after the abolition of chattel property, as citizens who had to seek legal redress before they could use the common facilities of the country — water fountains, public accommodations, restaurants, schools, and so on. There is no need to repeat this history; it is too well known, and the point I wish to make is more subtle than these specific issues, important as they may be.

In addition to the image and historical reality of Africa, one must add, as another persisting datum, the involuntary presence and orientation as a religious meaning. I have stated elsewhere the importance of the involuntary structure of the religious consciousness in the terms of oppugnancy.[44] In the case of the slaves, America presented a bizarre reality, not simply because of the novelty of a radical change of status and culture but equally because their presence as slaves pointed to a radical contradiction within the dominant culture itself. The impact of America was a discovery, but one had little ability to move from the bizarre reality of discovery to the level of general social rules of conduct, which happens in the case of other communities presented with an ultimate discovery. In addition to this, to normalize the condition of slavery would be to deny the existence of the slaves as human beings.

The slaves had to come to terms with the opaqueness of their condition and at the same time oppose it. They had to experience the truth of their negativity and at the same time transform and create *an-other* reality. Given the limitations imposed upon them, they created on the level of the religious consciousness. Not only did this transformation produce new cultural forms but its significance must be understood from the point of view of the creativity of the transforming process itself.

Three short illustrations of this phenomenon must suffice at this point. Listen to the words of this spiritual:

He's so high, you can't get over him,
He's so low, you can't get under him,
So round, you can't get around him,
You got to go right through the door.

Or this poem by a black poet:

Yet do I marvel at this curious thing,
To make a poet black and bid him sing.

Or a folk aphorism:

What do you mean I gotta do that?
Ain't but two things I got to do — Be black and die.

The musical phenomenon called the blues is another expression of the same consciousness. What is portrayed here is a religious consciousness that has experienced the "hardness" of life, whether the form of that reality is the slave system, God, or simply life itself. It is from such a consciousness that the power to resist and yet maintain one's humanity has emerged. Though the worship and religious life of blacks have often been referred to as forms of escapism, one must always remember that there has always been an integral relationship between the "hardness" of life and the ecstasy of religious worship. It is, in my opinion, an example of what Gaston Bachelard described in Hegelian language as the lithic imagination. Bachelard had reference to the imaginary structure of consciousness that arises in relationship to the natural form of the stone and the manner in which the volitional character of human consciousness is related to this imaginary form.[45] The black community in America has confronted the reality of the historical situation as immutable, impenetrable, but this experience has not produced passivity; it has, rather, found expression as forms of the involuntary and transformative nature of the religious consciousness. In connection with this point, I shall illustrate by returning to the meaning of the image and historical reality of Africa.

Over and over again this image has ebbed and flowed in the religious consciousness. It has found expression in music, dance, and political theorizing. There has been an equally persistent war against the image in the religion of black folk. This war against the image of Africa and blackness can be seen in the political and social movements connected with the stratagems of segregation and integration. Even more telling is the history of the names by which the community has chosen to call itself. From African to colored, to Negro, Afro-American, and, presently, black. The history of these designations can be seen as a religious history through which this community was coming to terms with a primary symbol of opacity.

Recall the words of Gerardus van der Leeuw. He said, "Religious experience, in other terms, is concerned with a 'Somewhat.' But this assertion often means no more than this 'Somewhat' is merely a vague 'something,' and in order that man may be able to make more significant statements about this 'Somewhat,' it must force itself upon him, oppose it to him as being Something Other. Thus the first statement we can make about religion is that it is a highly exceptional and extremely impressive 'Other.'"[46] From the point of view of religious history, one could say that this community in its own self-interpretation has moved from a vague "Somewhat" to the religious experience of a highly exceptional and *extremely impressive* "Other." The contemporary expressions of black power attest to this fact, and the universalizing of this notion in terms of pan-Africanism, negritude, or neo-Marxian and Christian conceptions must equally be noted.

The meaning of the involuntary structure or the opacity of the religious symbol has within this community held together eschatological hopes and the archaic religious consciousness. In both secular and religious groups, new expressions such as Moorish Temple, Black Jews, and Black Muslims retain an archaic structure in their religious consciousness, and this structure is never quite settled, for it is there as a datum to be deciphered in the context of their present experience.

The Experience and Symbol of God

The sources for my interpretation of the experience of the holy in this community are from the folkloric tradition. By this, I mean an oral tradition that exists in its integrity as an oral tradition, the writing down of which is a concession to scholarship.

These sources are slave narratives, sermons, the words and music of spirituals and the blues, the cycles of Brer Rabbit and High John, the Conqueror, stories. These materials reveal a range of religious meanings extending from trickster-transformer hero to High God.

To be sure, the imagery of the Bible plays a large role in the symbolic presentations, but to move from this fact to any simplistic notion of blacks as slaves or former slaves converted to Christianity would, I think, miss several important religious meanings.

The biblical imagery was used because it was at hand; it was adapted to and invested with the experience of the slave. Strangely enough, it was the slave who gave a religious meaning to the notions of freedom and land. The deliverance of the Children of Israel from the Egyptians became an archetype which enabled the slave to live with promise.

God for this community appears as an all-powerful and moral deity, though one hardly ever knows why he has willed this or that. God is never, or hardly ever, blamed for the situation of humanity, for somehow in an inscrutable manner there is a reason for all of this. By and large, a fundamental distinction is made between God and Jesus Christ. To the extent that the language of Christianity is used, black Americans have held to the Trinitarian distinction, but adherence to this distinction has been for experiential rather than dogmatic reasons. Historians of religions have known for a long time that the Supreme Being appears in differing forms. To be sure, God, the first person of the Trinity, is a powerful creator deity.

It is not so much the dogma of the Trinity as it is the modalities of experience of the Trinity which is most important. The experience of God is thus placed within the context of the other images and experiences of black religion. God, as first person of the Trinity, is, of course, a powerful Creator and Supreme deity. Though biblical language is used to speak of his historical presence and intervention in history, we have neither a clear Hebraic nor what has become a Christian interpretation of history. I am not implying that the deity is a *deus otiosus,* for there is an acceptance of historical reality, but in neither its Hebraic nor its traditional Christian mode. We must remember that the historicity of these two traditions was related to the possession of a land, and this has not been the case for blacks in America. In one sense, it is possible to say that their history in America has always presented to them a situation of crisis. The intervention of the deity into their community has not been synonymous with the confirmation of the reality of their being within the structures of America. God has been more often a transformer of their consciousness, the basis for a resource that enabled them to maintain the human image without completely acquiescing to the norms of the majority population. He provided a norm of self-criticism that was not derivative from those who enslaved them. I cite two examples as illustrations:

When I was very small my people thought I was going to die. Mama used to tell my sister that I was puny and that she didn't think that she would be able to raise me. I used to dream nearly all the time and see all kinds of wild-looking animals. I would nearly always get scared and nervous.

Some time later I got heavy one day and began to die. For days I couldn't eat, I couldn't sleep; even the water I drank seemed to swell in my mouth. A voice said to me one day, "Nora you haven't done what you promised." And again it said, "You saw the sun rise, but you shall die before it goes down." I began to pray. I was making up my bed. A light seemed to come down from heaven, and it looked like it just split me open from my head to my feet. A voice said to me, "Ye are freed and free indeed. My son set you free. Behold, I give you everlasting life."

During all this time I was just dumb. I couldn't speak or move. I heard a moaning sound, and a voice said, "Follow me, my little one, and I will show you the marvelous works of God." I got up it seems, and started to traveling. I was not my natural self but a little angel. We went and came to a sea of glass, and it was mingled with fire. I opened my mouth and began to pray, "Lord, I will perish in there." Then I saw a path that led through the fire, I journeyed in this path and came to a green pasture where there were a lot of sheep. They were all of the same size and bleated in a mournful tone. A voice spoke to me, and it sounded like a roar of thunder: "Ye are my workmanship and the creation of my hand. I will drive all fears away. Go, and I go with you. You have a deed to your name, and you shall never perish."[47]

Everybody seemed to be getting along well but poor me. I told him so. I said, "Lord, it looks like you come to everybody's house but mine. I never bother my neighbors or cause any disturbance. I have lived as it is becoming a poor widow woman to live and yet, Lord, it looks like I have a harder time than anybody." When I said this, something told me to turn around and look. I put my bundle down and looked towards the east part of the world. A voice spoke to me as plain as day, but it was inward and said, "I am a time-God working after the counsel of my own will. In due time I will bring all things to you. Remember and cause your heart to sing."

When God struck me dead with his power I was living on Fourteenth Avenue. It was the year of the Centennial. I was in my house alone, and I declare to you, when his power struck me I died. I fell out on the floor flat on my back. I could neither speak nor move, for my tongue stuck to the roof of my mouth; my jaws were locked and my limbs were stiff.[48]

These two narratives are illustrative of the inner dynamics of the conversion experience. The narratives combine and interweave the ordinary events with the transformation of the religious consciousness. It is not merely a case of God acting in history, for the historical events are not the locus of the activity but then neither do we have a complete lack of concern for historical events in favor of a mystification of consciousness. It is the combination of these two structures that is distinctive in these narratives; clues such as these might help us to understand the specific nature of the black religious consciousness.

But this structure of the deity is present in non-Christian movements among the blacks; the transforming power of the deity may be seen among the Black Muslims and the Black Jews. This quality of the presence of the deity has enabled blacks to affirm the historical mode by seeing it more in terms of an initiatory structure than in terms of a progressive or evolutionary understanding of temporality.

Continuing with the Christian language of the Trinity, Jesus has been experienced more in the form of a dema-deity[49] than as conquering hero. One could make the case that this understanding of Jesus Christ has always been present in the history of the Western church, but it is clear that this image of the Christ has not been experienced as a symbol of Western culture as a whole since the seventeenth century. Christ as fellow sufferer, as the little child, as the companion, as the man who understands — these symbols of Christ have been dominant. Consider, for example, the spirituals:

I told Jesus it would be all right if he changed my name,
Jesus told me that the world would hate me if he changed my name.

Or:

Poor little Jesus boy, made him to be born in a manger.
World treated him so mean,
Treats me mean too ...

But there is more than biblical imagery as a datum. In the folklore we see what appears as the trickster-transformer hero. More than often he appears in the Brer Rabbit cycle of stories, which seem related to similar West African stories of Ananse, the Spider.

This is one of the cycles of the Brer Rabbit stories.[50] Brer Rabbit, Brer Fox, and Brer Wolf were experiencing a season of drought. They met to decide the proper action to take. It was decided that they should dig a well so that they would have a plenteous supply of water. Brer Rabbit said that he thought this was a very good plan, although he did not wish to participate in the digging of the well, because, he said, he arose early in the morning and drank the dew from the grass and thus did not wish to participate in the arduous task of digging. Brer Fox and Brer Wolf proceeded with their task and completed the digging of the deep well. After the well was dug, Brer Rabbit arose early each morning and went to the well and drank his fill, pretending all the time that he was drinking the morning dew. After a while, Brer Fox and Brer Wolf became suspicious of Brer Rabbit and set about to spy upon him. Sure enough, they caught him one morning drinking from their well. They subjected him to some punishment, which we need not go into, for the point of the story has been made.

Brer Rabbit is not simply lazy and clever; it is clear that he feels that he has something else to do — that life cannot be dealt with in purely conventional terms and committee meetings. In many respects the preacher in the black community exhibits many of the traits of Brer Rabbit, and it was often the preacher who kept alive the possibility of another life, or who protested and affirmed by doing nothing.

One other instance should be mentioned: High John, the Conqueror. It is stated explicitly in the folklore that High John came dancing over the waves from Africa, or that he was in the hold of the slave ship. High John is a flamboyant character. He possesses great physical strength and conquers more by an audacious display of his power than through any subtlety or cunning. He is the folkloric side of a conquering Christ, though with less definite goals.

The essential element in the expression and experience of God is his transforming ability. This is true in the case of God as absolute moral ruler as well as in Brer Rabbit or High John, the Conqueror. Insofar as society at large was not an agent of transformation, the inner resources of consciousness and the internal structures of the blacks' own history and community became not simply the locus for new symbols but the basis for a new consciousness for the blacks.

It is therefore the religious consciousness of the blacks in America which is the repository of who they are, where they have been, and where they are going. A purely existential analysis cannot do justice to this religious experience. A new interpretation of American religion would come about if careful attention were given to the religious history of this strange American.

d. Questions

Comprehension

1. How does Long define "empirical others," and what does that mean?

2. In the section "Utopias and Hermeneutics," how does Long think the use of symbols and "geographical and cartographic images" combine, and what do they produce?

3. What does Long mean by his call to demythologize the "symbol of civilization" ("Primitive/Civilized" [1999] 2018: 115)?

4. Why does black religion need to be analyzed as its own specific tradition?

Analysis

5. What would you consider to be defining features or characteristics of "the West"? Do these features change depending on a specific time period? What is the conceptual relationship of the West to either "the Orient" or the "New World"?

6. Long observes that "scientific studies and reports on the primitives are usually made after some two hundred years of cultural contact with Europeans" ("Primitive/Civilized" [1999] 2018: 115). What difficulties emerge in attempting to study a religious tradition before colonial contact? Is this even a possible goal, and, if so, what would a study entail in such a pursuit?

7. Long writes: "Even more telling is the history of the names by which the community has chosen to call itself. From African to colored, to Negro, Afro-American, and, presently, black" ("Perspectives" [1999] 2018: 121). To this we might now add people of color. What does self-naming indicate in each of these examples, and why is the specific terminology important?

Synthesis

8. Both Douglas and Long deal with the concept of "primitive" peoples and practices. How does Long's discussion of the results of colonial contact agree with or challenge Douglas's formulation of dirt as a structuring mechanism of social value? How are their discussions similar? Where do their assumptions or goals separate?

Notes

1 Charles J. Adams, "The History of Religions and the Study of Islam," in *The History of Religions: Essays on the Problem of Understanding*, ed. Joseph Kitagawa, with the collaboration of Mircea Eliade and Charles H. Long (Chicago and London: University of Chicago Press, 1967), pp. 177–93.

2 Arthur O. Lovejoy and George Boas, *A Documentary History of Primitivism and Related Ideas* (Baltimore: Johns Hopkins Press, 1935), pp. 1–22.

3 Stanley Diamond argues that the power and influence of figures such as Darwin, Marx, Frazer, and Freud are due in substantial part to their ability as *imaginative* writers; see Stanley Hyman, *The Tangled Bank* (New York: Atheneum Publishers, 1962).

4 Ilza Veith, *Hysteria: The History of a Disease* (Chicago and London: University of Chicago Press, Phoenix Books, 1970).

5 Ibid., p. 6.

6 I am dependent on Richard Bernheimer's *Wild Men in the Middle Ages* (New York: Octagon Books, 1970). See also Edward J. Dudley and Maximillian E. Novak, eds., *The Wild Man Within: An Image in Western Thought from the Renaissance to Romanticism* (Pittsburgh: University of Pittsburgh Press, 1973), especially Hayden White, "The Forms of Wildness: Archaeology of an Idea," pp. 3–38; Stanley L. Robe, "Wild Men and Spain's Brave New World," pp. 39–54; and Geoffrey Symcox, "The Wild Man's Return: Enclosed Visions of Rousseau's *Discourses*," pp. 223–48.

7 Michel Foucault, *Madness and Civilization: A History of Insanity in the Age of Reason* (New York: Random House, Vintage Books, 1973).

8 Ibid., p. 11.

9 Ibid., chap. 7.

10 See Émile Benveniste, *Problems in General Linguistics,* trans. Mary Elizabeth Meek (Miami: University of Miami Press, 1971), chap. 28, "Civilization: A Contribution to the History of the Word," pp. 289–96.

11 Ibid., p. 293.

12 It is interesting to observe the influence of the Scottish moral philosophers' contribution to the discussion on civilization. Most prominent are Adam Smith and John Millar. Ronald Meek, *Social Science and the Ignoble Savage* (Cambridge: Cambridge University Press, 1976), credits this school with the stadial theory of cultural evolution.

13 Norbert Elias, *The Civilizing Process: The Development of Manners* (New York: Urizen Books, 1977).

14 Ibid., pp. 3–4.

15 See Paul Ricoeur, *Freud and Philosophy* (New Haven: Yale University Press, 1970), pp. 26, 32–36. I am employing "hermeneutics of suspicion" here because the meaning of primitive religion is couched within the Western ideological understanding of "primitivism." And given the history of modern Western civilization, the authenticity of the actual cultures and peoples called primitives has been conflated with "primitivism."

16 For a polemic on the discipline of anthropology and the "primitives," see Dell Hymes, ed., *Reinventing Anthropology* (New York: Random House, Vintage Books, 1974), especially William S. Willis Jr.'s essay, "Skeletons in the Anthropological Closet," pp. 121–52. For insight into the practical and disciplinary nature of this dilemma, see Wole Soyinka, *Myth, Literature and the African World* (Cambridge: Cambridge University Press, 1978), especially the preface.

17 Henri Baudet, *Paradise on Earth: Some Thoughts on European Images of Non-European Man,* trans. Elizabeth Wentholt (New Haven: Yale University Press, 1965), p. 6.

18 See John Parker, ed., *Merchants and Scholars* (Minneapolis: University of Minnesota Press, 1965). For an understanding of the aesthetic appeal of Renaissance cartography, see Joan Gadol, *Leon Battista Alberti: Universal Man of the Early Renaissance* (Chicago and London: University of Chicago Press, 1969).

19 For a thorough discussion of the transformation of the "three wise men," see J. Duchesne-Guillemin, "Die drei Weisen aus dem Morgenlande und die Anbetung der Zeit," *Antaios* 8, no. 5 (September, 1965): 234–52.

20 Edmundo O'Gorman, *The Invention of America* (Bloomington: Indiana University Press, 1961).

21 Ibid., p. 4.

22 Ibid., p. 117.

23 Ibid.

24 See Robert F. Berkhofer, Jr., *The White Man's Indian* (New York: Alfred A. Knopf, 1978); Benjamin Keen, *The Aztec Image* (New Brunswick, NJ: Rutgers University Press, 1971); Philip D. Curtin, *The Image of Africa* (Madison: University of Wisconsin Press, 1964).

25 Bernard Smith, *European Vision and the South Pacific* (Oxford: Clarendon Press, 1960).

26 The phrase is from Alan Moorehead, *The Fatal Impact: An Account of the Invasion of the South Pacific 1767–1840* (New York: Harper & Row, 1966); see also, for North America, Francis Jennings, *The Invasion of America: Indians, Colonialism, and the Cant of Conquest* (Chapel Hill: University of North Carolina Press, 1975).

27 Samuel Purchas, *Hakluytus Posthumus or Purchas his Pilgrimes...*, 4 vols. (1625); J. Hawkesworth, *An Account of the Voyages Undertaken by the Order of His Present Majesty for Making Discoveries in the Southern Hemisphere,* 3 vols. (London, 1773). Both were writers whose depictions of the New World were designed to attract investment and settlement. Hakluyt was Purchas's business partner.

28 The image of the New World found profuse expression on the learned and popular levels of European society, in philosophical discussion, in theater, and in literary creations. See Antonelli Gerbi, *The Dispute About America,* and Gilbert Chinard,

L'Amérique et le rêve exotique dans la littérature francaise au XVII et au XVIII siècle (Paris: E. Droz, 1934).

29   Nathan Wachtel, "The Vision of the Vanquished," in *Social Historians in Contemporary France: Essays from Annales,* ed. Marc Ferro (New York: Harper & Row, 1972), pp. 230–60.

30   Jacques Lafaye, *Quetzalcóatl and Guadalupe: The Formation of Mexican National Consciousness,* trans. Benjamin Keen (Chicago: University of Chicago Press, 1976).

31   Eva Hunt, *The Transformation of the Hummingbird* (Ithaca, NY: Cornell University Press, 1977); Gary H. Gossen, *Chamulas in the World of the Sun: Time and Space in a Maya Oral Tradition* (Cambridge: Harvard University Press, 1974).

32   Jennings, *The Invasion of America.*

33   Kenelm Burridge, *New Heaven, New Earth: A Study of Millenarian Activities* (New York: Schocken Books, 1969).

34   Jacques Derrida, *Of Grammatology,* trans. Gayatri Spivak (Baltimore: Johns Hopkins University Press, 1976). See especially pt. II.

35   W. E. B. DuBois, ed., *The Negro Church* (Atlanta: Atlanta University Press, 1903); Carter G. Woodson, *The History of the Negro Church* (Washington, DC: Associatcd Publishers, 1921); Benjamin E. Mays and Joseph W. Nicholson, *The Negro's Church* (New York: Russell & Russell, 1969); Arthur Fausct, *Black Gods in the Metropolis* (Philadelphia: University of Pennsylvania Press, 1944; London: Oxford University Press, 1944); E. Franklin Frazier, *The Negro Church in America* (New York: Schockcn Books, 1962); Howard Brotz, *The Black Jews of Harlem* (New York: Schocken Books, 1970); C. Eric Lincoln, *The Black Muslims in America* (New York: Beacon Press, 1961); and E. U. Essien-Udom, *Black Nationalism: The Search for an Identity in America* (Chicago and London: University of Chicago Press, 1962).

36   Pierre Verger, *Notes sur la culte des Orisa at Vodun à Bahia la Baie de tous les saints au Bresil et à l'ancienne Côte des esclaves en Afrique* (Dakar, 1957).

37   Alfred Métraux, *Le Vaudou haitien* (Paris, 1958).

38   See W. E. B. DuBois, *The Souls of Black Folk* (Basic Afro-American Reprint Library, Johnson reprint; originally published in Chicago: A. C. McClurg, 1903).

39   See Verger, *Notes sur le cults des Orisa.*

40   Daryll Forde, "The Cultural Map of West Africa: Successive Adaptations to Tropical Forests and Grassland," in *Cultures and Societies of Africa,* ed. Simon Ottenberg and Phoebe Ottenberg (New York: Random House, 1960).

41   Joseph Greenberg makes a similar argument for the structural similarity of West African languages in his *Studies in African Linguistic Classification* (New Haven: Yale University Press, 1955).

42   See especially Edward W. Blyden, *Christianity, Islam and the Negro Race* (London, 1887). Blyden, though born in the Virgin Islands and ordained as a Presbyterian minister, was one of the early leaders in pan-Africanism. It is interesting to note that he set the problem within a religious context. The publication of his work is directly related to the problems created in the 1840s by the passage of the Fugitive Slave Law and the Dred Scott decision of the United States Supreme Court.

43   See E. David Cronon, *Black Moses* (Madison: University of Wisconsin Press, 1962).

44   See Charles H. Long, "Prolegomenon to a Religious Hermeneutic," *History of Religion* 6, no. 3 (February, 1967): 254–64; chap. 2 in this volume.

45   See Gaston Bachelard, *La terre et les réveries de la volonté* (Paris, 1948).

46 Gerardus van der Leeuw, *Religion in Essence and Manifestation,* trans. J. E. Turner (London: George Allen & Unwin, 1938), p. 23.

47 Clifton H. Johnson, ed., *God Struck Me Dead,* Religious Conversion Experiences and Autobiographies of Ex-Slaves (Boston: Pilgrim Press, 1969), pp. 62–63.

48 Ibid., pp. 58–59.

49 Adolf E. Jensen defined this religious structure as a result of his researches in Ccram. See his *Hainuwele* (Frankfurt, 1939) and *Myth and Cult Among Primitive Peoples* (Chicago and London: University of Chicago Press, 1963). I do not wish to say that Jesus Christ is understood in any complete sense as a dema-deity in black religion; I am saying that it is from this religious structure that one should begin the deciphering of the meaning of Jesus. Essential to this structure is the notion of the deity as companion and creator, a diety related more to the human condition than deities of the sky, and the subjection of this deity in the hands of human beings.

50 See T. F. Crane, "Plantation Folklore," in *The Negro and His Folklore,* ed. Bruce Jackson (Austin: University of Texas Press, 1967), pp. 157–67.

7

Gender and Materiality: Caroline Walker Bynum

a. Introduction

Caroline Walker Bynum (1941–) is a US-based scholar of medieval Europe whose interdisciplinary work reveals the importance of the diversity of historical religious practices. Bynum was the first woman to be appointed University Professor at Columbia University in 1998, a distinction that allowed her to teach within multiple departments (Fairfield 1998). Bynum's recognition as a University Professor acknowledges the inherent interdisciplinarity of Bynum's work that, according to her, spans the fields of history, religion, art history, philosophy, comparative literature, and anthropology. Drawing on the methods and resources of all of these academic fields, Bynum explores particular texts and artifacts in medieval Europe. Through her analysis of these texts and artifacts, Bynum identifies themes such as the role of women's devotion, food, and materiality that had been underexplored in medieval and religious studies before Bynum's work. The selection that follows highlights one of these themes: that studying bodies is important for understanding both medieval and contemporary cultures. According to Bynum, attention to this theme shifts the study of medieval Christianity from theological abstractions toward the diversity of religious practices.

In the selection, Bynum expands the way the "body" is understood in academic literature. In particular, she hopes to broaden understandings of the body beyond its usually gendered social position, providing an alternative to assumptions about a Western history in which "the body" is denigrated in relation to the mind or spirit. Focusing on the dying body, Bynum offers a nuanced historical account of bodiliness that she suggests should challenge contemporary academic assumptions about the body in the past and in the present.

Bynum begins by discussing the literature on bodies emerging in the 1980s and 1990s, arguing that the use of the term body is often incommensurate across and sometimes even within disciplinary boundaries. Thus, historians and feminists might both use the term "body" but they generally have different meanings of this term. While academics use it in increasingly complicated and disparate ways, Bynum suggests that much popular culture approaches bodies in a way that is not unlike medieval approaches to the body in that both approach it through the lens of the uncertainty of death. Bynum rejects contemporary understandings of medieval thought that assume a kind of Cartesian mind/body split. She, in other words, challenges the assumption of contemporary scholars that medieval scholars both dualistically rejected the body and equated bodily terms with the feminine. As Bynum argues, "Nothing entitles us to say that medieval thinkers essentialized body as matter or essentialized either body or matter as female" (Bynum 1995: 17). She concludes the article by discussing how medieval authors grappled with the themes of identity or individuality, matter or physicality, and desire. According to Bynum, medieval questions about the body are both like and unlike contemporary questions about the body and, especially, its persistence after death.

Why all the Fuss builds on the themes of Bynum's second book, *Holy Feast and Holy Fast: The Religious Significance of Food to Medieval Women* (1987), in which Bynum explores the medieval connections between women, bodies, and food. She suggests that bodily religious practices are more accessible to women because of the (misogynistic) assumption that associates women with physicality and men with rationality. Rather than accept the connection between women and physicality as a limitation, medieval women writers used the association of flesh and female to express a level of religious devotion that was inaccessible to men. Women's religious practices, in other words, cannot be attributed to their internalized misogyny. With this argument, Bynum demonstrates the importance of bodies and bodily practices for religious devotion.

Further, the themes in this selection foreshadow the directions of Bynum's later work. In her 2011 *Christian Materiality*, Bynum shifts from her earlier focus on bodies to consider matter more broadly construed. She argues that later medieval religion (1100–1550 CE) is characterized not only by devotion to religious objects but also by the belief that religious objects are alive insofar as these objects bleed, walk, or weep. Thus, according to Bynum, religious objects in the late medieval period were not simply signifying or pointing to the divine. Rather, religious objects were understood to be powerful as objects in their own right. While Bynum's argument is about a specific time and place, and is thus distinct from these universalizing theories, *Christian Materiality* contributes to the expansion from a focus on bodies in the 1980s and 1990s to a more recent and ongoing exploration of the power of matter in religious traditions.

Although Bynum is not technically trained in the field of religious studies, the fields of medieval studies and religious studies maintain porous boundaries. Because the Christian Church played such a significant role in medieval Europe, scholars of the medieval such as Bynum often study religion whether or not they describe themselves as scholars of religion. Bynum, thus, is neither entirely inside nor outside of religious studies. Two of Bynum's books, *Wonderful Blood* (2007) and *Fragmentation and Redemption* (1991), have received awards from the American Academy of Religion. These and other awards recognize the importance of her medievalist work in the study of religion. In particular, over the course of her career, Bynum has developed two theories of religion. The first, represented in *Holy Feast and Holy Fast*, describes religion as embodied. The second, represented in *Christian Materiality*, expands Bynum's theory of embodiment to describe religion not only as embodied in living beings but also as embedded in material objects. Like Doniger's theory of myth and Bell's theory of ritual, Bynum's theories of embodiment and materiality offer explanations of religious traditions and what it means to be religious. Her work, like the contributions of Douglas and Walker, points to the importance of the interdisciplinarity of the study of religion.

b. Why All the Fuss about the Body?: A Medievalist's Perspective (*Critical Inquiry*) Caroline Walker Bynum[*]

In the Classroom and the Bookstore

A friend of mine is leaving for eastern Europe where she has been asked to establish a women's studies program. She is working on the reading list. Her students will come mostly from a city where a few years ago there was little to buy in the stores except a large selection of paprikas; now the stores are full, but many people whose days were formerly occupied in work are unemployed. The concerns are very different from those on American campuses where eating-disorder clinics proliferate and the place of gay studies or Western civilization in the curriculum are heated topics of debate. "There's so much written about the body," she groans, "but it all focuses on such a recent period. And in so much of it, the body dissolves into language. The body that eats, that works, that dies, that is afraid—that body just isn't there. Can't you write something for my students that would put things in a larger perspective?" I said I would try.[1]

In a sense, of course, "the body" is the wrong topic. It is no topic or, perhaps, almost all topics. As many contemporary theorists point out, we no longer think there is such a thing as the body—a kind of "flesh dress" we take up, or put off, or refurbish according to the latest style.[2] Whatever our position on "antiessentialism" (and it is certainly true that many of the recent attacks on "essentialists" have been both intellectually imprecise and cruel), no one in the humanities seems really to feel comfortable any longer with the idea of an essential "bodiliness." We tend to reject both a "bodiliness" that is in some way prior to the genderings, sexings, colorings, or handicappings particular persons are subject to and a body that is easily separable from the feelings, consciousness, and thoughts that occur in it.[3] Nor does it really help much to replace *the body* with *my body*, as Adrienne Rich and Diana Fuss have suggested we should do.[4] For if *my body* is not simply a synonym for *me*, I must, by using the term, raise questions about some particular aspects of the self. Which aspects? And why does the phrase suggest them? So I am stuck again with my original topic. But it, we are told, is the wrong category. What, then, is everybody writing about?

Perhaps some help is to be found in the usual scholarly move of surveying the literature. What does the phrase mean in the rapidly increasing number of books with *the body* in the title—an increase only too apparent to anyone who walks these days into a bookstore? A survey of recent Anglo-American scholarship turns up only a welter of confusing and contradictory usages.[5] In certain areas of philosophy, attention to the body means attention to the role of the senses in epistemology or to the so-called mind/body problem; in others it provides an opportunity to enter into discussion of essence or objectivity.[6] The most ambitious recent sociological treatment of the body defines it as "environment," "representation," and "sensuous potentiality"; it is, however, disease, especially anorexia nervosa, that furnishes Bryan Turner with his most frequent and telling example.[7] Discussing recent historical writing, Roy Porter and Susan Bordo each enumerate an amazing range of topics—from biology and demography to artistic depiction—under the rubric of body history.[8] A large number focus in some way on issues of reproduction or sexuality, or of the construction of gender and family roles, especially through medicine.[9] The work of Foucault and the "new historicist" approach of literary critic Stephen Greenblatt often lie behind the way the questions are posed in this sort of history, although New Historicism itself has not until recently been characterized by a focus on gender.[10] In a good deal of recent theological writing, particularly of the popular variety, *the body* raises issues of medical and/or sexual ethics, rather than more conventional questions of eschatology or soteriology.[11] In feminist theory, especially in the linguistic and/or psychoanalytic turn it has taken in the past decade, the body as "discovered" or "constructed" has been replaced by bodies as "performative" (as becoming what they are by performing what they "choose" or must choose).[12] In much of this writing, *body* refers to speech acts or discourse; this is what my friend meant when she said: "The lived body seems to disappear."[13] In art history, the proliferation of recent work on the body refers not so much to the formal qualities of depicted figures as to the way in which what is seen is constructed by the viewer's gaze.[14] For literary criticism, philosophy, sociology, history, and theology, the body is a recent enthusiasm. A full survey would have to include as well such fields as biology, medicine, and behaviorist psychology, whose well-established and familiar understandings of the body as physiology are often the object of intense criticism by the new literary and historical approaches.[15]

Thus, despite the enthusiasm for the topic, discussions of the body are almost completely incommensurate—and often mutually incomprehensible—across the disciplines. There is no clear set of structures, behaviors, events, objects, experiences, words, and moments to which *body* currently refers. Rather, it seems to me, the term conjures up two sharply different groups of phenomena. Sometimes *body, my body,* or *embodiedness* seems to refer to limit or placement, whether biological or social. That is, it refers to natural, physical structures (such as organ systems or chromosomes), to environment or locatedness, boundary or definition, or to role (such as gender, race, class) as constraint. Sometimes—on the other hand—it seems to refer precisely to lack of limits, that is, to desire, potentiality, fertility, or sensuality/sexuality (whether "polymorphously perverse," as Norman O. Brown puts it, or genital), or to person or identity as malleable representation or construct.[16] Thus *body* can refer to the organs on which a physician operates or to the assumptions about race and gender implicit in a medical textbook, to the particular trajectory of one person's desire or to inheritance patterns and family structures.

Such discussions have, in their details, almost nothing to do with each other. Three general observations can, however, be made. The first is that an extraordinarily large amount of this recent discussion of the body is in fact a discussion of sex and gender. This is in part true because, as Porter and Ludmilla Jordanova have pointed out, so much of the good recent work has been done by feminists.[17] But the equation of body with sex and gender is now also found in discussions that are not really feminist in inspiration. A recent popular work entitled *Body Theology*, for example, includes three sections: one on human sexuality; one on "men's issues" (or gender); and a third entitled "medical issues," which deals primarily with reproductive choice. If my count is correct, the entire book devotes only about seventeen pages to what was surely, in earlier times, theology's major preoccupation with bodies: suffering and death.[18]

The second observation is that both of the current sets of understandings of the body seem characterized by discomfort. Some writers express profound unease with any self-definition, whether based on biological structures or on cultural and social position; others are made nervous by potency. Indeed, advances in reproductive medicine and in contraception seem to have brought in their wake greater agony about both personal reproductive decisions and worldwide overpopulation; AIDS and sexually transmitted diseases have darkened the promise of sexual liberation; subtle analyses of knowledge as perspectival and situated, devised to defeat the omniscient observer, seem to have left viewers not free and creative but rather caught in— because constructed by—their vantage points. For all the contemporary castigation of earlier concepts of embodiment, present discussion reveals surprisingly often its own version of body-as-trap.

Third, it is worth noting that many of these current analyses, different from each other though they be, share a characterization of earlier Western history. From Plato to Descartes, the Western tradition was—in this interpretation—dualist.[19] It despised the body (however defined). Moreover, it in some way identified the body with nature and the female; dualism was thus by definition misogyny. Sweeping two thousand years of history into what can only be called a vast essentialization, some scholars—ostensibly in the name of antiessentialism—have even gone so far as to identify woman with what cannot be said, thus gagging themselves with their own historical generalization. When my friend asks for a wider perspective on the body, she is asking, I think, to be freed not just from a body that "dissolves into language" but also from a self that reduces to an identity-position and a past that dwindles into one or two implausible generalizations.

In the rest of this article I want to put back on the table, so to speak, some issues relating to bodies and embodiment that have been eclipsed in present theorizing.

I shall do so through a discussion of my own research on the European Middle Ages. I do this not in order to denigrate or trivialize the recent scholarly concern with sex and gender nor to suggest that the Middle Ages had no such concerns.[20] Rather, by giving a much more complex view of the past than is usually presented, I suggest that the present, whose ancestor it is, may be more complex as well. "Medieval people" (as vague a notion, by the way, as "modern people") did not have "a" concept of "the body" any more than we do; nor did they "despise" it (although there is reason to think that they feared childbirth, or having their teeth pulled, or the amputation of limbs without anaesthesia). Like the modern world, the Middle Ages was characterized by a cacophony of discourses. Doctors took a completely different view of sexuality from theologians, sometimes prescribing extramarital sex as a cure for disease.[21] Secular love poets and ascetic devotional writers meant something radically different by *passion*. *Pissing* and *farting* did not have the same valence in the grim monastic preaching of the years around 1100 and in the cheerfully scatological, although still misogynistic, fabliaux of two centuries later.[22] Alchemists studied the properties of minerals and gems in an effort to precipitate chemical change and prolong life, whereas students of the Bible saw in these same objects lessons about fortitude and truth.[23]

Even within what we would call discourse communities, ideas about matter, body, and person could conflict and contradict. Galenic and Aristotelian ideas of reproduction disagreed sharply about the importance of the female seed, and the new attention to the structure of organs that emerged in the Renaissance was very different from earlier understandings of the physical body as humors and fluids.[24] Dualist Cathar preachers, and some orthodox monks, disapproved of marriage and meat eating, whereas hagiographers often praised the obedience of women who married.[25] Eastern and Western theologians disagreed about whether there was a purgatory for separable souls; and even within the Western tradition, the pope and his cardinals broke for a time over whether resumption of body in the afterlife was necessary before the beatific vision.[26] It would be no more correct to say that medieval doctors, rabbis, alchemists, prostitutes, wet nurses, preachers, and theologians had "a" concept of "the body" than it would be to say that Charles Darwin, Beatrix Potter, a poacher, and the village butcher had "a" concept of "the rabbit."

Nonetheless I would like to describe three aspects of a widespread medieval concern about a particular kind of body—the body that dies. I do so not because the Middle Ages thought the body was corpse, pain, and death rather than pleasure, sex, and life; not because theologies and rituals of death were without controversy in the Middle Ages; not because I think the topics I shall treat are the only proper topics for a discussion of the many bodies of the Middle Ages; and not because I think modern attitudes are the direct descendants of medieval ones (although I shall argue below that there is an important connection). Rather, I do so to correct certain prevalent generalizations about the medieval past and thus, by bringing forward a more nuanced understanding of that past, to suggest that we in the present would do well to focus on a wider range of topics in our study of body or bodies.

At the Movies

To introduce my topic I return for a moment to the late twentieth century. I have argued in an earlier article that the pulp fiction and popular movies of the last two decades, as well as formal work in the philosophy of mind, raise an interesting question about embodiment through repeated exploration of the problem of body-hopping. Films such as *Heaven Can Wait, Maxie, All of Me, Freejack, Death Becomes Her, The Switch, Heart Condition,* or *Robocop,* and TV serials such as *Max Headroom* or *Star Trek,* explore the problem of identity and personal survival through asking whether "I" will still be "I" if transplanted into a body clearly marked by the personal characteristics (the race and sex markers, the scars and aging, and so on) of "someone else." Issues of gender have been particularly prominent in this questioning: can Caroline Bynum still be Caroline Bynum if, having defined her as her stream of memory or her consciousness, we transplant "her" into the body (which comes close here to meaning the identity-position) of Michael Jackson? Or, more simply, do we react as if it is a transplanted "she"—however we define her—if we see what looks like Michael Jackson in front of us? In contrast to the popular literature of the turn of the century, or even the 1950s, when table tipping, spiritualism, multiple personalities, etc., provided the medium for exploring issues of personal survival, today's popular culture worries about bodies. Its stories and images tend to erase the kind of line between mind and body that would make the transplanting or disembodying of consciousness or memory a satisfactory conception of personal continuity.[27]

As Bordo and Robert Nozick have pointed out, a fear of body swapping as destruction of person pervades recent films. In *Invasion of the Body Snatchers* the pods attack "us" by occupying our bodies; it is "we the bodies" who are afraid. In the remake of *The Fly,* what was in the earlier version a mechanical joining of human and fly parts is now the eruption from within of an alien and uncontrollable "something" that, by replacing the material of the body, destroys the previous self. Popular fiction, such as *Who Is Julia?* or *Memories of Amnesia,* suggests that transplant of a body part (and it is not only the brain that is at stake here) could be transplant of self.[28] Moreover, it is in my view significant not only that religious groups differ in their responses to organ transplants but also that they consider the matter a deeply fraught ethical issue, not merely a medical matter. To come back to the movies: medieval and modern conceptions find a strange and explicit mirroring in the recent film *Jesus of Montreal,* where the modern Christ figure saves others after his death through heart and cornea transplants. Suggesting that organ transplantation *is* the modern translation of resurrection, the film raises complex questions about part and whole, survival and self, familiar to any student of medieval saints' lives and reliquaries. I shall return to them. My point here, however, is less the conclusions reached by filmmakers and audiences than the fact that we ask the question this way. For every ghost in a contemporary film or TV series, one can list dozens of bodily divisions and transplantations that query the nature of personal survival.

Much of this recent concern does in fact focus on gender or sexual identity. Almost any episode of *Star Trek* these days seems to raise in some form the question whether it is possible to change sex, sexual orientation, or identity-position by radical change of physical stuff—questions that much sophisticated feminist philosophy, such as that of Bordo or Judith Butler, explores on another level. But such films and stories raise as well other issues of identity and self. They ask not only to what extent is my identity-position "me" but also how can "I" still be "me" next week? Can I, if I die? In other words, they deal with death. It is this aspect of our contemporary concern with body that, I argue, we academics have tended to overlook.

I turn finally then to *Truly, Madly, Deeply*, a lovely film that raises in complex ways the question of death and identity (in both senses of the word *identity*—that is, What makes me an individual? and what accounts for my continuing the same over time and space?). Although it plays humorously and gently with the thousand-year-old theme of our fear that the dead may walk again, it is not a ghost story. The plot of the film is simple: a young woman, grieving passionately for her dead lover, finds him in the house again. As long as her desire and grief encounter and relate to her complicated and full memory of him, all is, in some sense, well. But when he and his buddies return, really playing the cellos and violins they used in life, he is decidedly in the way. So much indeed is physical stuff the problem that in a moving early scene, when the heroine's sister asks for the dead man's cello for her son, the heroine replies in anguish: "It's as if you asked for his body."[29]

I do not have the space here to provide a full analysis of *Truly, Madly, Deeply*.[30] But I want to use the film to argue that popular culture is at the moment asking three profound questions about body that we academics have not really noticed, or at least not noticed correctly, nor have we understood how central the fact of death is to their urgency. I will call them identity, matter, and desire.

By this I mean, first, that questions of the return or transfer of bodies raise for us issues about how we conceptualize identity in both the sense of individuality and the sense of spatiotemporal continuity. Unless the person I love is present in body, does the person continue? Can "she" or "he" really exist in a radically different body (or perhaps one could say identity-position) or in no body (perhaps one could say as spirit or consciousness)? How would you know it was "she"?

Moreover, as Jean-Claude Schmitt has reminded us, remembering someone else after his or her death is at least as much a way of letting go as of retaining.[31] I construct my memory of what I have lost in order to be at peace with it; before the peace comes, the ghosts walk. But I am not inclined to think that (either before or after your death) *you* are in my mind when I remember what you meant to me. I may remember you, or not; but if you exist, you are someplace other than in my mind.

Films such as *Truly, Madly, Deeply* also raise the issue of our bodies in another sense; and here the cello is crucial. What difference does it make that we leave behind clothes, papers, a favorite brooch or mixing bowl, a corpse? In a sense the dead lover of *Truly, Madly, Deeply* returns because the heroine cannot let go of his cello. But do we ever easily let go of the cello? Do we not need transitional objects to cope with death as much as with our initial formation of self? And isn't their very "stuffness" important? As grief therapists tell us, the relatives of MIAs and of victims of air crashes in which no bodies survive must travel a much more complex route in grieving than that travelled by those who can cremate or bury a body. When medieval thinkers spoke of the saints as "in the tomb (or reliquary)" and "in heaven," they understood (as Giles of Rome tells us) that they used synecdoche in both cases; but they understood something else as well. Whereas remembering lets the spirits rest and be forgotten, relics (including what the Middle Ages called contact relics—physical bits that were not body but touched the body—clothes, that is, or cellos) keep the person present.[32] In our own decade, those who have created the AIDS quilt seem to me to evidence a sophisticated understanding of the role physical transitional objects can play in carrying our love and our grief as we mourn.[33]

Third, *Truly, Madly, Deeply* raises the question of desire. The heroine falls in love again; the real problem with the physical presence of the dead lover is that, by the end of the film, he's one lover too many. The dead lover is not, in other words, just an identity in the sense of an individual, particular self, nor just an identity whose continuation seems guaranteed by his physical body; he is also the object of desire—a straining, expanding, pulling of self toward other that seems to have something to do with "body" (*body* in both the senses we find in contemporary writing, that is, body as "locatedness" and body as potentiality). For the heroine's conflicted, troubling, and guilty desire to disappear, what must disappear is not her memory of the departed but the particular, embodied self, complete with cello, that is occupying her house. Bodies are both the subject and the object of desire.

I have certainly not exhausted here either *Truly, Madly, Deeply* or modern literature on the body. But I hope I have suggested that, for all the proliferating number of body books on the shelves of American bookstores, theorists are not discussing much of what our popular culture indicates we in fact worry about. For we do worry about survival, about bodily stuff, about desire. And the films and TV shows we choose for our entertainment suggest that we often think about these things in the context of the possibility or impossibility of defeating death. Gayatri Spivak has said: "Death as such can only be thought via essence or rupture of essence... I cannot approach death as such."[34] This is undoubtedly true, but it is not "death as such" that is the threat for most of us. Theoretical impossibility neither stills the need to approach and ask questions nor provides solace for our fears.

What I am proposing therefore is that body or embodiment is an aspect of many conversations we are now having—including conversations about death—and was part of many such conversations in the European past. I wish to broaden our awareness and understanding of both sets of conversations by broadening our awareness of each.

In the Middle Ages

I return then to the stereotype, common in textbooks, of the Middle Ages as "dualistic"—that is, as despising and fleeing "matter" or "the body," which in this interpretation is often understood to be gendered "female" because "passive," "negative," and "irrational."

Medieval thinkers did, of course, speak of "the body" (corpus) or "the flesh" (caro) in certain contexts, although as I explained above corpus meant something very different to a doctor looking at a flask of urine and to a priest consecrating the eucharist. But even if we stay for a moment within orthodox Christian discourses in which there was some agreed upon moral and ontological significance for the word corpus, the understanding of "medieval attitudes" as "dualistic" in the sense of "despising" or "recommending flight from" the body is wrong for three reasons.

First, even when discussing soul (anima) and body (corpus) as components of person, medieval theologians and philosophers did not discuss anything at all like the Cartesian mind/body problem (any more, by the way, than Aristotle did).[35] Late medieval philosophy used the Aristotelian concept of soul as life principle.[36] Thus both in metaphysics and in embryology there was argument over whether the person had one soul or many. Indeed, dualities or binaries were frequently not at stake. Many discussions of knowing and seeing used a threefold categorization of body (corpus), spirit (animus or spiritus), and soul (anima) that placed experiencing either sense data or even dreams and visions in corpus or spiritus, not anima. Under the influence of the Arab philosopher Avicenna, psychologists also tried to work out a theory of "powers" located between anima and corpus to connect the activities of the two. These discussions often, as I have explained elsewhere, drew a sharper distinction between levels of soul than between soul and body.[37] Moreover, knowing, feeling, and experiencing were located in body. As David Morris (among others) has pointed out, these thinkers would not have understood the question (frequent in modern circles): Is pain in my body or in my mind?[38] Even in the late medieval dialogues that personify two clear components of person as Soul and Body, the Body character often "wins" the debate by charging that evil is lodged in the Soul's willing, not in the Body's senses.[39] As I shall show in a moment, the debates in high scholasticism over identity involved in some real sense rejection of soul and body as separable parts of "person." What I wish to stress here is that such discussion was embedded in larger discussions in which trinary or multifold categories were basic ways of thinking about psychology or anthropology.[40]

We must also reject the characterization of most medieval literature and art as dualistic in a second sense of the word dualism. Even in the most (to our tastes) macabre of late medieval poems and images—the Dances of Death or the transi tombs that depict their occupants as putrefying corpses—one can hardly with accuracy speak of "rejection of the body." I do not mean to argue here that modern accounts have concentrated too much on sensationalist and morbid themes in medieval literature, although that is to some extent true. Historians such as Jean Delumeau and Robert Bultot, who have chronicled the theme of contemptus mundi, themselves admit that it was frequently complemented in medieval treatises by discussions of the glory of creation and of "man."[41] Many historians of funerary practices point out that the injunction of memento mori was embedded in imagery that promised resurrection to the same corpse that moldered in the grave.[42] My argument here, however, is different. It is that the extravagant attention to flesh and decay characteristic of the period is not "flight from" so much as "submersion in." The attitudes and practices of religious specialists in the late Middle Ages, and the reverence they won from a wide spectrum of the population, assumed the flesh to be the instrument of salvation (in many senses of the word *instrument*—musical instrument, kitchen implement, instrument of torture, etc.). In *Holy Feast and Holy Fast,* I cited examples of religious women who spoke of striking music from their flesh through extravagant asceticisms such as flagellation or self-mutilation.[43] Technical theological tractates and works of popular piety in the thirteenth century described Christ's body on the cross as suffering more exquisite pain than any other body because it was the most perfect of all bodies.[44] One can even interpret the eucharistic theology of the high Middle Ages as a sort of cannibalism—a literal incorporation of the power of a tortured god.[45] My point is simply that, whatever the technical terms that circulated around such practices, the cultivation of bodily experience as a place for encounter with meaning, a locus of redemption, is not "flight from" the body. Nor could it have been in a religion whose central tenet was that the divine had chosen to offer redemption by becoming flesh.

Third, it is inaccurate to see medieval notions of *corpus, caro, materia, mundus, tellus, limus,* or *stercus* as gendered feminine. Both Butler and Luce Irigaray, who have built complex and highly politicized readings around a collapsing of woman and heterosexuality into the receptacle of Plato's *Timaeus* (conflated then with Aristotle's matter), admit that such collapsing is a deliberate misreading.[46] It is not useful for my purposes to pursue the complicated issues of psychoanalysis, politics, and philosophy they raise, although (as I shall explain below) I have sympathy with Butler's idea of the performative body. But somehow a misinterpretation of their argument has left, in more journalistic treatments (feminist and nonfeminist), the notion that vast binaries— reducible to a male/female binary—marched through the medieval past from Plato to Descartes. (In some accounts, Augustine and an Aristotle in rather curious seventeenth-century garb play bit parts in the intellectual drama as well.) This generalization is not tenable. Medieval ritual, practice, story, and belief made use of many binary contrasts, some of which corresponded with a male/ female opposition. In formal theological and devotional writing, these contrasts often associated women with body and matter, especially in a number of highly complicated treatments of the incarnation of Christ and the role of the Virgin in the economy of salvation. But symbolic patterns do not, of course, fit into only a single grid. Moreover, in medieval writing, they can be shown to have undercut as well as undergirded traditional understandings of gender. Much of the serious work on medieval sources from the past fifteen years has shown us how polymorphous are medieval uses of gender categories and images.[47]

To say this is not to argue that there was no widespread misogyny in the Middle Ages.[48] Within monastic didactic literature and folktales, there was fear of female sexuality; within medical discourse, there was curiosity and wonder, tinged with fear, about female anatomy; and of course legal codes treated female property-holding and economic opportunities as less than those of males (although with complex differences of time and place I will not go into here).[49] In embryology the father's seed was associated with form, the mother's seed (or, in other theories, her menstrual matter) with potency. Such attitudes did carry over in complex ways into religious ritual to produce symbolic usages in which female was seen as below and above reason— as witch or saintly visionary—whereas male was seen as a rather pedestrian middle, incapable of direct contact either with angelic or with demonic power.[50] But soul (*anima*) was gendered feminine far more often than *corpus* (in part of course because of the grammar itself). The contrast between male and female was sometimes connected to Genesis 1:7 and 1:21–24, in which God created Adam from mud but Eve from flesh. Female characteristics (that is, characteristics that our sources suggest were understood by contemporaries, both male and female, to be feminine) were used to describe God in his/her ruling as well as nurturing capacity.[51] Rarely in any period has religious poetry provided such androgynous or complexly erotic images of desire.[52]

Nothing entitles us to say that medieval thinkers essentialized body as matter or essentialized either body or matter as female. Indeed, philosophically speaking, body as subsisting was always form as well as matter. Although it is true that medieval discussions, from natural philosophy to secular love poetry, often reveal a profound distrust for fertility and biological process, this is not at all the same thing as essentialized physicality. Medieval visionaries sometimes saw life as a river filled with muck or hell as eternal digestion.[53] Monks such as Hermann of Reun warned that human beings were in the process of aging, corrupting, and dying from the first moment of birth.[54] Innocent III, like many other moralists, spoke of our origins in "vile sperm."[55] Exegetes felt it important to underline that the earth God created on the third day did not contain seeds; rather, God first created the plant life that then shed seeds into the earth.[56] Cathar and Catholic preachers accused each other of denigrating the world and the flesh and of not caring properly for the bodies of the dead.[57] The profound discomfort with biological process betrayed in all this needs more research and elucidation.[58] But medieval theorists did not reduce embodiment either to matter or to female matter. (Peter Damian's statement about embracing a corpse when one embraces a female body is notorious, but as the quotation from Innocent III given above suggests, male sexuality and matter could also be identified with putrefaction, physical or moral.)[59]

As I shall try to show in a moment, some antique and medieval thinkers put forward a technical conception of embodiment that departs (for better or worse) as radically as do the theories of Judith Butler from an understanding of body as stuff or physicality. And while it is true that medieval philosophers sometimes tried to define person (and it is important that this was their category for thinking about the human, not essence [*esse*]), they did not usually in these discussions deal with gender. Those passages where they do deal with what we would consider identity in the sense of individual (or identity-position) are not about definition at all and are certainly not essentialist. They are about death and triumph over it—and, as I shall show, the metaphysical principles that are put into play have surprising implications.

I have, however, spent too much time now on characterizations to be rejected. Hardly a way to broaden the conversation! So I shall turn to my own recent work on eschatology and funerary practice, not because I think the topics I shall now treat are the only proper subjects for a conversation about the many bodies of the Middle Ages, but because even a few new topics may begin to expand our rather cramped and limited picture of the medieval past. I use the somewhat inelegant categories I used to discuss *Truly, Madly, Deeply:* identity, stuff or matter, and desire.

In the Afterlife

In my recent book *The Resurrection of the Body in Western Christianity,* I chronicle both technical discussions of what it means for the body to return at the end of time and the spread of burial practices that treat the corpse, whether its parts are carefully united or deliberately divided, as an object of great cultural significance. From this complicated story I wish here to extract three points, which I intend to place in conversation with certain of the recent theoretical positions discussed above. The first concerns identity.

Throughout the Middle Ages theorists who dealt with eschatology tended to talk of the person not as soul but as soul and body. (As a number of scholars have established, Platonic definitions of the person as the soul were explicitly rejected by the middle of the twelfth century.)[60] Of course theologians and philosophers knew the corpse was in the grave; they buried corpses, and they revered as relics bits of holy corpses that remained above ground (a point to which I shall return). Moreover, they thought the souls of the dead sometimes walked abroad; and occasionally they imagined these spirits or ghosts in other than recognizable bodily form (as lights or doves). But ghost stories and other-world visions came increasingly in the course of the Middle Ages to depict the dead—even immediately after death—as already in their totally particular earthly bodies (or at least ghostly versions thereof).[61] And Catholic theologians very early rejected the idea of metempsychosis—the idea that we find in Plato's *Republic,* for example, that soul or spirit can inhabit a body other than "its own."[62] The doctrine that the same body we possess on earth will rise at the end of time and be united to our soul was part of the Christian creeds from the early third century on.[63] That doctrine almost immediately forced a good deal of sophisticated speculation about how the resurrected body can be "the same" as the earthly one.

From the end of the second century, certain theologians felt it necessary to respond to philosophical doubts about the resurrection of the flesh. Both pagan critics and Christian theorists of a Gnostic and Docetist persuasion argued that corpses are prey not only to decay in the earth but also to destruction by wild beasts or even, in the case of cannibalism, by other human beings; therefore, the same body cannot come back. Moreover, they argued, we are not even the same body from one day to the next, certainly not from one decade to another; the matter turns over. What can it mean therefore to be the same?

I do not intend here to explain all the answers this question elicited.[64] What I want to demonstrate, however, is that, through discussion of eschatology, a number of thinkers grappled with the issue of how identity, in the sense of spatiotemporal continuity, is maintained; they also came, in the process, to give an answer to the question of identity as individuality.

To give two examples. The great third-century theologian Origen formulated a complex theory of body as an *eidos* that carried within itself a potentially unfolding pattern; the idea is not unlike modern notions of DNA. Origen thought this *eidos* might unfold into versions of body very different from those of earth; no particle of the original body was to him necessary for the body to be the same, and Origen vacillated a good deal over how much of its earthly structure (organs, scars, and so on) it would retain.[65] In the middle of the thirteenth century, Thomas Aquinas adumbrated a theory (which was worked out by the next generation of scholars) that soul, the single form or principle of the person, carried all the specificity of that person with it; it then, at the resurrection, informed or activated matter to be that person's body. Thus any matter at all, if informed by the form of Harry, would be Harry's body (even particles that had once been in the living body, or the corpse, of a specific Joe or Jane). That body, restored at the resurrection, retained all the specific structures it had in earthly life (organs, height, even—in certain cases—scars).[66] If it was the body of one of the elect, it was "glorified," that is, subtle, beautiful, and impassable, in heaven.[67] My point here is not to explain these abstruse theories fully, although they are shrewd and complex and should not be caricatured. Rather, my point is to show that, in any commonsense understanding of the word *matter*, Origen has eliminated "matter" but retained "body," whereas Aquinas appears on some level to have retained "the same matter" by a philosophical trick (defining "my matter" as anything activated by "my soul"). The bodies they put forward "dissolve into language" as thoroughly—and in as sophisticated a fashion—as the recent theories deplored by my friend. And in a not dissimilar way, they made those who read them uncomfortable. Theologians contemporary with Origen and Aquinas, drawing in some cases explicitly on popular practices concerning the care and reverencing of corpses, protested the idea of such a divorce of self and stuff.

Yet in some ways, early fourteenth-century theological discussion saw the triumph of Aquinas's idea of the specificity or "whatness" of the self as packed into the form, or soul, or principle of identity (in the sense of continuity). And with a very interesting consequence. The soul of the person starts to look like what we would call today his or her identity-position. Soul is not a sort of rational essence to be only incidentally or accidentally sexed, gendered, colored, handicapped, and aged in various unequal ways. Soul carries the structure of the "me" that will rise at the end of time—with all my organs, and even my acquired characteristics, at least if these wrinkles and scars are the result of bearing up virtuously under hardship. It is no accident then that such a soul cannot body-hop! No accident that it is repeatedly said in the literature to yearn for its "own" body. Nor is it an accident that Dante, in canto 25 of his *Purgatorio*, works out a complex analogy to embryology when he explains that, even in the separated state between death and resurrection, the soul generates an aerial body with all the particularities of its earthly condition.[68] If there *is* a sense in which one can say that soul carries identity in late medieval theories of the person, one must also note that much of what was traditionally meant by body has been packed into soul. Soul is not some sort of essential humanness to which gender, say, is attached—whether in equal or unequal varieties. Nor is soul "me," any more (says Aquinas) than my foot is me. To Aquinas, "me" is carried in soul when body is absent. (This is the abnormal situation.) "Me" is expressed in body when things are as they should be (that is, in life and after the resurrection). But "I" am not soul or body; I am a person. Moreover, "I" am a person with an identity in both senses of the term *identity*.[69] We have to do here with a theory of person not so different really from much late twentieth-century talk about body.[70]

My second point about medieval eschatology can be made much more succinctly. It is simply that certain Christian beliefs and practices of the late Middle Ages (and there are parallels in Jewish practice and belief although I shall not treat them here) pulled radically against any theoretical position that led to the dissolution of either person or body into discourse. Not only did a good deal of preaching and storytelling stress resurrection as the literal reassembling of every bit that went into the tomb at death; it is also true that dead bodies were extraordinarily charged objects—fields of force from which emanated miracles or the work of demons.

As is well known, holy bodies were revered as relics, as places where supernatural power was especially present; they were deliberately divided in order to produce more such objects for veneration. Not only they, but even objects they had touched (their clothes, utensils, even their bodily effluvia, such as milk, spittle, or wash water) were revered. From the tenth century on, in certain parts of Europe, bodily partition was practiced on the dead of high secular status as well. The corpses of kings and nobles were fragmented in order to be buried in several places, the practice being accompanied by complex arguments about the need to garner more prayers and also about the presence of the person's power where his or her body part resided.[71]

These practices seem to have assumed a kind of assimilation of resurrected body to corpse, for which the texts give confirmation. Pious Christians sometimes said that the bodies they placed in graves or reliquaries "were" the saints, although they said simultaneously (as Simon Tugwell and Thomas Head have reminded us) that the saints "were" also in heaven.[72] Such usages are found in many cultures. What is more interesting for my argument is the fact that hagiographers, preachers, and artists fairly often said that the body in the grave or reliquary "was" "the resurrection body."[73] Such locutions were used to argue both that bodies could be divided (that is, their specific treatment in burial did not matter because God had promised resurrection to all bodies in whatever condition they might be found) and that they should be buried without disturbance (that is, that because exactly this stuff would rise, it should be kept close to its resurrection condition as long as possible).

These practices and beliefs are very complicated and I cannot deal with them fully here. It should by now at least be clear how and why they pulled in a countervailing direction from theories of person to which material continuity was not necessary. The doctrine of formal identity could solve technical issues of personhood and survival, it is true. But to late thirteenth-century theologians, a theory of body had also to account for continuity between living person and cadaver, both in order to make relic veneration veneration of the saint and in order to make Christ's body in the triduum between his crucifixion and resurrection "really" his body and therefore really the redemption of our bodiliness.

It should also be clear that there are parallels in all this to modern concerns about disposal of bodies, organ transplants, artificial intelligence, and so on. As new work in the field of medical ethics and cultural studies has emphasized, many in the late twentieth century hope (or fear) that self is transferred with body part (especially but not exclusively with the brain) in transplants, autopsies, or disposals.[74] The body that dies is also the body that remains; whether, and how, we handle it makes a difference. Those who have experienced the loss of loved ones in the violent disappearances of spacecraft explosions, air crashes, drownings, or war can understand how Jewish and Christian resurrection belief arose in the context of persecutions that threatened to make it impossible to reassemble the shattered bodies of the martyrs for burial.[75] They can also understand the power of medieval veneration of remains and the complex insistence of medieval hagiography and eucharistic theology that, with God, *pars* not only stands *pro toto* but is truly *totum.*

All this is clear. What is perhaps less clear and should therefore be underlined is that, whether or not the concern for identity and the concern for material continuity were fully compatible, both were deeply related to the fear of biological change I noted above. The resurrection body, reassembled from its earlier physical bits and conforming in every detail to its earthly structure, was a guarantee that change has limits; process is under control; development stops at death. Butterflies may come from cocoons and worms from corpses, but we will not be, in the afterlife, something we cannot recognize.

One does not have to essentialize body as matter to feel that the spiritualized and glorified body of scholastic theology is something of an oxymoron. A body that cannot age, corrupt, feel pain, or change in any way that would involve incurring or filling a lack, is a curious sort of body—which may be one of the reasons why theorists, especially in the early modern period, moved as much as they possibly could of the senses into heaven.[76] But this theory of a resurrection body reconstructed from the same physical bits and according to the same plan it had in life (and it is significant that high medieval thinkers were, when they dealt with the physical stuff of creation, atomists) implied that redemption had something to do with stasis.

This leads me to my final point, which concerns desire. For stasis was not the only image of the afterlife in the late Middle Ages. Especially in the poetry and visions of mystical women, heaven was ever-expanding desire. Such a notion was, however, long in coming.

In the visions and tales of the early Middle Ages, heaven was the realm of gold, gems, and crystal, whereas hell was the place of digestion and excretion, process, metamorphosis, and fluids. Exegetes were even reluctant to use biblically authorized images of flowers and seeds to describe either resurrection or reward. According to most scholastic theory (at least before the fourteenth century), heaven was *requies aeterna,* where longing was satiated and stilled. After the final Judgment, motion ceased (Apocalypse 10:6); eternity, as Boethius had said, is life *tota simul.*[77] Indeed, complex arguments, which I will not describe, circled around the texts in which Peter Lombard, Bernard of Clairvaux, and Bonaventure (themselves building on Augustine's *Literal Commentary on Genesis*) spoke of the separated soul as "retarded" by longing for its body after death.[78] What is important for my purposes here is that, in thirteenth-century university discussions, this longing was lodged in soul and was understood as a distraction from the peace of salvation. As Tugwell has recently reminded us, Aquinas held that the beatific vision was "decisive arrival. Once it is attained, there is no more change. Beatitude is a participation in eternity."[79]

And yet there were other ideas. Devotional literature and religious poetry (which often borrowed rhythms and vocabulary from secular love lyrics) spoke increasingly of a desire that would never be stilled.[80] Cracks appeared in the crystalline heaven of the scholastics.

In the final lines of the *Paradiso,* for example, Dante's heaven is not a gem but a flower. And at the heart of the heavenly rose is the great wheeling motion of love.

> Thus my mind, all rapt, was gazing … ever enkindled by its gazing….
>
> My own wings were not sufficient … save that my mind was smitten by a flash wherein its wish came to it. Here power failed …; but already my desire and my will were revolved, like a wheel that is evenly moved, by the Love which moves the sun and the other stars.[81]

Mystical women such as Hadewijch, Mechtild of Magdeburg, Angela of Foligno, and Marguerite of Oingt spoke of selves (body and soul together) yearning in heaven with a desire that was piqued and delighted into ever greater frenzy by encounter with their lover, God. Angela described Jesus as "love and inestimable satiety, which, although it satiated, generated at the same time insatiable hunger, so that all her [that is, Angela's own] members were unstrung."[82] Mechtild indeed wrote that she wished to remain in her body forever in order to suffer and yearn forever toward God.[83]

My point is not merely that writing about desire becomes more complex and fervent in the twelfth and thirteenth centuries, although this is true. It is that such desire is not only *for* bodies; it is lodged *in* bodies. When Mechtild and Marguerite speak of being lifted into the arms of God, tasting his goodness, seeing themselves reflected in his shining surface, they make it explicit that they speak of embodied persons, not of souls. All their senses are in play. And if certain of the university theologians of the thirteenth century would not fully have comprehended or accepted their poetry, there were already in the twelfth century Cistercian monks who wrote of the development of empathy through the encounter of our embodied selves with the body of Christ; they would have understood.[84]

It should be clear that this medieval idea of desire is both like and unlike the notion of desire I discussed when I considered *Truly, Madly, Deeply.* I do not wish to strain for parallels. I merely suggest that the sort of presence we usually mean by body and the sort of tug we usually mean by desire are radically related to each other in both the medieval and the modern periods. We do not usually speak of desire for a ghost or a memory, or think of our desire as in our minds. *Truly, Madly, Deeply* is not about ghosts but about persons.

Nor is late medieval discussion of personal survival, whether popular or learned, mostly about ghosts. In devotional writing, as in medieval love poetry, body and desire are connected. Thus not only do we see that body (in the sense of particular identity) is packed into soul by the theories of the scholastics; we also discover in the mystics a hint that passionate and ever unfolding love of God lodges fully in souls only when they get their bodies back.

Medieval discussions of the body that desires and the body that dies must of course be understood in the context of many other ideas. For a full picture of the many bodies of the Middle Ages we would need to consider understandings of disease and health, of growth and decay, of nature, the supernatural, the sacramental and the magical, of reproduction, contraception and birthing, of sexuality and rape, of pain and pleasure, of gender expectations, group affiliations, and social roles, of lineage and work, mothering and childhood. Moreover, as I have suggested in the discussion above, ideas differed according to who held them and where and when. The philosophy, the practices, the stories of late antiquity, of the twelfth and thirteenth centuries, of the age of Dante and Christine de Pisan, were not the same. Not only did mystical women and scholastic theologians differ; each group varied and disagreed among themselves. Experiences as basic as birthing and being born, working and eating, aging and dying were very different in the fens of England, the forests of Brittany, and the bustling cities of the Rhineland and the north of Italy.

Nonetheless I hope I have made it clear that medieval theories about the body that dies addressed philosophical issues of identity and individuality that still bother us today. I wish now to suggest how these theories relate to the contemporary debate over essentialism and especially to the performative feminism of Judith Butler (with which, as I said above, I have some sympathy). I will not attempt to provide a full discussion of the emerging field of gender studies (any more than I have treated fully either medieval scholasticism or the current cinema). Rather, I wish to make two general points about how medievalists should approach the plethora of body theory out of which my friend in eastern Europe (like many of her contemporaries) is struggling to build a course syllabus.

In Theory

In current philosophical and historical discussion, "identity" refers to two related issues: spatiotemporal continuity and identity-position. It refers, that is, to the question of how a thing survives in time and space as "the same thing" (for example, Bynum as Bynum), and the question of what makes two separate things describable by the same grouping noun (for example, Native American). The recent debate over essentialism is really an effort to find understandings that do not assume a common essence or nature (or, in some theories, even a common definition) for identity in both senses.[85]

The effort stems in part from the desire of certain groups (self-identified *as* groups) to seize control of descriptions that had been imposed on them by outsiders,[86] in part from dissatisfaction with the sex/gender distinction (understood as a distinction between the biologically given and the culturally constructed) so popular in the early 1980s.[87] The antiessentialism of many recent theorists, and especially the performative feminism of Butler, are impressive efforts to explain how the categories with which we live are created by us as we live them. No one, Butler argues, is born "woman" or "black" or "lesbian," nor are these categories "cultural interpretations" of biological "facts." Yet one does not simply choose an identity-position. One becomes a lesbian by living as a lesbian, changing the category as one incorporates and inspires it (the echoes of *corpus* and *spiritus* in the verbs I have chosen here are intentional).

Seen in a slightly longer perspective, the antiessentialist position is, of course, a reaction to Cartesian and Enlightenment dichotomies: mind versus body, authority versus liberty, society (or nurture) versus nature, and so on.[88] For all its energy and intelligence, it sometimes seems to flail in its analysis from one pole to the other— from performance to regulation, mind to matter, socialization to physical structure— as if both were traps from which something (but what?) might escape. In my own more ludic moments, I find the discussion empowering; in gloomier times I too (like the theorists themselves) feel trapped by categories. By and large, as the best of contemporary feminists enjoin me, I try to listen to the voices of others. But does any of this have anything to do with the Middle Ages?

The debate about essentialism that has so dominated feminist and gender studies over the past five years is clearly an event in contemporary politics. As Bordo and Jane Martin (among others) have argued, it has unfortunately sometimes been used to repress empirical historical research. Historians have been accused of silencing past voices when they fail to find in them decidedly 1990s sensibilities,[89] of essentializing categories when they have instead (often after long and painstaking research) discovered an unfamiliar attitude in the past. Such charges are abusive, both of the historical record and of the contemporary diversity they purport to foster. But does this mean that current feminist theories, especially the debate over essentialism, have no relevance—or even destructive implications—for the study of remote periods such as the European Middle Ages? I suggest on the contrary that there is something to be learned, but in two quite specific ways.[90]

First, if we situate our own categories in the context of our own politics, we must situate those of the Middle Ages in theirs. The relationship between then and now will thus be analogous and proportional, not direct. It seems to me, that is, that the fruitful question to explore is not likely to be, How is Origen (or Christine de Pisan or Aquinas) like or not like Butler (or Spivak or Foucault)? Posed in this simple way, the answer (whether we applaud it or condemn it) is almost certain to be, not very like. It is far more fruitful to think along the lines: Origen is to Origen's context as Butler is to Butler's. By understanding the relationship of figures to contexts, and then the relationship of those relationships, we will often see that there is a large and developing issue with which both figures struggle, each in his or her own vocabulary and circumstances.

Or, to put it another way, the past is seldom usefully examined by assuming that its specific questions or their settings are the same as those of the present. What may, however, be the same is the way in which a question, understood in its context, struggles with a perduring issue such as, for example, group affiliation. Origen asked, What of our bodily self survives into the realm of resurrection? Butler asks, How is a sexual orientation constituted by a way of being in the world? That is, Origen dealt with identity in the sense of spatiotemporal continuity; Butler deals with an identity-position. For Origen, the continuing of body into the afterlife seems to involve the transcending of what we call gender; for Butler, it is unimaginable that we could be "we" without performing what we call gender. Moreover, Origen's context was martyrdom, persecution, and debate over how we know the truth; Butler's is homophobia, the academy, and debate over who has the power to define. Neither the issues nor their contexts are the same. If we assume they are, we get only boring results. We learn very little that is important about the third or the twentieth century if we ask, for example, What does Origen think about transvestites or Butler about angels (although it is clear that each would condemn the views of the other)? Yet I would suggest that Origen, struggling with the categories he inherited and the traumas of his world, can be seen as "solving" an issue of identity in a way surprisingly similar to the solution Butler forges from her inheritance and her experience. Both Butler and Origen speak of a labile, active, unfolding body that somehow becomes more what it is by behaving as it does; both have trouble explaining how what we think of as "physical stuff" fits in.[91]

Second, we must recognize that we are, at least in part, the heirs of many earlier discourses.[92] The conversation about nature and difference, about individuality and identity, that is so heated today has roots in centuries of debate. Our current concerns have not sprung full-blown from the 1970s. I do not, of course, argue that Origen of Alexandria, Aquinas, and Angela of Foligno had twentieth-century notions of difference and desire, but I do insist that, by the early fourteenth century, mystical and scholastic understandings of body implied that both physicality and sensuality lodge squarely in person. If there had been no sophisticated discussion of identity and survival, of gender and longing, before *The Feminine Mystique,* recent discussions would not be so nuanced and powerful. It is partly because premodern Western philosophy is not dualistic, not essentialist, that we struggle so hard today with certain issues of philosophical vocabulary inherited from the Enlightenment. Much (I did not say all) of what we include in an identity-position (especially gender) was already in the late Middle Ages established as intrinsic to self exactly because it was understood to return at the moment of bodily resurrection. Debates about spatiotemporal continuity and personal survival came to imply notions of the individual that foreshadowed the modern concern with identity-position (although the term has no medieval equivalent).

My friend in eastern Europe asked me to write something for her students. In the face of arguments that seemed to make the premodern past irrelevant, irretrievable, and irredeemable, she wanted an example of what it might mean to relate feminist theory to the Middle Ages. One of my purposes here has been to provide such an example. I might indeed suggest that it is impossible not to. For the only past we can know is one we shape by the questions we ask; yet these questions are also shaped by the context we come from, and our context includes the past. Thus my picture of medieval concerns is as influenced by current feminist debates as those debates are influenced by the ideas from which they partly descend.

It is not only possible, it is imperative to use modern concerns when we confront the past. So long as we reason by analogy rather than merely rewriting or rejecting, the present will help us see past complexity and the past will help us to understand ourselves. Thus we need not succumb to the despair or solipsism to which modern historians are sometimes reduced by the plethora of new approaches. Nor need we abandon the study of the Middle Ages in favor of the study of other medievalists.[93] We must never forget to watch ourselves knowing the otherness of the past, but this is not the same as merely watching ourselves.

Indeed, awareness of our individual situations and perspectives can be freeing rather than limiting, for it removes the burden of trying to see everything. The enterprise of the historian becomes, of necessity, more cooperative and therefore more fun.[94] Recent theorizing has surely taught us that our knowledge is "situated," that the effort to understand "the other" is fraught with danger.[95] But any medievalist who tackles her professional subject matter writes, and must write, about what is other—radically, terrifyingly, fascinatingly other—from herself. If we no longer believe that the *pars* elucidated by any one historian stands *pro toto*, we must nonetheless not surrender our determination to reach outside ourselves in our encounter with the part. Exactly because we recognize *pars* for *pars,* we can have greater confidence—and greater pleasure—in a kaleidoscopic whole that is far larger than the limited vision of any one of us. The sources are there to be deciphered, the charnel houses to be excavated, the reliquaries to be studied in terms of their contents as well as their design. We can, I think, bring recent theoretical discussion to bear on the Middle Ages without doing violence to the nuances of medieval texts and images or to the slow, solid efforts of medievalists to understand them.

In closing, then, I return to medieval ideas and images of the body. I have considered them (as should now be clear) in the light of a modern concern with identity and individuality, physicality and desire. What, if anything, has emerged from this encounter of present and past?

In Conclusion

Certain philosophical theories about the body that developed in late antiquity and the high Middle Ages answered the question, How can "I" continue to be "I" through time, both the time of earth and the time of the eschaton? But they were understood by contemporaries to do this at the expense of taking lived life very abstractly, at the expense of jettisoning the stuffness of "me." These theories did not essentialize "me" as a general human abstraction. Even for Origen, the "I" that unfolds in heaven carries with it some of my particularity. And for thirteenth-century followers of Aquinas, "my" particularity—not only my sex but also personal characteristics, such as beauty or size—were understood to be carried by soul or form. Although Origen's contemporaries feared that he opened the way to metempsychosis, by the thirteenth century no philosophical theory of the person admitted any possibility of transmigration of soul. Body was individual and immediately recognizable as such; for better or worse, one could not shed gender or appearance; one could not body-hop in this life or in the afterlife.

In such a theory, however, body became an expression of soul; indeed, body could be expressed in any stuff. As a number of more conservative thinkers of the late thirteenth century noticed, this raised questions for religious practice. No less a figure than the Archbishop of Canterbury pointed out that there would be no reason for revering the relics of a saint if any stuff could provide his or her body at the end of time.[96] It is remarkable that we find scholastics in the years around 1300 raising questions about relic cult and burial practices as ways of objecting to technical philosophical theories, since in the Middle Ages (as today), practice and the discourse of university intellectuals were seldom explicitly related to each other.

The new philosophical theories did more than threaten specific religious practices. They tended to make body itself into a concept, to dissolve body into theory. And they made salvation repose or stasis. The goal of human existence became crystalline permanence. Yet the period that produced such theories saw an explosion of poetry, religious and secular, in which labile, physical, agile, yearning body received new articulation. The abstractions of the philosophers and theologians were not so much defeated as simply and very effectively ignored by the poets and mystics, preachers and storytellers, of the later Middle Ages. (Even in the universities, the new theory received remarkably little attention outside certain circles.) To the singers, preachers, and lovers of the fourteenth century, the self is a person whose desire rolls and tumbles from fingertips as well as genitals, whose body is not only instrument, expression, and locus of self, but in some sense self itself.

My friend suspected that a conversation between medieval ideas and modern ones might reintroduce into her classroom something of the stuffness of body that she found missing in contemporary literary and feminist theory. As I have tried to show, that expectation is only partly right. Medieval theories too could be highly abstract; some at least of the many bodies of the Middle Ages themselves dissolved into discourse. But there was also resistance to such discourse. And I hope I have demonstrated that there was as well, in social and religious practice, a sense of the immediacy of bodies, living and dead, that provides some of what my friend wanted to show her students.

The roots of modern notions of a particular embodied self that cannot, we feel, body-hop despite the intellectual and technical opportunities presented by organ transplants and artificial intelligence, thus lie in the later Middle Ages. Hundreds of years of controversy, in which person was seen as a unity (not a mind/body duality), a particular individual (not an essence), and a yearning stuff (not—and here despite the theologians—a form for which any matter can be its matter) have profoundly shaped the Western tradition. Compared to this, the real mind/body dualism introduced by early modern philosophers is a small blip on the long curve of history.[97] For better and for worse, we are the heirs of Aquinas's notion of a particular self (not an essence) carried in soul but expressed in body, as we are of those long lines of pilgrims who kissed relics of fingers and garments, or of Angela's, Dante's, and Mechtild's dreams of insatiable desire.

Finally, however, I stress not parallels between medieval and modern understandings— or the roots of present and past in each other—but the diversity within each period. Medieval writings about *corpus* or *caro*—or even *materia* or *tellus*—were as multiple and multivalent as the varying discourses found in modern writing about the body. If I have pulled from my own detailed research certain themes concerning death and survival, it is because I think modern treatments of person and body have recently concentrated rather too much on issues of gender and sexuality to the detriment of our awareness of other things (such as death and work) that are also at stake.[98]

Indeed, if (as I have asserted above) we are all shaped by our many presents and pasts, I may be merely *reflecting* the broader understanding of body for which I appear to be calling. Why all the fuss about the body? Perhaps because I am not, after all, alone in noticing—in *Truly, Madly, Deeply,* the AIDS quilt, or the controversy over organ transplants—the complex link between body, death, and the past.

c. Questions

Comprehension

1. What are the "issues relating to bodies and embodiment that have been eclipsed in present theorizing" that Bynum wants to correct?

2. Explain the three aspects—identity or individuality, matter or physicality, and desire—that concern people about "the body." How does Bynum use them when talking about *Truly, Madly, Deeply,* and in what ways are these similar to or different from her discussions in medieval examples?

3. What are the three different stereotypes of the Middle Ages that Bynum says must be rejected? In what ways do each of them rely on the assumption of a binary?

Analysis

4. What dimensions of identity and bodies does Bynum examine in her scholarship and why are these particularities important?

5. Bynum makes specific, historical, arguments about medieval Christianity. What can scholars of religion who study different religions or historical periods use or

learn from Bynum's argument? What aspects of her argument should they not use across contexts?

Synthesis

6. Although we have encountered the important contributions of scholars trained outside of the field of religious studies in earlier chapters, Bynum's work highlights the interdisciplinary nature of religious studies in a new way. Why does the study of religion require so much interdisciplinary work? What do interdisciplinary contributions to the study of religion illuminate about religious traditions and people? How is Bynum's work different than the previous theorists? Are there any drawbacks to the interdisciplinary study of religion?

Notes

*   For help with this essay, I thank Elaine Combs-Schilling, Arnold Davidson, Tilman Habermas, Jeffrey Hamburger, Bruce Holsinger, Jean Howard, Lynn Hunt, Hans Medick, Hilary Putnam, Guenther Roth, Nancy Leys Stepan, and Stephen D. White. Although in some cases their suggestions cancelled each other out, I profited immensely from the diverse readings they provided.

Critical Inquiry 22 (Autumn 1995)

1   My friend's point is echoed in Susan Bordo, "Feminism, Postmodernism, and Gender-Scepticism," in *Feminism/Postmodernism,* ed. Linda Nicholson (New York, 1990), p. 145: "What sort of body is it that is free to change its shape and location at will, that can become anyone and travel anywhere? If the body is a metaphor for our locatedness in space and time and thus for the finitude of human perception and knowledge, then the postmodern body is no body at all." As I mention in n. 67 below, medieval debates over the glorified body of the resurrection consider some of the same issues.

2   Margaret Atwood uses the idea of a flesh dress in her novel *The Robber Bride* (Toronto, 1993). The idea comes from a poem by James Reaney called "Doomsday, or the Red Headed Woodpecker," *Poems,* ed. Germaine Warkentin (Toronto, 1972), pp. 112–13.

3   For recent discussions of essentialism, especially with regard to feminist issues, see Diana Fuss, *Essentially Speaking: Feminism, Nature, and Difference* (New York, 1989); Bordo, "Feminism, Postmodernism, and Gender-Scepticism," pp. 133–56; Ellen Rooney, interview with Gayatri Chakravorty Spivak, "In a Word: *Interview,*" in *Outside in the Teaching Machine* (New York, 1993), esp. pp. 14–23; and Jane Roland Martin, "Methodological Essentialism, False Difference, and Other Dangerous Traps," *Signs* 19 (Spring, 1994): 630–57. All four authors deplore recent uses of the charge of essentialism to attack empirical, historical research. All four show courage in speaking out; I find myself most in sympathy with the specific formulations of Susan Bordo.

4 See Fuss, *Essentially Speaking,* pp. 51–53. When I say it doesn't help much, I mean precisely this; it does, of course, help some. Focusing on the variety of individual experiences, and guarding against generalizing from self to other, produce a more nuanced understanding of both the present and the past.

5 In the survey of literature that follows I deliberately bring together authors who never read each other. The books and articles I cite below often speak with great assurance of what "the body" is and yet display little awareness of each others' conversations— conversations in which totally diverse assumptions and definitions figure. It is thus part of my purpose here to serve as a historian of our present moment, calling attention both to the ghettoization of contemporary discourses and to their common emphases. It is *not* part of my purpose either to provide a complete survey of recent literature or to recommend as serious and valuable every title I cite.

6 For several recent (and very different) examples, see *The Philosophy of the Body: Rejections of Cartesian Dualism,* ed. Stuart F. Spicker (Chicago, 1970); Mark Johnson, *The Body in the Mind: The Bodily Basis of Meaning, Imagination, and Reason* (Chicago, 1987); Bordo, *The Flight to Objectivity: Essays on Cartesianism and Culture* (Albany, NY, 1987); Judith Butler, *Gender Trouble: Feminism and the Subversion of Identity* (New York, 1990) and *Bodies That Matter: On the Discursive Limits of "Sex"* (New York, 1993); Patrick Quinn, "Aquinas's Concept of the Body and Out of Body Situations," *Heythrop Journal* 34 (October 1993): 387–400; and Jean-Luc Nancy, "Corpus," trans. Claudette Sartiliot, in *Thinking Bodies,* ed. Juliet Flower MacCannell and Laura Zakarin (Stanford, CA, 1994), pp. 17–31.

7 See Bryan S. Turner, *The Body and Society: Explorations in Social Theory* (Oxford, 1984). Important recent works that are, properly speaking, part of the new field of cultural studies but have much in common with what was the enterprise of sociology a generation ago are Elaine Scarry, *The Body in Pain: The Making and Unmaking of the World* (Oxford, 1985), and David B. Morris, *The Culture of Pain* (Berkeley, 1991). See also Jakob Tanner, "Körpererfahrung, Schmerz, und die Konstruktion des Kulturellen," *Historische Anthropologie: Kultur, Gesellschaft, Alltag* 2, no. 3 (1994): 489–502.

8 See Roy Porter, "History of the Body," in *New Perspectives on Historical Writing,* ed. Peter Burke (University Park, PA, 1991), pp. 206–32, and Bordo, *"Anorexia Nervosa:* Psychopathology as the Crystallization of Culture," in *Feminism and Foucault: Reflections on Resistance,* ed. Irene Diamond and Lee Quinby (Boston, 1988), pp. 87–90. An older survey that is still powerful and convincing is Natalie Zemon Davis, "Women's History in Transition: The European Case," *Feminist Studies* 3 (Spring–Summer, 1976): 83–103.

9 See, for example, *Feminism and Foucault; The Making of the Modern Body: Sexuality and Society in the Nineteenth Century,* ed. Catherine Gallagher and Thomas Laqueur (Berkeley, 1987); Emily Martin, *The Woman in the Body: A Cultural Analysis of Reproduction* (Boston, 1987); *Body/Politics: Women and the Discourses of Science,* ed. Mary Jacobus, Evelyn Fox Keller, and Sally Shuttleworth (New York, 1990); and Ludmilla Jordanova, *Sexual Visions: Images of Gender in Science and Medicine between the Eighteenth and Twentieth Centuries* (New York, 1989). Martin is an anthropologist but her method is similar to that of the historians cited here. An important recent work that takes a somewhat different approach is Barbara Duden, *Geschichte unter der Haut: Ein Eisenacher Arzt und seine Patientinnen um 1730* (Stuttgart, 1987); trans. Thomas Dunlap, under the misleading title *The Woman beneath the Skin: A Doctor's Patients in Eighteenth-Century Germany* (Cambridge, MA, 1991).

10 See Martha C. Howell, "A Feminist Historian Looks at the New Historicism: What's So Historical about It?" *Women's Studies* 19 (Spring, 1991): 139–47; and John E. Toews, "Stories of Difference and Identity: New Historicism in Literature and History," *Monatshefte für deutschen Unterricht, deutsche Sprache und Literatur* 84 (Spring, 1992): 193–211.

11 See, for example, Lawrence E. Sullivan, "Body Works: Knowledge of the Body in the Study of Religion," *History of Religions* 30 (August, 1990): 86–99; Antoine Vergote, "The Body as Understood in Contemporary Thought and Biblical Categories," *Philosophy Today* 35 (Spring, 1991): 93–105; James B. Nelson, *Body Theology* (Louisville, KY, 1992); and James F. Keenan, "Christian Perspectives on the Human Body," *Theological Studies* 55 (June, 1994): 330–46.

12 See Butler, *Gender Trouble* and *Bodies That Matter.* Butler is herself aware of the criticism and takes skilful steps to avoid some of the problems pointed out by her critics. I return to discussion of this below.

13 See n. 1 above. The major place where the body that dies receives extensive treatment in contemporary scholarship is in gay studies. See, for example, Randy Shilts, *And the Band Played On: Politics, People, and the AIDS Epidemic* (New York, 1987), and Eve Kosofsky Sedgwick, *Tendencies* (Durham, NC, 1993).

14 See, for example, Margaret Miles, *Carnal Knowing: Female Nakedness and Religious Meaning in the Christian West* (Boston, 1989).

15 See, for example, Emily Martin, *The Woman in the Body.*

16 See Norman O. Brown, *Love's Body* (New York, 1966). The two senses of body— as constraint and as potentiality—are in certain ways two sides of the same coin. Debate about the extent to which body can be altered, overthrown, and so on (or to put it another way, the extent to which we can be liberated from body) is lodged in debates over authority and freedom, society (or nurture) and nature, that go back to the Enlightenment. There are also, however, current discussions about bodies (especially but not exclusively around issues of reproduction) that have roots in pre-Enlightenment concerns.

17 See Porter, "History of the Body," pp. 207, 224–25, and Jordanova, *Sexual Visions,* pp. 10–13.

18 See Nelson, *Body Theology.* Teresa L. Ebert points out that recent work tends also to leave out the laboring body. See Teresa L. Ebert, "Ludic Feminism, the Body, Performance, and Labor: Bringing *Materialism* Back into Feminist Cultural Studies," *Cultural Critique,* no. 23 (Winter, 1992–93): 5–50.

19 The cliche is found in some form in most of the books cited above. Porter in his review essay, for example, sees the contemporary interest in body history as a result of our new freedom from such dualism; Bordo, whose *The Flight to Objectivity* brilliantly protests the conventional misreading of medieval thought as Cartesian, nonetheless repeats the generalization in her work on anorexia nervosa. For the standard formulation, see Elizabeth V. Spelman, "Woman as Body: Ancient and Contemporary Views," *Feminist Studies* 8 (Spring, 1982): 109–31, and Jacques Le Goff, "Corps et idéologie dans l'Occident médiéval," *L'Imaginaire médiéval: Essais* (Paris, 1985), pp. 123–27.

20 Among much splendid work on sexuality and gender in the Middle Ages, I single out Peter Brown, *The Body and Society: Men, Women, and Sexual Renunciation in Early Christianity* (New York, 1988); Danielle Jacquart and Claude Thomasset, *Sexuality and Medicine in the Middle Ages,* trans. Matthew Adamson (Princeton, NJ, 1988); and Joan Cadden, *The Meanings of Sex Difference in the Middle Ages: Medicine,*

Science, and Culture (Cambridge, 1993). For a discussion of gender and sexuality in rabbinic Judaism, see Daniel Boyarin, *Carnal Israel: Reading Sex in Talmudic Culture* (Berkeley, 1993).

21 See Jacquart and Thomasset, *Sexuality and Medicine in the Middle Ages,* pp. 83–138; Cadden, *The Meanings of Sex Difference in the Middle Ages,* pp. 271–77; and Mary Frances Wack, *Lovesickness in the Middle Ages: The Viaticum and Its Commentaries* (Philadelphia, 1990), pp. 68–70, 79, and 131.

22 See the works cited in nn. 41 and 80 below, and R. Howard Bloch, *The Scandal of the Fabliaux* (Chicago, 1986).

23 See Agostino Paravicini Bagliani, "Rajeunir au Moyen Age: Roger Bacon et le mythe de la prolongation de la vie," *Revue médicale de la Suisse Romande* 106, no. 1 (1986): 9–23 and "Storia della scienza e storia della mentalità: Ruggero Bacone, Bonifacio VIII e la teoria della 'prolongatio vitae,' " in *Aspetti della Letteratura latina nel secolo XIII,* ed. Claudio Leonardi and Giovanni Orlandi (Perugia, 1985), pp. 243–80; and Christel Meier, *Gemma spiritalis: Methode und Gebrauch der Edelsteinallegorese vom frühen Christentum bis ins 18. Jahrhundert* (Munich, 1977).

24 See Jacquart and Thomasset, *Sexuality and Medicine in the Middle Ages,* and Cadden, *The Meanings of Sex Difference in the Middle Ages,* esp. pp. 167–227. For the new emphasis on organ systems found in Renaissance medicine, see Laqueur's splendid study, *Making Sex: Body and Gender from the Greeks to Freud* (Cambridge, MA, 1990). The critique by Katharine Park and Robert A. Nye suggests that Laqueur has not taken sufficient account of earlier Galenic notions that would make the body more a matter of fluids and humors. See Katharine Park and Robert A. Nye, "Destiny Is Anatomy," review of *Making Sex,* by Laqueur, *New Republic* 18 (February 1991): 53–57.

25 For these "mixed messages" to medieval women (and some men as well), see Donald Weinstein and Rudolph M. Bell, *Saints and Society: The Two Worlds of Western Christendom, 1000–1700* (Chicago, 1982), pp. 73–99.

26 On purgatory, see Le Goff, *The Birth of Purgatory,* trans. Arthur Goldhammer (Chicago, 1984). On the beatific vision controversy, see Simon Tugwell, *Human Immortality and the Redemption of Death* (London, 1990), pp. 125–56, and my own *The Resurrection of the Body in Western Christianity, 200–1336* (New York, 1995), pp. 279–91.

27 See my *Fragmentation and Redemption: Essays on Gender and the Human Body in Medieval Religion* (New York, 1991), pp. 244–52 and *The Resurrection of the Body in Western Christianity, 200–1336,* pp. 14–17.

28 See Robert Nozick, *Philosophical Explanations* (Cambridge, MA, 1981), pp. 29–70, esp. 41–42 and 58–59, and Bordo, "Reading the Slender Body," in *Body/Politics,* pp. 87–94. For a discussion of the carrying of race and "racial characteristics" with a body part, see bell hooks [Gloria Watkins], *Black Looks: Race and Representation* (Boston, 1992), p. 31, who argues that the theme in the movie *Heart Condition* is a white fantasy. See also my discussion in *Fragmentation and Redemption,* pp. 245–49, and *The Mind's I: Fantasies and Reflections on Self and Soul,* ed. Douglas R. Hofstadter and Daniel C. Dennett (New York, 1981).

29 *Truly, Madly, Deeply,* BBC, 1990; Samuel Goldwyn Company, Los Angeles, 1992.

30 For example, the film raises interesting, and unresolved, gender issues: Why are the returned figures all male? Moreover, although the ending clearly suggests that the returned Jamie has come back exactly in order to release his lover, nothing in his character suggests why he might act thus.

31 See Jean-Claude Schmitt, *Les Revenants: Les Vivants et les morts dans la société mediévale* (Paris, 1994).

32 For a general discussion of relics in the Middle Ages, see Peter Brown, *The Cult of the Saints: Its Rise and Function in Latin Christianity* (Chicago, 1981); Patrick J. Geary, *Furta Sacra: Thefts of Relics in the Central Middle Ages* (Princeton, NJ, 1978) and *Living with the Dead in the Middle Ages* (Ithaca, NY, 1994), esp. pp. 42–44 and 163–218; and Nicole Hermann-Mascard, *Les Reliques des saints: Formation coutumière d'un droit* (Paris, 1975). The remark of Giles of Rome is found in *Quodlibeta* 4, q. 4, fol. 47va; quoted in Kiernan Nolan, *The Immortality of the Soul and the Resurrection of the Body According to Giles of Rome: A Historical Study of a Thirteenth-Century Theological Problem* (Rome, 1967), p. 60 n. 49. For a fascinating example of medieval contact relics, see the late sixth-century account of a pilgrimage to the Holy Land written by a traveller from Piacenza: *Antonini Placentini Itinerarium*, ed. P. Geyer, in *Itineraria et alia geographica*, 2 vols. (Turnhout, 1965), 1:129–74. The account includes such objects as "manna" from the Sinai, dew from Mount Hermon, rocks from Mount Carmel (supposed to prevent miscarriages), and "measures" of Jesus's body (that is, strips of cloth measured and cut to fit what was supposedly the body's imprint and then worn around the neck of the pilgrim).

33 For a sensitive discussion of what I am calling here physical transitional objects, see Sedgwick, "White Glasses," *Tendencies*, pp. 252–66. I am grateful to Tilman Habermas for discussion of these matters at a crucial moment in my thinking.

34 Rooney, "In a Word," p. 20.

35 See Wallace I. Matson, "Why Isn't the Mind-Body Problem Ancient?" in *Mind, Matter, and Method: Essays in Philosophy and Science in Honor of Herbert Feigl*, ed. Paul K. Feyerabend and Grover Maxwell (Minneapolis, 1966), pp. 92–102; Hilary Putnam, "How Old Is the Mind?" and (with Martha C. Nussbaum), "Changing Aristotle's Mind," *Words and Life*, ed. James Conant (Cambridge, MA, 1994), pp. 3–21 and 22–61, esp. pp. 23–28. In certain ways I agree here with the more theologically formulated position of Vergote, "The Body," pp. 93–105.

36 To Aquinas, who made historically accurate use of Aristotle's ideas, soul is the substantial form of the organized living body. For Bonaventure and others who held the doctrine of a multiplicity of forms, the question is more complicated. I discuss these technical philosophical issues in *The Resurrection of the Body in Western Christianity, 200–1336*, pp. 229–78. In order to avoid overloading this article with notes, I refer my reader to the book. I give here only citations for quoted primary sources or material not referred to in the book.

37 See my *Fragmentation and Redemption*, pp. 226–27, for a discussion of ways in which medieval thinkers blurred the soul/body contrast or used trinary rather than binary models. On medieval psychology of vision, which made use of trinary categories, see Sixten Ringbom, *Icon to Narrative: The Rise of the Dramatic Close-Up in Fifteenth-Century Devotional Painting* (Abo, 1965), pp. 15–22, and Schmitt, *Les Revenants*, pp. 38–40 and 223–26. On functions shared by body and soul in Aristotle's account, see Putnam (with Nussbaum), "Changing Aristotle's Mind," pp. 38–43; on Aquinas, see Putnam, "How Old Is the Mind?" pp. 4–7.

38 See Morris, *Culture of Pain*, p. 152, although elsewhere he tends to interpret the Middle Ages more dualistically; see, for example, pp. 131–34. See also Wack, *Lovesickness in the Middle Ages*, pp. 7–9; Putnam (with Nussbaum), "Changing

Aristotle's Mind" and "Aristotle after Wittgenstein," *Words and Life,* pp. 38–43, 69–78; and Stanley Cavell, "Natural and Conventional," *The Claim of Reason: Wittgenstein, Skepticism, Morality, and Tragedy* (Oxford, 1979), pp. 86–125.

39 On the genre, see Robert W. Ackerman, *"The Debate of the Body and the Soul* and Parochial Christianity," *Speculum* 37 (October, 1962): 541–65.

40 I leave aside here for the moment positions—such as the theology of some thirteenth-century Cathars—that were in a technical sense ontological and cosmic dualism, that is, they argued for two sorts of reality, material and spiritual, created by two distinct and opposing ultimate powers. In *The Resurrection of the Body in Western Christianity, 200–1336,* pp. 214–25, I show how orthodox and Cathar discussions were in many ways animated by the same fears and argue that orthodox theologians were working out their own understandings of matter in their polemics against heretics.

41 See Jean Delumeau, *Le Peur en Occident: Une Cité assiégée* (Paris, 1978) and *Sin and Fear: The Emergence of a Western Guilt Culture, Thirteenth–Eighteenth Centuries,* trans. Eric Nicholson (New York, 1990); and Robert Bultot, *Christianisme et valeurs humaines: La Doctrine du mépris du monde, en Occident, de S. Ambroise à Innocent III,* 6 vols. (Paris, 1963–64), vol. 4, pts. 1 and 2.

42 See, for example, Kathleen Cohen, *Metamorphosis of a Death Symbol: The Transi Tomb in the Late Middle Ages and the Renaissance* (Berkeley, 1973).

43 See Bynum, *Holy Feast and Holy Fast: The Religious Significance of Food to Medieval Women* (Berkeley, 1987). And see Keenan, "Christian Perspectives on the Human Body." The radical physicality of medieval religion provides the context for such genuinely new somatic events as stigmata and miraculous inedia.

44 For example, see Bonaventure, *Breviloquium,* in vol. 7 of *Opera omnia,* ed. A. C. Peltier (Paris, 1866), pt. 4, chap. 9, pp. 292–94.

45 There is an obvious parallel between the late medieval devotion to the suffering Christ and the cannibalistic practice of torturing a captured hero before consuming him. In many cannibal cultures, the one to be eaten was seen to gain in power the longer he held out under torture. See Peggy Reeves Sanday, *Divine Hunger: Cannibalism as a Cultural System* (New York, 1986); Louis-Vincent Thomas, *Le Cadavre: De la biologie à l'anthropologie* (Brussels, 1980), pp. 159–69; Georges Bataille, *Consumption,* trans. Robert Hurley, vol. 1 of *The Accursed Share: An Essay on General Economy* (New York, 1988), pp. 45–61; Maggie Kilgour, *From Communion to Cannibalism: An Anatomy of Metaphors of Incorporation* (Princeton, NJ, 1990); Gananath Obeyesekere, " 'British Cannibals': Contemplation of an Event in the Death and Resurrection of James Cook, Explorer," *Critical Inquiry* 18 (Summer, 1992): 630–54, trans. Sibylle Brändli, under the title " 'Britische Kannibalen': Nachdenkliches zur Geschichte des Todes und der Auferstehung des Entdeckers James Cook," *Historische Anthropologie: Kultur, Gesellschaft, Alltag* 1, no. 2 (1993): 273–93; and Philippe Buc, *L'Ambiguïté du livre: Prince, pouvoir, et peuple dans les commentaires de la Bible au moyen âge* (Paris, 1994), pp. 206–31 and 406.

46 See Luce Irigaray, "Une Mère de glace," *Speculum of the Other Woman,* trans. Gillian Gill (Ithaca, NY, 1985), pp. 168–79, and Butler, *Bodies That Matter,* pp. 32–55, esp. nn. 22, 28, 31, and 34. And see the essays in *The Concept of Matter in Greek and Medieval Philosophy,* ed. Ernan McMullin (Notre Dame, IN, 1965).

47 I have touched on these issues in my *Jesus as Mother: Studies in the Spirituality of the High Middle Ages* (Berkeley, 1982), pp. 110–69 and *Fragmentation and*

Redemption, pp. 151–79. Recent and sensitive examples of such argument are Karma Lochrie, *Margery Kempe and Translations of the Flesh* (Philadelphia, 1991); Sarah Beckwith, *Christ's Body: Identity, Culture, and Society in Late Medieval Writings* (London, 1993); Jeffrey M. Hamburger, "The Visual and the Visionary: The Image in Late Medieval Monastic Devotions," *Viator* 20 (1989): 161–82 and *Nuns as Artists in Fifteenth-Century Franconia: Devotional Drawings from the Convent of St. Walburg in Eichstätt* (forthcoming).

48 See Diane Bornstein, "Antifeminism," *Dictionary of the Middle Ages,* ed. Joseph R. Strayer, 13 vols. (New York, 1982–89), 1:322–25, and R. Howard Bloch, *Medieval Misogyny and the Invention of Western Romantic Love* (Chicago, 1992). There have been several recent attempts to read medieval texts against themselves and find women's voices raised against the misogyny built into the accounts by both male and female authors; see, for example, E. Jane Burns, *Bodytalk: When Women Speak in Old French Literature* (Philadelphia, 1993). More successful, in my judgment, are the sophisticated technical studies that actually discover women's voices in texts written by male scribes. See, for example, Anne L. Clark, *Elisabeth of Schönau: A Twelfth-Century Visionary* (Philadelphia, 1992), and Catherine M. Mooney, "The Authorial Role of Brother A. in the Composition of Angela of Foligno's Revelations," in *Creative Women in Medieval and Early Modern Italy: A Religious and Artistic Renaissance,* ed. E. Ann Matter and John Coakley (Philadelphia, 1994), pp. 34–63.

49 Especially good, among much good recent work, are Marie-Christine Pouchelle, *Corps et chirurgie à l'apogée du moyen âge: Savoir et imaginaire du corps chez Henri de Mondeville, chirugien de Phillipe le Bel* (Paris, 1983); James A. Brundage, *Law, Sex, and Christian Society in Medieval Europe* (Chicago, 1987); Pierre J. Payer, *The Bridling of Desire: Views of Sex in the Later Middle Ages* (Toronto, 1993); Dyan Elliott, *Spiritual Marriage: Sexual Abstinence in Medieval Wedlock* (Princeton, NJ, 1993); and Howell, *Women, Production, and Patriarchy in Late Medieval Cities* (Chicago, 1986).

50 Still useful on this is the older work of Eleanor C. McLaughlin, "Equality of Souls, Inequality of Sexes: Women in Medieval Theology," in *Religion and Sexism: Images of Woman in the Jewish and Christian Traditions,* ed. Rosemary Radford Ruether (New York, 1974), pp. 213–66. Buc, *L'Ambiguité du livre,* esp. pp. 323–66 and 401–6, has recently shown that there was a tradition of questioning hierarchy in medieval exegesis.

51 See Bynum, *Jesus as Mother,* pp. 110–262, for many citations.

52 See Lochrie, *Margery Kempe and Translations of the Flesh;* Beckwith, *Christ's Body;* Hamburger, "The Visual and the Visionary"; and Danielle Régnier-Bohler, "Voix littéraires, voix mystiques," in *Le Moyen âge,* ed. Christiane Klapisch-Zuber, vol. 2 of *Histoire des femmes en occident,* ed. Georges Duby and Michelle Perrot (Paris, 1991), pp. 443–500.

53 See, for example, Eadmer's account of a vision received by Anselm in which the life of the world is a river full of detritus but the monastery is a vast cloister of pure silver; see Eadmer, *The Life of St. Anselm, Archbishop of Canterbury* [Latin and English], trans. and ed. R. W. Southern (Oxford, 1962), pp. 35–36. Anselm returns to the image in his own preaching, where he compares life to a rushing stream; the safety of the monastic life is imaged both as a mill and as a vessel holding the milled flour; see ibid., pp. 74–76. The idea of life as a river, and safety as a building by its side, is also found in Peter Damian; see Bultot, *La Doctrine du mépris du monde,* 4:2:84, 90. The contrast of flow and stasis as evil and good is very clear. On hell as digestion, see my *The Resurrection of the Body in Western Christianity, 200–1336,* plates 3, 6, 12–16, and 28–32, and Robert M. Durling, "Deceit and Digestion in the Belly of Hell," in *Allegory and Representation,* ed. Stephen J. Greenblatt (Baltimore, 1980), pp. 61–93.For medieval understandings of "matter" as a philosophical concept, see *The Concept of Matter in Greek and Medieval Philosophy* and *The Concept of Matter in Modern Philosophy,* ed. McMullin (Notre Dame, IN, 1963), pp. 5–14.

54 Hermann of Reun, sermon 67, *Sermones festivales,* ed. Edmund Mikkers et al. (Turnhout, 1986), chaps. 4–5, pp. 306–10.

55 Innocent III, *De contemptu mundi sive de miseria humanae conditionis,* in vol. 217 of *Patrologia latina,* ed. J.-P. Migne (Paris, 1890), bk. 1, chaps. 1–5, col. 702. Innocent also says, quoting Jeremiah, "[ist] mihi mater mea sepulcrum" (ibid.). And see the many passages cited in Bultot, *La Doctrine du mépris du monde,* and Delumeau, *Sin and Fear,* pp. 9–34.

56 See Augustine, *The Literal Meaning of Genesis,* trans. and ed. John Hammond Taylor, 2 vols. (New York, 1982), bk. 5, chap. 4, 1:150–53. The idea was repeated in later discussions.

57 See my *The Resurrection of the Body in Western Christianity, 200–1336,* pp. 214–20, and M. D. Lambert, "The Motives of the Cathars: Some Reflections," in *Religious Motivation: Biographical and Sociological Problems for the Church Historian* (Oxford, 1978), pp. 49–59.

58 On this fear of decay, see Piero Camporesi, *The Incorruptible Flesh: Bodily Mutation and Mortification in Religion and Folklore,* trans. Tania Croft-Murray and Helen Elsom (Cambridge, 1988).

59 See Peter Damian, letter 15, *Epistolarum libri octo,* in *Patrologia Latina,* vol. 144, bk. 1, cols. 232D–233A. And see Bultot, *La Doctrine du mépris du monde,* 4:1:25 n. 27.

60 See Richard Heinzmann, *Die Unsterblichkeit der Seele und die Auferstehung des Leibes: Eine problemgeschichtliche Untersuchung der frühscholastischen Sentenzen- und Summenliteratur von Anselm von Laon bis Wilhelm von Auxerre* (Munster, 1965).

61 See Schmitt, *Les Revenants;* Ronald C. Finucane, *Appearances of the Dead: A Cultural History of Ghosts* (London, 1982); Carol Zaleski, *Otherworld Journeys: Accounts of Near-Death Experiences in Medieval and Modern Times* (New York, 1987); and Peter Dinzelbacher, "Reflexionen irdischer Sozialstrukturen in mittelalterlichen Jenseitsschilderungen," *Archiv für Kulturgeschichte* 61, no. 1 (1979): 16–34.

62 See Plato, *The Republic,* trans. Paul Shorey, 2 vols. (Cambridge, MA, 1935), 2:505–21 (10.15–16.617E–621D). In *The Resurrection of the Body in Western Christianity, 200–1336,* I suggest that, in certain ways, the early Christian fear of being eaten was tantamount to a fear of transmigration of souls; see pp. 86–91 and 108–14. See also Kilgour, *From Communion to Cannibalism.*

63 The profession of faith that became the so-called Apostles' Creed required Christians to believe in *resurrectio carnis;* see J. N. D. Kelly, *Early Christian Creeds* (New York, 1950). By the high Middle Ages, this was glossed as meaning: "all rise with their own individual bodies, that is, the bodies which they now wear"; see Heinrich Denzinger, *Enchiridion symbolorum, definitionum, et declarationum de rebus fidei et morum,* 11th ed., ed. Clemens Bannwart (Freiburg, 1911), pp. 189, 202–3.

64 For a survey, see H. Cornélis, et al., *The Resurrection of the Body,* trans. M. Joselyn (Notre Dame, IN, 1964); Joanne E. McWilliam Dewart, *Death and Resurrection* (Wilmington, Del., 1986); Gisbert Greshake and Jacob Kremer, *Resurrectio* *mortuorum: Zum theologischen Verständnis der leiblichen Auferstehung* (Darmstadt, 1986); and Antonius H. C. van Eijk, *La Résurrection des morts chez les pères apostoliques* (Paris, 1974).

65   See Mark Edwards, "Origen No Gnostic; or, On the Corporeality of Man," *Journal of Theological Studies,* n. s., 43 (April, 1992): 23–37, and Elizabeth A. Clark, "New Perspectives on the Origenist Controversy: Human Embodiment and Ascetic Strategies," *Church History* 59 (June, 1990): 145–62.

66   See Vergote, "The Body," pp. 93–105; Quinn, "Aquinas's Concept of the Body and Out of Body Situations," pp. 387–400; Tugwell, *Human Immortality and the Redemption of Death;* and Bernardo C. Bazán, "La Corporalité selon saint Thomas," *Revue philosophique de Louvain* 81, 4th ser., no. 51 (1983): 369–409.

67   Technical theological discussion saw the glorified body as dowered with four gifts: agility (a sort of weightlessness that enabled it to move with the speed of light), subtlety (a sort of incorporeality—if one can use such a term for body), clarity (which seems to have meant beauty), and impassibility (an inability to suffer). These technical terms are carried over into the mystical descriptions of desire I discuss below. On the four dowries, see Nikolaus Wicki, *Die Lehre von der himmlischen Seligkeit in der mittelalterlichen Scholastik von Petrus Lombardus bis Thomas von Aquin* (Freiburg, 1954), and Joseph Goering, "The *De dotibus* of Robert Grosseteste," *Mediaeval Studies* 44 (1982): 83–109.

68   See Dante Alighieri, *Purgatorio,* in *The Divine Comedy,* trans. Charles S. Singleton, 3 vols. (Princeton, NJ, 1977), canto 25, 1:1:269–77. See also Étienne Gilson, "Dante's Notion of a Shade: *Purgatorio* XXV," *Mediaeval Studies* 29 (1967): 124–42; Rachel Jacoff, "Transgression and Transcendence: Figures of Female Desire in Dante's *Commedia,*" *Romantic Review* 29, no. 1 (1988): 129–42, rpt. in *The New Medievalism,* ed. Marina S. Brownlee, Kevin Brownlee, and Stephen G. Nichols (Baltimore, 1991), pp. 183–200; and Bynum, "Faith Imagining the Self: Somatomorphic Soul and Resurrection Body in Dante's *Divine Comedy,*" in *Imagining Faith: A Festschrift for Richard Reinhold Niebuhr,* ed. Wayne Proudfoot, Sang Hyun Lee, and Albert Blackwell (forthcoming).

69   See, for example, Thomas Aquinas, *On First Corinthians,* vol. 21 of *Opera omnia,* ed. S. E. Fretté (Paris, 1876), chap. 15, lect. 2, pp. 33–34: "anima...non est totus homo, et anima mea non est ego." See also Aquinas, *Summa contra Gentiles,* vol. 12 of *Opera omnia,* bk. 4, chap. 79, p. 592 and *Summa theologiae* Ia, trans. and ed. Timothy Suttor (New York, 1970), vol. 11, q. 75, art. 4, reply to obj. 2, pp. 20–21, in both of which Aquinas asserts that the soul is only a part of the person, like the hand or foot. Hence: "It is more correct to say that soul contains body [continet corpus] and makes it to be one, than the converse" (ibid., q. 76, art. 3, pp. 60–61; trans. mod.). By connecting Aristotelianism and sexism, Prudence Allen has raised a very important issue; it is true that the idea of woman as defective man had a long and unfortunate history. But my interpretation of Aquinas's use of Aristotle differs from hers: see Prudence Allen, *The Concept of Woman: The Aristotelian Revolution, 750 B.C.–A.D. 1250* (Montreal, 1985). And see Buc, *L'Ambiguïté du livre,* p. 108.

70   Butler in *Gender Trouble,* citing Foucault, *Discipline and Punish,* comments: "In Foucault's terms, the soul is not imprisoned by or within the body, as some Christian imagery would suggest, but 'the soul is the prison of the body' " (p. 135). She is of course correct that some Christian imagery suggests that the body is a prison; what is interesting here, however, is that there is a sense in which Aquinas makes the same move as Foucault and imprisons body in soul.

71 See Elizabeth A. R. Brown, "Death and the Human Body in the Later Middle Ages: The Legislation of Boniface VIII on the Division of the Corpse," *Viator* 12 (1981): 221–70 and "Authority, the Family, and the Dead in Late Medieval France," *French Historical Studies* 16 (Fall, 1990): 803–32; and Bynum, *The Resurrection of the Body in Western Christianity, 200–1336,* pp. 200–25 and 318–29.

72 See Tugwell, *Human Immortality and the Redemption of Death,* pp. 125–34, and Thomas Head, *Hagiography and the Cult of the Saints: The Diocese of Orleans, 800–1200* (Cambridge, 1990), pp. 144, 268. And see Arnold Angenendt, *"Corpus incorruptum:* Eine Leitidee der mittelalterlichen Reliquienverehrung," *Saeculum* 42, nos. 3–4 (1991): 320–48.

73 See, for example, Goscelin, *Life of St. Ivo,* in *Acta sanctorum,* ed. the Bollandists, *June:* vol. 2 (Paris, 1867), pp. 286–87.

74 See Renée C. Fox and Judith P. Swazey, *The Courage to Fail: A Social View of Organ Transplants and Dialysis* (Chicago, 1974), pp. 27–32.

75 See Bynum, "Images of the Resurrection Body in the Theology of Late Antiquity," *Catholic Historical Review* 80 (April, 1994): 215–37, and Lionel Rothkrug, "German Holiness and Western Sanctity in Medieval and Modern History," *Historical Reflections/Réflexions historiques* 15, no. 1 (1988): 215–29.

76 See Camporesi, *Incorruptible Flesh,* esp. pp. 46–63 and 179–207.

77 See Tugwell, *Human Immortality and the Redemption of Death,* pp. 152–54, and Bynum, *The Resurrection of the Body in Western Christianity, 200–1336,* pp. 164–65, 264–71, and 303–5.

78 See Augustine, *The Literal Meaning of Genesis,* bk. 12, chap. 35, 2:228–29; Peter Lombard, *Sententiae in IV libris distinctae,* 2 vols. (Grottaferrata, 1971), bk. 4, dist. 49, chap. 4, art. 3, 2:553; Bernard of Clairvaux, *De diligendo Deo,* in *Sancti Bernardi Opera,* ed. J. Leclercq and H. M. Rochais, 8 vols. (Rome, 1957–77), chaps. 10–11, 3:143–47; and Bonaventure, *Commentary on the Sentences,* vol. 6 of *Opera omnia,* dist. 49, pt. 2, p. 578.

79 Tugwell, *Human Immortality and the Redemption of Death,* p. 153.

80 There has been much debate over the borrowings and mutual influence of secular and religious literature. On the idea of passion as ecstatic desire and suffering—an idea developed by religious writers—see Erich Auerbach, "Excursus: *Gloria passionis,*" in *Literary Language and Its Public in Late Latin Antiquity and in the Middle Ages,* trans. Ralph Manheim (New York, 1965), pp. 67–81.

81 Dante, *Paradiso,* in *The Divine Comedy,* canto 33, 11. 97–99, 139–45, 3:1:359–81.

82 Angela of Foligno, *Le Livre de l'expérience des vrais fidèles: Texte latin publié d'après le manuscript d'Assise,* ed. M.-J. Ferré and L. Baudry (Paris, 1927), pp. 156–58.

83 See Mechtild of Magdeburg, *Das fliessende Licht der Gottheit: Nach der Einsiedler Handschrift in kritischem Vergleich mit der gesamten Überlieferung,* ed. Hans Neumann (Munich, 1990), esp. p. 222; and see also Marguerite of Oingt, *Les Oeuvres de Marguerite d'Oingt,* ed. Antonin Duraffour, P. Gardette, and P. Durdilly (Paris, 1965).

84 See Karl F. Morrison, *"I Am You": The Hermeneutics of Empathy in Western Literature, Theology, and Art* (Princeton, NJ, 1988) and *Understanding Conversion* (Charlottesville, VA, 1992).

85 On the difference between essentialism of words and of things, see Jane Roland Martin, "Methodological Essentialism, False Difference, and Other Dangerous Traps," and Fuss, *Essentially Speaking.*

86 For examples of resistance to misuses of identity-positions, images, or stereotypes, see Denise Riley, *"Am I That Name?" Feminism and the Category of "Women" in History* (New York, 1989), and Ann duCille, "The Occult of True Black Womanhoood: Critical Demeanor and Black Feminist Studies," *Signs* 19 (Spring, 1994): 591–629.

87 For an early expression of dissatisfaction with the distinction, see Davis and Elizabeth Fox-Genovese, "Call for Papers," *Common Knowledge* 1 (Spring, 1992): 5.

88 See Bordo, *The Flight to Objectivity.*

89 Although I have my own criticisms of Bloch's recent *Medieval Misogyny and the Invention of Western Romantic Love* (chiefly of its failure to take sufficient account of chronological change), I find many of the attacks on it examples of this second type of fallacious charge. For warnings against such attacks, see Jane Roland Martin, "Methodological Essentialism, False Difference, and Other Dangerous Traps," and Bordo, "Feminism, Postmodernism, and Gender-Scepticism."

90 It should be clear that my focus in this article is "body theory," not gender theory. For a survey of recent applications of gender theory to the study of the past, see the important article by Joan W. Scott, "Gender: A Useful Category for Historical Analysis," *American Historical Review* 91 (December, 1986): 1053–75. See also n. 8 above.

91 See Butler, *Bodies That Matter,* pp. 1–11.

92 Those since the Enlightenment are also, of course, important. See, for example, Richard Rorty, "Religion as Conversation-Stopper," *Common Knowledge* 3 (Spring, 1994): 1–6.

93 That a number of recent authors have turned, in a kind of despair, to studying medievalism or medievalists rather than the Middle Ages will be obvious to anyone who reads the journals. A joke going the rounds in anthropological circles makes the point I make here. It is a joke that has only a punch line. The informant says to the anthropologist: "Don't you think it's time we talked about me?"

94 I made the same point four years ago in the introduction to *Fragmentation and Redemption,* pp. 11–16. In *The Flight to Objectivity,* Bordo argues, similarly, that we must be careful lest a rejection of the omniscient observer merely leads feminists to offer arrogant (and inadvertently universalizing) critiques from the margins.

95 See Donna Haraway, "Situated Knowledges: The Science Question in Feminism and the Privilege of Partial Perspective," *Feminist Studies* 14 (Fall, 1988): 575–99. A recent and powerful defense of historical research against the extreme claims of deconstructionism is Joyce Appleby, Lynn Hunt, and Margaret Jacob, *Telling the Truth about History* (New York, 1994); see also Lawrence Stone and Gabrielle M. Spiegel, "History and Post-Modernism," *Past and Present* 135 (May, 1992): 189–208.

96 See John Peckham, *Registrum epistolarum fratris Johannis Peckham, archiepiscopi cantuariensis,* ed. Charles T. Martin, 3 vols. (London, 1882–85), 3:921–23.

97 See Putnam, *Words and Life,* pp. 4–6.

98 For perceptive remarks on our modern fear of death, see Geary, *Living with the Dead in the Middle Ages,* pp. 1–5.

PART THREE

Expanding Boundaries

8

Mestiza Language of Religion: Gloria Anzaldúa

a. Introduction

Gloria Anzaldúa (1942–2004) was a Chicana, feminist, lesbian poet, essayist, and activist whose work on borderlands, indigenous spirituality, and questioning of lesbian woman of color identity have pushed scholars toward intersectional analyses of religious traditions. She died from diabetes-related complications while she was in the process of completing her PhD in literature at the University of California, Santa Cruz. As her work reveals, her death cannot be understood outside of the institutionalized structures of whiteness, straightness, capitalism, and nationalism. Anzaldúa is considered to be one of the most formative figures who insisted that race, nation, sexuality, gender, imperialism, and capital could not be analytically separated. Reading her work is likely to be an experience unlike the rest of the selections gathered in this volume. One of Anzaldúa's biographers writes: "She wanted the words to move in readers' bodies and transform them, from the inside out, and she revised repeatedly to achieve this impact. She revised for cadence, musicality, nuanced meaning, and metaphoric complexity" (Anzaldúa 2015: xii). Anzaldúa uses the histories and languages that coalesce in her own body as an entré to theorizing interpersonal and social relationships.

In the selection, "La Conciencia de la Mestiza/Towards a New Consciousness" ([1987] 2007), Anzaldúa stops consistently translating into English the Spanish she uses to craft her point. There are words, phrases, and sentences that remain in Spanish; this movement between English and Spanish a space of flexibility and fluidity in reading for the reader who is fluent in Spanish. For the reader who does not know Spanish, these spaces tend to mark disruption, difficulty, and perhaps frustration. This linguistic combination unfolds through her continued use of autobiography, developing further key themes such as "*la raza cósmica*" from which the "*mestiza*," emerges—a specific, unique entity she simultaneously analyzes and calls into existence along with the *mestiza*'s new consciousness. The Spanish-English language relationship that points to both fluidity and difficulty shows what Anzaldúa means when she writes about ambiguity and *mestiza* as method. She notes that ambiguity causes "a swamping of her psychological borders . . . [and/yet] the new *mestiza* copes by developing a tolerance for contradictions, a tolerance for ambiguity . . . [and/yet] she can be jarred out of ambivalence" ([1987] 2007: 101). Even the role that ambiguity plays provides no clear-cut answer or single shape. Anzaldúa describes multiple borderlands—geographical, sexual, racial, linguistic, and religious— and the complexity present in each instance. Methodologically, the scholar of religion is challenged to learn from personal narrative and then move beyond to identify other site-specific, local, social, historical, and individual forces in power at a given time. Looking at life on the Mexico-Texas border, Anzaldúa explains: "Cradled in one culture, sandwiched between two cultures, straddling all three cultures and their value systems, *la mestiza* undergoes a struggle of flesh, a struggle of borders, an inner war" ([1987] 2018: 155). Being attentive to such a constellation of aspects that produce creativity and violence acknowledges the realities of borders present in every situation, necessarily nuancing explorations of religious traditions.

Anzaldúa assumes religion to be an integral aspect when writing about identity, such that it is not merely added on as another feature to a previously existing, self-contained person. As becomes clear throughout her writings, rituals such as the December 2 celebration of "*el día de la Chicana y Chicano*" and deities such as Coatlalopeuh and Coatlicue are as deeply tied to one's sense of self. Such religious, cultural traditions and celebrations are as important and interrelated to a person's identity as who one loves and sleeps with, where one is born and the physical land of 'home,' and what language one speaks, dreams, and writes in. Because of this dense integration of religion, history, family, race, and nation as features of identity, Anzaldúa's work provides rich theoretical engagement for the scholar of religion. Anzaldúa offers herself as an object—as a primary source—which can be set in dialogue with other traditions and other stories. This is distinct from the way that Doniger places herself within the external tradition she analyzes. Anzaldúa claims the kinship and intimacy of a practitioner, which has a different set of implications than residing in the scholarly position. Yet, Anzaldúa is not only herself a primary source; she also provides a constructive synthesis or framework that other scholars can follow in form. In this second role, scholars studying religion create and identify new aspects of their own work when they look at borderlands and bring together figures, traditions, and materials that are still too often separated by scholarly work.

b. La conciencia de la mestiza/Towards a New Consciousness (*Borderlands/La Frontera: The New Mestiza*) *Gloria Anzaldúa*

Por la mujer de mi raza hablará el espíritu.[1]

José Vasconcelos, Mexican philosopher, envisaged *una raza mestiza, una mezcla de razas afines, una raza de color—la primera raza síntesis del globo.* He called it a cosmic race, *la raza cósmica,* a fifth race embracing the four major races of the world.[2] Opposite to the theory of the pure Aryan, and to the policy of racial purity that white America practices, his theory is one of inclusivity. At the confluence of two or more genetic streams, with chromosomes constantly "crossing over," this mixture of races, rather than resulting in an inferior being, provides hybrid progeny, a mutable, more malleable species with a rich gene pool. From this racial, ideological, cultural and biological cross-pollinization, an "alien" consciousness is presently in the making—a new *mestiza* consciousness, *una conciencia de mujer.* It is a consciousness of the Borderlands.

Una Lucha de Fronteras / *A Struggle of Borders*

Because I, a *mestiza,*
continually walk out of one culture and into another,
because I am in all cultures at the same time, *alma entre dos mundos, tres,*
cuatro, me zumba la cabeza con lo contradictorio. Estoy norteada por todas las
voces que me hablan simultáneamente.

The ambivalence from the clash of voices results in mental and emotional states of perplexity. Internal strife results in insecurity and indecisiveness. The *mestiza's* dual or multiple personality is plagued by psychic restlessness.

In a constant state of mental nepantilism, an Aztec word meaning torn between ways, *la mestiza* is a product of the transfer of the cultural and spiritual values of one group to another. Being tricultural, monolingual, bilingual, or multilingual, speaking a patois, and in a state of perpetual transition, the *mestiza* faces the dilemma of the mixed breed: which collectivity does the daughter of a darkskinned mother listen to?

El choque de un alma atrapado entre el mundo del espíritu y el mundo de la técnica *a veces la deja entullada.* Cradled in one culture, sandwiched between two cultures, straddling all three cultures and their value systems, *la mestiza* undergoes a struggle of flesh, a struggle of borders, an inner war. Like all people, we perceive the version of reality that our culture communicates. Like others having or living in more than one culture, we get multiple, often opposing messages. The coming together of two self-consistent but habitually incompatible frames of reference[3] causes *un choque,* a cultural collision.

Within us and within *la cultura chicana,* commonly held beliefs of the white culture attack commonly held beliefs of the Mexican culture, and both attack commonly held beliefs of the indigenous culture. Subconsciously, we see an attack on ourselves and our beliefs as a threat and we attempt to block with a counterstance.

But it is not enough to stand on the opposite river bank, shouting questions, challenging patriarchal, white conventions. A counterstance locks one into a duel of oppressor and oppressed; locked in mortal combat, like the cop and the criminal, both are reduced to a common denominator of violence. The counterstance refutes the dominant culture's views and beliefs, and, for this, it is proudly defiant. All reaction is limited by, and dependent on, what it is reacting against. Because the counterstance stems from a problem with authority—outer as well as inner—it's a step towards liberation from cultural domination. But it is not a way of life. At some point, on our way to a new consciousness, we will have to leave the opposite bank, the split between the two mortal combatants somehow healed so that we are on both shores at once and, at once, see through serpent and eagle eyes. Or perhaps we will decide to disengage from the dominant culture, write it off altogether as a lost cause, and cross the border into a wholly new and separate territory. Or we might go another route. The possibilities are numerous once we decide to act and not react.

A Tolerance for Ambiguity

These numerous possibilities leave *la mestiza* floundering in uncharted seas. In perceiving conflicting information and points of view, she is subjected to a swamping of her psychological borders. She has discovered that she can't hold concepts or ideas in rigid boundaries. The borders and walls that are supposed to keep the undesirable ideas out are entrenched habits and patterns of behavior; these habits and patterns are the enemy within. Rigidity means death. Only by remaining flexible is she able to stretch the psyche horizontally and vertically. *La mestiza* constantly has to shift out of habitual formations; from convergent thinking, analytical reasoning that tends to use rationality to move toward a single goal (a Western mode), to divergent thinking,[4] characterized by movement away from set patterns and goals and toward a more whole perspective, one that includes rather than excludes.

The new *mestiza* copes by developing a tolerance for contradictions, a tolerance for ambiguity. She learns to be an Indian in Mexican culture, to be Mexican from an Anglo point of view. She learns to juggle cultures. She has a plural personality, she operates in a pluralistic mode—nothing is thrust out, the good the bad and the ugly, nothing rejected, nothing abandoned. Not only does she sustain contradictions, she turns the ambivalence into something else.

She can be jarred out of ambivalence by an intense, and often painful, emotional event which inverts or resolves the ambivalence. I'm not sure exactly how. The work takes place underground—subconsciously. It is work that the soul performs. That focal point or fulcrum, that juncture where the *mestiza* stands, is where phenomena tend to collide. It is where the possibility of uniting all that is separate occurs. This assembly is not one where severed or separated pieces merely come together. Nor is it a balancing of opposing powers. In attempting to work out a synthesis, the self has added a third element which is greater than the sum of its severed parts. That third element is a new consciousness—a *mestiza* consciousness—and though it is a source of intense pain, its energy comes from continual creative motion that keeps breaking down the unitary aspect of each new paradigm.

En unas pocas centurias, the future will belong to the *mestiza.* Because the future depends on the breaking down of paradigms, it depends on the straddling of two or more cultures. By creating a new mythos—that is, a change in the way we perceive reality, the way we see ourselves, and the ways we behave—*la mestiza* creates a new consciousness.

The work of *mestiza* consciousness is to break down the subject-object duality that keeps her a prisoner and to show in the flesh and through the images in her work how duality is transcended. The answer to the problem between the white race and the colored, between males and females, lies in healing the split that originates in the very foundation of our lives, our culture, our languages, our thoughts. A massive uprooting of dualistic thinking in the individual and collective consciousness is the beginning of a long struggle, but one that could, in our best hopes, bring us to the end of rape, of violence, of war.

La encrucijada / *The Crossroads*

A chicken is being sacrificed
    at a crossroads, a simple mound of earth
a mud shrine for *Eshu,*
    Yoruba god of indeterminacy,
who blesses her choice of path.
    She begins her journey.

Su cuerpo es una bocacalle. La mestiza has gone from being the sacrificial goat to becoming the officiating priestess at the crossroads.

As a *mestiza* I have no country, my homeland cast me out; yet all countries are mine because I am every woman's sister or potential lover. (As a lesbian I have no race, my own people disclaim me; but I am all races because there is the queer of me in all races.) I am cultureless because, as a feminist, I challenge the collective cultural/religious male-derived beliefs of Indo-Hispanics and Anglos; yet I am cultured because I am participating in the creation of yet another culture, a new story to explain the world and our participation in it, a new value system with images and symbols that connect us to each other and to the planet. *Soy un amasamiento,* I am an act of kneading, of uniting and joining that not only has produced both a creature of darkness and a creature of light, but also a creature that questions the definitions of light and dark and gives them new meanings.

We are the people who leap in the dark, we are the people on the knees of the gods. In our very flesh, (r)evolution works out the clash of cultures. It makes us crazy constantly, but if the center holds, we've made some kind of evolutionary step forward. *Nuestra alma el trabajo,* the opus, the great alchemical work; spiritual *mestizaje,* a "morphogenesis,"[5] an inevitable unfolding. We have become the quickening serpent movement.

Indigenous like corn, like corn, the *mestiza* is a product of crossbreeding, designed for preservation under a variety of conditions. Like an ear of corn—a female seed-bearing organ—the *mestiza* is tenacious, tightly wrapped in the husks of her culture. Like kernels she clings to the cob; with thick stalks and strong brace roots, she holds tight to the earth—she will survive the crossroads.

Lavando y remojando el maíz en agua de cal, despojando el pellejo. Moliendo, mixteando, amasando, haciendo tortillas de masa.[6] She steeps the corn in lime, it swells, softens. With stone roller on *metate,* she grinds the corn, then grinds again. She kneads and moulds the dough, pats the round balls into *tortillas.*

> We are the porous rock in the stone *metate*
> squatting on the ground.
> We are the rolling pin, *el maíz y agua,*
> *la masa harina. Somos el amasijo.*
> *Somos lo molido en el metate.*
> We are the *comal* sizzling hot,
> the hot *tortilla,* the hungry mouth.
> We are the coarse rock.
> We are the grinding motion,
> the mixed potion, *somos el molcajete.*
> We are the pestle, the *comino, ajo, pimienta,*
> We are the *chile colorado,*
> the green shoot that cracks the rock.
> We will abide.

El camino de la mestiza / *The Mestiza Way*

Caught between the sudden contraction, the breath sucked in and the endless space, the brown woman stands still, looks at the sky. She decides to go down, digging her way along the roots of trees. Sifting through the bones, she shakes them to see if there is any marrow in them. Then, touching the dirt to her forehead, to her tongue, she takes a few bones, leaves the rest in their burial place.

She goes through her backpack, keeps her journal and address book, throws away the muni-bart metromaps. The coins are heavy and they go next, then the greenbacks flutter through the air. She keeps her knife, can opener and eyebrow pencil. She puts bones, pieces of bark, *hierbas,* eagle feather, snakeskin, tape recorder, the rattle and drum in her pack and she sets out to become the complete *tolteca.*

Her first step is to take inventory. *Despojando, desgranando, quitando paja.* Just what did she inherit from her ancestors? This weight on her back—which is the baggage from the Indian mother, which the baggage from the Spanish father, which the baggage from the Anglo?

Pero es difícil differentiating between *lo heredado, lo adquirido, lo impuesto.* She puts history through a sieve, winnows out the lies, looks at the forces that we as a race, as women, have been a part of. *Luego bota lo que no vale, los desmientos, los desencuentos, el embrutecimiento. Aguarda el juicio, hondo y enraízado, de la gente antigua.* This step is a conscious rupture with all oppressive traditions of all cultures and religions. She communicates that rupture, documents the struggle. She reinterprets history and, using new symbols, she shapes new myths. She adopts new perspectives toward the darkskinned, women and queers. She strengthens her tolerance (and intolerance) for ambiguity. She is willing to share, to make herself vulnerable to foreign ways of seeing and thinking. She surrenders all notions of safety, of the familiar. Deconstruct, construct. She becomes a *nahual,* able to transform herself into a tree, a coyote, into another person. She learns to transform the small "I" into the total Self. *Se hace moldeadora de su alma. Según la concepción que tiene de sí misma, así será.*

Que no se nos olviden los hombres

"Tú no sirves pa'nada—
you're good for nothing.
Eres pura vieja."

"You're nothing but a woman" means you are defective. Its opposite is to be *un macho.* The modern meaning of the word "machismo," as well as the concept, is actually an Anglo invention. For men like my father, being "macho" meant being strong enough to protect and support my mother and us, yet being able to show love. Today's macho has doubts about his ability to feed and protect his family. His "machismo" is an adaptation to oppression and poverty and low self-esteem. It is the result of hierarchical male dominance. The Anglo, feeling inadequate and inferior and powerless, displaces or transfers these feelings to the Chicano by shaming him. In the Gringo world, the Chicano suffers from excessive humility and self-effacement, shame of self and self-deprecation. Around Latinos he suffers from a sense of language inadequacy and its accompanying discomfort; with Native Americans he suffers from a racial amnesia which ignores our common blood, and from guilt because the Spanish part of him took their land and oppressed them. He has an excessive compensatory hubris when around Mexicans from the other side. It overlays a deep sense of racial shame.

The loss of a sense of dignity and respect in the macho breeds a false machismo which leads him to put down women and even to brutalize them. Coexisting with his sexist behavior is a love for the mother which takes precedence over that of all others. Devoted son, macho pig. To wash down the shame of his acts, of his very being, and to handle the brute in the mirror, he takes to the bottle, the snort, the needle, and the fist.

Though we "understand" the root causes of male hatred and fear, and the subsequent wounding of women, we do not excuse, we do not condone, and we will no longer put up with it. From the men of our race, we demand the admission/ acknowledgment/disclosure/testimony that they wound us, violate us, are afraid of us and of our power. We need them to say they will begin to eliminate their hurtful put-down ways. But more than the words, we demand acts. We say to them: We will develop equal power with you and those who have shamed us.

It is imperative that *mestizas* support each other in changing the sexist elements in the Mexican-Indian culture. As long as woman is put down, the Indian and the Black in all of us is put down. The struggle of the *mestiza* is above all a feminist one. As long as *los hombres* think they have to *chingar mujeres* and each other to be men, as long as men are taught that they are superior and therefore culturally favored over *la mujer,* as long as to be a *vieja* is a thing of derision, there can be no real healing of our psyches. We're halfway there—we have such love of the Mother, the good mother. The first step is to unlearn the *puta/virgen* dichotomy and to see *Coatlalopeuh-Coatlicue* in the Mother, *Guadalupe.*

Tenderness, a sign of vulnerability, is so feared that it is showered on women with verbal abuse and blows. Men, even more than women, are fettered to gender roles. Women at least have had the guts to break out of bondage. Only gay men have had the courage to expose themselves to the woman inside them and to challenge the current masculinity. I've encountered a few scattered and isolated gentle straight men, the beginnings of a new breed, but they are confused, and entangled with sexist behaviors that they have not been able to eradicate. We need a new masculinity and the new man needs a movement.

Lumping the males who deviate from the general norm with man, the oppressor, is a gross injustice. *Asombra pensar que nos hemos quedado en ese pozo oscuro donde el mundo encierra a las lesbianas. Asombra pensar que hemos, como femenistas y lesbianas, cerrado nuestros corazónes a los hombres, a nuestros hermanos los jotos, desheredados y marginales como nosotros.* Being the supreme crossers of cultures, homosexuals have strong bonds with the queer white, Black, Asian, Native American, Latino, and with the queer in Italy, Australia and the rest of the planet. We come from all colors, all classes, all races, all time periods. Our role is to link people with each other— the Blacks with Jews with Indians with Asians with whites with extraterrestrials. It is to transfer ideas and information from one culture to another. Colored homosexuals have more knowledge of other cultures; have always been at the forefront (although sometimes in the closet) of all liberation struggles in this country; have suffered more injustices and have survived them despite all odds. Chicanos need to acknowledge the political and artistic contributions of their queer. People, listen to what *your jotería* is saying.

The *mestizo* and the queer exist at this time and point on the evolutionary continuum for a purpose. We are a blending that proves that all blood is intricately woven together, and that we are spawned out of similar souls.

Somos una gente

Hay tantísimas fronteras
que dividen a la gente,
pero por cada frontera
existe también un puente.

—Gina Valdés[7]

<u>Divided Loyalties</u>. Many women and men of color do not want to have any dealings with white people. It takes too much time and energy to explain to the downwardly mobile, white middle-class women that it's okay for us to want to own "possessions," never having had any nice furniture on our dirt floors or "luxuries" like washing machines. Many feel that whites should help their own people rid themselves of race hatred and fear first. I, for one, choose to use some of my energy to serve as mediator. I think we need to allow whites to be our allies. Through our literature, art, *corridos*, and folktales we must share our history with them so when they set up committees to help Big Mountain Navajos or the Chicano farmworkers or *los Nicaragüenses* they won't turn people away because of their racial fears and ignorances. They will come to see that they are not helping us but following our lead.

Individually, but also as a racial entity, we need to voice our needs. We need to say to white society: We need you to accept the fact that Chicanos are different, to acknowledge your rejection and negation of us. We need you to own the fact that you looked upon us as less than human, that you stole our lands, our personhood, our self-respect. We need you to make public restitution: to say that, to compensate for your own sense of defectiveness, you strive for power over us, you erase our history and our experience because it makes you feel guilty—you'd rather forget your brutish acts. To say you've split yourself from minority groups, that you disown us, that your dual consciousness splits off parts of yourself, transferring the "negative" parts onto us. (Where there is persecution of minorities, there is shadow projection. Where there is violence and war, there is repression of shadow.) To say that you are afraid of us, that to put distance between us, you wear the mask of contempt. Admit that Mexico is your double, that she exists in the shadow of this country, that we are irrevocably tied to her. Gringo, accept the doppelganger in your psyche. By taking back your collective shadow the intra-cultural split will heal. And finally, tell us what you need from us.

By Your True Faces We Will Know You

I am visible—see this Indian face—yet I am invisible. I both blind them with my beak nose and am their blind spot. But I exist, we exist. They'd like to think I have melted in the pot. But I haven't, we haven't.

The dominant white culture is killing us slowly with its ignorance. By taking away our self-determination, it has made us weak and empty. As a people we have resisted and we have taken expedient positions, but we have never been allowed to develop unencumbered—we have never been allowed to be fully ourselves. The whites in power want us people of color to barricade ourselves behind our separate tribal walls so they can pick us off one at a time with their hidden weapons; so they can whitewash and distort history. Ignorance splits people, creates prejudices. A misinformed people is a subjugated people.

Before the Chicano and the undocumented worker and the Mexican from the other side can come together, before the Chicano can have unity with Native Americans and other groups, we need to know the history of their struggle and they need to know ours. Our mothers, our sisters and brothers, the guys who hang out on street corners, the children in the playgrounds, each of us must know our Indian lineage, our afro-*mestizaje,* our history of resistance.

To the immigrant *mexicano* and the recent arrivals we must teach our history. The 80 million *mexicanos* and the Latinos from Central and South America must know of our struggles. Each one of us must know basic facts about Nicaragua, Chile and the rest of Latin America. The Latinoist movement (Chicanos, Puerto Ricans, Cubans and other Spanish-speaking people working together to combat racial discrimination in the marketplace) is good but it is not enough. Other than a common culture we will have nothing to hold us together. We need to meet on a broader communal ground.

The struggle is inner: Chicano, *indio,* American Indian, *mojado, mexicano,* immigrant Latino, Anglo in power, working class Anglo, Black, Asian—our psyches resemble the bordertowns and are populated by the same people. The struggle has always been inner, and is played out in the outer terrains. Awareness of our situation must come before inner changes, which in turn come before changes in society. Nothing happens in the "real" world unless it first happens in the images in our heads.

El día de la Chicana

I will not be shamed again
Nor will I shame myself.

I am possessed by a vision: that we Chicanas and Chicanos have taken back or uncovered our true faces, our dignity and self-respect. It's a validation vision.

Seeing the Chicana anew in light of her history. I seek an exoneration, a seeing through the fictions of white supremacy, a seeing of ourselves in our true guises and not as the false racial personality that has been given to us and that we have given to ourselves. I seek our woman's face, our true features, the positive and the negative seen clearly, free of the tainted biases of male dominance. I seek new images of identity, new beliefs about ourselves, our humanity and worth no longer in question.

Estamos viviendo en la noche de la Raza, un tiempo cuando el trabajo se hace a lo quieto, en lo oscuro. El día cuando aceptamos tal y como somos y para donde vamos y porque—ese día será el día de la Raza. Yo tengo el conpromiso de expresar mi visión, mi sensibilidad, mi percepción de la revalidación de la gente mexicana, su mérito, estimación, honra, aprecio, y validez.

On December 2nd when my sun goes into my first house, I celebrate *el día de la Chicana y el Chicano.* On that day I clean my altars, light my *Coatlalopeuh* candle, burn sage and copal, take *el baño para espantar basura,* sweep my house. On that day I bare my soul, make myself vulnerable to friends and family by expressing my feelings. On that day I affirm who we are.

On that day I look inside our conflicts and our basic introverted racial temperament. I identify our needs, voice them. I acknowledge that the self and the race have been wounded. I recognize the need to take care of our personhood, of our racial self. On that day I gather the splintered and disowned parts of *la gente mexicana* and hold them in my arms. *Todas las partes de nosotros valen.*

On that day I say, "Yes, all you people wound us when you reject us. Rejection strips us of self-worth; our vulnerability exposes us to shame. It is our innate identity you find wanting. We are ashamed that we need your good opinion, that we need your acceptance. We can no longer camouflage our needs, can no longer let defenses and fences sprout around us. We can no longer withdraw. To rage and look upon you with contempt is to rage and be contemptuous of ourselves. We can no longer blame you, nor disown the white parts, the male parts, the pathological parts, the queer parts, the vulnerable parts. Here we are weaponless with open arms, with only our magic. Let's try it our way, the *mestiza* way, the Chicana way, the woman way."

On that day, I search for our essential dignity as a people, a people with a sense of purpose—to belong and contribute to something greater than our *pueblo.* On that day I seek to recover and reshape my spiritual identity. *¡Anímate! Raza, a celebrar el día de la Chicana.*

El retorno

> All movements are accomplished in six stages,
> and the seventh brings return.
>
> —I Ching[8]

> *Tanto tiempo sin verte casa mía,*
> *mi cuna, mi hondo nido de la huerta.*
>
> — "Soledad"[9]

I stand at the river, watch the curving, twisting serpent, a serpent nailed to the fence where the mouth of the Rio Grande empties into the Gulf.

I have come back. *Tanto dolor me costó el alejamiento.* I shade my eyes and look up. The bone beak of a hawk slowly circling over me, checking me out as potential carrion. In its wake a little bird flickering its wings, swimming sporadically like a fish. In the distance the expressway and the slough of traffic like an irritated sow. The sudden pull in my gut, *la tierra, los aguaceros*. My land, *el viento soplando la arena, el lagartijo debajo de un nopalito. Me acuerdo como era antes. Una región desértica de vasta llanuras, costeras de baja altura, de escasa lluvia, de chaparrales formados por mesquites y huizaches.* If I look real hard I can almost see the Spanish fathers who were called "the cavalry of Christ" enter this valley riding their *burros,* see the clash of cultures commence.

Tierra natal. This is home, the small towns in the Valley, *los pueblitos* with chicken pens and goats picketed to mesquite shrubs. *En las colonias* on the other side of the tracks, junk cars line the front yards of hot pink and lavender-trimmed houses— Chicano architecture we call it, self-consciously. I have missed the TV shows where hosts speak in half and half, and where awards are given in the category of Tex-Mex music. I have missed the Mexican cemeteries blooming with artificial flowers, the fields of aloe vera and red pepper, rows of sugar cane, of corn hanging on the stalks, the cloud of *polvareda* in the dirt roads behind a speeding pickup truck, *el sabor de tamales de rez y venado.* I have missed *la yegua colorada* gnawing the wooden gate of her stall, the smell of horse flesh from Carito's corrals. *Hecho menos las noches calientes sin aire, noches de linternas y lechuzas* making holes in the night.

I still feel the old despair when I look at the unpainted, dilapidated, scrap lumber houses consisting mostly of corrugated aluminum. Some of the poorest people in the U.S. live in the Lower Rio Grande Valley, an arid and semi-arid land of irrigated farming, intense sunlight and heat, citrus groves next to chaparral and cactus. I walk through the elementary school I attended so long ago, that remained segregated until recently. I remember how the white teachers used to punish us for being Mexican.

How I love this tragic valley of South Texas, as Ricardo Sánchez calls it; this borderland between the Nueces and the Rio Grande. This land has survived possession and ill-use by five countries: Spain, Mexico, the Republic of Texas, the U.S., the Confederacy, and the U.S. again. It has survived Anglo-Mexican blood feuds, lynchings, burnings, rapes, pillage.

Today I see the Valley still struggling to survive. Whether it does or not, it will never be as I remember it. The borderlands depression that was set off by the 1982 peso devaluation in Mexico resulted in the closure of hundreds of Valley businesses. Many people lost their homes, cars, land. Prior to 1982, U.S. store owners thrived on retail sales to Mexicans who came across the border for groceries and clothes and appliances. While goods on the U.S. side have become 10, 100, 1000 times more expensive for Mexican buyers, goods on the Mexican side have become 10, 100, 1000 times cheaper for Americans. Because the Valley is heavily dependent on agriculture and Mexican retail trade, it has the highest unemployment rates along the entire border region; it is the Valley that has been hardest hit.[10]

"It's been a bad year for corn," my brother, Nune, says. As he talks, I remember my father scanning the sky for a rain that would end the drought, looking up into the sky, day after day, while the corn withered on its stalk. My father has been dead for 29 years, having worked himself to death. The life span of a Mexican farm laborer is 56—he lived to be 38. It shocks me that I am older than he. I, too, search the sky for rain. Like the ancients, I worship the rain god and the maize goddess, but unlike my father I have recovered their names. Now for rain (irrigation) one offers not a sacrifice of blood, but of money.

"Farming is in a bad way," my brother says. "Two to three thousand small and big farmers went bankrupt in this country last year. Six years ago the price of corn was $8.00 per hundred pounds," he goes on. "This year it is $3.90 per hundred pounds." And, I think to myself, after taking inflation into account, not planting anything puts you ahead.

I walk out to the back yard, stare at *los rosales de mamá.* She wants me to help her prune the rose bushes, dig out the carpet grass that is choking them. *Mamagrande Ramona también tenía rosales.* Here every Mexican grows flowers. If they don't have a piece of dirt, they use car tires, jars, cans, shoe boxes. Roses are the Mexican's favorite flower. I think, how symbolic—thorns and all.

Yes, the Chicano and Chicana have always taken care of growing things and the land. Again I see the four of us kids getting off the school bus, changing into our work clothes, walking into the field with Papi and Mami, all six of us bending to the ground. Below our feet, under the earth lie the watermelon seeds. We cover them with paper plates, putting *terremotes* on top of the plates to keep them from being blown away by the wind. The paper plates keep the freeze away. Next day or the next, we remove the plates, bare the tiny green shoots to the elements. They survive and grow, give fruit hundreds of times the size of the seed. We water them and hoe them. We harvest them. The vines dry, rot, are plowed under. Growth, death, decay, birth. The soil prepared again and again, impregnated, worked on. A constant changing of forms, *renacimientos de la tierra madre.*

> This land was Mexican once
> was Indian always
> and is.
> And will be again.

c. Questions

Comprehension

1. What are the benefits of ambiguity for Anzaldúa?

2. If you don't already know what it says, spend some time working to translate Anzaldúa's statement: "Estamos viviendo en la noche de la Raza, un tiempo cuando el trabajo se hace a lo quieto, en lo oscuro" ([1987] 2018: 186). Explain what she means.

3. What does Anzaldúa mean when she directs the United States to "admit that Mexico is your double, that she exists in the shadow of this country, that we are irrevocably tied to her" ([1987] 2018: 161)?

Analysis

4. What is your response to Anzaldúa's claim: "Nothing happens in the 'real' world unless it first happens in the images in our heads" ([1986] 2018: 162).

Synthesis

5. What are some of the differences (if any) between Anzaldúa's use of Spanish and Nahuatl in her writings and other scholars, such as Doniger, who include non-English terms in their analyses? What is the purpose for each author in including these languages?

Notes

1 This is my own "take off" on José Vasconcelos' idea. José Vasconcelos, *La Raza Cósmica: Misión de la Raza Ibero-Americana* (México: Aguilar S.A. de Ediciones, 1961).

2 Vasconcelos.

3 Arthur Koestler termed this "bisociation." Albert Rothenberg, *The Creative Process in Art. Science, and Other Fields* (Chicago, IL: University of Chicago Press, 1979), p. 12.

4 In part, I derive my definitions for "convergent" and "divergent" thinking from Rothenberg, pp. 12–13.

5 To borrow chemist Ilya Prigogine's theory of "dissipative structures." Prigogine discovered that substances interact not in predictable ways as it was taught in science, but in different and fluctuating ways to produce new and more complex structures, a kind of birth he called "morphogenesis," which created unpredictable innovations. Harold Gilliam, "Searching for a New World View," *This World* (January, 1981), 23.

6 *Tortillas de masa harina:* corn tortillas are of two types, the smooth uniform ones made in a tortilla press and usually bought at a tortilla factory or supermarket, and *gorditas,* made by mixing *masa* with lard or shortening or butter (my mother sometimes puts in bits of bacon or *chicharrones*).

7 Gina Valdés, *Puentes y Fronteras: Coplas Chicanas* (Los Angeles, CA: Castle Lithograph, 1982), p. 2.

8 Richard Wilhelm, *The I Ching or Book of Changes*, trans. Cary F. Baynes (Princeton, NJ: Princeton University Press, 1950), p. 98.

9 *"Soledad"* is sung by the group *Haciendo Punto en Otro Son.*

10 Out of the twenty-two border counties in the four border states, Hidalgo County (named for Father Hidalgo who was shot in 1810 after instigating Mexico's revolt against Spanish rule under the banner of *la Virgen de Guadalupe*) is the most poverty-stricken county in the nation as well as the largest home base (along with Imperial in California) for migrant farmworkers. It was here that I was born and raised. I am amazed that both it and I have survived.

9

Performative, Queer Theories for Religion: Judith Butler

a. Introduction

Judith Butler (1956–) is a philosopher whose writings challenge accepted notions of gender, sexuality, subjectivity, and secularism. Trained at Yale University, Butler has been the Maxine Elliot Professor in the Department of Comparative Literature and the Program of Critical Theory at the University of California, Berkley, since 1998. She has authored over a dozen books, collaborated as coeditor and coauthor with a wide range of scholars, and maintains an international academic and activist presence. Among her distinctions, Butler was both a Guggenheim Fellow and a Fellow at the Institute for Advanced Study at Princeton and has received nine honorary degrees. The selection here comes from *Gender Trouble*, highlighting Butler's early emphasis on the formation and maintenance of gendered subjects.

The selection from *Gender Trouble: Feminism and the Subversion of Identity*, "Bodily Inscriptions, Performative Subversions" ([1990] 2006), presents a set of difficulties that Butler wrestles with in her writings over the following decades, namely how to conceptualize and interpret the body and the production/performance of the subject. According to Butler, one mistake that emerges in formulating identity categories arises from a misreading of the body as a pre-given biological reality, which external cultural forces shape. In other words, Butler argues that assigning "sex" as a biological given and "gender" as a cultural category read onto the sexed body is an unhelpful and problematic division. Butler writes: "The sex/gender distinction and the category of sex itself appear to presuppose a generalization of 'the body' that preexists the acquisition of its sexed significance" ([1990] 2018: 169). Assuming a foundational, stable "body" that exists as if in a vacuum chamber, simply waiting for culture to be added on to it is part of the problematic presupposition; assuming that this pre-cultural body is either biologically male or female is what reinforces the seemingly immutable gender binary—a binary that ultimately reinforces compulsory heterosexuality. This mistake subsequently carries forth into creating political, social, and interpersonal hierarchies. Where other scholars suggest a distinction between nature and nurture,

Butler argues that what appears to be natural is actually nurtured. The personal and social forces that inextricably link cultural interpretations of the body with identity (female/male, homosexual/heterosexual) can be used to identify forces at work in religious traditions.

The sex/gender distinction continues to operate because it relies on a whole constellation of other distinctions associated with it. Butler proposes that traditional binary thinking—inner/outer, self/other, male/female, nature/culture ([1990] 2006: 182–183)—sets up a false opposition in which one category is presumed to be the "original" while the other is a mere (and thus devalued) "copy." Combining psychoanalytic argument, structural linguistics, and Hegelian philosophy, Butler shows the circularity, and hence failure, of the origin-copy argument. Revealing, then challenging, the notion of relationship is a foundational theme to the assumptions and arguments Butler crafts—philosophy and culture have no concept of female without male, no homosexuality without heterosexuality. Because nothing exists outside of relationship, because nothing takes it identity in a vacuum, we cannot make pure assertions about the "being" (or ontology) of a single subject. In other words, "man" relies on the opposite conceptual category of "woman." Yet, this creation-through-opposition does not happen only once at the moment of birth and it is not attached to specific genitalia. Rather, as Butler argues, interpretation of bodies as sexed/gendered is a "construction that regularly conceals its genesis . . . the construction 'compels' our belief in its necessity and naturalness" ([1990] 2006: 190).

Drag is one mechanism that Butler uses to reveal the ongoing production of discrete categories of gender, sex, and sexuality to illustrate a philosophically dense argument. The tendency when thinking about drag is to revert to binary categories of the body of the drag performer as one aspect and the clothes/accouterments donned by the performer as another distinct aspect. Yet, Butler argues that this binary is not accurate. We must realize that the subject only comes to subjectivity through the embodied, enclothed, ensouled repetition of thought and action in relation to a larger matrix of preestablished rules and expectations. Drag proves to be illustrative because its performative attempt to draw close to gendered norms "implicitly reveals the imitative structure of gender itself—as well as its contingency" (Butler [1990] 2006: 187). She acknowledges in another article: "To claim that there is no performer prior to the performed, that the performance is performative, that the performance constitutes the appearance of the 'subject' as its effect is difficult to accept. This difficulty is the result of a predisposition to think of sexuality and gender as 'expressing' in some indirect or direct way a psychic reality that precedes it" (Butler 1993: 315). Humans do not exist apart from their actions, thoughts, interactions, decisions, and relationships; there is no "psychic reality" that ever exists untouched by the world.

Butler's queer performativity offers a theory for studying religion, leading to questions about repetition with which scholars across the field of religious studies continue to wrestle. For example, how does a ritual or a set of relationships not only reproduce itself, but what acts, assumptions, and histories of gendered power does it rely on to come to fruition? Butler's methods also prompt questions about structural relationships in religious acts and ideas: what must be excluded in the production of prayer, ritual, family, worship, pilgrimage, or money? Her method of performativity calls for scholars to look at the interconnected forces present in the development of subjects and to understand that both they and the subject of study are implicated in complex relationships.

b. Bodily Inscriptions, Performative Subversions (*Gender Trouble: Feminism and the Subversion of Identity*) *Judith Butler*

"Garbo 'got in drag' whenever she took some heavy glamour part, whenever she melted in or out of a man's arms, whenever she simply let that heavenly-flexed neck … bear the weight of her thrown-back head… How resplendent seems the art of acting! It is all impersonation, *whether the sex underneath is true or not."*
—PARKER TYLER, "THE GARBO IMAGE" QUOTED IN ESTHER NEWTON, *Mother Camp*

Categories of true sex, discrete gender, and specific sexuality have constituted the stable point of reference for a great deal of feminist theory and politics. These constructs of identity serve as the points of epistemic departure from which theory emerges and politics itself is shaped. In the case of feminism, politics is ostensibly shaped to express the interests, the perspectives, of "women." But is there a political shape to "women," as it were, that precedes and prefigures the political elaboration of their interests and epistemic point of view? How is that identity shaped, and is it a political shaping that takes the very morphology and boundary of the sexed body as the ground, surface, or site of cultural inscription? What circumscribes that site as "the female body"? Is "the body" or "the sexed body" the firm foundation on which gender and systems of compulsory sexuality operate? Or is "the body" itself shaped by political forces with strategic interests in keeping that body bounded and constituted by the markers of sex?

The sex/gender distinction and the category of sex itself appear to presuppose a generalization of "the body" that preexists the acquisition of its sexed significance. This "body" often appears to be a passive medium that is signified by an inscription from a cultural source figured as "external" to that body. Any theory of the culturally constructed body, however, ought to question "the body" as a construct of suspect generality when it is figured as passive and prior to discourse. There are Christian and Cartesian precedents to such views which, prior to the emergence of vitalistic biologies in the nineteenth century, understand "the body" as so much inert matter, signifying nothing or, more specifically, signifying a profane void, the fallen state: deception, sin, the premonitional metaphorics of hell and the eternal feminine. There are many occasions in both Sartre's and Beauvoir's work where "the body" is figured as a mute facticity, anticipating some meaning that can be attributed only by a transcendent consciousness, understood in Cartesian terms as radically immaterial. But what establishes this dualism for us? What separates off "the body" as indifferent to signification, and signification itself as the act of a radically disembodied consciousness or, rather, the act that radically disembodies that consciousness? To what extent is that Cartesian dualism presupposed in phenomenology adapted to the structuralist frame in which mind/body is redescribed as culture/nature? With respect to gender discourse, to what extent do these problematic dualisms still operate within the very descriptions that are supposed to lead us out of that binarism and its implicit hierarchy? How are the contours of the body clearly marked as the taken-for-granted ground or surface upon which gender significations are inscribed, a mere facticity devoid of value, prior to significance?

Wittig suggests that a culturally specific epistemic *a priori* establishes the naturalness of "sex." But by what enigmatic means has "the body" been accepted as a *prima facie* given that admits of no genealogy? Even within Foucault's essay on the very theme of genealogy, the body is figured as a surface and the scene of a cultural inscription: "the body is the inscribed surface of events."[1] The task of genealogy, he claims, is "to expose a body totally imprinted by history." His sentence continues, however, by referring to the goal of "history"—here clearly understood on the model of Freud's "civilization"—as the "destruction of the body" (148). Forces and impulses with multiple directionalities are precisely that which history both destroys and preserves through the *Entstehung* (historical event) of inscription. As "a volume in perpetual disintegration" (148), the body is always under siege, suffering destruction by the very terms of history. And history is the creation of values and meanings by a signifying practice that requires the subjection of the body. This corporeal destruction is necessary to produce the speaking subject and its significations. This is a body, described through the language of surface and force, weakened through a "single drama" of domination, inscription, and creation (150). This is not the *modus vivendi* of one kind of history rather than another, but is, for Foucault, "history" (148) in its essential and repressive gesture.

Although Foucault writes, "Nothing in man [*sic*]—not even his body—is sufficiently stable to serve as the basis for self-recognition or for understanding other men [*sic*]" (153), he nevertheless points to the constancy of cultural inscription as a "single drama" that acts on the body. If the creation of values, that historical mode of signification, requires the destruction of the body, much as the instrument of torture in Kafka's "In the Penal Colony" destroys the body on which it writes, then there must be a body prior to that inscription, stable and self-identical, subject to that sacrificial destruction. In a sense, for Foucault, as for Nietzsche, cultural values emerge as the result of an inscription on the body, understood as a medium, indeed, a blank page; in order for this inscription to signify, however, that medium must itself be destroyed—that is, fully transvaluated into a sublimated domain of values. Within the metaphorics of this notion of cultural values is the figure of history as a relentless writing instrument, and the body as the medium which must be destroyed and transfigured in order for "culture" to emerge.

By maintaining a body prior to its cultural inscription, Foucault appears to assume a materiality prior to signification and form. Because this distinction operates as essential to the task of genealogy as he defines it, the distinction itself is precluded as an object of genealogical investigation. Occasionally in his analysis of Herculine, Foucault subscribes to a prediscursive multiplicity of bodily forces that break through the surface of the body to disrupt the regulating practices of cultural coherence imposed upon that body by a power regime, understood as a vicissitude of "history." If the presumption of some kind of precategorial source of disruption is refused, is it still possible to give a genealogical account of the demarcation of the body as such as a signifying practice? This demarcation is not initiated by a reified history or by a subject. This marking is the result of a diffuse and active structuring of the social field. This signifying practice effects a social space for and of the body within certain regulatory grids of intelligibility.

Mary Douglas's *Purity and Danger* suggests that the very contours of "the body" are established through markings that seek to establish specific codes of cultural coherence. Any discourse that establishes the boundaries of the body serves the purpose of instating and naturalizing certain taboos regarding the appropriate limits, postures, and modes of exchange that define what it is that constitutes bodies:

> ideas about separating, purifying, demarcating and punishing transgressions have as their main function to impose system on an inherently untidy experience. It is only by exaggerating the difference between within and without, above and below, male and female, with and against, that a semblance of order is created.[2]

Although Douglas clearly subscribes to a structuralist distinction between an inherently unruly nature and an order imposed by cultural means, the "untidiness" to which she refers can be redescribed as a region of *cultural* unruliness and disorder. Assuming the inevitably binary structure of the nature/culture distinction, Douglas cannot point toward an alternative configuration of culture in which such distinctions become malleable or proliferate beyond the binary frame. Her analysis, however, provides a possible point of departure for understanding the relationship by which social taboos institute and maintain the boundaries of the body as such. Her analysis suggests that what constitutes the limit of the body is never merely material, but that the surface, the skin, is systemically signified by taboos and anticipated transgressions; indeed, the boundaries of the body become, within her analysis, the limits of the social *per se*. A poststructuralist appropriation of her view might well understand the boundaries of the body as the limits of the socially *hegemonic*. In a variety of cultures, she maintains, there are

> pollution powers which inhere in the structure of ideas itself and which punish a symbolic breaking of that which should be joined or joining of that which should be separate. It follows from this that pollution is a type of danger which is not likely to occur except where the lines of structure, cosmic or social, are clearly defined.

A polluting person is always in the wrong. He [sic] has developed some wrong condition or simply crossed over some line which should not have been crossed and this displacement unleashes danger for someone.[3]

In a sense, Simon Watney has identified the contemporary construction of "the polluting person" as the person with AIDS in his Policing Desire: AIDS, Pornography, and the Media.[4] Not only is the illness figured as the "gay disease," but throughout the media's hysterical and homophobic response to the illness there is a tactical construction of a continuity between the polluted status of the homosexual by virtue of the boundary-trespass that is homosexuality and the disease as a specific modality of homosexual pollution. That the disease is transmitted through the exchange of bodily fluids suggests within the sensationalist graphics of homophobic signifying systems the dangers that permeable bodily boundaries present to the social order as such. Douglas remarks that "the body is a model that can stand for any bounded system. Its boundaries can represent any boundaries which are threatened or precarious."[5] And she asks a question which one might have expected to read in Foucault: "Why should bodily margins be thought to be specifically invested with power and danger?"[6]

Douglas suggests that all social systems are vulnerable at their margins, and that all margins are accordingly considered dangerous. If the body is synecdochal for the social system per se or a site in which open systems converge, then any kind of unregulated permeability constitutes a site of pollution and endangerment. Since anal and oral sex among men clearly establishes certain kinds of bodily permeabilities unsanctioned by the hegemonic order, male homosexuality would, within such a hegemonic point of view, constitute a site of danger and pollution, prior to and regardless of the cultural presence of AIDS. Similarly, the "polluted" status of lesbians, regardless of their low-risk status with respect to AIDS, brings into relief the dangers of their bodily exchanges. Significantly, being "outside" the hegemonic order does not signify being "in" a state of filthy and untidy nature. Paradoxically, homosexuality is almost always conceived within the homophobic signifying economy as both uncivilized and unnatural.

The construction of stable bodily contours relies upon fixed sites of corporeal permeability and impermeability. Those sexual practices in both homosexual and heterosexual contexts that open surfaces and orifices to erotic signification or close down others effectively reinscribe the boundaries of the body along new cultural lines. Anal sex among men is an example, as is the radical re-membering of the body in Wittig's The Lesbian Body. Douglas alludes to "a kind of sex pollution which expresses a desire to keep the body (physical and social) intact,"[7] suggesting that the naturalized notion of "the" body is itself a consequence of taboos that render that body discrete by virtue of its stable boundaries. Further, the rites of passage that govern various bodily orifices presuppose a heterosexual construction of gendered exchange, positions, and erotic possibilities. The deregulation of such exchanges accordingly disrupts the very boundaries that determine what it is to be a body at all. Indeed, the critical inquiry that traces the regulatory practices within which bodily contours are constructed constitutes precisely the genealogy of "the body" in its discreteness that might further radicalize Foucault's theory.[8]

Significantly, Kristeva's discussion of abjection in *Powers of Horror* begins to suggest the uses of this structuralist notion of a boundary-constituting taboo for the purposes of constructing a discrete subject through exclusion.[9] The "abject" designates that which has been expelled from the body, discharged as excrement, literally rendered "Other." This appears as an expulsion of alien elements, but the alien is effectively established through this expulsion. The construction of the "not-me" as the abject establishes the boundaries of the body which are also the first contours of the subject. Kristeva writes:

> *nausea* makes me balk at that milk cream, separates me from the mother and father who proffer it. "I" want none of that element, sign of their desire; "I" do not want to listen, "I" do not assimilate it, "I" expel it. But since the food is not an "other" for "me," who am only in their desire, I expel *myself*, I spit *myself* out, I abject *myself* within the same motion through which "I" claim to establish myself.[10]

The boundary of the body as well as the distinction between internal and external is established through the ejection and transvaluation of something originally part of identity into a defiling otherness. As Iris Young has suggested in her use of Kristeva to understand sexism, homophobia, and racism, the repudiation of bodies for their sex, sexuality, and/or color is an "expulsion" followed by a "repulsion" that founds and consolidates culturally hegemonic identities along sex/race/sexuality axes of differentiation.[11] Young's appropriation of Kristeva shows how the operation of repulsion can consolidate "identities" founded on the instituting of the "Other" or a set of Others through exclusion and domination. What constitutes through division the "inner" and "outer" worlds of the subject is a border and boundary tenuously maintained for the purposes of social regulation and control. The boundary between the inner and outer is confounded by those excremental passages in which the inner effectively becomes outer, and this excreting function becomes, as it were, the model by which other forms of identity-differentiation are accomplished. In effect, this is the mode by which Others become shit. For inner and outer worlds to remain utterly distinct, the entire surface of the body would have to achieve an impossible impermeability. This sealing of its surfaces would constitute the seamless boundary of the subject; but this enclosure would invariably be exploded by precisely that excremental filth that it fears.

Regardless of the compelling metaphors of the spatial distinctions of inner and outer, they remain linguistic terms that facilitate and articulate a set of fantasies, feared and desired. "Inner" and "outer" make sense only with reference to a mediating boundary that strives for stability. And this stability, this coherence, is determined in large part by cultural orders that sanction the subject and compel its differentiation from the abject. Hence, "inner" and "outer" constitute a binary distinction that stabilizes and consolidates the coherent subject. When that subject is challenged, the meaning and necessity of the terms are subject to displacement. If the "inner world" no longer designates a topos, then the internal fixity of the self and, indeed, the internal locale of gender identity, become similarly suspect. The critical question is not *how* did that identity become *internalized*? as if internalization were a process or a mechanism that might be descriptively reconstructed. Rather, the question is: From what strategic position in public discourse and for what reasons has the trope of interiority and the disjunctive binary of inner/outer taken hold? In what language is "inner space" figured? What kind of figuration is it, and through what figure of the body is it signified? How does a body figure on its surface the very invisibility of its hidden depth?

From Interiority to Gender Performatives

In *Discipline and Punish* Foucault challenges the language of internalization as it operates in the service of the disciplinary regime of the subjection and subjectivation of criminals.[12] Although Foucault objected to what he understood to be the psychoanalytic belief in the "inner" truth of sex in *The History of Sexuality*, he turns to a criticism of the doctrine of internalization for separate purposes in the context of his history of criminology. In a sense, *Discipline and Punish* can be read as Foucault's effort to rewrite Nietzsche's doctrine of internalization in *On the Genealogy of Morals* on the model of *inscription*. In the context of prisoners, Foucault writes, the strategy has been not to enforce a repression of their desires, but to compel their bodies to signify the prohibitive law as their very essence, style, and necessity. That law is not literally internalized, but incorporated, with the consequence that bodies are produced which signify that law on and through the body; there the law is manifest as the essence of their selves, the meaning of their soul, their conscience, the law of their desire. In effect, the law is at once fully manifest and fully latent, for it never appears as external to the bodies it subjects and subjectivates. Foucault writes:

> It would be wrong to say that the soul is an illusion, or an ideological effect. On the contrary, it exists, it has a reality, it is produced permanently *around, on, within,* the body by the functioning of a power that is exercised on those that are punished. (my emphasis)[13]

The figure of the interior soul understood as "within" the body is signified through its inscription *on* the body, even though its primary mode of signification is through its very absence, its potent invisibility. The effect of a structuring inner space is produced through the signification of a body as a vital and sacred enclosure. The soul is precisely what the body lacks; hence, the body presents itself as a signifying lack. That lack which *is* the body signifies the soul as that which cannot show. In this sense, then, the soul is a surface signification that contests and displaces the inner/outer distinction itself, a figure of interior psychic space inscribed *on* the body as a social signification that perpetually renounces itself as such. In Foucault's terms, the soul is not imprisoned by or within the body, as some Christian imagery would suggest, but "the soul is the prison of the body."[14]

The redescription of intrapsychic processes in terms of the surface politics of the body implies a corollary redescription of gender as the disciplinary production of the figures of fantasy through the play of presence and absence on the body's surface, the construction of the gendered body through a series of exclusions and denials, signifying absences. But what determines the manifest and latent text of the body politic? What is the prohibitive law that generates the corporeal stylization of gender, the fantasied and fantastic figuration of the body? We have already considered the incest taboo and the prior taboo against homosexuality as the generative moments of gender identity, the prohibitions that produce identity along the culturally intelligible grids of an idealized and compulsory heterosexuality. That disciplinary production of gender effects a false stabilization of gender in the interests of the heterosexual construction and regulation of sexuality within the reproductive domain. The construction of coherence conceals the gender discontinuities that run rampant within heterosexual, bisexual, and gay and lesbian contexts in which gender does not necessarily follow from sex, and desire, or sexuality generally, does not seem to follow from gender—indeed, where none of these dimensions of significant corporeality express or reflect one another. When the disorganization and disaggregation of the field of bodies disrupt the regulatory fiction of heterosexual coherence, it seems that the expressive model loses its descriptive force. That regulatory ideal is then exposed as a norm and a fiction that disguises itself as a developmental law regulating the sexual field that it purports to describe.

According to the understanding of identification as an enacted fantasy or incorporation, however, it is clear that coherence is desired, wished for, idealized, and that this idealization is an effect of a corporeal signification. In other words, acts, gestures, and desire produce the effect of an internal core or substance, but produce this *on the surface* of the body, through the play of signifying absences that suggest, but never reveal, the organizing principle of identity as a cause. Such acts, gestures, enactments, generally construed, are *performative* in the sense that the essence or identity that they otherwise purport to express are *fabrications* manufactured and sustained through corporeal signs and other discursive means. That the gendered body is performative suggests that it has no ontological status apart from the various acts which constitute its reality. This also suggests that if that reality is fabricated as an interior essence, that very interiority is an effect and function of a decidedly public and social discourse, the public regulation of fantasy through the surface politics of the body, the gender border control that differentiates inner from outer, and so institutes the "integrity" of the subject. In other words, acts and gestures, articulated and enacted desires create the illusion of an interior and organizing gender core, an illusion discursively maintained for the purposes of the regulation of sexuality within the obligatory frame of reproductive heterosexuality. If the "cause" of desire, gesture, and act can be localized within the "self" of the actor, then the political regulations and disciplinary practices which produce that ostensibly coherent gender are effectively displaced from view. The displacement of a political and discursive origin of gender identity onto a psychological "core" precludes an analysis of the political constitution of the gendered subject and its fabricated notions about the ineffable interiority of its sex or of its true identity.

If the inner truth of gender is a fabrication and if a true gender is a fantasy instituted and inscribed on the surface of bodies, then it seems that genders can be neither true nor false, but are only produced as the truth effects of a discourse of primary and stable identity. In *Mother Camp: Female Impersonators in America*, anthropologist Esther Newton suggests that the structure of impersonation reveals one of the key fabricating mechanisms through which the social construction of gender takes place.[15] I would suggest as well that drag fully subverts the distinction between inner and outer psychic space and effectively mocks both the expressive model of gender and the notion of a true gender identity. Newton writes:

> At its most complex, [drag] is a double inversion that says, "appearance is an illusion." Drag says [Newton's curious personification] "my 'outside' appearance is feminine, but my essence 'inside' [the body] is masculine." At the same time it symbolizes the opposite inversion; "my appearance 'outside' [my body, my gender] is masculine but my essence 'inside' [myself] is feminine."[16]

Both claims to truth contradict one another and so displace the entire enactment of gender significations from the discourse of truth and falsity.

The notion of an original or primary gender identity is often parodied within the cultural practices of drag, cross-dressing, and the sexual stylization of butch/femme identities. Within feminist theory, such parodic identities have been understood to be either degrading to women, in the case of drag and cross-dressing, or an uncritical appropriation of sex-role stereotyping from within the practice of heterosexuality, especially in the case of butch/femme lesbian identities. But the relation between the "imitation" and the "original" is, I think, more complicated than that critique generally allows. Moreover, it gives us a clue to the way in which the relationship between primary identification—that is, the original meanings accorded to gender—and subsequent gender experience might be reframed. The performance of drag plays upon the distinction between the anatomy of the performer and the gender that is being performed. But we are actually in the presence of three contingent dimensions of significant corporeality: anatomical sex, gender identity, and gender performance. If the anatomy of the performer is already distinct from the gender of the performer, and both of those are distinct from the gender of the performance, then the performance suggests a dissonance not only between sex and performance, but sex and gender, and gender and performance. As much as drag creates a unified picture of "woman" (what its critics often oppose), it also reveals the distinctness of those aspects of gendered experience which are falsely naturalized as a unity through the regulatory fiction of heterosexual coherence. *In imitating gender, drag implicitly reveals the imitative structure of gender itself—as well as its contingency.* Indeed, part of the pleasure, the giddiness of the performance is in the recognition of a radical contingency in the relation between sex and gender in the face of cultural configurations of causal unities that are regularly assumed to be natural and necessary. In the place of the law of heterosexual coherence, we see sex and gender denaturalized by means of a performance which avows their distinctness and dramatizes the cultural mechanism of their fabricated unity.

The notion of gender parody defended here does not assume that there is an original which such parodic identities imitate. Indeed, the parody is *of* the very notion of an original; just as the psychoanalytic notion of gender identification is constituted by a fantasy of a fantasy, the transfiguration of an Other who is always already a "figure" in that double sense, so gender parody reveals that the original identity after which gender fashions itself is an imitation without an origin. To be more precise, it is a production which, in effect—that is, in its effect—postures as an imitation. This perpetual displacement constitutes a fluidity of identities that suggests an openness to resignification and recontextualization; parodic proliferation deprives hegemonic culture and its critics of the claim to naturalized or essentialist gender identities. Although the gender meanings taken up in these parodic styles are clearly part of hegemonic, misogynist culture, they are nevertheless denaturalized and mobilized through their parodic recontextualization. As imitations which effectively displace the meaning of the original, they imitate the myth of originality itself. In the place of an original identification which serves as a determining cause, gender identity might be reconceived as a personal/cultural history of received meanings subject to a set of imitative practices which refer laterally to other imitations and which, jointly, construct the illusion of a primary and interior gendered self or parody the mechanism of that construction.

According to Fredric Jameson's "Postmodernism and Consumer Society," the imitation that mocks the notion of an original is characteristic of pastiche rather than parody:

> Pastiche is, like parody, the imitation of a peculiar or unique style, the wearing of a stylistic mask, speech in a dead language: but it is a neutral practice of mimicry, without parody's ulterior motive, without the satirical impulse, without laughter, without that still latent feeling that there exists something *normal* compared to which what is being imitated is rather comic. Pastiche is blank parody, parody that has lost it humor.[17]

The loss of the sense of "the normal," however, can be its own occasion for laughter, especially when "the normal," "the original" is revealed to be a copy, and an inevitably failed one, an ideal that no one *can* embody. In this sense, laughter emerges in the realization that all along the original was derived.

Parody by itself is not subversive, and there must be a way to understand what makes certain kinds of parodic repetitions effectively disruptive, truly troubling, and which repetitions become domesticated and recirculated as instruments of cultural hegemony. A typology of actions would clearly not suffice, for parodic displacement, indeed, parodic laughter, depends on a context and reception in which subversive confusions can be fostered. What performance where will invert the inner/outer distinction and compel a radical rethinking of the psychological presuppositions of gender identity and sexuality? What performance where will compel a reconsideration of the *place* and stability of the masculine and the feminine? And what kind of gender performance will enact and reveal the performativity of gender itself in a way that destabilizes the naturalized categories of identity and desire.

If the body is not a "being," but a variable boundary, a surface whose permeability is politically regulated, a signifying practice within a cultural field of gender hierarchy and compulsory heterosexuality, then what language is left for understanding this corporeal enactment, gender, that constitutes its "interior" signification on its surface? Sartre would perhaps have called this act "a style of being," Foucault, "a stylistics of existence." And in my earlier reading of Beauvoir, I suggest that gendered bodies are so many "styles of the flesh." These styles all never fully self-styled, for styles have a history, and those histories condition and limit the possibilities. Consider gender, for instance, as *a corporeal style,* an "act," as it were, which is both intentional and performative, where *"performative"* suggests a dramatic and contingent construction of meaning.

Wittig understands gender as the workings of "sex," where "sex" is an obligatory injunction for the body to become a cultural sign, to materialize itself in obedience to a historically delimited possibility, and to do this, not once or twice, but as a sustained and repeated corporeal project. The notion of a "project," however, suggests the originating force of a radical will, and because gender is a project which has cultural survival as its end, the term *strategy* better suggests the situation of duress under which gender performance always and variously occurs. Hence, as a strategy of survival within compulsory systems, gender is a performance with clearly punitive consequences. Discrete genders are part of what "humanizes" individuals within contemporary culture; indeed, we regularly punish those who fail to do their gender right. Because there is neither an "essence" that gender expresses or externalizes nor an objective ideal to which gender aspires, and because gender is not a fact, the various acts of gender create the idea of gender, and without those acts, there would be no gender at all. Gender is, thus, a construction that regularly conceals its genesis; the tacit collective agreement to perform, produce, and sustain discrete and polar genders as cultural fictions is obscured by the credibility of those productions—and the punishments that attend not agreeing to believe in them; the construction "compels" our belief in its necessity and naturalness. The historical possibilities materialized through various corporeal styles are nothing other than those punitively regulated cultural fictions alternately embodied and deflected under duress.

Consider that a sedimentation of gender norms produces the peculiar phenomenon of a "natural sex" or a "real woman" or any number of prevalent and compelling social fictions, and that this is a sedimentation that over time has produced a set of corporeal styles which, in reified form, appear as the natural configuration of bodies into sexes existing in a binary relation to one another. If these styles are enacted, and if they produce the coherent gendered subjects who pose as their originators, what kind of performance might reveal this ostensible "cause" to be an "effect"?

In what senses, then, is gender an act? As in other ritual social dramas, the action of gender requires a performance that is *repeated.* This repetition is at once a reenactment and reexperiencing of a set of meanings already socially established; and it is the mundane and ritualized form of their legitimation.[18] Although there are individual bodies that enact these significations by becoming stylized into gendered modes, this "action" is a public action. There are temporal and collective dimensions to these actions, and their public character is not inconsequential; indeed, the performance is effected with the strategic aim of maintaining gender within its binary frame—an aim that cannot be attributed to a subject, but, rather, must be understood to found and consolidate the subject.

Gender ought not to be construed as a stable identity or locus of agency from which various acts follow; rather, gender is an identity tenuously constituted in time, instituted in an exterior space through a *stylized repetition of acts.* The effect of gender is produced through the stylization of the body and, hence, must be understood as the mundane way in which bodily gestures, movements, and styles of various kinds constitute the illusion of an abiding gendered self. This formulation moves the conception of gender off the ground of a substantial model of identity to one that requires a conception of gender as a constituted *social temporality.* Significantly, if gender is instituted through acts which are internally discontinuous, then the *appearance of substance* is precisely that, a constructed identity, a performative accomplishment which the mundane social audience, including the actors themselves, come to believe and to perform in the mode of belief. Gender is also a norm that can never be fully internalized; "the internal" is a surface signification, and gender norms are finally phantasmatic, impossible to embody. If the ground of gender identity is the stylized repetition of acts through time and not a seemingly seamless identity, then the spatial metaphor of a "ground" will be displaced and revealed as a stylized configuration, indeed, a gendered corporealization of time. The abiding gendered self will then be shown to be structured by repeated acts that seek to approximate the ideal of a substantial ground of identity, but which, in their occasional discontinuity, reveal the temporal and contingent groundlessness of this "ground." The possibilities of gender transformation are to be found precisely in the arbitrary relation between such acts, in the possibility of a failure to repeat, a de-formity, or a parodic repetition that exposes the phantasmatic effect of abiding identity as a politically tenuous construction.

If gender attributes, however, are not expressive but performative, then these attributes effectively constitute the identity they are said to express or reveal. The distinction between expression and performativeness is crucial. If gender attributes and acts, the various ways in which a body shows or produces its cultural signification, are performative, then there is no preexisting identity by which an act or attribute might be measured; there would be no true or false, real or distorted acts of gender, and the postulation of a true gender identity would be revealed as a regulatory fiction. That gender reality is created through sustained social performances means that the very notions of an essential sex and a true or abiding masculinity or femininity are also constituted as part of the strategy that conceals gender's performative character and the performative possibilities for proliferating gender configurations outside the restricting frames of masculinist domination and compulsory heterosexuality.

Genders can be neither true nor false, neither real nor apparent, neither original nor derived. As credible bearers of those attributes, however, genders can also be rendered thoroughly and radically *incredible.*

c. Questions

Comprehension

1. Describe the concept of the "abject." What does the abject create, or what is it used to establish?

2. Butler writes that "for Foucault, as for Nietzsche, cultural values emerge as the result of an inscription on the body, understood as a medium, indeed, a blank page" ([1990] 2018: 170). What does she mean by this image of the body as a blank page? Why does she think this is a problematic image?

3. How does Foucault describe the relationship between the soul and the body? How does this affect our understanding of the interior and exterior of a person?

4. Why does Butler sometimes write "I" with quotation marks? What does she hope to indicate with that grammatical construction?

Analysis

5. Butler writes that "gender is an identity tenuously constituted in time, instituted in an exterior space through a *stylized repetition of acts*" ([1990] 2018: 179); emphasis in original). What are some implications of this discussion of "copy" and "origin" and what other places might it apply?

Synthesis

6. Mary Douglas writes that "dirt [is] matter out of place . . . [that] implies two conditions: a set of ordered relations and a contravention of that order" ([1966] 2002: 44). How does Douglas's identification of the desire for order and hierarchy relate to Butler's description of the formation of gendered subjects?

7. Caroline Bynum uses three aspects to discuss the body in her article: identity or individuality, matter or physicality, and desire. She also admits to finding aspects of Butler's work helpful, even though she is suspicious of the usefulness of other aspects of it. How might Butler respond in applying concepts of performativity to the bodily categories of identity, matter, and desire that Bynum delineates?

Notes

1 Michel Foucault, "Nietzsche, Geneaology, History," in *Language, Counter-Memory, Practice: Selected Essays and Interviews by Michel Foucault*, trans. Donald F. Bouchard and Sherry Simon, ed. Donald F. Bouchard (Ithaca: Cornell University Press, 1977), p. 148. References in the text are to this essay.

2 Mary Douglas, *Purity and Danger* (London, Boston, and Henley: Routledge and Kegan Paul, 1969), p. 4.

3 Ibid., p. 113.

4 Simon Watney, *Policing Desire: AIDS, Pornography, and the Media* (Minneapolis: University of Minnesota Press, 1988).

5 Douglas, *Purity and Danger*, p. 115.

6 Ibid., p. 121.

7 Ibid., p. 140.

8 Foucault's essay "A Preface to Transgression" (in *Language, Counter-Memory, Practice*) does provide an interesting juxtaposition with Douglas' notion of body boundaries constituted by incest taboos. Originally written in honor of Georges Bataille, this essay explores in part the metaphorical "dirt" of transgressive pleasures and the association of the forbidden orifice with the dirt-covered tomb. See pp. 46–48.

9 Kristeva discusses Mary Douglas's work in a short section of *Powers of Horror: An Essay on Abjection,* trans. Leon Roudiez (New York: Columbia University Press, 1982), originally published as *Pouvoirs de l'horreur* (Paris: Éditions de Seuil, 1980). Assimilating Douglas' insights to her own reformulation of Lacan, Kristeva writes, "Defilement is what is jettisoned from the *symbolic system.* It is what escapes that social rationality, that logical order on which a social aggregate is based, which then becomes differentiated from a temporary agglomeration of individuals and, in short, constitutes a *classification system* or a *structure*" (p. 65).

10 Ibid., p. 3.

11 Iris Marion Young, "Abjection and Oppression: Dynamics of Unconscious Racism, Sexism, and Homophobia," paper presented at the Society of Phenomenology and Existential Philosophy Meetings, Northwestern University, 1988. In *Crises in Continental Philosophy,* eds. Arleen B. Dallery and Charles E. Scott with Holley Roberts (Albany: SUNY Press, 1990), pp. 201–14.

12 Parts of the following discussion were published in two different contexts, in my "Gender Trouble, Feminist Theory, and Psychoanalytic Discourse," in *Feminism/Postmodernism,* ed. Linda J. Nicholson (New York: Routledge, 1989) and "Performative Acts and Gender Constitution: An Essay in Phenomenology and Feminist Theory," *Theatre Journal* 20, no. 3 (Winter, 1988).

13 Michel Foucault, *Discipline and Punish: the Birth of the Prison,* trans. Alan Sheridan (New York: Vintage, 1979), p. 29.

14 Ibid., p. 30.

15 See the chapter "Role Models" in Esther Newton, *Mother Camp: Female Impersonators in America* (Chicago: University of Chicago Press, 1972).

16 Ibid., p. 103.

17 Fredric Jameson, "Postmodernism and Consumer Society," in *The Anti-Aesthetic: Essays on Postmodern Culture,* ed. Hal Foster (Port Townsend, WA: Bay Press, 1983), p. 114.

18 See Victor Turner, *Dramas, Fields and Metaphors* (Ithaca: Cornell University Press, 1974). See also Clifford Geertz, "Blurred Genres: The Refiguration of Thought," in *Local Knowledge, Further Essays in Interpretive Anthropology* (New York: Basic Books, 1983).

10

Disrupting Secular Power and the Study of Religion: Saba Mahmood

a. Introduction

Saba Mahmood (1962–2018) was an anthropologist whose fieldwork focused on Muslim women mainly in Egypt; yet the theoretical questions that drove her work address larger topics, such as female agency and the construction of secularism, that are widely relevant to the historical and ongoing study of religion. She received her PhD from Stanford University in 1998 and taught and researched in the field of sociocultural anthropology at the University of California, Berkeley, from 2004 until her death in 2018. Previously, Mahmood worked for four years at the University of Chicago Divinity School and as an architect in Seattle, Washington. Mahmood received several awards, including the Henry Luce Foundation's Initiative on Religion and International Affairs award that funded the global project, "Politics of Religious Freedom."

The following selection comes from Mahmood's work in *Politics of Piety: The Islamic Revival and the Feminist Subject* ([2005] 2012), a book that emerges from fieldwork she completed in Cairo, Egypt, and from questions about global feminist contradictions she experienced growing up in Pakistan. The chapter "Agency, Gender, and Embodiment" concludes the book and theorizes the work of the piety (*da'wa*) movement in relation to questions of agency. Mahmood focuses on the women's mosque movement to examine the tensions that arise from two different, and perhaps ultimately noncompatible, subject formations—between Islamic fundamentalist, nonliberal subject formation and Western, secular-liberal subject formation. She writes that "any discussion of the issue of [feminist inflected] transformation must begin with an analysis of the specific practices of subjectivation that make the subjects of a particular social imaginary possible" (Mahmood [2005] 2018: 185). In other words, scholars cannot use a one-size-fits-all model of Western liberal subject formation to engage and adjudicate the process and outcomes of producing subjects, or "subjectivation." Put baldly, there are other systems that form and embody people differently than in Western democracies. Western feminism, however, does not do a good job in acknowledging the possibility of other systems of subject formation. Rather, it narrowly identifies feminist agency from the perspective of resistance—resistance to being held back from accessing traditionally identified democratic ideals such as freedom, choice, opportunity, and liberty. Mahmood notes that identifying feminist agency only as resistance cannot account for how systems of ethics, choices in behavior, and the attempts to match exterior actions and interior thoughts complicate discussions of subordination, violence, and agency. These realizations become critical when discussing religious traditions because the vast majority of critical analysis has relied on this assumed universal model of liberal subjecthood.

Mahmood's discussions of the construction of secularism and identity reveals that the analytic categories that scholars tend to take for granted, such as "woman," "secular," and "religion," all rely on specific historic, geographic constructions. In pointing out how scholarship has taken only one part—Western liberal ideals of personhood and secularism—and used it to analyze the whole world, regardless of context, Mahmood redefines boundaries for studying religion. She uses these traditions in order to reappraise the historical relationship of secularism. Her project is a large-scale investigation into the boundaries of subjecthood, agency, interreligious relationship, modernity, and the secular.

b. Agency, Gender, and Embodiment (*Politics of Piety: The Islamic Revival and the Feminist Subject*) Saba Mahmood

While in the earlier chapters of this book I explored how the ethical practices of the mosque movement have been shaped by, and in turn transformed, the social field of Egyptian secularity in unexpected ways, here I want to focus on how we might think about these ethical practices in the context of relations of gender inequality. Given the overwhelming tendency of mosque movement participants to accept the patriarchal assumptions at the core of the orthodox Islamic tradition, this chapter is animated by the following questions: What were the terms the mosque participants used to negotiate the demands of the orthodox Islamic tradition in order to master this tradition? What were the different modalities of agency that were operative in these negotiations? What difference does it make analytically if we attend to the terms internal to this discourse of negotiation and struggle? And what challenges do these terms pose to notions of agency, performativity, and resistance presupposed within liberal and poststructuralist feminist scholarship?

[Earlier], I argued for uncoupling the analytical notion of agency from the politically prescriptive project of feminism, with its propensity to valorize those operations of power that subvert and resignify the hegemonic discourses of gender and sexuality. I have argued that to the extent that feminist scholarship emphasizes this politically subversive form of agency, it has ignored other modalities of agency whose meaning and effect are not captured within the logic of subversion and resignification of hegemonic terms of discourse. In this chapter, I want to attend not only to the different meanings of agency as they emerge within the practices of the mosque movement, but also to the kinds of analytical questions that are opened up when agency is analyzed in some of its other modalities—questions that remain submerged, I would contend, if agency is analyzed in terms of resistance to the subordinating function of power.

I should make clear that my exploration of the multiple forms agency takes is not simply a hermeneutical exercise, one that is indifferent to feminism's interest in theorizing about the possibility of transforming relations of gender subordination. Rather, I would argue that any discussion of the issue of transformation must begin with an analysis of the specific practices of subjectivation that make the subjects of a particular social imaginary possible.[1] In the context of the mosque movement, this means closely analyzing the scaffolding of practices—both argumentative and embodied—that secured the mosque participants' attachment to patriarchal forms of life that, in turn, provided the necessary conditions for both their subordination and their agency. One of the questions I hope to address is: how does the particularity of this attachment challenge familiar ways of conceptualizing "subordination" and "change" within liberal and poststructuralist feminist debates?

Finally, since much of the analytical labor of this book is directed at the specificity of terms internal to the practices of the mosque movement, I would like to remind the reader that the force of these terms derives not from the motivations and intentions of the actors but from their inextricable entanglement within conflicting and overlapping historical formations. My project is therefore based on a double disavowal of the humanist subject. The first disavowal is evident in my exploration of certain notions of agency that cannot be reconciled with the project of recuperating the lost voices of those who are written out of "hegemonic feminist narratives," to bring their humanism and strivings to light—precisely because to do so would be to underwrite all over again the narrative of the sovereign subject as the author of "her voice" and "her-story."

My project's second disavowal of the humanist subject is manifest in my refusal to recuperate the members of the mosque movement either as "subaltern feminists" or as the "fundamentalist Others" of feminism's progressive agenda. To do so, in my opinion, would be to reinscribe a familiar way of being human that a particular narrative of personhood and politics has made available to us, forcing the aporetic multiplicity of commitments and projects to fit into this exhausted narrative mold. Instead, my ruminations on the practices of the women's mosque movement are aimed at unsettling key assumptions at the center of liberal thought through which movements of this kind are often judged. Such judgments do not always simply entail the ipso facto rejection of these movements as antithetical to feminist agendas (e.g., Moghissi 1999); they also at times seek to embrace such movements as forms of feminism, thus enfolding them into a liberal imaginary (e.g., Fernea 1998). By tracing in this chapter the multiple modalities of agency that informed the practices of the mosque participants, I hope to redress the profound inability within current feminist political thought to envision valuable forms of human flourishing outside the bounds of a liberal progressive imaginary.

Ethical Formation

In order to begin tugging at the multiple twines that hold this object called agency in its stable locution, let me begin with an ethnographic vignette that focuses on one of the most feminine of Islamic virtues, *al-ḥayā'* (shyness, diffidence, modesty), a virtue that was considered necessary to the achievement of piety by the mosque participants I worked with. In what follows, I want to examine the kind of agency that was involved when a novice tried to perfect this virtue, and how its performance problematizes certain aspects of current theorizations within feminist theory about the role embodied behavior plays in the constitution of the subject.

In the course of my fieldwork, I had come to spend time with a group of four working women, in their mid- to late thirties, who were employed in the public and private sectors of the Egyptian economy. In addition to attending the mosque lessons, the four also met as a group to read and discuss issues of Islamic ethical practice and Quranic exegesis. Given the stringent demands their desire to abide by high standards of piety placed on them, these women often had to struggle against the secular ethos that permeated their lives and made their realization of piety somewhat difficult. They often talked about the pressures they faced as working women, which included negotiating close interactions with unrelated male colleagues, riding public transportation in mixed-sex compartments, overhearing conversations (given the close proximity of their coworkers) that were impious in character and tone, and so on. Often this situation was further compounded by the resistance these women encountered in their attempts to live a pious life from their family members—particularly from male members—who were opposed to stringent forms of religious devotion.

When these women met as a group, their discussions often focused on two challenges they constantly had to face in their attempts to maintain a pious lifestyle. One was learning to live amicably with people—both colleagues and immediate kin—who constantly placed them in situations that were far from optimal for the realization of piety in day-to-day life. The second challenge was in the internal struggle they had to engage in within themselves in a world that constantly beckoned them to behave in unpious ways.

On this particular day, the group had been reading passages from the Quran and discussing its practical significance for their daily conduct. The Quranic chapter under discussion was "The Story" (Surat al-Qaṣaṣ), which discusses the virtue of shyness or modesty (al-ḥayā'), a coveted virtue for pious Muslims in general and women in particular. To practice al-ḥayā' means to be diffident, modest, and able to feel and enact shyness. While all of the Islamic virtues are gendered (in that their measure and standards vary when applied to men versus women), this is particularly true of shyness and modesty (al-ḥayā'). The struggle involved in cultivating the virtue of shyness was brought home to me when, in the course of a discussion about the exegesis of "The Story," one of the women, Amal, drew our attention to verse 25. This verse is about a woman walking shyly—with al-ḥayā'—toward Moses to ask him to approach her father for her hand in marriage. Unlike the other women in the group, Amal was particularly outspoken and confident, and would seldom hesitate to assert herself in social situations with men or women. Normally I would not have described her as shy, because I considered shyness to be antithetical to qualities of candidness and self-confidence in a person. Yet, as I was to learn, Amal had learned to be outspoken in a way that was in keeping with Islamic standards of reserve, restraint, and modesty required of pious Muslim women. The conversation proceeded as follows.

Contemplating the word *istiḥyā'*, which is form ten of the substantive *ḥayā'*,[2] Amal said, "I used to think that even though shyness [al-ḥayā'] was required of us by God, if I acted shyly it would be hypocritical [*nifāq*] because I didn't actually feel it inside of me. Then one day, in reading verse 25 in Surat al-Qaṣaṣ ["The Story"] I realized that al-ḥayā' was among the good deeds [*huwwa min al-a'māl al-ṣaliḥa*], and given my natural lack of shyness [al-ḥayā'], I had to make or create it first. I realized that making [*ṣana'*] it in yourself is not hypocrisy, and that eventually your inside learns to have al-ḥayā' too." Here she looked at me and explained the meaning of the word *istiḥyā'*: "It means making oneself shy, even if it means creating it [*Ya'ni ya Saba, yi'mil nafsu yitkisif ḥatta lau ṣana'ti*]." She continued with her point, "And finally I understood that once you do this, the sense of shyness [al-ḥayā'] eventually imprints itself on your inside [*as-shu'ūr yiṭba' 'ala guwwwaki*]."

Another friend, Nama, a single woman in her early thirties, who had been sitting and listening, added: "It's just like the veil [*ḥijāb*]. In the beginning when you wear it, you're embarrassed [*maksūfa*] and don't want to wear it because people say that you look older and unattractive, that you won't get married, and will never find a husband. But you *must* wear the veil, first because it is God's command [*ḥukm allah*], and then, with time, because your inside learns to feel shy without the veil, and if you take it off, your entire being feels uncomfortable [*mish rāḍī*] about it."

To many readers this conversation may exemplify an obsequious deference to social norms that both reflects and reproduces women's subordination. Indeed, Amal's struggle with herself to become shy may appear to be no more than an instance of the internalization of standards of effeminate behavior, one that contributes little to our understanding of agency. Yet if we think of "agency" not simply as a synonym for resistance to social norms but as a modality of action, then this conversation raises some interesting questions about the kind of relationship established between the subject and the norm, between performative behavior and inward disposition. To begin with, what is striking here is that instead of innate human desires eliciting outward forms of conduct, it is the sequence of practices and actions one is engaged in that determines one's desires and emotions. In other words, action does not issue forth from natural feelings but *creates* them. Furthermore, pursuant to the behaviorist tradition of Aristotelian moral philosophy discussed [earlier], it is through repeated *bodily acts* that one trains one's memory, desire, and intellect to behave according to established standards of conduct.[3] Notably, Amal *does not* regard simulating shyness in the initial stages of her self-cultivation to be hypocritical, as it would be in certain liberal conceptions of the self where a dissonance between internal feelings and external expressions would be considered a form of dishonesty or self-betrayal (as captured in the phrase: "How can I do something sincerely when my heart is not in it?"). Instead, taking the absence of shyness as a marker of an incomplete learning process, Amal further develops the quality of shyness by synchronizing her outward behavior with her inward motives until the discrepancy between the two is dissolved. This is an example of a mutually constitutive relationship between body learning and body sense—as Nama says, your body literally comes to feel uncomfortable if you do *not* veil.

Secondly, what is also significant in this program of self-cultivation is that bodily acts—like wearing the veil or conducting oneself modestly in interactions with people (especially men)—do not serve as manipulable masks in a game of public presentation, detachable from an essential interiorized self. Rather they are the *critical markers* of piety as well as the *ineluctable means* by which one trains oneself to be pious. While wearing the veil serves at first as a means to tutor oneself in the attribute of shyness, it is also simultaneously integral to the practice of shyness: one cannot simply discard the veil once a modest deportment has been acquired, because the veil itself is part of what defines that deportment.[4] This is a crucial aspect of the disciplinary program pursued by the participants of the mosque movement, the significance of which is elided when the veil is understood solely in terms of its symbolic value as a marker of women's subordination or Islamic identity.

A substantial body of literature in feminist theory argues that patriarchal ideologies—whether nationalist, religious, medical, or aesthetic in character—work by objectifying women's bodies and subjecting them to masculinist systems of representation, thereby negating and distorting women's own experience of their corporeality and subjectivity (Bordo 1993; Göle 1996; Mani 1998; E. Martin 1987). In this view, the virtue of al-ḥayā' (shyness or modesty) can be understood as yet another example of the subjection of women's bodies to masculinist or patriarchal valuations, images, and representational logic. A feminist strategy aimed at unsettling such a circumscription would try to expose al-ḥayā' for its negative valuation of women, simultaneously bringing to the fore alternative representations and experiences of the feminine body that are denied, submerged, or repressed by its masculinist logic.

A different perspective within feminist theory regards the recuperation of "women's experience" to be an impossible task, since the condition for the possibility of any discourse, or for that matter "thought itself" (Colebrook 2000b, 35), is the rendering of certain materialities and subjectivities as the constitutive outside of the discourse. In this view, there is no recuperable ontological "thereness" to this abjected materiality (such as "a feminine experience"), because the abject can only be conceived in relation to hegemonic terms of the discourse, "at and as its most tenuous borders" (Butler 1993, 8). A well-known political intervention arising out of this analytic aims to demonstrate the impossibility of "giving voice" to the subalterity of any abject being—thereby exposing the violence endemic to thought itself. This intervention is famously captured in Gayatri Spivak's rhetorical question, "Can the Subaltern Speak?" (Spivak 1988).

The analysis I have presented of the practice of al-ḥayā' (and the practice of veiling) departs from both these perspectives: I do not regard female subjectivity as that which belies masculinist representations; nor do I see this subjectivity as a sign of the abject materiality that discourse cannot articulate. Rather, I believe that the body's relationship to discourse is variable and that it seldom simply follows either of the paths laid out by these two perspectives within feminist theory. In regard to the feminist argument that privileges the role representations play in securing male domination, it is important to note that even though the concept of al-ḥayā' embeds a masculinist understanding of gendered bodies, far more is at stake in the practice of al-ḥayā' than this framework allows, as is evident from the conversation between Amal and her friend Nama. Crucial to their understanding of al-ḥayā' as an embodied practice is an entire conceptualization of the role the body plays in the making of the self, one in which the outward behavior of the body constitutes both the potentiality and the means through which interiority is realized. A feminist strategy that seeks to unsettle such a conceptualization cannot simply intervene in the system of representation that devalues the feminine body, but must also engage the very armature of attachments between outward behavioral forms and the sedimented subjectivity that al-ḥayā' enacts. Representation is only one issue among many in the ethical relationship of the body to the self and others, and it does not by any means determine the form this relationship takes.

Similarly, I remain skeptical of the second feminist framing, in which the corporeal is analyzed on the model of language, as the constitutive outside of discourse itself. In this framework, it would be possible to read al-ḥayā' as an instantiation of the control a masculinist imaginary must assert over the dangerous supplement femininity signifies in Islamic thought. Such a reading is dissatisfying to me because the relationship it assumes between the body and discourse, one modeled on a linguistic theory of signification, is inadequate to the imaginary of the mosque movement. Various aspects of this argument will become clear in the next section when I address the notion of performativity underlying the Aristotelian model of ethical formation the mosque participants followed. Suffice it to say here that the mosque women's practices of modesty and femininity do not signify the abjectness of the feminine within Islamic discourse, but articulate a positive and immanent discourse of being in the world. This discourse requires that we carefully examine the *work that bodily practices perform* in creating a subject that is pious in its formation.

To elucidate these points, it might be instructive to juxtapose the mosque participants' understanding of al-ḥayā' with a view that takes the pietists to task for making modesty dependent upon the particularity of attire (such as the veil). The contrastive understanding of modesty or al-ḥayā' (also known as *iḥtishām*) that results from such a juxtaposition was articulated forcefully by a prominent Egyptian public figure, Muhammad Said Ashmawi, who has been a leading voice for "liberal Islam" in the Arab world.[5] He is a frequent contributor to the liberal-nationalist magazine *Rūz al-Yūsuf,* which I quoted from earlier. In a series of exchanges in this magazine, Ashmawi challenged the then-mufti of Egypt, Sayyid Tantawi, for upholding the position that the adoption of the veil is obligatory upon all Muslim women (farḍ) (Ashmawi 1994a,

1994b; Tantawi 1994). Ashmawi's general argument is that the practice of veiling was a regional custom in pre-Islamic Arabia that has mistakenly been assigned a divine status. His writings represent one of the more eloquent arguments for separating the virtue of modesty from the injunction to veil in Egypt today:

> The real meaning of the veil [ḥijāb] lies in thwarting the self from straying toward lust or illicit sexual desires, and keeping away from sinful behavior, without having to conjoin this [understanding] with particular forms of clothing and attire. As for modesty [iḥtishām] and lack of exhibitionism ['adam al-tabarruj] in clothing and outward appearance [maẓhar], this is something that is imperative, and any wise person would agree with it and any decent person would abide by it. (Ashmawi 1994b, 25)

Note that for Ashmawi, unlike for the women I worked with, modesty is less a divinely ordained virtue than it is an attribute of a "decent and wise person," and in this sense is similar to any other human attribute that marks a person as respectable. Furthermore, for Ashmawi the proper locus of the attribute of modesty is the interiority of the individual, which then has an effect on outward behavior. In other words, for Ashmawi modesty is not so much an attribute of the body as it is a characteristic of the individual's interiority, which is then expressed in bodily form. In contrast, for the women I worked with, this relationship between interiority and exteriority was almost reversed: a modest bodily form (the veiled body) did not simply express the self's interiority but was the means by which it was acquired. Since the mosque participants regarded outward bodily markers as an ineluctable means to the virtue of modesty, the body's precise movements, behaviors, and gestures were all made the object of their efforts to live by the code of modesty.

Performativity and the subject

It might seem to the reader that the differences between these two perspectives are minor and inconsequential since, ultimately, both understandings of modesty have the same effect on the social field: they both proscribe what Ashmawi calls "illicit sexual desires and sinful behavior." Disagreement about whether or not one should veil may appear to be minor to those who believe it is the moral principle of the regulation of sexuality, shared by Ashmawi and the mosque participants, that matters. The idea that such differences are minor accords with various aspects of the Kantian model of ethics discussed [previously]; however, from an Aristotelian point of view, the difference between Ashmawi's understanding of modesty and that of the mosque participants is immense. In the Aristotelian worldview, ethical conduct is not simply a matter of the effect one's behavior produces in the world but depends crucially upon the precise form that behavior takes: both the acquisition and the consummation of ethical virtues devolve upon the proper enactment of prescribed bodily behaviors, gestures, and markers (MacIntyre 1966). Thus, an act is judged to be ethical in this tradition not simply because it accomplishes the social objective it is meant to achieve but also because it enacts this objective in the manner and form it is supposed to: an ethical act is, to borrow J. L. Austin's term, "felicitous" only if it achieves its goals in a prescribed behavioral form (Austin 1994).

Certain aspects of this Aristotelian model of ethical formation resonate with J. L. Austin's concept of the performative, especially as this concept has been conjoined with an analysis of subject formation in Judith Butler's work (1993, 1997a), which I touched upon briefly in [the beginning]. It is instructive to examine this resonance closely for at least two reasons: one, because such an examination reveals the kinds of questions about bodily performance and subjectivity that are important to foreground in order to understand the force this Aristotelian tradition of ethical formation commands among the mosque participants; and two, because such an examination reveals the kind of analytical labor one needs to perform in order to make the ethnographic particularity of a social formation speak generatively to philosophical concepts—concepts whose anthropological assumptions are often taken for granted.

A performative, which for Austin is primarily a speech act, for Butler includes both bodily and speech acts through which subjects are formed. Butler, in her adoption of Derrida's interpretation of performativity as an "iterable practice" (Derrida 1988), formulates a theory of subject formation in which performativity becomes "one of the influential rituals by which subjects are formed and reformulated" (1997a, 160). Butler is careful to point out the difference between performance as a "bounded act," and performativity, which "consists in a reiteration of norms which precede, constrain, and exceed the performer and in that sense cannot be taken as the fabrication of the performer's 'will' or 'choice' " (Butler 1993, 234).[6] In *Excitable Speech,* Butler spells out the role bodily performatives play in the constitution of the subject. She argues that "bodily habitus constitutes a tacit form of performativity, a citational chain lived and believed at the level of the body" (1997a, 155) such that the materiality of the subject comes to be enacted through a series of embodied performatives.[7]

As I discussed earlier, Butler's conception of performativity is also at the core of her theory of agency: she claims that the iterable and repetitive character of the performatives makes the structure of norms vulnerable and unstable because the reiteration may fail, be resignified, or be reappropriated for purposes other than the consolidation of norms. This leads Butler to argue: "That no social formation can endure without becoming reinstated, and that every reinstatement puts the 'structure' in question at risk suggests the possibility of its undoing is at once the condition of possibility of the structure itself" (1997b, 14). In other words, what makes the structure of norms stable—the reiterative character of bodily and speech performatives—is also that which makes the structure susceptible to change and resignification.[8]

Butler's notion of performativity and the labor it enacts in the constitution of the subject may at first glance seem to be a useful way of analyzing the mosque participants' emphasis on embodied virtues in the formation of a pious self. Both views (the mosque participants' and Butler's) suggest that it is through the repeated performance of virtuous practices (norms in Butler's terms) that the subject's will, desire, intellect, and body come to acquire a particular form. The mosque participants' understanding of virtues may be rendered in Butlerian terms in that they regard virtuous performances not so much as manifestations of their will but more as actions that produce the will in its particularity. In this conception, one might say that the pious subject does not precede the performance of normative virtues but is enacted through the performance. Virtuous actions may well be understood as performatives; they enact that which they name: a virtuous self.

Despite these resonances between Butler's notion of performativity and the mosque participants' understanding of virtuous action, it would be a mistake to assume that the logic of piety practices can be so easily accommodated within Butler's theoretical language. Butler herself cautions against such a "technological approach" to theory wherein "the theory is articulated on its self-sufficiency, and then shifts register only for the pedagogical purpose of illustrating an already accomplished truth" (Butler, Laclau, and Žižek 2000, 26). Such a perfunctory approach to theory is inadequate, Butler argues, because theoretical formulations often ensue from particular examples and are therefore constitutively stained by that particularity. In order to make a particular theoretical formulation travel across cultural and historical specificities, one needs to rethink the structure of assumptions that underlies a theoretical formulation and perform the difficult task of translation and reformulation.[9] If we take this insight seriously, then the question we need to ask of Butler's theorization of performativity is: how does a consideration of the mosque participants' understanding of virtuous action make us rethink the labor performativity enacts in the constitution of the pious subject?

To address this question, I believe that it is necessary to think through three important dimensions of the articulation of performativity in regard to subject formation: (a) the sequencing of the performatives and their interrelationship; (b) the place of language in the analysis of performativity; and (c) different articulations of the notions of "subversion," "change," or "destabilization" across different models of performativity. One of the crucial differences between Butler's model of the performative and the one implicitly informing the practices of the mosque movement lies in how each performative is related to the ones that follow and precede it. The model of ethical formation followed by the mosque participants emphasizes the sedimented and cumulative character of reiterated performatives, where each performative builds on prior ones, and a carefully calibrated system exists by which differences between reiterations are judged in terms of how successfully (or not) the performance has taken root in the body and mind. Thus the mosque participants—no matter how pious they were—exercised great vigilance in scrutinizing themselves to gauge how well (or poorly) their performances had actually taken root in their dispositions (as Amal and Nama do in the conversation described earlier in this chapter).

Significantly, the question of the disruption of norms is posed differently in the model governing the mosque movement from how it is posed in the model derived from the examples that Butler provides. Not only are the standards by which an action is perceived to have failed or succeeded different, but the practices that *follow* the identification of an act (as successful or failed) are also distinct. Consider for example Butler's discussion of drag queens (in "Gender Is Burning") who parody dominant heterosexual norms and in so doing expose "the imitative structure by which hegemonic gender is itself produced and disputes heterosexuality's claim on naturalness and originality" (Butler 1993, 125). What is significant here is that as the drag queen becomes more successful in her approximation of heterosexual norms of femininity, the challenge her performance poses to the stability of these norms also increases. The excellence of her performance, in other words, exposes the vulnerability of heterosexual norms and puts their naturalized stability at risk. For the mosque participants, on the other hand, excellence at piety does not put the structure that governs its normativity at risk but rather consolidates it.

Furthermore, when, in Butler's example, a drag queen's performance fails to approximate the ideal of femininity, Butler reads this failure as a sign of the intrinsic inability of the performative structure of heteronormativity to realize its own ideals. In contrast, in the model operative among the mosque participants, a person's failure to enact a virtue successfully is perceived to be the marker of an inadequately formed self, one in which the interiority and exteriority of the person are improperly aligned. The recognition of this disjuncture in turn requires one to undertake a specific series of steps to rectify the situation—steps that build upon the rooted and sedimented character of prior performances of normative virtues. Amal, in the conversation cited above, describes how she followed her initial inability to simulate shyness successfully with repeated acts of shyness that in turn produced the cumulative effect of a shy interiority and disposition. Drag queens may also expend a similar kind of effort in order to better approximate dominant feminine norms, but what is different is that they take the disjuncture between what is socially performed and what is biologically attributed as necessary to the very structure of their performance. For the mosque participants, in contrast, the relevant disjuncture is that between a religious norm (or ideal) and its actual performance: their actions are aimed at precisely *overcoming* this disjuncture.

One reason these two understandings of performative behavior differ from each other is based in the contrastive conceptions of embodied materiality that underlie them. Butler understands the materiality of the body on the model of language, and analyzes the power of bodily performatives in terms of processes of signification whose disruptive potential lies in the indeterminate character of signs. In response to those who charge her with practicing a kind of linguistic reductionism, Butler insists that the body is not reducible to discourse or speech, since "the relationship between speech and the body is that of a chiasmus. Speech is bodily, but the body exceeds the speech it occasions; and speech remains irreducible to the bodily means of its enunciation" (Butler 1997a, 155–56). So how are we to understand this chiasmus? For Butler, the answer lies in formulating a theory of signification that is always operative— whether acknowledged or not—when one tries to speak about this chiasmus, because in speaking one renders discursive what is extra- or nondiscursive (Butler 1993, 11). The discursive terms, in turn, become constitutive of the extra-discursive realms of the body because of the formative power of language to constitute that which it represents.[10] Butler remains skeptical of approaches that leave the relationship between discursive and extra-discursive forms of materiality open and untheorized, and seeks to demonstrate the power of an analysis that foregrounds the significatory aspects of the body.[11]

It is important to point out here that there are a range of theorists who may agree with Butler about the chiasmic relationship between the body and discourse, but for whom a theory of signification does not quite address a basic problem: how do we develop a vocabulary for thinking conceptually about forms of corporeality that, while efficacious in behavior, do not lend themselves easily to representation, elucidation, and a logic of signs and symbols (see, for example, T. Asad 1993; Connolly 1999; Grosz 1994; Massumi 2002). For these scholars, a theory of linguistic signification does not quite apprehend the power that corporeality commands in the making of subjects and objects. These scholars, of course, speak from within a long philosophical tradition that extends from Spinoza to Bergson to Merleau-Ponty and, more recently, to Deleuze.

In light of this ongoing debate, a consideration of the mosque participants' understanding of virtuous action raises yet another set of interesting questions regarding Butler's emphasis on the significatory aspects of bodily performatives. As I mentioned earlier, the mosque participants do not understand the body as a sign of the self's interiority but as a means of developing the self's potentiality. (Potentiality here refers not to a generic human faculty but to the abilities one acquires through specific kinds of embodied training and knowledge.) As described [previously], the mosque participants are in fact strongly critical of the nationalist-identitarian interpretations of religiosity because these views treat the body primarily as a sign of the self rather than as a means to its formation. One might say that for the mosque participants, therefore, the body is not apprehensible through its ability to function as a sign but encompasses an entire manner of being and acting in which the body serves as the developable means for its consummation. In light of this, it is important to ask whether a theory of embodied performativity that assumes a theory of linguistic signification (as necessary to its articulation) is adequate for analyzing formulations of the body that insist on the inadequacy of the body to function as a sign?

The fact that the mosque participants treat the body as a medium for, rather than a sign of, the self also has consequences for how subversion or destabilization of norms might operate within such an imaginary. Note that the mosque participants regard both *compliance to* and *rebellion against* norms as dependent upon the teachability of the body—what I called the "docility of the body"—such that both virtuous and unvirtuous dispositions are neccesarily learned. This means that the possibility for disrupting the structural stability of norms depends upon *literally* retutoring the body rather than on destabilizing the referential structure of the sign, or, for that matter, positing an alternative representational logic that challenges masculinist readings of feminine corporeality. Thus, anyone interested in reforming this tradition cannot simply assume that resignifying Islamic practices and virtues (like modesty or donning the veil) would change the meaning of these practices for the mosque participants; rather, what is required is a much deeper engagement with the architecture of the self that undergirds a particular mode of living and attachment, of which modesty/veiling are a part.

The recalcitrant character of the structure of orthodox Islamic norms contrasts dramatically with the politics of resignification that Butler's formulation of performativity presupposes. Butler argues that the body is knowable through language (even if it is not reducible to language); corporeal politics for her often ensue from those features of signification and reference that destabilize the referential structure. In Butler's conception, insofar as the force of the body is knowable through the system of signification, challenges to the system come from interventions in the significatory features of that system. For example, Butler analyzes the reappropriation of the term "queer," which was historically used as a form of hate speech against lesbians and gays, but which has now come to serve as a positive term of self-identification. For Butler the appropriation of the term "queer" works by redirecting the force of the reiterative structure of homophobic norms and tethering the term to a different context of valences, meanings, and histories. What is notable for the purpose of my argument here is that it is a change in the referential structure of the sign that destabilizes the normative meaning and force of the term "queer." In the case of the mosque movement, as I have argued above, a change in the referential structure of the system of signs cannot produce the same effect of destabilization. Any attempt to destabilize the normative structure must also take into account the specificity of embodied practices and virtues, and the kind of work they perform on the self, recognizing that any transformation of their meaning requires an engagement with the technical and embodied armature through which these practices are attached to the self.

My somewhat long foray into Butler's theory of embodied performativity elucidates, I hope, the range of productive questions that are generated through an encounter between philosophical "generality" and ethnographic "particularity"—an encounter that makes clear the constitutive role "examples" play in the formulation of theoretical concepts. Moreover, an analysis of the historical and cultural particularity of the process of subjectivation reveals not only distinct understandings of the performative subject but also the perspectival shifts one needs to take into account when talking about politics of resistance and subversion.

To Endure Is To Enact?

In this section I would like to return to the exploration of different modalities of agency whose operations escape the logic of resistance and subversion of norms. In what follows I will investigate how suffering and survival—two modalities of existence that are often considered to be the antithesis of agency—came to be articulated within the lives of women who live under the pressures of a patriarchal system that requires them to conform to the rigid demands of heterosexual monogamy. Given that these conditions of gender inequality uniformly affect Egyptian women, regardless of their religious persuasion, I am particularly interested in understanding how a life lived in accordance with Islamic virtues affects a woman's ability to inhabit the structure of patriarchal norms. What resources and capacities does a pious lifestyle make available to women of the mosque movement, and how do their modes of inhabiting these structures differ from women for whom the resources of survival lie elsewhere? In particular I want to understand the practical and conceptual implications of a religious imaginary in which humans are considered to be only partially responsible for their own actions, versus an imaginary in which humans are regarded as the sole authors of their actions. It is not so much the epistemological repercussions of these different accounts of human action that interest me (cf. Chakrabarty 2000; Hollywood 2004), but how these two accounts affect women's ability to survive within a system of inequality and to flourish despite its constraints.

In what follows, I will juxtapose an example drawn from the life of a woman who was part of the mosque movement with another taken from the life of a woman who considered herself a "secular Muslim," and who was often critical of the virtues that the mosque participants regard as necessary to the realization of their ability to live as Muslims. I want to highlight the strikingly different ways in which these two women dealt with the pressures of being single in a society where heterosexual marriage is regarded as a compulsory norm. Even though it would be customary to consider one of these strategies "more agentival" than the other, I wish to show that such a reading is in fact reductive of the efforts entailed in the learning and practicing of virtues—virtues that might not be palatable to humanist sensibilities but are nonetheless constitutive of agency in important ways.

The full extent to which single women in Egypt are subjected to the pressure to get married was revealed to me in a conversation with Nadia, a woman I had come to know through her work in the mosques. Nadia was in her mid-thirties and had been married for a couple of years, but did not have any children; she and her husband lived in a small apartment in a lower-middleincome neighborhood of Cairo. She taught in a primary school close to her home, and twice a week after work she taught Quranic recitation to young children in the Nafisa mosque as part of what she considered her contribution to the ongoing work of da'wa. Afterward, she would often stay to attend the lesson at the mosque delivered by one of the better-known dā'iyat. Sometimes, after the lesson, I would catch a bus back with her and her friends. The ride was long and we would often have a chance to chat.

During one of these rides, I observed a conversation between Nadia and her longtime friend Iman, who was in her late twenties and who also volunteered at the mosque. Iman seemed agitated that day and, upon getting on the bus, immediately spoke to Nadia about her dilemma. A male colleague who was married to another woman had apparently approached her to ask her hand in marriage.[12] By Egyptian standards Iman was well over the marriageable age. Iman was agitated because although the man was very well respected at her place of work and she had always held him in high regard, he already had a first wife. She was confused about what she should do, and was asking Nadia for advice. Much to my surprise, Nadia advised Iman to tell this man to approach her parents formally to ask for her hand in marriage, and to allow her parents to investigate the man's background in order to ascertain whether he was a suitable match for her.

I was taken aback by this response because I had expected Nadia to tell Iman not to think about this issue any further, since not only had the man broken the rules for proper conduct by approaching Iman directly instead of her parents, but he was also already married. I had come to respect Nadia's ability to uphold rigorous standards of pious behavior: on numerous occasions I had seen her give up opportunities that would have accrued her material and social advantages for the sake of her principles. So a week later, when I was alone with Nadia, I asked her the question that had been bothering me: why did she not tell Iman to cut off any connection with this man?

Nadia seemed a little puzzled and asked me why I thought this was proper advice. When I explained, she said, "But there is nothing wrong in a man approaching a woman for her hand in marriage directly as long as his intent is serious and he is not playing with her. This occurred many times even at the time of the Prophet."

I interrupted her and said, "But what about the fact that he is already married?" Nadia looked at me and asked, "You think that she shouldn't consider marriage to an already married man?" I nodded yes. Nadia gave me a long and contemplative look, and said, "I don't know how it is in the United States, but this issue is not that simple here in Egypt [*il-mas'ila di mish sahla fi maṣr*]. Marriage is a very big problem here. A woman who is not married is rejected by the entire society as if she has some disease [*il-maraḍ*], as if she is a thief [*ḥarāmi*]. It is an issue that is very painful indeed [*hadhahi mas'ila muẓlima jiddan, jiddan ḥaqīqi*]."

I asked Nadia what she meant by this. She replied: "If you are unmarried after the age of say late teens or early twenties—as is the case with Iman—everyone around you treats you like you have a defect [*al-naqṣ*]. Wherever you go, you are asked, 'Why didn't you get married [*matgawwaztīsh ley*]?' Everyone knows that you can't offer to marry a man, that you have to wait until a man approaches you. Yet they act as if the decision is in your hands! You know I did not get married until I was thirty-four years old: I stopped visiting my relatives, which is socially improper, because every time I would go I would encounter the same questions. What is even worse is that your [immediate] family starts to think that you have some failing [*il- 'ēb*] in you because no man has approached you for marriage. They treat you as if you have a disease."

Nadia paused reflectively for a moment and then continued: "It's not as if those who are married necessarily have a happy life. For marriage is a blessing [*na'ma*], but it can also be a trial/problem [fitna]. For there are husbands who are cruel [*qāṣi*: they beat their wives, bring other wives into the same house, and don't give each an equal share. But these people who make fun of you for not being married don't think about this aspect of marriage, and only stress marriage as a blessing [*na'ma*]. Even if a woman has a horrible husband, and has a hard married life, she will still make an effort to make you feel bad for not being married."

I was surprised at Nadia's clarity about the injustice of this situation toward women and the perils of marriage. I asked Nadia if single men were treated in the same way. Nadia replied resoundingly, "Of course not! For the assumption is that a man, if he wanted to, could have proposed to any woman: if he is not married it's because he *didn't want* to, or there was no woman who deserved him. But for the woman it is assumed that no one wanted *her* because it's not up to her to make the first move." Nadia shook her head again, and went on, "No, this situation is very hard and a killer [*il-mauḍū' ṣa'b wi qātil*], O Saba. You have to have a very strong personality [*shakhṣiyya qawiyya*] for all of this not to affect you because eventually you also start thinking that there is something deeply wrong with you that explains why you are not married."

I asked her what she meant by being strong. Nadia said in response, "You must be patient in the face of difficulty [*lāzim tikūni ṣābira*], trust in God [*tawwwakali 'ala allah*], and accept the fact that this is what He has willed as your fate [*qaḍā'*]; if you complain about it all the time, then you are denying that it is only God who has the wisdom to know why we live in the conditions we do and not humans." I asked Nadia if she had been able to achieve such a state of mind, given that she was married quite late. Nadia answered in an unexpected manner. She said, "O Saba, you don't learn to become patient [*ṣābira*] or trust in God [*mutawakkila*] only when you face difficulties. There are many people who face difficulties, and may not even complain, but they are not *ṣābirīn* [patient, enduring]. You practice the virtue of patience [*ṣabr*] because it is a good deed [*al-'amal al-ṣāliḥ*], regardless of your situation: whether your life is difficult or happy. In fact, practicing patience in the face of happiness is even more difficult."

Noting my look of surprise, Nadia said: "Yes, because think of how often people turn to God only when they have difficult times, and often forget Him in times of comfort. To practice patience in moments of your life when you are happy is to be mindful of His rights [*ḥaqqahu*] upon you at all times." I asked Nadia, "But I thought you said that one needs to have patience so as to be able to deal with one's difficulties?" Nadia responded by saying, "It is a secondary consequence [*al-natīja al-thānawiyya*] of your doing good deeds, among them the virtue of patience. God is merciful and He rewards you by giving you the capacity to be courageous in moments of difficulty. But you should practice ṣabr [patience] because this is the right thing to do in the path of God [*fi sabīl lillah*]."

I came back from my conversation with Nadia quite struck by the clarity with which she outlined the predicament of women in Egyptian society: a situation created and regulated by social norms for which women were in turn blamed. Nadia was also clear that women did not deserve the treatment they received, and that many of those she loved (including her kin) were equally responsible for the pain that had been inflicted on her when she was single. While polygamy is allowed in Islam, Nadia and other participants of the mosque movement would often point out that, according to the Quran, marriage to more than one woman is conditional upon the ability of a man to treat all his wives equally (emotionally and materially), a condition almost impossible to fulfill.[13] For this reason, polygamous marriages are understood to create difficult situations for women, and the mosque participants generally advise against it.[14] Nadia's advice to Iman that she consider marriage to a married man, however, was based on a recognition of the extreme difficulty entailed in living as a single woman in Egypt.

While Nadia's response about having to make such choices resonated with other, secular, Egyptian friends of mine, her advocacy of the cultivation of the virtue of ṣabr (roughly meaning "to persevere in the face of difficulty without complaint") was problematic for them.[15] Ṣabr invokes in the minds of many the passivity women are often encouraged to cultivate in the face of injustice. My friend Sana, for example, concurred with Nadia's description of how difficult life could be for a single woman in Egypt, but strongly disagreed with her advice regarding ṣabr.

Sana was a single professional woman in her mid-thirties who came from an upper-middle-class family—a self-professed "secular Muslim" whom I had come to know through a group of friends at the American University in Cairo. In response to my recounting of the conversation with Nadia, Sana said, "Ṣabr is an important Islamic principle, but these religious types [*mutadayyinīn*] think it's a solution to everything. It's such a passive way of dealing with this situation." While Sana, too, believed that a woman needed to have a "strong personality" (*shakhṣiyya qawiyya*) in order to be able to deal with such a circumstance, for her this meant acquiring self-esteem or self-confidence (*thiqa fil-nafs wal-dhāt*). As she explained, "Self-esteem makes you independent of what other people think of you. You begin to think of your worth not in terms of marriage and men, but in terms of who you *really are,* and in my case, I draw pride from my work and that I am good at it. Where does ṣabr get you? Instead of helping you to improve your situation, it just leads you to accept it as fate—passively."

While Nadia and Sana shared their recognition of the painful situation single women face, they differed markedly in their respective engagements with this suffering, each enacting a different modality of agency in the face of it. For Sana the ability to survive the situation she faced lay in seeking self-empowerment through the cultivation of self-esteem, a psychological capacity that, in her view, enabled one to pursue self-directed choices and actions unhindered by other people's opinions. In this view, self-esteem is useful precisely because it is a means to achieving self-directed goals.[16] For Sana one of the important arenas for acquiring this self-esteem was her professional career and achievements. Nadia also worked, but clearly did not regard her professional work in the same manner.

Importantly, in Nadia's view, the practice of ṣabr does not necessarily make one immune to being hurt by others' opinions: one undertakes the practice of ṣabr first and foremost because it is an essential attribute of a pious character, an attribute to be cultivated regardless of the situation one faces. Rather than alleviating suffering, ṣabr allows one to bear and live hardship *correctly* as prescribed by one tradition of Islamic self-cultivation.[17] As Nadia says, if the practice of ṣabr fortifies one's ability to deal with social suffering, this is a secondary, not essential, consequence. Justification for the exercise of ṣabr, in other words, resides neither in its ability to reduce suffering nor in its ability to help one realize one's self-directed choices and/or goals. When I pressed Nadia for further explanation, she gave me the example of Ayyub, who is known in Islam for his exemplary patience in the face of extreme physical and social hardship (Ayyub is the equivalent of Job in the Judeo-Christian tradition). Nadia noted that Ayyub is famous *not* for his ability to rise above the pain, but precisely for the manner in which he *lived* his pain. Ayyub's perseverance did not decrease his suffering: it ended only when God had deemed it time for it to end. In this view, it is not only the lack of complaint in the face of hardship, but the way in which ṣabr infuses one's life and mode of being that makes one a ṣābira (one who exercises ṣabr). As Nadia notes in the conversation reported earlier, while ṣabr is realized through practical tasks, its consummation does not lie in practice alone.

Importantly, Nadia's conception of ṣabr is linked to the idea of divine causality, the wisdom of which cannot be deciphered by mere human intelligence. Many secular-oriented Muslims,[18] like Sana above, regard such an approach to life as defeatist and fatalist—as an acceptance of social injustice whose real origins lie in structures of patriarchy and social arrangements, rather than in God's will manifest as fate (qaḍā'). According to this logic, holding humans responsible for unjust social arrangements allows for the possibility of change, which a divine causality forecloses. Note, however, that the weight Nadia accords to fate does not absolve humans from responsibility for the unjust circumstances single women face. Rather, as she pointed out to me later, predestination is one thing and choice another (al-qadr shai' wal-ikhtiyār shai' ākhir): while God determines one's fate (for example, whether someone is poor or wealthy), human beings still choose how to deal with their situations (for example, one can either steal or use lawful means to ameliorate one's situation of poverty). What we have here is a notion of human agency, defined in terms of individual responsibility, that is bounded by both an eschatological structure *and* a social one. Importantly, this account privileges neither the relational nor the autonomous self so familiar to anthropologists (Joseph 1999), but a conception of individual ethics whereby each person is responsible for her own actions.[19]

Just as the practice of self-esteem structured the possibilities of action that were open to Sana, so did the realization of ṣabr for Nadia, enabling certain ways of being and foreclosing others. It is clear that certain virtues (such as humility, modesty, and shyness) have lost their value in the liberal imagination and are considered emblematic of passivity and inaction, especially if they don't uphold the autonomy of the individual: ṣabr may, in this view, mark an inadequacy of action, a failure to act under the inertia of tradition. But ṣabr in the sense described by Nadia and others does not mark a reluctance to act. Rather, it is integral to a constructive project: it is a site of considerable investment, struggle, and achievement. What Nadia's and Sana's discussions reveal are two different modes of engaging with social injustice, one grounded in a tradition that we have come to value, and another in a nonliberal tradition that is being resuscitated by the movement I worked with.

Note that even though Nadia regarded herself as only partially responsible for the actions she undertook (the divine being at least equally responsible for her situation), this should not lead us to think that she was therefore less likely to work at changing the social conditions under which she lived. Neither she nor Sana, for a variety of reasons, could pursue the project of reforming the oppressive situation they were forced to inhabit. The exercise of ṣabr did not hinder Nadia from embarking on a project of social reform any more than the practice of self-esteem enabled Sana to do so. One should not, therefore, draw unwarranted correlations between a secular orientation and the ability to transform conditions of social injustice. Further, it is important to point out that to analyze people's actions in terms of realized or frustrated attempts at social transformation is necessarily to reduce the heterogeneity of life to the rather flat narrative of succumbing to or resisting relations of domination. Just as our own lives don't fit neatly into such a paradigm, neither should we apply such a reduction to the lives of women like Nadia and Sana, or to movements of moral reform such as the one discussed here.

The Paradoxes of Piety

As I suggested [previously], it is possible to read many of the practices of the mosque participants as having the effect of undermining the authority of a variety of dominant norms, institutions, and structures. Indeed, my analysis of the overall aims of the mosque movement shows that challenging secular-liberal norms—whether of sociability or governance—remains central to the movement's self-understanding. Moreover, regardless of the movement's self-understanding, the objective effects that the movement has produced within the Egyptian social field de facto pose stiff impediments to the process of secularization. Despite this acknowledgment, as I suggested before, it would be a mistake to analyze the complexity of this movement through the lens of resistance insomuch as such a reading flattens out an entire dimension of the force this movement commands and the transformations it has spawned within the social and political fields.

  This caution against reading the agency of this movement primarily in terms of resistance holds even more weight when we turn our attention to the analysis of gender relations. In what follows, I want to show why this is the case through ethnographic examples in which women may be seen as resisting aspects of male kin authority. While conceding that one of the effects of the mosque participants' pursuit of piety is the destabilization of certain norms of male kin authority, I want to argue that attention to the terms and concepts deployed by women in these struggles directs us to analytical questions that are closed off by an undue emphasis on resistance. The discourse of the mosque movement is shot through, of course, with assumptions that secure male domination: an analysis that focuses on terms internal to the discourse of piety must also engage the entire edifice of male superiority upon which this discourse is built. Indeed, my analysis of the mosque participants' practices of pedagogy and ritual observance is in part an exposition of this point. But the fact that discourses of piety and male superiority are ineluctably intertwined does not mean that we can assume that the women who inhabit this conjoined matrix are motivated by the desire to subvert or resist terms that secure male domination; neither can we assume that an analysis that focuses on the subversive effects their practices produce adequately captures the meanings[20] of these practices, that is, what these practices "do" within the discursive context of their enactment. Let me elaborate.

The pursuit of piety often subjected the mosque participants to a contradictory set of demands, the negotiation of which often required maintaining a delicate balance between the moral codes that could be transgressed and those that were mandatory. One common dilemma the mosque participants faced was the opposition they encountered to their involvement in da'wa activities from their immediate male kin, who, according to the Islamic juristic tradition, are supposed to be the guardians of women's moral and physical well-being. In order to remain active in the field of da'wa, and sometimes even to abide by rigorous standards of piety, these women often had to go against their male kin, who exercised tremendous authority in their lives, authority that was sanctioned not only by divine injunctions but also by Egyptian custom.

Consider for example the struggles a woman called Abir had with her husband regarding her involvement in da'wa activities. I had met Abir during one of the lessons delivered in the low-income Ayesha mosque and, over a period of a year and a half, came to know her and her family quite well. Abir was thirty years old and had three children at the time. Her husband was a lawyer and worked two jobs in order to make ends meet. Abir would sew clothes for her neighbors to supplement their income, and also received financial help from her family, who lived only a few doors down from her. Like many young women of her classed and background, Abir was not raised to be religiously observant, and showed me pictures from her youth when she, like other neighborhood girls, wore short skirts and makeup, flaunting the conventions of modest comportment. Abir recounted how, as a young woman, she had seldom performed any of the obligatory acts of worship and, on the occasions when she did, she did so more out of custom ('āda) than out of an awareness of all that was involved in such acts. Only in the last several years had Abir become interested in issues of piety, an interest she pursued actively by attending mosque lessons, reading the Quran, and listening to taped religious sermons that she would borrow from a neighborhood kiosk. Over time, Abir became increasingly more diligent in the performance of religious duties (including praying five times a day and fasting during Ramadan). She donned the headscarf, and then, after a few months, switched to the full body and face veil (niqāb). In addition, she stopped socializing with Jamal's male friends and colleagues, refusing to help him entertain them at home.

Abir's transformation was astonishing to her entire family, but it was most disturbing to her husband, Jamal. Jamal was not particularly religious, even though he considered himself a Muslim—if an errant one. He seldom performed any of his religious obligations and, much to Abir's consternation, sometimes drank alcohol and indulged his taste for X-rated films. Given his desire for upward mobility—which required him to appear (what Abir called) "civilized and urbane" (mutahaḍḍir) in front of his friends and colleagues—Jamal was increasingly uncomfortable with the orthodox Islamic sociability his wife seemed to be cultivating at an alarming rate, the full face and body veil (niqāb) being its most "backward" (mutakhallif) sign. He was worried, and let Abir know in no uncertain terms that he wanted a more worldly and stylish wife who could facilitate his entry and acceptance into a class higher than his own.

Things became far more tense between them when Abir enrolled in a two year program at a nongovernmental institute of da'wa so she could train to become a dā'iya. She had been attending the local mosque lessons, and felt that she would make a more effective teacher than the local dā'iyāt if she had the proper training. Jamal did not take her seriously at first, thinking that she would soon grow tired of the study this program required, coupled with the long commute and daily child care and housework. But Abir proved to be resolute and tenacious: she knew that if she was lax in her duties toward the house, her children, or Jamal, she did not stand a chance. So she was especially diligent in taking care of all household responsibilities on the days she attended the da'wa institute, and even took her son with her so that Jamal would not have to watch him when he returned from work.

Jamal tried several tactics to dissuade Abir. He learned quickly that his sarcastic remarks about her social "backwardness" did not get him very far: Abir would retort by pointing out how shortsighted he was to privilege his desire for worldly rewards over those in the Hereafter. She would also ridicule his desire to appear "civilized and urbane," calling it a blind emulation of Western values. Consequently, Jamal changed his tactic and started to use religious arguments to criticize Abir, pointing out that she was disobeying Islamic standards of proper wifely conduct when she disobeyed the wishes and commands of her husband. He would also occasionally threaten to take a second wife, as part of his rights as a Muslim man, if she did not change her ways. On one occasion, when he had just finished making this threat in front of her family and myself, Abir responded by saying, "You keep insisting on this right God has given you [to marry another woman]. Why don't you first take care of *His* rights over *you* [*ḥaqq allāh 'ēlaik*]?" It was clear to everyone that she was talking about Jamal's laxity in the performance of prayers, particularly since just an hour before, Abir had asked him, as the man of the household, to lead the evening prayer (*ṣalāt al-maghrib*)—a call he had ignored while continuing to watch television. Abir had eventually led the prayers herself for the women present in the house. Jamal was silenced by Abir's retort, but he did not refrain from continuing to harass her. At one point, after a particularly harsh argument between the two of them, I asked Abir, when we were alone, if she would consider giving up her da'wa studies due to Jamal's opposition. She answered resolutely, "No! Even if he took an absolute stand on the issue [*hatta lau kān itmassik il-mauqif*], I would not give up da'wa."

In response to Jamal's increasing pressure, Abir adjusted her own behavior. Much to her family's surprise, she became uncharacteristically gentle with Jamal, while using other means of persuasion with him. In particularly tense moments, she would at times cajole or humor him, and at times embarrass him by taking the higher moral ground (as in the scene just described). She also started to pray regularly for Jamal to his face, pointedly asking for God's pardon (*maghfira*) and blessings (*baraka*), not only in this life but in the Hereafter. The phrase "rabbinna yihdīk, ya rabb!" ("May our Lord show you the straight path, O Lord!") became a refrain in her interactions with Jamal. Sometimes she would play tape-recorded sermons at full volume in the house, especially on Fridays when he was home, that focused on scenes of death, tortures in hell, and the day of final reckoning with God. Thus, in order to make Jamal feel vulnerable, Abir invoked destiny and death (reminding him of the Hereafter when he would face God), urging him to accord these their due by being more religiously observant.

All of these strategies eventually had a cumulative effect on Jamal and, even though he never stopped pressuring Abir to abandon her studies at the da'wa institute, the intensity with which he did so declined. He even started to pray more regularly, and to visit the mosque occasionally with her. More importantly for Abir, he stopped indulging his taste for alcohol and X-rated films at home.

What is important to note in this account is that none of Abir's arguments would have had an effect on Jamal had he not shared with her some sort of a commitment to their underlying assumptions—such as belief in the Hereafter, the inevitability that God's wrath will be unleashed on those who habitually disobey His commands, and so on. Abir's persuasion worked with Jamal in part because he considered himself to be a Muslim, albeit one who was negligent in his practice and prone to sinful acts. As an example of this, even when he did not pray in response to her repeated enjoinders, he did not offer a reasoned argument for his refusal in the way an unbeliever might have when faced with a similar situation. Certain shared moral orientations structured the possibilities of the argument, and thus the shape of the conflict, between them. When confronted with the moral force of Abir's arguments, Jamal could not simply deny their truth. As Abir once explained to me, for Jamal to reject her moral arguments would be tantamount "to denying God's truth, something even he is not willing to risk." The force of Abir's persuasion lay partly in her perseverance, and partly in the tradition of authority she invoked to reform her husband, who was equally—if errantly—bound to the sensibilities of this tradition. In other words, Abir's effectiveness was not an individual but a collaborative achievement, a product of the shared matrix of background practices, sensibilities, and orientations that structured Jamal and Abir's exchanges.

Secondly, it is also important to note that Abir's enrollment in the da'wa institute against the wishes of her husband would not be condoned by majority of the dā'iyāt and Muslim jurists. This is because, as I explained [earlier], while da'wa is regarded a voluntary act for women, obedience to one's husband is considered an obligation to which every Muslim woman is bound.[21] Abir was aware of the risks she was taking in pursuing her commitment to da'wa: Jamal's threats to divorce her, or to find a second wife, were not entirely empty since he was within his rights as a Muslim man to do so in the eyes of the sharī'a. Abir was able to hold her position in part because she could claim a higher moral ground than her husband. Her training in da'wa had given her substantial authority from which to speak and challenge her husband on issues of proper Islamic conduct. For example, as she learned more about the modern interpretation of da'wa from the institute where she attended classes, she started to justify her participation in da'wa using the argument, now popular among many Islamist thinkers, that da'wa was no longer considered a collective duty but an individual duty that was incumbent upon each and every Muslim to undertake—a change that had come about precisely because people like Jamal had lost the ability to know what it meant to live as Muslims.[22] Paradoxically, Abir's ability to break from the norms of what it meant to be a dutiful wife were predicated upon her learning to perfect a tradition that accorded her a subordinate status to her husband. Abir's divergence from approved standards of wifely conduct, therefore, did not represent a break with the significatory system of Islamic norms, but was saturated with them, and enabled by the capacities that the practice of these norms endowed her with.

It is tempting to read Abir's actions through the lens of subordination and resistance: her ability to pursue da'wa work against her husband's wishes may well be seen as an expression of her desire to resist the control her husband was trying to exert over her actions. Or, from a perspective that does not privilege the sovereign agent, Abir's use of religious arguments may be understood as a simultaneous reiteration and resignification of religious norms, whereby patriarchal religious practices and arguments are assigned new meanings and valences. While both analyses are plausible, they remain inadequately attentive to the forms of reasoning, network of relations, concepts, and practices that were internal to Abir's actions. For example, what troubled Abir was not the authority Jamal commanded over her (upheld by divine injunctions), but his impious behavior and his attempts to dissuade her from what she considered to be her obligations toward God. For Abir, the demand to live piously required the practice of a range of Islamic virtues and the creation of optimal conditions under which they could be realized. Thus Abir's complicated evaluations and decisions were aimed toward goals whose sense is not captured by terms such as *obedience* versus *rebellion, compliance* versus *resistance,* or *submission* versus *subversion.* These terms belong more to a feminist discourse than to the discourse of piety precisely because these terms have relevance for certain actions but not others. Abir's defiance of social and patriarchal norms is, therefore, best explored through an analysis of the ends toward which it was aimed, and the terms of being, affectivity, and responsibility that constituted the grammar of her actions.[23]

da'wa and kinship demands

The significance of an analysis that attends to the grammar of concepts within which a set of actions are located may be further elaborated through another example, one that is well known and often cited among those who are familiar with the figure of Zaynab al-Ghazali. As I mentioned [previously], Zaynab al-Ghazali is regarded as a pioneering figure in the field of women's da'wa in Egypt; she is also well known for having served as a leader of the Islamist political group the Muslim Brotherhood in the 1950s and 1960s. Given her public profile and political activism, al-Ghazali has been seen as a paradoxical figure who urged other women to abide by their duties as mothers, wives, and daughters, but lived her own life in a manner that challenged these traditional roles (Ahmed 1992; Hoffman 1985). An often-cited example of this seeming contradiction is al-Ghazali's account of how she divorced her first husband whom she claimed interfered with her "struggle in the path of God" (*jihād fi sabīl lillāh*), and then married her second husband on the condition that he not intervene in her work of da'wa (Z. al-Ghazali 1995; Hoffman 1985, 236–37).

In her well-known autobiographical account, *Days from My Life* (*Ayyām min ḥayātī*), al-Ghazali reports an exchange with her second husband, who, upon seeing the frequency of her meetings with male members of the Muslim Brotherhood increase, had inquired about the nature of her work. According to al-Ghazali, since the Brotherhood was under strict government surveillance, with many of its leaders in Egyptian jails, her work with the Brotherhood had to be performed clandestinely, and she refused to share the exact nature of this work with her husband. When he probed, she conceded that her work with the Brotherhood could endanger her life, but reminded him of the agreement they had come to before their marriage:

> I cannot ask you today to join me in this struggle [jihād] but it is within my rights to stipulate [*ashtaraṭ 'alayka*] that you not prevent me from my struggle in the path of God [jihādi fi sabīl lillāh], and that the day this [task] places upon me the responsibility of joining the ranks of the strugglers [*mujāhidīn*] you do not ask me what I am doing. But let the trust be complete between us, between a man who wanted to marry a woman who has offered herself to the struggle in the name of God and the establishment of the Islamic state since she was eighteen years old. If the interests of marriage conflict with the call to God [*al-da'wa 'ila allāh*], then marriage will come to an end and the call [to God] [da'wa] will prevail in my whole being/existence… I know it is within your rights to order me, and it is incumbent upon me to grant you [your wishes], but God is greater in us than ourselves and His call is dearer to us than our existence. (Z. al-Ghazali 1995, 34–35)

In commenting on this passage, feminist historian Leila Ahmed points out that al-Ghazali's own choices in life "flagrantly undercut her statements on the role of women in Islamic society" (Ahmed 1992, 199–200). This contradiction is most apparent, in Ahmed's view, when al-Ghazali gives herself permission to place her work above her "obligations to raise a family," but does not extend the same right to other Muslim women (Ahmed 1992, 200).[24] While I do not deny that al-Ghazali's life has entailed many contradictions,[25] I think it is possible to understand her prescriptions for Muslim women as consistent with the conditions she stipulated in her own marriage. Notably, al-Ghazali does not argue that the pursuit of *any* kind of work in a woman's life permits her to excuse herself from familial duties (as Ahmed suggests): only her work "in the path of God" (fi sabīl lillāh) allows her to do so, and only in those situations where her kinship responsibilities interfere with her commitment to serving God. According to al-Ghazali, had she been able to bear children, her choices would have been more complicated because, as she expressed to me in one of my interviews with her, this would not have left her "free to devote herself to the path of God" (Cairo, 22 July 1996). She also talks about this in an interview that was published in a Saudi women's magazine called *Sayyidati* (Hindawi 1997). In this interview, al-Ghazali explains her decision to seek divorce from her first husband by saying, "It was God's wisdom that

He did not divert me from my [religious] activities by endowing me with a son, or blessing me with children. I was, however, and still am, a mother to all Muslims. Thus, confronted with the treasure and ardor of this call [to da'wa], I was not able to keep myself from responding to it. When my [first] husband refused to let me continue my da'wa activities, I asked him for a divorce and this was how it happened" (Hindawi 1997, 72).

Two doctrinal presuppositions are at the core of Zaynab al-Ghazali's argument. One is the position within Islamic jurisprudence, and commonly espoused by contemporary dā'iyāt and the 'ulamā', that a woman's foremost duty is to her parents before marriage, and to her husband and offspring after marriage, and that this responsibility is second only to her responsibility toward God. Only in situations where a woman's loyalty to God is compromised by her obligations toward her husband and family is there space for debate on this issue, and it is within this space that al-Ghazali formulates her dissent against her husband.

Zaynab al-Ghazali's argument also turns upon another important distinction made by Muslim jurists between one's *material* and *spiritual* responsibilities toward one's kin—both of which are organized along lines of age, gender, and kinship hierarchy. In this moral universe, while women are responsible for the *physical well-being* of both their husbands and children in the eyes of God, they are accountable only for their own and their children's *moral conduct*—not that of their husbands. Husbands, on the other hand, by virtue of the authority they command over their wives and children, are accountable for their *moral conduct* as well as their *social and physical well-being*. Thus, while inferiors and superiors have mutual *material* responsibilities toward each other (in the sense that wives, husbands, and children are obligated to care for one another's material comforts, albeit in different ways), it is husbands who are accountable for their wives' virtue, while wives are accountable only for the moral conduct of their children. This distinction allowed al-Ghazali to argue that her inability to bear children had "freed her" to pursue da'wa activities, something she would have been unable to do if she were encumbered by the responsibility for her children's moral and physical well-being.

Al-Ghazali's ability to break successfully from traditional norms of familial duty should be understood, as I suggested [earlier], within the context of her considerable exposure to a well-developed discourse of women's rights at the turn of the twentieth century, a discourse that had been crucial to her formation as an activist. Indeed, it is quite possible to read al-Ghazali's ability to stipulate conditions in both her marriages as a function of the opportunities that were opened up for women of her socioeconomic background in the 1930s and 1940s in Egypt and the new consciousness this had facilitated regarding the role women had come to play in the public domain.

While this social and historical context is undoubtedly important for explicating al-Ghazali's actions in her personal and public life, it would be a mistake to ignore the specificity of doctrinal reasoning and its governing logic that accorded her actions a particular force—a force whose valence would be quite different if her arguments had relied upon the claim that women should be granted rights equal to those enjoyed by men within Islam in regard to marriage, divorce, and other kinship responsibilities. Al-Ghazali's actions and her justifications for her actions did not, in fact, depend on such an argument for equal rights. Instead her argument pivoted upon the concept of "moral and physical responsibility" that she as a Muslim woman owed to her immediate kin. In al-Ghazali's reasoning, her ability to break from these responsibilities was a function of her childless status. Whether we agree with the politics this reasoning advances or not, the discursive effects that follow from her invocation of this concept of moral responsibility explain both the power she commands as an "Islamic" (rather than a "feminist") activist in the Muslim world today and the immense legitimacy her life story has accorded juristic Islamic discourse on kinship—particularly for those who want to pursue a lifestyle that breaks from the traditional demands of this discourse while at the same time abiding by its central tenets and principles.

Here I do not mean to suggest that the effect of al-Ghazali's abidance by the terms of juristic discourse is best understood in terms of the lifestyles it has legitimized; rather, my point is that her narrative account should be analyzed in terms of the particular field of arguments it has made available to Muslim women and the possibilities for action these arguments have opened and foreclosed for them. It is this dimension of al-Ghazali's reasoning that I have wanted to emphasize, particularly because it is often ignored and elided in accounts that explain her actions in terms of the universal logic of "structural changes" that modernity has heralded in non-Western societies like Egypt. While these "structural changes" provide an important backdrop for understanding al-Ghazali's speech and actions, they have little power when it comes to explicating the force her life story commands in the field of Islamist activism.

Doctrinal (ir)resolutions

While many of the problems that al-Ghazali and Abir faced in their pursuit of piety were related to their goal of becoming trained dā'iyāt, women who did not have such ambitions also encountered structurally similar problems. Given that Islamic jurisprudence regards men to be the moral and physical guardians of women,[26] participants in the mosque movement often complained that living with male kin who were not as religiously devout compromised their own standards of piety. The problem seemed to be particularly acute for a woman who was married to what the mosque participants called "al-zauj al-'āṣi" (a disobedient husband)—this concern was widely discussed not only in the mosque circles but also in religious advice columns in newspapers. In the eyes of the sharī'a, even though a woman is not responsible for her husband's moral conduct but only her own and her children's, her husband's behavior nonetheless profoundly affects her own pursuit of a virtuous life, given the moral authority he commands over her and his offspring as their custodian. Faced with such a situation, it is not easy for a woman to challenge her husband's conduct or to seek divorce, given the stigma of being a divorcée in Egyptian society and the restrictions Islamic law places on a woman's right to divorce. It was, therefore, very common during the mosque lessons to hear the audiences ask the dā'iyāt what a woman should do if she was married to a husband who lived a sinful existence by the standards of virtuous Muslim conduct.

There is no simple doctrinal resolution to this problem. The responses of the dā'iyāt varied and the women were urged to pursue a variety of means to come to terms with the contradictions posed by the conflicting demands of loyalty to God versus fidelity to one's (sinful) husband. Most dā'iyāt, whether at the upper-middle-, middle-, or lower-income mosques, argued that since men are the custodians (auliyā'; singular: wali) of female kin in Islam, and not the other way around, women are not accountable in the eyes of God for the actions of their adult male kin. They advised women to try persuading their "disobedient husbands" to reform their behavior, and in the event they failed, to continue living with them with the understanding that they would have to be extra vigilant in monitoring their own conduct.

I questioned some of the dā'iyāt and the mosque participants about the contradictions this advice generated in a woman's life, since living with an impious husband would force her into situations that compromised her ability to live by acceptable standards of virtuous conduct. Most of them acknowledged that their recommendations did not constitute the best solution to the problem at hand, but insisted that most women had no choice. Some of the dā'iyāt said, "If we advised women to seek divorce from disobedient husbands, we would de facto be asking half the population of married Egyptian women to be divorcées!"—implying that they thought a large number of Egyptian men were impious. Some argued that the fact that women are not held accountable for their husband's conduct is a blessing God has bestowed upon women—one that frees them to pursue piety without having to worry about the conduct of male kin—while men are burdened with having to account for their wives' actions as well as their own.

Other dā'iyāt, such as Hajja Asma, who had been Zaynab al-Ghazali's student and now served as a dā'iya in a local mosque, answered the question very differently.[27] During an afternoon lesson, when Hajja Asma was presented with this question by a woman in her mid-thirties from among a group of twelve middle-class housewives, she started by inquiring about the nature of the husband's sins. Once it was established that they were "grave sins" (al-kabā'ir—such as refusing to pray regularly (qaṣr al-ṣalāt qāṣiran), engaging in illicit sexual activity (zinā'), and drinking alcohol—she advised the woman to employ a variety of strategies to convince her husband to change his conduct. She said:

The first step is to cry in front of your husband, and make him realize that you are worried for him because of what God will do to him given his conduct. Don't think that this crying is in vain [mafish fā'ida bi] because crying is known to have melted the hearts of many. One of my neighbors convinced her husband to start praying regularly this way. She also brought other pressures to bear on him by having me talk to him, because she knows that he respects me and would be embarrassed [maksūf] if I were to question him about prayers. But if you find that crying does not seem to have results, then the next step you can take is to stop sharing meals with him [*baṭṭali it-ta'm ma'a*]. Eventually this is bound to have an effect, especially because men usually have stronger willpower than women and when a man sees a woman stronger than him he is moved by her persistence and strength [*istimrāriha wi quwwatiha*].

At this point one of the women listening to Hajja Asma asked, "What if none of this has an effect on him [*matit'ashirīsh bi*]?" Hajja Asma replied, "The final and last thing you can try is to refuse to sleep with him [*baṭṭali al-ishr'a ma'a*]." There was a palpable silence among the women at this point, and then a woman in her early thirties said in a low voice, "What if that doesn't work?" An older woman in her late sixties added loudly in response, "Yes, this happens a lot! [*'aiwa, da ḥaṣal kitīr*]." Hajja Asma nodded in agreement and said, "If none of this works, and you are certain that you have tried everything—and *only you can judge how hard you have tried*—and he still does not change his ways, then you have the right to demand a divorce from him [*'alēyki ḥaqq tuṭlubi it-ṭalāq minnu*]."

Some of the women gasped in surprise: "Yā!" ("Yā!" is an expression of surprise women often use in Egyptian colloquial Arabic). Noting this reaction, Hajja Asma responded, "Of course—what else can you do [*ḥati'mli 'ēh*]? Live with a sinning husband, raise your children in a sinful atmosphere—who will then grow up to be like him? How can you be obedient to God if you are living with a man like this [*tikūni fi-ṭ-ṭā'at allāh izāy lamma tikūni ma'a rāgil zayyu*]?" She continued, "If it was only a matter of him being harsh with you [*lau kān qāṣi ma'aki*], or having a rough temperament [*tabī'atu kān khishn*], then you could have endured it [*titṣabbiri 'alēy*]. But this is something you cannot be patient about or forebear: it is an issue between you and your God."

Hajja Asma's words were received with somber silence, since divorce is not something that is easy for Egyptian women to contemplate given the social taboos associated with it, the bias against women in Egyptian law regarding child custody, and the economic hardship a divorcée must face in raising her children. Moreover, as I mentioned earlier, Islamic law does not make it easy for a woman to seek divorce, even in such a situation. In talking to Hajja Asma later, it was obvious to me that divorce was not something she took lightly either. Notably, Hajja Asma emphasized (as she does above) that if a woman was faced with a husband who had a harsh temperament, it was her obligation to be patient, given that patience (ṣabr) is an Islamic virtue that she should cultivate as a pious Muslim. But to practice forbearance in a situation where *God's claims over her* were being compromised, was to place her own interests (in terms of the security and safety marriage provides) above her commitment to God. When I asked the other dā'iyāt and their audiences what they thought of Hajja Asma's response, they argued that not all women would have the courage and strength to risk the scorn and hardship a divorcée would be subjected to in Egyptian society in order to uphold high standards of virtuous conduct. Among the dā'iyāt who took such a position, some of them said that women like Hajja Asma "were true slaves of God [*humma 'ibād allāh ḥaqīqiyyan*]!"

As is clear from these disparate answers, the choice between submission to God's will and being obedient to one's husband did not follow a straightforward rule, and at times placed contradictory demands on the mosque participants. As a result, women were called upon to make complex judgments that entailed an interpretation of the Islamic corpus as well as their own sense of responsibility in the situation.[28] The questions the audience members posed, and the answers the dā'iyāt provided, assumed that a woman is responsible for herself and her moral actions; the anguish underlying these queries was a product of both the sense of moral responsibility these women felt and the limited scope of choices available to them within orthodox Islamic tradition.

Within the moral-ethical framework articulated by Hajja Asma, a woman must, prior to asking for divorce, have a clear understanding of the order of priorities entailed in God's commands so that she challenges her husband only on those issues that compromise her ability to live as a dutiful Muslim. According to Hajja Asma's framework, if husbands interfere with matters pertaining to voluntary, rather than obligatory, acts (such as praying in a mosque instead of at home, practicing supererogatory fasts, undertaking da'wa, or wearing the full face and body veil), then women are advised to give up these practices and to not disobey their husbands' wishes and commands. Similarly, a husband's harsh treatment of his wife is not regarded as sufficient reason to seek a divorce (although Egyptian women have been known to do so). Only when the nature of a husband's conduct is such that it violates key Islamic injunctions and moral codes, making it impossible for a woman to realize the basic tenets of virtuous conduct in her own and her children's lives, is she allowed to resort to divorce.

When viewed from a feminist perspective, the choices open to the mosque participants appear quite limited. The constraining nature of these alternatives notwithstanding, I would argue that they nonetheless represent forms of reasoning that must be explored on their own terms if one is to understand the structuring conditions of this form of ethical life and the forms of agency they entail. Note that the various paths followed by the women do not suggest the application of a universal moral rule (in the Kantian sense), but are closer to what Foucault calls ethics: the careful scrutiny one applies to one's daily actions in order to shape oneself to live in accordance with a particular model of behavior. Thus, Hajja Asma's advice entails a variety of techniques of introspection and argument, including: examining oneself to determine whether one has exhausted all possible means of persuading one's husband prior to asking for a divorce; being honest with oneself in such an examination, since no one else can make such a judgment; and employing a variety of techniques of persuasion, both oral and embodied, to change the immoral ways of the husband. This stands in contrast to the kind of self-scrutiny applied by a woman who chooses to stay with an impious husband: such a woman must constantly watch that she does not use her husband's behavior as an excuse for her own religious laxity, assess her intentions and motivations for the actions she pursues, make sure she does everything in her capacity to raise her children in accord with standards of pious conduct, and so on. In both situations, moral injunctions are not juridically enforced but are self-monitored and entail an entire set of ascetic practices in which the individual engages in an interpretive activity, in accord with sharī'a guidelines, to determine how best to live by Islamic moral codes and regulations.

Only through attention to these kinds of specificities can we begin to grasp the different modalities of agency involved in enacting, transgressing, or inhabiting ethical norms and moral principles. The analysis I have presented here should not be confused with a hermeneutical approach, one that focuses on the meanings that particular utterances, discourses, and practices convey. Rather, the framework I have suggested analyzes the *work* that discursive practices perform in making possible particular kinds of subjects. From this perspective, when assessing the violence that particular systems of gender inequality enact on women, it is not enough to simply point out, for example, that a tradition of female piety or modesty serves to give legitimacy to women's subordination. Rather it is only by exploring these traditions in relation to the practical engagements and forms of life in which they are embedded that we can come to understand the significance of that subordination to the women who embody it.

Finally, in respect to agency, my arguments in this chapter show that the analytical payback in detaching the concept of agency from the trope of resistance lies in the series of questions such a move opens up in regard to issues of performativity, transgression, suffering, survival, and the articulation of the body within different conceptions of the subject. I have insisted that it is best not to propose *a* theory of agency but to analyze agency in terms of the different modalities it takes and the grammar of concepts in which its particular affect, meaning, and form resides. Insomuch as this kind of analysis suggests that different modalities of agency require different kinds of bodily capacities, it forces us to ask whether acts of resistance (to systems of gender hierarchy) also devolve upon the ability of the body to behave in particular ways. From this perspective, transgressing gender norms may not be a matter of transforming "consciousness" or effecting change in the significatory system of gender, but might well require the retraining of sensibilities, affect, desire, and sentiments—those registers of corporeality that often escape the logic of representation and symbolic articulation.

c. Questions

Comprehension

1. How does Mahmood define "agency" in *Politics of Piety*?

2. How does Mahmood understand the relationship between interiority and exteriority in the subjecthood of the *da'wa* movement? How does she assert

this subject formation differs from conceptions of interiority and exteriority in liberal subject formation?

Analysis

3. What is lost when secular-liberal feminism thinks of agency only in terms of resistance to the dominant power structures?

4. Is it possible to have debates about agency and subordination across cultural formations of personhood? What resources might Mahmood seem to offer when discussing gendered violence across disparate understandings of the "subject"? What cautions does she warn that we should take seriously in such discussions?

Synthesis

5. Both Long and Mahmood examine the ways in which scholarly and popular categories rely on binaries to structure social power. In what ways do their accounts rely on similar strategies? What are the differences either in their process or in the outcomes?

6. Mahmood argues that Butler's theory of performativity differs when thinking about drag performers and women in the mosque movement: "A drag queen's performance fails to approximate the ideal of femininity, [and] Butler reads this failure as a sign of the intrinsic inability of the performative structure of heteronormativity to realize its own ideals. In contrast, in the model operative among the mosque participants, a person's failure to enact a virtue successfully is perceived to be the marker of an inadequately formed self, one in which the interiority and exteriority of the person are improperly aligned" ([2005] 2018: 193). How is the work of "failure" in performativity different or similar in Butler and Mahmood's theories? How do the goals of performativity change when we talk about it in the context of a drag show, a heterosexual couple, or a mosque participant?

Notes

1 I am in agreement with anthropologists such as Jane Collier, Marilyn Strathern, and Sylvia Yanagisako who have argued that all cultures and societies are predicated upon relations of gender inequality, and that the task of the anthropologist is to show how a culturally specific system of inequality (and its twin, equality) is constructed, practiced, and maintained (Collier 1988, 1997; Collier and Yanagisako 1989; Strathern 1988). My only caveat is that I do not believe that there is a single arrangement of gender inequality that characterizes a particular culture; rather, I believe that different arrangements of

gender inequality often coexist within a given culture, the specific forms of which are a product of the particular discursive formation that each arrangement is a part of.

2   Most Arabic verbs are based on a triconsonantal root from which ten verbal forms (and sometimes fifteen) are derived.

3   It is interesting to note that the women I worked with did not actually employ the body-mind distinction I use in my analysis. In referring to shyness, for example, they talked about it as a way of being and acting such that any separation between mind and body was difficult to discern. I have retained the mind-body distinction for analytical purposes, the goal being to understand the specific relation articulated between the two in this tradition of self-formation.

4   This concept can perhaps be illuminated by analogy to two different models of dieting: an older model in which the practice of dieting is understood to be a temporary and instrumental solution to the problem of weight gain; and a more contemporary model in which dieting is understood to be synonymous with a healthy and nutritious lifestyle. The second model presupposes an ethical relationship between oneself and the rest of the world and in this sense is similar to what Foucault called "practices of the care of the self." The differences between the two models point to the fact that it does not mean much to simply note that systems of power mark their truth on human bodies through disciplines of self-formation. In order to understand the force these disciplines command, one needs to explicate the conceptual relationship articulated between different aspects of the body and the particular notion of the self that animates distinct disciplinary regimes.

5   Ashmawi served as the chief justice of the Criminal Court of Egypt and as a professor of Islamic and Comparative Law at Cairo University. For an overview of his work on Islamic legal theory, see Hallaq 1997, 231–54.

6   An important aspect of Butler's formulation of performativity is its relationship to concepts in psychoanalytic theory. On this relationship, see the chapter "Critically Queer" in Butler 1993.

7   See Amy Hollywood's excellent discussion of Butler's analysis of embodied performativity and its relationship to the concept of ritual (2002).

8   While Butler remains indebted to Derrida in this formulation, she also departs from him by placing a stronger emphasis on the historically sedimented quality of performatives. See Butler 1997a, 147–50.

9   Butler argues this point eloquently in her recent work: "no assertion of universality takes place apart from a cultural norm, and, given the array of contesting norms that constitute the international field, no assertion can be made without at once requiring a cultural translation. Without translation, the very concept of universality cannot cross the linguistic borders it claims, in principle, to be able to cross. Or we might put it another way: without translation, the only way the assertion of universality can cross a border is through colonial and expansionist logic" (Butler, Laclau, and Žižek 2000, 35).

10   Note that Butler's focus on the formative power of discourse posits a strong critique of a representational model of language. Her objections are twofold: one, that this model incorrectly presupposes that language is anterior to the object it represents, when it in fact constitutes the object as well; two, that this model presumes a relationship of exteriority between language and power, when, in essence, language is not simply a tool for power but is itself a form of power. On these points, see

Butler's critique of Bourdieu's representational theory of language in Butler 1997c; also see Butler and Connolly 2000.

11 In response to a question posed by William Connolly about the nondiscursive character of bodily practices, Butler argues: "To focus on linguistic practice here and non-linguistic practice there, and to claim that both are important is still not to focus on the relation between them. It is that relation that I think we still do not know how to think… It will not be easy to say that power backs language when one form that power takes is language. Similarly, it will not be possible to look at non-discursive practices when it turns out that our very way of delimiting and conceptualizing the practice depends on the formative power of a certain conceptual discourse. We are in each of these cases caught in a chiasmus relation, one in which the terms to be related also partake of one another, but do not collapse into one another" (Butler and Connolly 2000).

12 Islamic jurisprudence permits men to have up to four wives.

13 Both the Hanbali and Maliki schools of Islamic jurisprudence permit a woman to stipulate in her marriage contract that if the husband takes a second wife, she has the right to seek divorce. What is quite clear is that none of the schools give the woman the legal right to prevent her husband from taking a second wife. For recent debates on polygamy among contemporary religious scholars in Egypt, see Skovgaard-Petersen 1997, 169–70, 232–33.

14 This is further augmented by the liberal ideal of nuclear family and companionate marriage, which, as Lila Abu-Lughod points out (1998), has increasingly become the norm among Islamists as well as secular-liberal Egyptians.

15 I have retained the use of ṣabr in this discussion rather than its common English translation, "patience," because ṣabr communicates a sense not quite captured by the latter: one of perseverance, endurance of hardship without complaint, and steadfastness.

16 In the language of positive freedom, Sana may be understood to be a "free agent" because she appears to formulate her projects in accord with her own desires, values, and goals, and not those of others.

17 For contemporary discussions of ṣabr among leaders of the Islamic Revival, see M. al-Ghazali 1990; al-Qaradawi 1989.

18 As I indicated, I am using "secular-oriented Muslims" as shorthand to refer to those for whom religious practice has limited relevance outside of personal devotion. See [my text] for my discussion of how the term "secularism" is used by the mosque participants in Egypt today.

19 Notably, Sunni Islam shares with Protestantism two central ideas. First, they both share the assumption that each follower of the tradition is potentially capable of inculcating the highest virtues internal to the tradition and is responsible for the self-discipline necessary to achieve this goal (even though divine grace plays a central role in both traditions). Second, they both share the assumption that the highest virtues of the tradition must be pursued while one is immersed in the practicalities of daily life, rather than through seclusion in an enclosed community (of nuns, priests, or monks), or a predefined religious order (as is the case in certain strains of Christianity, Hinduism, and Buddhism). Consequently all of life is regarded as the stage on which these values and attitudes are enacted, making any separation between the secular and the sacred difficult to maintain.

20 Obviously, my use of the term "meaning" here goes well beyond mere sense and reference.

21 Even among those writers who argue that da'wa in the modern period has acquired the status of an individual duty (farḍ al-'ain) rather than a collective duty (farḍ al-kifāya), da'wa is still considered, for women, an obligation secondary to their duties as wives, mothers, and daughters. This position is upheld not only by men but also by women, like Zaynab al-Ghazali, who have advocated for women's increased participation in the field of da'wa (see Z. al-Ghazali 1996a, 39; al-Hashimi 1990, 237).

22 Jamal could have countered this argument by pointing out that most proponents of da'wa consider it to be a woman's duty only if da'wa does not interfere with her service to her husband and children (see note above). But since Jamal was unfamiliar with these debates about da'wa, he was unable to make this argument.

23 My insistence throughout this book that we attend to the terms and concepts informing the actions of the mosque participants does not aim to simply reproduce "folk categories." Rather, my argument is that attention to these terms and concepts is necessary to rethinking analytical questions about regnant notions of agency in the social sciences and feminist theory. In this sense, my approach to the analysis of concepts is informed by the philosopher Ian Hacking who notes, "a concept is nothing other than a word in its sites. That means attending to a variety of types of sites: the sentences in which the word is actually (not potentially) used, those who speak those sentences, with what authority, in what institutional settings, in order to influence whom, with what consequences for the speakers" (Hacking 2002, 17).

24 Hoffman (1985) offers a similar reading of these passages.

25 In her two-volume book addressed to Muslim women in Egypt, al-Ghazali calls on women to enter the field of da'wa (Z. al-Ghazali 1994a, 1996a). However, she advises a woman dā'iya to concentrate her efforts on other women because "she can understand their temperaments, circumstances and characteristics, and therefore will succeed in reaching their hearts and solving their problems, and [be able] to follow their issues" (1994a, 2). While al-Ghazali conducted da'wa among women for a period of thirteen years, she also worked with men when she joined the Muslim Brotherhood as part of what she considered her work in da'wa. She rose to a position of leadership among the Muslim Brothers during a period when the majority of its top leaders were in jail and played a key role in coordinating the activities of the Brothers, a role for which she was later imprisoned. Clearly, her advice to women dā'iyāt—to primarily focus on other women—was not something she followed in her own life.

26 The Quranic verse often cited to support this position states, "Men shall take full care of women with the bounties which God has bestowed more abundantly on the former than on the latter" (al-rijāl qawwamūn 'ala al-nisā', verse 34 from Sūrat al-Nisā' ["The Woman"]).

27 Hajja Asma was the only dā'iya I worked with who talked openly about her sympathies with the Muslim Brotherhood. As a result, she often had to move from mosque to mosque under government pressure and was only able to offer lessons sporadically.

28 To make informed decisions about such an issue, Muslims often turn to a mufti (juriconsult) who, after consulting various established opinions and evaluating the individual situation, issues a fatwa that is legally nonbinding. In the context of the mosque lessons, the dā'iyāt, though not trained to be muftis, in practice enact this role by helping women interpret the sharī'a in light of their personal situations. For more complex issues, the dā'iyāt often refer their audiences to a qualified mufti.

References

Abu-Lughod, Lila. (1998), "The Marriage of Feminism and Islamism in Egypt: Selective Repudiation as a Dynamic of Postcolonial Cultural Politics." In *Remaking Women: Feminism and Modernity in the Middle East*, ed. L. Abu-Lughod, 243–69. Princeton, NJ: Princeton University Press.

Ahmed, Leila. (1992), *Women and Gender in Islam: Historical Roots of a Modern Debate*. New Haven, CT: Yale University Press.

Asad, Talal. (1993), *Genealogies of Religion: Discipline and Reasons of Power in Christianity and Islam*. Baltimore, MD: Johns Hopkins University Press.

Ashmawi, Said Muhammed. (1994a), Fatwa al-ḥijāb ghair shar'iyya. *Rūz al-Yūsuf*, August 8, 28.

Ashmawi, Said Muhammed. (1994b), al-ḥijāb laisa farīḍla. *Rūz al-Yūsuf*, June 13, 22.

Austin, J. L. (1994), *How to Do Things with Words*. Ed. J. O. Urmson and M. Sbisà. Cambridge, MA: Harvard University Press.

Bordo, Susan. (1993), *Unbearable Weight: Feminism, Western Culture, and the Body*. Berkeley and Los Angeles: University of California Press.

Butler, Judith. (1993), *Bodies That Matter: On the Discursive Limits of "Sex."* New York: Routledge.

Butler, Judith. (1997a), *Excitable Speech: A Politics of the Performative*. New York: Routledge.

Butler, Judith. (1997b), "Further Reflections on Conversations of Our Time." *Diacritics* 27 (1): 13–15.

Butler, Judith. (1997c), *The Psychic Life of Power: Theories in Subjection*. Stanford, CA: Stanford University Press.

Butler, Judith, and William Connolly. (2000), "Politics, Power and Ethics: A Discussion between Judith Butler and William Connolly." *Theory and Event* 24 (2), http:// muse.jhu. edu/journals/theory_and_event/v004/4.2butler.html.

Butler, Judith, Ernesto Laclau, and Slavoj Žižek. (2000), *Contingency, Hegemony, Universality: Contemporary Dialogues on the Left*. London: Verso Press.

Chakrabarty, Dipesh. (2000), *Provincializing Europe: Postcolonial Thought and Historical Difference*. Princeton, NJ: Princeton University Press.

Colebrook, Claire. (2000b), "Incorporeality: The Ghostly Body of Metaphysics." *Body and Society* 6 (2): 25–44.

Collier, Jane. (1988), *Marriage and Inequality in Classless Societies*. Stanford, CA: Stanford University Press.

Collier, Jane. (1997), *From Duty to Desire: Remaking Families in a Spanish Village*. Princeton, NJ: Princeton University Press.

Collier, Jane, and Sylvia Yanagisako. (1989), "Theory in Anthropology since Feminist Practice." *Critique of Anthropology* IX (2): 27–37.

Connolly, William. (1999), *Why I Am Not a Secularist*. Minneapolis: University of Minnesota Press.

Derrida, Jacques. (1988), "Signature Event Context." In Limited Inc, 1–23. Evanston, IL: Northwestern University Press.

Fernea, Elizabeth, ed. (1998), *In Search of Islamic Feminism: One Woman's Global Journey.* New York: Doubleday Press.

Göle, Nilüfer. (1996), *The Forbidden Modern: Civilization and Veiling.* Ann Arbor: University of Michigan Press.

Grosz, Elizabeth. (1994), *Volatile Bodies: Toward a Corporeal Feminism.* Bloomington: Indiana University Press.

Hacking, Ian. (2002), *Historical Ontology.* Cambridge, MA: Harvard University Press.

Hallaq, Wael. (1997), *A History of Islamic Legal Theories: An Introduction to Sunnī usūl al-fiqh.* Cambridge: Cambridge University Press.

Hindawi, Khayriyya. (1997), Naṣīḥat Zaynab al-Ghazali lil-mar'a al-muslima: al-Zauja la taqūl "la" li-zaujiha abadan illa fi ma yaghḍab allāh. *Sayyidati,* January 24, 70–75.

Hoffman, Valerie. (1985), "An Islamic Activist: Zaynab al-Ghazali." In *Women and the Family in the Middle East: New Voices of Change,* ed. E. Fernea, 233–54. Austin: University of Texas Press.

Hollywood, Amy. (2002), "Performativity, Citationality, Ritualization." *History of Religions* 42 (2): 93–115.

Hollywood, Amy. (2004), "Gender, Agency, and the Divine in Religious Historiography." *The Journal of Religion* 84 (4).

Joseph, Suad, ed. (1999), *Intimate Selving in Arab Families: Gender, Self, and Identity.* Syracuse: Syracuse University Press.

al-Ghazali, Muhammed. (1990), *al-Jānib al-'āṭifi min al-Islām.* Alexandria: Dār al-da'wa.

al-Ghazali, Zaynab. (1994a), *'ila ibnati: al juz' al-awwal.* Cairo: Dār al-tauzī' wal-nashr al-islāmi.

al-Ghazali, Zaynab. (1995), *Ayyām min ḥayāti.* Cairo: Dār al-shurūq.

al-Ghazali, Zaynab. (1996a), *'ila ibnati: al juz' al-thāni.* Cairo: Dār al-tauzī' wal-nashr al-islāmiyya.

al-Hashimi, Ibn, ed. (1990), *Humūm al-mar'a al-muslima wal-dā'iya Zaynab al-Ghazali.* Cairo: Dār al-i'tiṣām.

MacIntyre, Alisdair. (1966), *A Short History of Ethics: A History of Moral Philosophy from the Homeric to the Twentieth Century.* New York: Macmillan.

Mani, Lata. (1998), *Contentious Traditions: The Debate on Sati in Colonial India.* Berkeley and Los Angeles: University of California Press.

Martin, Emily. (1987), *The Woman in the Body: A Cultural Analysis of Reproduction.* Boston: Beacon Press.

Massumi, Brian. (2002), *Parables for the Virtual: Movement, Affect, Sensation.* Durham, NC: Duke University Press.

Moghissi, Haideh. (1999), *Feminism and Islamic Fundamentalism: The Limits of Postmodern Analysis.* New York: Zed Books.

al-Qaradawi, Yusuf. (1989). *al-Ṣabr fi al-Qur'ān.* Cairo: Maktabat wahba.

Skovgaard-Petersen, Jakob. (1997), *Defining Islam for the Egyptian State Muftis and fatwas of the Dār al-Iftā.* Leiden: Brill.

Spivak, Gayatri. (1988), "Can the subaltern speak?" In *Marxism and the Interpretation of Culture,* ed. C. Nelson and L. Grossberg, 271–313. Urbana: University of Illinois Press.

Strathern, Marilyn. (1988), *The Gender of the Gift: Problems with Women and Problems with Society in Melanesia.* Berkeley and Los Angeles: University of California Press.

Tantawi, Muhammed Sayyid. (1994), Bal al-ḥijāb farīḍa islāmiyya. *Rūz al-Yūsuf,* June 27, 68.

Index